LIGHT *of Her* CHILDREN

LIGHT *of Her* CHILDREN

RONALD JAMES NEWTON

Copyright © 2015 by Ronald James Newton.

Library of Congress Control Number: 2015916119
ISBN: Hardcover   978-1-5144-1255-8
         Softcover   978-1-5144-1256-5
         eBook   978-1-5144-1257-2

All rights reserved. No part of this book may be reproduced or transmitted in any form or by any means, electronic or mechanical, including photocopying, recording, or by any information storage and retrieval system, without permission in writing from the copyright owner.

Any people depicted in stock imagery provided by Thinkstock are models, and such images are being used for illustrative purposes only. Certain stock imagery © Thinkstock.

Print information available on the last page.

Rev. date: 06/08/2016

To order additional copies of this book, contact:
Xlibris
1-888-795-4274
www.Xlibris.com
Orders@Xlibris.com

Contents

Chapter 1: Leaving Home 1
Chapter 2: Elmer 12
Chapter 3: Elmer and Johnnie 21
Chapter 4: The Twenties 30
Chapter 5: The Depression 42
Chapter 6: Surprise Threesome 50
Chapter 7: Sons of War 61
Chapter 8: War Home Front 74
Chapter 9: War's End 82
Chapter 10: Expanding Family 95
Chapter 11: Come Spring 107
Chapter 12: Communion Prayer 112
Chapter 13: Chickens 117
Chapter 14: Occasions of Summer 123
Chapter 15: Halloween 131
Chapter 16: Wheels 141
Chapter 17: Church Picnic 149
Chapter 18: Feeding the Family 165
Chapter 19: Way it Bounces 178
Chapter 20: Warriors 186
Chapter 21: Winter's Children 198
Chapter 22: Picture Show 207
Chapter 23: Pool Hall 220

Chapter 24: Hoedown 229
Chapter 25: Beet Dividend 244
Chapter 26: Up the Mountain 252
Chapter 27: Down the Creek 262
Chapter 28: On the Creek 275
Chapter 29: On the River 288
Chapter 30: Highland Lake 297
Chapter 31: Big Band 307
Chapter 32: Independence 313
Chapter 33: Departing 326
Chapter 34: Losing 339
Chapter 35: Summer Job 347
Chapter 36: Agnes 355
Chapter 37: Christmas 367
Chapter 38: Winning 374
Chapter 39: Dragging Main 382
Chapter 40: Time to Go 390
Chapter 41: Leaving Town 394

Epilogue 403
Bibliography 411
Index 415

With deep thanksgiving to my parents and siblings, the people who made me and shaped me.

To the love of my life, Mary Weingarth Newton, who supported me as I remembered, researched, wrote, and rewrote. She is my guiding polestar.

To my two children, Courtney and Brooke, now residing in the Lone Star State of their birth with their respective spouses, Jennifer and Scott. The shining lives of all four of them continue to provide me with inspiration and incentive.

To my grandchildren, Hazel, Sam, Grace, and Sage, whose own light will shine in ways and places that I cannot even imagine.

For you were once darkness, but now you are light in the Lord. Walk, then, as children of light.

—Ephesians 5:8

LIST OF ILLUSTRATIONS

1. Map of Mead, Colorado
2. Map of Northeastern Colorado
3. Map of Fox Creek and Rock Creek
4. Map of Fox Creek, Rock Creek, and the North Saint Vrain River

Yal

Dear reader,

In your hands you hold a special universe. This book started out as a family memoir written by one member of a quite remarkable Northeastern Colorado family. There is a clear beginning and a traceable—although meandering—path. But that indirect and sometimes convoluted path really just mirrors life as we know it. Oh yes, narrative in a book often has a much more direct course, wherein causes and effects, interrelationships of people, and events are quite evident. In that sense, books are *easier,* and life itself is *harder* to decode.

Ron Newton's text starts with a frontier flavor as early family antecedents move into Colorado. These are **tough** and **resilient** individuals because they had to be. Two of these antecedents, whom you will meet in Ron's narrative, are his parents, who had twenty children. No, that is not a typo. So this story really is a family universe, densely layered and complex. Some threads that are part of the Weld County tapestry are being on public assistance, Horatio Alger–like rising above circumstance, powerful and pervasive Roman Catholicism, creativity and resourcefulness, love, sports, deep connection with nature, mental illness, an emerging array of adult role models (within and without the family), a Tiger Mom—long before that term was coined—the turning of seasons and the passage of time, and an awareness and attraction to physical beauty, dreams, and ambitions. What is it that creates patterns in this tapestry? What qualities set apart Ron's sharp sensory memories from similar descriptions of hundreds of other families?

Ron's narrative is a loving chronicle of the ebb and flow of human relationship. All the "threads" listed above are the woof shuttled back and forth on the loom. It is that warp of human relationship that holds everything together. The chapters, at time, tend to feel quite discrete. The reader meets people and learns about events that seemingly have little direct connection, but that quality in Ron's narrative is just the antiphony of life, the call and response of human interaction. The stories are not just simple paeans to small-town life in the mid–twentieth century. There is honesty and pain. There is personal revelation, perhaps courageous, perhaps trivial. But there is authenticity. What mattered to Ron or to his family begins to matter to all of us. We begin to share the disappointments, the hunger and hardships, and eventually, the triumphs. The reader learns a lot about family life in an abandoned public building, sugar-beet farming, religious faith, small-town schools, fishing, and more. The reader begins to hear the speech patterns and learn the lingo of Northeastern Colorado. Maine's "ayeah" and South Texas's "yup" for "yes" are joined by rural Colorado's "yal." We acquire a new vocabulary, and perhaps most significantly, we connect and care.

Ron Newton's tapestry, his personal **universe**, becomes ours.

It has been said that "all politics is local." It might also be said that any narrative, even one as diverse as Ron's, might be the global distilled to the familial. This story "reads" in two quite different ways: Ron's family story has undoubted macrocosmic intimations. The reader moves **outward** from a specific Newton family narrative to the complexity of our shared global family story. But the "big" story simultaneously occupies an intimate, almost secret, corner of the heart: all good stories are personal. And the galaxy of stars that peoples this narrative illuminates the universal human condition and provides light for our paths.

Yal,
Lorraine Hale Robinson

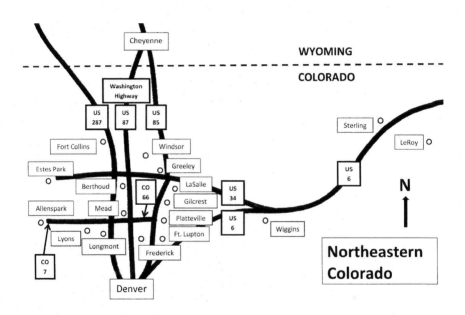

| Businesses and Public Buildings | (Residents [Subsequent Residents]) |

Businesses and Public Buildings

A. EUB Church
B. Kuner-Empson Pea Huller
C. Mead Dehydrating Company
D. Town Park
E. Jail-Library
F. Firehouse
G. Mead Motor Company
H. Bunton's Red & White
I. Mead Appliance Store
J. Mead Blacksmith Shop
K. Denver Elevators Co.
L. Jones Auto Service
M. Pool Hall and Barber Shop
N. Baker's Store
O. Post Office
P. Snider's Drugstore
Q. Clark Lumber Company
R. Town Hall
S. Texaco Gas Station
T. Mead Inn
U. Mead Consolidated Schools
V. Athletic Field
W. Denver Elevators Co.
X. Conoco Gas Station
Y. Guardian Angel Church
YY. State Highway Department
Z. Train Depot.
ZZ. Kuner-Empson Pickle Tanks

(Residents [Subsequent Residents])

1. Dulcinea and Unrita Gallegos
2. Parsonage of EUB Church
3. Mr. and Mrs. Moore
4. James Elmer and Laura Newton
5. Mr. and Mrs. Stephen Weeks
6. Grover and Ethel Roberts
7. Leo and Ruby Bencomo
8. Richard and Glenda Benevidez
9. Melvin Boro
10. Howard and Bonnie Widger
11. Mr. and Mrs. Jack Pierce
12. James and Mona Logan (Unrein)
13. Clare "Curly" and Emily Newman
14. Isaac and Grace Doke (Russell Schaefer)
15. Mr. and Mrs. Yakel (Roy and Esther Weber)
16. William and Francis Howard
17. Benjamin and Anna Ballinger (Jake Amen Jr.)
18. John and Edna Moehler
19. Mamie Howlett
20. Joseph and Molly Hernandez
21. Ralph and Margaret Alexander
22. Ed and Annely Dempewolf
23. Anthony and Margaret Dempewolf
24. Bernard "Duck" Newman
25. John Olsberg
26. Dale and Virginia Baker
27. Wilse and Glenna Lamberson
28. William and Alice Bunton
29. Jim and Mary Halpin
30. Effie and Charles Markham
31. Glen and Lillie Leonard
32. Edwin and Lillian Spencer (Samuel Stewart)
33. George and Elizabeth Snider
34. Mrs. Johnson (Jack Adams)
35. Mr. and Mrs. Ben McCoy
36. Mrs. Cleveland
37. Iva Stotts
38. Joe and Lila Jones
39. Ansel and Ruth Clark
40. Charles and Eva Dempsey
41. Carl and Mary Carlson
42. Frank and Ethel Kruger
43. Wally and Gladys Fredericksen
44. Mary Johnson
45. Rodney and Hester Markham
46. James and Hazel Trimble
47. Jake and Katherine Amen (Sander Adler) Fred and Elizabeth Petersen
48. (Delbert Thompson)
49. Marion and Esther Humphrey
50. John and Christina Gust
51. John and Fay Maestes

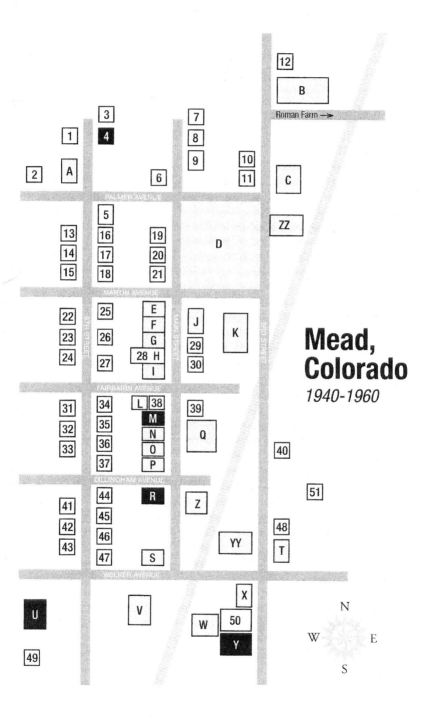

This story is factual, but in almost any story, facts are filtered through personal experience—refracted through the lens of memory. So my story may be more "real and authentic" than narrowly "accurate." I have tried to write honestly—charitably, yes, I hope—but honestly.

Very few books are the products of just one individual. This one has resulted largely from the contribution of my sister Helen Newton Teter, who provided many of the photos, which she took with her box camera beginning in 1948 and many photos of others that she has assembled into the Newton family album over the years. Most importantly, this book could not have been factually, historically, and accurately written without the contribution of Helen's painstaking research of the last two decades on the genealogy of the Dreier and Newton families. My thanks go to my cousin Laurel Dreier Williams, who provided narrations and documents on Dreier family history. Lastly, the stories included in this book have resulted from conversations I've had with Helen Newton Teter, Patricia Newton French, Richard Newton, Roland Newton, Marc Newton, Forrest Newton, Laurel Dreier Williams, and friends and classmates.

My sincere thanks goes to my classmate Irene Stotts Hayward, who provided twelve annual volumes of the *Mead High School Yearbook*; my niece Patricia Thornton Lewis, who scanned and digitized the family album photos, edited the text, and designed the book cover; my photographer Sheila Koenig, who has shot photos with black-and-white film of Mead and the surrounding community; my editor, Lorraine Hale Robinson, who has critiqued and corrected my manuscript and provided suggestions and narrative input and who has been an inspirational and collaborative colleague and friend; and to my journalist brother, Marc Newton, whose critical, scrutinizing eye for extraneous words has encouraged me to write more succinctly—my apologies to all the rest of my family who think otherwise.

Laura Dreier Newton with triplet sons, Richie, Rollie, and Ronnie, 1943, *Newton Family Album*

CHAPTER 1

Leaving Home

My mother, Laura Dreier Newton, was fifty-six years old when I left home to attend college. She had given birth to my two triplet brothers and me in 1939, and we were the fifteenth, sixteenth, and seventeenth of the twenty children whom she and my father brought into this world. Our arrival was sandwiched in between the tail end of the Great Depression and the beginning of World War II. Her excitement at being the mother of the second set of triplets born in the state of Colorado must have been dampened by the realization that her two eldest sons, Orbin and Raymond, had enlisted to fight in the war. Those two were the first of a long line of children whom my mother would bid good-bye to over the next eighteen years, and now in 1957, she was saying farewell to the three of us, all at the same time.

Earlier in her married life, my mother said final good-byes to two of her children. With no suitable drugs available, my brother Robert succumbed to erysipelas when he was just one year old, and my week-old sister Martha was unable to survive complications of an undeveloped intestinal tract. There was no hint of sadness or sorrow when our mother spoke to us about their deaths. Her true feelings were tempered by time, and wallowing in self-pity was not Laura Dreier Newton—meeting hardship and difficulty head-on was. Her mental toughness was constant, but it was tested each time her nest was emptied.

My seven sisters were all older than we triplets. When the girls left home to take jobs or to get married, they all settled in close-by towns and cities. We knew that when they left, it was only for a short time, and we would soon see them again. However, with my older brothers, we were separated by time and distance as they left for military service. Each time they left, my mother would peck them on the cheek just as they stepped out the door and then retire to her bedroom to sob in solitude.

Kissing them good-bye was the only time I ever saw my mother express her love for my older siblings. Hugging and embracing us stopped when we were very young. The last time I remembered my mother touching me affectionately was when I was four years old. It was a summer evening, and she had been gone for most of the day with a next-door neighbor to shop for groceries in nearby Longmont. She didn't get home until way after dark, and my two triplet brothers, Richie and Rollie, and I had been put to bed by our sisters Pat and Helen. Despite our age of four years, we were still drinking condensed milk from a bottle and were sleeping in our baby cribs. Richie and Rollie had already gone to sleep, but I was still awake, longing for my mother. From our bedroom next to the living room in the front part of the house, I could hear my mother telling my brother Tom to bring in the sacks of groceries and baskets of peaches and pears that remained in the trunk of our neighbor's car. I then heard her talking to my older sisters Helen and Pat as she entered the house, checking to see what had transpired and if everyone had been fed supper.

"MOM!" I yelled from my crib as I stood upright, hanging on to the railing and looking out the open bedroom door into the lighted living room. It was the sound of a very familiar "distress call," one that my mother heard from her children many times in the middle of the night when we were cold, scared, lonely, feeling abandoned, or feeling uncomfortable and embarrassed, realizing we had wet the bed.

With the light from the adjacent room streaming through the doorway, she could clearly see me standing forlornly. She came to my crib, stooped down to me, and put one arm around my shoulders while leaning on the railing with the other. She kissed me on the cheek, and I, feeling the moisture from her lips on my skin, quickly took my hand and rubbed it away. My mother said, "Don't do that—it's not nice to wipe your cheek after someone kisses you." Then she added, "They might think that you don't like them."

I always knew my mother cared deeply for all of us, and I never felt that we were shortchanged by her reserve in expressing her love with words or physical contact. However, I perceived then that we Newtons were different from other families. Our friend Allen Thompson and his sister and brothers were doted upon by their mother. Each one of them seemed to be very special to Mrs. Thompson, and she could be seen sitting on their living-room couch with her arms around one of them. Mr. and Mrs. Thompson watched TV with arms around each other's shoulders—something I never saw my mother and father do. I simply concluded that this difference in behavior between my mother and father must be because we had a larger family than they did. After all, my mother and father had so much to do they didn't have time to display affection—and if they did, they were not the type of people who would do it for others to see.

I had often heard conversations of adults who said, "Daughters grow up to be like their mothers," and "I knew that she would turn out like that—she's just like her mother." Now I don't know for sure if this can be said unequivocally about my own mother, because I never really knew my grandmother Lydia Dreier. I only saw her a few times when my aunt Ernestine and my uncle Earl brought her to visit, and then I never really talked to her.

My knowledge of my grandfather Ernest Dreier was even more clouded than the knowledge of my grandmother, because he died when my mother was five, leaving my grandmother with the responsibility of raising my mother, seven other daughters, and one son. With a toddler and teenage children to rear, my grandmother remained on the wheat farm that she and my grandfather homesteaded in Northeastern Colorado. Making a living on a half-section of dry land was a harsh life for her and her brood of eight.

A cousin told me she heard our aunts say on many occasions that Grandma Dreier was not an affectionate person and was not prone to shower her children with displays of maternal love. "I'm willing to bet" (as my mother would say when she thought she had special insight into a situation) that my own mother, like her mother before her, most likely demonstrated little affection toward her children out of concern that this might lessen the self-esteem of those not recognized. If this happened, it could destroy the morale of the whole family—because with large families (especially rural ones), there is much work to be done and all have to share the burden. Motivating everyone to work for a family's common good requires that all siblings have a strong sense of self-worth.

However, not showing favoritism to any of her children was not easy for my mother. She faced a real dilemma when it came to her triplet sons. We were the center of attention—we were a novelty—we were the ones whom visitors to our home wanted to see. It made no difference that she had a set of twins and other children to show to the inquisitive public—people were most interested in the triplets. With both reluctance and pride, she would parade the three of us in front of them and smile tolerantly as they voiced admiring comments.

"They're not identical—but you can tell they're brothers," one would say.

"Boy, they have pretty, straight teeth," said another.

Teenage girls would innocently ask each other, "Who do you think is the cutest?" The other would whisper the answer in the ear of the inquirer so we wouldn't hear.

"Who's the toughest?" asked an adult male. We would say nothing, only smile and laugh, embarrassed by their special interest in us as well as by the question. Only Richie and I responded. We both pointed to Rollie.

For us children, speaking to strangers and adults was difficult and was never encouraged by our mother. She reminded us, "Children are to be seen and not heard."

Most often, we would let her answer for us. On the other hand, if our mother thought that any of the three of us was enjoying the notoriety too much, she would say, "Remember, you are not the only star that twinkles." And after eighteen years, it was clear in my mind that the stars of my two brothers and me had been more than just a flickering glimmer—far from it—in my way of thinking, our stars had been immutable beams of brightness, reflecting the lustrous essence that radiated from the family of my parents, James Elmer and Laura Dreier Newton.

But in 1957, our stars were starting to fade in our hometown of Mead; we triplets were leaving—leaving behind our families and friends and a familiar landscape of buildings that housed our nurturing activities of worship, education, and recreation. Other than the Catholic Church, to us, the most important structures in the town were the Mead Consolidated Schools building and its attached gymnasium. These were the buildings where we had spent many hours of the past twelve years, and the gym was where we played basketball for Mead High School. That gym was also where we learned how to play so well that Coach John Bunn later recruited us to play for Colorado State College of Education.

Coach Bunn had visited our high school before graduation and invited all three of us to play for him.

"However," he said, "I only have only one scholarship—I can't give one to all three of you. I'm going to offer it to Ronnie."

Rollie then said emphatically, "That's okay—I'm not sure I'm even goin' to college. If I do, I'll probably go to Colorado A&M."

Richie said, "The scholarship doesn't matter to me—I'm still goin' to CSCE—I'll pay for everything myself."

There was much to be done before that September day when we were due to depart. With Rollie not having to be at A&M until the next week, Richie and I arranged for him to take us to CSCE. We would go in the '49 Ford the three of us had purchased together.

My mother washed and pressed a dozen or so sport shirts for each one of us. She washed and pressed our white cords—dress pants that we were required by Coach Adams to wear to every basketball game. Numerous pairs of socks, shorts, jeans, and T-shirts had been washed and hung out to dry before she folded them in neat piles for each of us.

Richie and I loaded hangers full of shirts and pants into the backseat of the car, leaving a small space for one of us to sit. On a hook over one back window, we hung our high school graduation suits, along with two sport coats that once belonged to our older brothers Tom and Jerry. We loaded T-shirts, jockey shorts, socks, jeans, and tennis shoes into brown paper grocery bags and placed them in the trunk.

"What jacket are ya takin'?" Richie asked me.

"I've got my gray plaid coat, that's enough," I answered, referring to the coats the three of us had bought in our junior year—the last pieces of look-alike clothing we wore as triplets.

"You're not takin' your letter jacket, are ya?" Richie asked.

"Nah," I said. "I'm leavin' it here for Dave or Marc—they'll make good use of it."

I was proud and comforted knowing that one of my younger brothers would be wearing the leather-sleeved orange-and-black jacket I was leaving behind.

Our mother descended the two steps leading from the back porch and stood on the broad sidewalk area in front of the car to assess our departure status. Standing with elbows outward and both hands clasping the waist of her tall frame as she watched us put our belongings into the car, she said, "Okay, you birds—behave yourself." She then wistfully commented like she did to all her departing children, "I guess I'll expect ya back when I see ya."

She walked up to Richie and kissed him on his cheek. She then kissed me and turned away as she started to sob, loudly and uncontrollably, as she hurried back into the house. She was not there to watch us drive away—she carried her sorrow into the seclusion of her bedroom.

Our mother's sudden outburst of tears as we left home was unexpected—we were surprised and didn't understand the complex feelings that a mother has as she sends her children into the world. We said nothing as Rollie backed our car out of the driveway and then onto the street, taking us southward through Mead. We paused just for a moment at the Stop sign on the south end of town, giving us a short glimpse of the school and the gym one more time before we turned east to catch the Washington Highway, just a mile away.

As we drove north toward Greeley, I thought how much I would miss my mother. I was very devoted to her, and I knew that Richie and Rollie felt the same way. I recalled a conversation I had with my girlfriend, Kathy Nottingham, when I asked her, "What would you do if your mother died?"

"I would die too," she answered.

I then said to her, "I read that one of the major causes of teenage death is suicide."

Kathy said, "I think that's what I'd do if I lost my mom."

Through the years, I had done everything I could to earn and maintain my mother's respect. I knew she was very proud of everything my brothers and I had accomplished, so I wanted to please her by continuing my success in basketball as well as my studies. I was excited with the prospect of "learning a lot" in college. Going to college was a great opportunity, I thought, and I was going to do everything I could to make it my advantage. Studying had been a way of life for me at Mead High School, and I knew I would do the same at CSCE. Although I had little confidence that I could meet the rigorous standards of college work or make the college basketball team, I wanted to coach. I wanted to be like Mead's Jack Adams, who had coached me and my four brothers and our teammates to many basketball championships.

Many times I had asked myself, "If I don't become a coach, how 'bout bein' a priest?" I remembered what Sister Marjorie told our catechism class one day, "Priests and nuns often come from large families—they've learned early on how to sacrifice and serve others."

I knew that I had served my family members well, and I had willingly shared my financial resources with them. "Young men most often become priests because they are inspired by their mothers," continued Sister Marjorie. "More than anyone else," she added, "their mothers influence their decision."

I knew my mother, a faithful believer after conversion to Catholicism, would be very proud if I donned the collar of a priest. In my mind, the priesthood had become probable since I had parted from Kathy, the only human being up until then I had ever told that I loved. A week earlier, we had separated our lives—she was leaving to attend college in Missouri.

Five miles north of Mead, we triplets still had no words to say as our car passed Hart's Corner Bar and Restaurant and then rolled out onto the open plains of fruitful cropland. To the west, we caught a final glance of Mount Meeker and Long's Peak, two majestic triangles that towered over the horizon of the Rockies' Front Range. We crossed over the Big Thompson River, once a torrential tributary from the melting ice and snow of summer but now just a trickle in the autumn season.

Light of Her Children

Finally, Rollie broke our silence with a question, "How much money do you guys have to start out with?" He added, "I don't have very much, maybe less than a hundred dollars in my bank account."

"I have $240," said Richie.

"I saved over $500," I said. "Tuition is $37.50 a quarter, but I get mine free—the dormitory room is $198, but we don't know yet what our meals will cost. I can make it through the first two quarters with the job Coach Bunn said they'd give me in the dining hall or in the student union."

"I'll find something in a restaurant near the college," said Richie. "I'll have enough."

Rollie steered the car off the interstate, and we headed eastward toward Greeley—the seat of Weld County and the home of CSCE. We drifted by stubbled fields of wheat and pens of fattening slaughter cattle. We passed rows of sugar beets, just weeks away from being harvested, and we navigated by fields of parched cornstalks with ears waiting to be picked. We saw tall cottonwoods lined along deep furrows of winding and wandering ravines, the only remnants of the plains of yesteryear. Their gnarled branches were silhouetted against the clear eastern sky, reigning like memorial statues over the fertile farmlands of Weld County.

Farming was the primary way of life in Weld, and it was a dominant force in the lives of my brothers and me. Farms surrounded the small town of Mead, where we and two hundred other townspeople had lived the past eighteen years. Farm produce had put many meals on our dinner table. Farm work and an hourly wage had provided us money to buy our clothes and our car and now to pay for college tuition and board. Mead farmers were not only the ones who paid us—they were also the ones who cheered for us on the basketball court. Farming had been our life and our livelihood, and now this was about to change.

Moving east, our car slowly ascended a long, shallow hill, and at its top, I saw the low-lying Greeley skyline just ahead. Greeley, with the CSCE campus, would now be my home. The town of Mead—Mead High School—Mead farms—the Rocky Mountains—they were now all behind me to the west; the first eighteen years of my life had passed, and now they too were behind me.

I recalled once again what my mother had said many times, "You've made your own bed—and now you have to sleep in it." In my short life of just eighteen years, I hoped I had made mine well. I knew then, more than ever, that my star would not be the only one that twinkled—I just hoped that my star would shine once again.

Rollie, Richie, and Ronnie Newton, 1957. *Mead Consolidated Schools Yearbook*

Southside of Rademacher house (formerly the Newton home) in Mead, 2011. Sheila Koenig

Mead Consolidated Schools Building, 1957. *Mead Consolidated Schools Yearbook*

North side of Mead Elementary School gymnasium (formerly Mead High School gymnasium), 2011. Sheila Koenig

Laura Dreier Newton, 1957. *Newton Family Album*

Chapter 2

Elmer

My father was not there to say good-bye when we triplets left home. I hadn't expected him to be—we both understood that I would be gone for a few weeks and would soon return for a weekend visit. That day, like every other day, he had risen early and milked the cow—washed up, shaved, dressed, and walked downtown. At age 67, he was fully retired and now participated in his favorite pastime—playing pool. My mother had pressed a clean shirt and tie for him, and she made sure he had pants back from the cleaners. His clothing style alternated from "Jacque Penne'" purchased at JCPenney's in neighboring Longmont to "military marine" left behind by my brother Orbin, a captain in the Marine Corps. With the brown khaki shirt, green cotton tie, and green wool pants, coupled with his newly shined Florsheim shoes, my father would have passed inspection of a hard-nosed drill sergeant. If you passed him walking down the street, he would call you "Captain"—the name he used for every male he directly addressed. Raising his hand to the brim of his tan fedora, he would salute you as he walked by.

I seldom talked to my father. When I had problems, I went first to my mother. When I needed money for tablets or pencils at school, I asked her, but if she had none, she would say, "Go ask your dad."

My father never refused—he always had change in his pocket. Because he was a disabled veteran from World War I, he received a check every month from the US government.

"How did Dad get that scar on his arm?" I asked my mother.

"He was shot by the Germans in the war," she said.

I pictured in my naive young mind that a German soldier had raised himself from a trench, took aim at my father, and shot him in the arm with a single bullet. Being wounded, my father received a commendation from President Woodrow Wilson. My mother framed it and hung it on our living-room wall. The commendation showed a soldier on one knee holding a rifle upright with the butt on the ground and the barrel with an attached bayonet. The thought of my father sticking a German in the stomach with something like a large butcher knife and killing him was unthinkable, so I convinced myself that this was something my father had not done.

Unlike my brothers and me, my father had never been an athlete. The closest he came to sports was as a spectator, watching the Kentucky Derby or attending a baseball game. "The greatest baseball player I ever saw was Mickey Cochrane," he told us one time. "He was a left-handed catcher for the Philadelphia Athletics. He had such a strong arm he could throw a runner out at second base without standing up."

Although my brothers and I played a lot of softball in our backyard in our younger days, my father never participated, nor did he try his hand at basketball or football. It might have been that his disability interfered with his ability to throw. Perhaps it was the fifty years difference in our ages, and he could no longer muster the energy to play sports with my brothers and me. Or maybe he was simply too tired at the end of the day to do anything that required more exertion. Most likely, he was well aware that he had not had an opportunity to develop his own athletic skills, and it was too late in his life to start. Most likely too, he knew he would be of no help to his precocious athlete sons.

My interaction with my father was minimal. When I needed help and guidance, there were always others whom I turned to—my mother, my brothers, and my sisters—never my father. It was always others, brothers-in-law and friends, who took my brothers and me fishing and swimming and to softball games. It was my older brother Jack who erected our basketball goal, and it was my brother Tom who taught me and my brothers to make and fly a kite. My father was always far removed from activities and from any personal issues I was facing. As a consequence, I spent very little time with him, and I had little opportunity to have conversations about his ancestry and his own life. What little I knew about him, I learned from others.

My father was one of seven sons born to my grandparents Benedict and Ida Newton on a small farm in Central Kentucky. The Civil War had ended just thirty-four years before he was born in 1889. However, the bitter memories of the war still lingered in the mind of every Kentuckian, including that of my grandfather Benedict Newton. As a child, young Ben had experienced—firsthand—the pain and suffering of the War between the States. His father and my great-grandfather James Irvin Newton, fought on the side of the North. The war was especially painful to Ben and his family because Kentucky, a border state that was neutral, was one of the primary places where "brother against brother and neighbor against neighbor" was most prevalent.

My aunt Mary, a feisty and jolly redhead from Kentucky and the wife of my uncle Spaulding, my father's brother, often came to visit my mother, and I would hear Aunt Mary reminisce about her life and that of her husband back in Kentucky. One afternoon, she told my brothers and me a story about our great-grandfather as a Union soldier—Corporal James Irvin Newton.

* * *

James Irvin Newton was at his home in Big Springs, Kentucky, lodged in a tiny ravine in the Appalachian foothills. He sat down with his family at the table to eat the evening meal that his wife, Ellenda, and his older daughters had prepared. It was 1865, three months after Lee surrendered to Grant at Appomattox. With the war presumably over, James Irvin had returned home to resume his blacksmithing. As a cavalryman with his portable forge, he made shoes for his regiment's horses. He repaired caissons and wagons, guns and cannons, breastplates and bits, and stirrups and harnesses. Now he was glad to be back with his wife and their nine children, including his eight-year-old son, Benedict.

James Irvin had worked late that evening, and darkness surrounded his tiny four-room house standing next to his shop. The nearby shoemaker had closed his doors and gone home, and there was no one at the spring drawing water. Horses in the livery lay quiet in slumber. The stagecoach had already passed through town, and the innkeeper, certain he would not be awakened by a weary traveler, had snuffed out the office candle and retired. No one was expected to be moving on the road through Big Springs that night.

Suddenly in the silence, James Irvin and his family heard hoof beats as horses and riders approached the house. The Newtons heard men talking and dozens of footsteps on the wooden floor of the front porch. They heard a knock.

"Who are these night riders? Why are they here? What do they want?" said James Irvin to himself as he got up from the table. He opened the door and stepped into the doorway. A lone man shook hands with him with one hand and pulled a pistol with the other. A loud gunshot pierced the evening stillness as a bullet from the revolver two feet in front of him entered his chest. James Irvin fell backward onto the floor as Ellenda and her children watched with horror. The masked riders rode off into the night, with their identity and true motives never to be known.

Hearing the shot, neighbors came to the family's aid, and they carried James Irvin's body up the hill to be buried in a Protestant cemetery. They buried him that night, wanting to keep his final resting place secret. If his killers were embittered Confederates, it was certain they would be back to desecrate his body and his grave.

Said Aunt Mary, "I guess your great-grandma was really worried that your great-grandpa was not goin' to heaven—he didn't get the last rites, and there was no funeral. They say she prayed every night for the rest of her life for God to save his soul. Your grandpa Benedict always remembered seein' his dad's bloodstains on the floor of their house. He never forgot watchin' his dad die."

"Who were those masked riders?" I asked.

"No one knew for sure," said Aunt Mary. "Some people thought that they were supporters of the North—they said that the night riders shot your great-grandpa because they thought he was givin' away secrets to the South. But I don't think so—I think they were farmers from around the county and they wore masks because they didn't want anybody to know who they were. I think they thought your great-grandpa was a traitor for fighting for the North. Until this day no one knows for sure."

I took boyish pride in learning that my great-grandfather had fought on the winning side. Winning was of significant importance—after all, my father and two brothers had also had been "victors" in war.

Later, however, my sense of triumph became confused when one of my classmates asked my fourth-grade teacher, Mrs. Jepperson, about World War II.

"Who won?" he asked.

"You know, no one ever wins a war," she answered.

Aunt Mary's stories about Kentucky and the Newton family were fascinating to us, and we encouraged her to tell us more every time we saw her. Whenever our mother could get a word in, she would also add to the conversation. From Aunt Mary and my mother, I learned how it came to be that my father

Light of Her Children

ended up in Mead, Colorado, where he spent most of his adult life and where I grew up.

* * *

James Elmer Newton left Kentucky in 1905 and spent the next twelve years working as a railroad locomotive fireman. The rails took him all over the United States. "I've been to every state in the Union," my father boasted to us one day. Said my mother, "There were a lot of relatives of your dad's named James—so when he was growin' up, they started callin' him Elmer—that's what he's always called himself."

In 1917, Elmer became weary of the nomadic railway life, and he decided to take up farming. He headed west—hoping to gain the opportunity to buy land, set up a farming operation, marry, and start a family. Elmer followed in the footsteps of his four brothers and his sister. Three of his siblings had married and moved west with their spouses and families to test their luck with farming. They joined folks from everywhere—Kansas, Missouri, Nebraska, Canada, Germany, and Russia—folks who migrated to the northeastern plains of Colorado to grow wheat and sugar beets on grasslands that once were the home of the buffalo and the antelope. Citizens and immigrants had been enticed to go west by eastern newspaper editors such as Nathan C. Meeker of the *New York Tribune* who, in 1869, wrote,

> If people would settle in Colorado and cultivate the sands of the Great American Desert by means of irrigation, they would receive health and happiness by inhaling the tonic of its rare bracing atmosphere, bathing in its almost perpetual sunshine, and would avoid the loneliness and inconvenience generally experienced by other settlers on the frontier.

"You can find work here," Elmer's sister, Minnie Newton Horrel, wrote from Colorado. "They always need somebody.

Zack is working on a farm near Mead. The mountains are just twenty miles from here."

It was midsummer when Elmer stepped off the Union Pacific in Denver. He had boarded the UP in Kansas City, and as it moved westward across the Kansas wheatlands, he saw the vigorous harvest activity that was taking place all across the land, all the way to Colorado.

He saw harvest crews working from dusk to dawn. Horse-drawn reapers moved across fields, scissoring wheat stems and collecting them into shocks, and binding them with twine. Shocks fell gently to the stubbled ground, later to be stacked into clusters, heads upward, for the precious grain to dry. Men pitched shocks into horse-drawn wagons and hauled them to the steam-powered thresher. There they pitched the shocks onto conveyer belts, carrying them into the belly of a large tin-covered machine, propped up on four wheels, and roaring and spewing steam like a monstrous dragon. Within its bowels, grain was separated from chaff and straw, and the galvanized giant ejected the straw from its spout, shooting straw into the air into tall stacks scattered all over the plains.

In Denver, Elmer took the Union Pacific Omaha-Chicago train to Sterling, a Northeastern Colorado railroad town surrounded by irrigated farms along the South Platte River. Wheat crops were lush near the river, and heavy spring rains had bathed the dry lands north and east of Sterling, yielding a bountiful grain crop, now ripe for harvesting. Farmers from Haxtun, Holyoke, Fleming, and LeRoy were in a hurry to get their crop harvested before the grain fell to the ground. But threshing operations were expensive—they required a water tank, a coal wagon, and a thresher. Many farmers could not afford these, so they were dependent upon entrepreneurial operators who had purchased the machines and hired crews. Furthermore, the operator had to be a steam engineer as well as a farmer. Joe Dullaghan from Peetz was just that—a business-minded farmer and mechanic who could also manage people.

Dullaghan hired Elmer Newton. Elmer and the rest of the crew followed the thresher from farm to farm, harvesting from sunup to sundown. At night, they slept in hotels in Fleming, Haxtun, and Holyoke—towns whose skyline was just a tall silo. In these cylindrical structures, grain from the harvest from miles around was stored. From there it was loaded onto railcars of the Chicago, Burlington, and Quincy Railroad and transported to Omaha or to Sterling and then on to Denver and towns along the Front Range of the Rockies.

It was dusk when Dullaghan's threshing crew with its wagons and horses pulled into the yard of Lydia Dreier's farmhouse on a hill above a ravine lined with outcroppings of limestone.

"Your grandma Lydia wanted her house on the hill so she could see across the plains," my mother said one night as we were eating supper. "It took her and your grandpa Ernest a couple of years to get it built. When they first got to Colorado after leaving Canada, they had to live in a dugout that they carved out of a limestone bluff on their homestead. So when they built the house, they used that same limestone. They made large blocks out of it and cemented them together with mortar that they made out of ground-up limestone and water."

Said my mother, "Your grandpa dug the well first—then he and your grandma built the house—and later they built the barn. But the barn didn't last long—got hit by a tornado. We were eating supper when it hit—'bout ready to eat our dessert—a bowl of strawberries and cream. The wind blew the kitchen door right off its hinges—it hit your grandma, but it didn't hurt her. When it passed, we went outside to see what happened. The barn had disappeared—the only thing left standin' was our horse tied to the manger post."

"How old were you?" I asked.

"I was 'bout five then," she said. "I remember there was so much dirt blown into the house—it covered all my strawberries—I was real unhappy that I couldn't eat 'em. Your uncle Emerit and your grandma built a new barn—it's still there."

Benedict and Ida Newton with son James Elmer Newton, 1889. *Newton Family Album*

James Elmer Newton, 1906. *Newton Family Album*

Childhood home of James Elmer Newton in Clarkson, KY, circa 1920. *Newton Family Album*

James Elmer Newton in the US Army, 1918. *Newton Family Album*

Threshing crew, James Elmer Newton, *far right*, circa 1920. *Newton Family Album*

Chapter 3

Elmer and Johnnie

Lydia Dreier was widowed when her husband, Ernest, died with typhoid fever in '06, and now she and her only son, Emerit, were managing the farm. Ernest himself had been a threshing operator, using a machine that he constructed and powered with horses. But now after his death, Lydia was dependent on others to thresh her wheat crop.

Wheat harvest was an exciting time for Lydia Dreier—it always had been. As a young girl on her father's Canadian farm, she had gathered the wheat into bunches, following behind her father as he swathed with a cradle and scythe. Now with mechanization, Lydia guided two horses pulling a machine that cut the stalks and bound them into bunches before casting them to the ground, doing what she had watched her father do with his horses. She was plowing and harrowing ground and planting seed. Soon the harvest would be over, and she would do what her father had done, disking the stubble from the past year's crop and preparing the land for the next planting season.

It was mid-July, and Lydia was ready for the threshing to begin. Weeks earlier, she and Emerit and her four youngest daughters had stood the shocks upright for drying. Daughters

Maggie, Petie, Freddie, and Sammie (Ernest Dreier had affectionately given male nicknames to all his daughters) were married and gone, but Mikie, Johnnie, Jimmie, and Ernie were still at home.

It was a common practice within the LeRoy farming community for the contracting farmer to provide an evening meal for the threshing crew. So the next morning, Lydia Dreier and her four daughters had much work to do after they did the usual morning chores. Chickens had to be killed, plucked, cleaned, and fried. Corn needed pulling, shucking, and boiling. Cream had to be churned into butter. Potatoes had to be brought up from the cellar, cleaned, peeled, boiled, and mashed. Garden-grown green beans and cabbage both needed boiling with onions and hog fat. Strawberries needed picking and washing. Extra pails of water needed to be drawn from the well, and a pot of coffee needed to be brewed. The kitchen floor had to be scrubbed, and the table had to be set for eight hungry guests.

As the men devoured the meal served by Lydia and her four daughters, the two oldest, Mikie and Johnnie, did not go unnoticed by the guests. Johnnie, especially, attracted Elmer's attention. Her long black hair was tied with two large white bows on each side just above her ears. Like her father and all her sisters, her lips drooped on each side, giving her a saddened look, masking the real happiness she felt inside. She did not have the sculptured and well-proportioned facial features of her mother but, instead, displayed the long jaw and downward arched nose of her father. However, she was radiantly beautiful when she smiled. The whiteness of her well-aligned teeth contrasted with the smooth summer tan on her face. A long-sleeved shirt and bib overalls hung loosely on her five-foot-eight frame. Underneath was the body of a sixteen-year-old with muscles sharply toned by the toil and sweat of farm work.

Johnnie had finished her eight years of schooling two years before, and now just as her older sisters had done, she remained at home to help Lydia with farming and keeping house, learning the skills of a farmer's wife. She planted gardens in the spring, canned fruits and vegetables all summer, helped with wheat harvests in July, sewed for herself and her sisters in the cold of winter, milked cows in the morning, baked bread on Saturdays, and sang in the church choir and played the organ on Sundays. Her older sisters had learned their lessons well and married men all destined to be farmers: Maggie and Gus, Petie and Peter, Freddie and Bill, and Sammie and Leonard. Harry was now courting Mikie, and soon Elmer would be courting Johnnie.

When the grain harvest was over in Logan County, Elmer went back to LeRoy, where there was plenty of opportunity for work on the farms of Johnnie's brothers-in-law. They gave him a bed to sleep in, fed him, and took him along to the family gatherings at Lydia's house. After the service at the LeRoy Evangelical Church, it was commonplace for Lydia to assemble her growing and extended family for Sunday dinner. In Lydia's home, Elmer saw Johnnie once again.

Lydia began to notice this "stranger" in her house. She admired his work ethic and his spiritual nature.

"Your grandma thought a lot of your dad," said my mother one time to us. "She liked him because he was a hard worker. Your dad was real strong—he could lift almost anything. She liked him too because he went to church. Every Sunday morning, your uncle Harry would give your dad a ride to St. Peter's, the Catholic Church in St. Petersburg, and he always dressed up in a suit and bow tie."

Elmer, at twenty-seven years of age, was short and compact. His 160 pounds was disproportionally distributed over his shoulders and upper arms—his upper torso bulging underneath his long-sleeved shirts. By most women's standards, and certainly those of Johnnie, he was a handsome man with a slightly arched nose, gray eyes, and contracted lips. His lower lip curled upward on the left side, perhaps indicating an indifference to the world but, mostly, portraying his confident self. In summer, his usually fair complexion was tanned, and his head was swept with waves of curled brown hair, parted on the left side. A gold chain dangled in an arc from his chest, attached to a gold watch that was hidden in the bib pocket of his strapped overalls. A tagged string from a Bull Durham bag hung over the top of the other chest pocket, which held the tobacco sack, a small folder of cigarette papers, and a dozen or so wooden matches.

When he ran out of work in Logan County, Elmer took the train to Denver and hitchhiked to Mead. His brothers, Robert and Spaulding, and sister, Minnie, boarded him while he stacked hay, picked corn, and topped sugar beets. When winter set in, he repaired fences, built barns, painted houses, and loaded grain into railcars. He returned to LeRoy and helped the Dreiers, the Looses, the Hagemeiers, and the Sonnenburgs. They all planted windbreak cedar, slaughtered pigs, fed cattle, and repaired barns and machinery. Once again in LeRoy, Elmer found time to see Johnnie.

But Elmer's pursuit of the farming life in Colorado was interrupted in early May of 1918 when he received a letter from his mother, Ida, telling him that he was about to be drafted and he should return to Kentucky. The Grayson County Board notified him at his home in Clarkson on May 21. He was to report to Leitchfield, the county seat, on May 26.

Elmer left Colorado with his future uncertain—his quest for the farming life was now on hold. He did not know when or if he would return. But he knew that he wanted to be back in Colorado, if he survived the war. He knew that he wanted to go back again to see Johnnie.

* * *

It was 1918, and James Elmer Newton's infantry regiment was already in France fighting the Germans when he boarded the train from Leitchfield to Camp Zachary Taylor near Louisville, Kentucky. The war had been going on for more than three years, and replacements were needed on the Western Front right away—there was little time to train. Draftees from all over, especially from the South, were transported to Camp Taylor, and except for Elmer Newton, most had hunted with a rifle. They already knew how to shoot to kill. Unlike Elmer, these men knew what it was like to pursue and destroy life with a bullet. Another difference between Elmer and the other draftees was age; Elmer was twenty-eight, and most of the draftees were teenage boys who had kissed their mothers good-bye and left home for the first time.

After only three months of training, Elmer's platoon took the train to New York. There in the harbor, a convoy of transport ships waited to carry him and several thousand hastily prepared troops across the Atlantic to England. Seasick when he arrived, it was several days before he could bring himself to eat anything, and then the only food that was available was the British ration of bread and cheese and "meat" of unknown origin.

The platoon boarded a train to a British camp and then hiked to the English Channel, where British ships carried the soldiers across to France. Elmer's unit caught up with Company E of the 355th Infantry—a regiment of the Eighty-Ninth Division of the US Army. It was late September, and Company E, along with the Eighty-Ninth, was resting on the edge of the Argonne Forest, close to the Belgian border and west of the Meuse River. Elmer took his assigned position with a four-man machine-gun unit. The Eighty-Ninth received continuous shelling from German airplanes, and it had to hunker down for three days before it could be trucked to the front to replace the battle-worn Thirty-Second, now exhausted from several unsuccessful tries at overcoming a German stronghold.

At the front, a huge rain cloud had settled over the forest where the Germans had dug in, and it poured for days as the Eighty-Ninth fought to advance. Bogged down in rain-filled trenches, Company E troops constantly battled rats, insects, lice, dysentery, and mud. On the edge of the forest at Bantheville, the Eighty-Ninth met heavy enemy artillery fire and fierce machine-gun resistance—the worst encountered by Company E in the war. Two lieutenants were wounded, and another was killed by a large shell fragment. An infantry private, the "company barber," died from a hand-grenade explosion. In three days of battle, Company E lost forty men to wounds and death.

Company E faced barrages of artillery and machine-gun fire. There was the continuous whine of bullets and the odor of gas as white puffballs moved overhead. The night lighted up as if it were day, and the earth shook. Under relentless fire and without protection except for the narrow trench, Elmer witnessed the bloodbath. He was numbed by the sight of bodies without heads, foreheads blown away, legs missing, and holes in the chests and abdomens of fallen comrades. He heard the moaning of wounded soldiers and the screams of horses and men in anguish. He gagged with the stench of dead bodies and human excrement—he could find relief only by wearing his gas mask.

On the third day, in midafternoon, Elmer heard a loud whistling from a distance, a sound he had heard many times. Instantly, he dropped the box of ammunition he was carrying and crunched his body together—he knew he needed protection from the debris that was about to explode around him. Every explosion produced thousands of projectiles searching for human targets.

Feeling an instant pain in his right bicep, he grabbed his upper arm with his left hand, only to see blood spurting between his fingers. His whole arm twinged with pain. He fell to his knees and leaned backward against the side of the trench, water up to his thighs. He unbuttoned his shirt, pulled the shirttail out of his pants, and stuffed it into the gaping hole in his bicep. Holding tightly to his arm, he got to his feet and crouched, supporting himself against the trench wall. Feet immersed in water, Elmer remained there in a crouched position until the next morning when Company E was relieved by an Eighty-Ninth machine-gun battalion. Company E, now with only 130 men, retreated from the front to Bois de Gaines for a needed rest.

Exhausted from combat and loss of blood, Elmer fell into formation for the long march to safety, his upper arm crudely bandaged. He was suffering from the lack of food and water, and the rolling and forested terrain of the march challenged his weakened body even more. Parched with dehydration, Elmer and his fellow soldiers fell out of formation to drink rainwater that had collected in shell holes. Finally reaching their position, Company E dug in and pitched its tents. However, the kitchen unit had not arrived with them, so the men went to sleep without being fed. The mess sergeant and cooks stayed behind—foraging the countryside, where they found cabbage and turnips in an abandoned field.

Years later, when our family was sitting down to eat supper with hot chocolate in our glasses, my father casually stated, "This reminds me when I was shot in the war. I went to sleep for a long time, and when I woke up, they served me boiled cabbage and hot cocoa. They told me that the chocolate was good for the 'runs' I had." That was the only time I heard my father make any reference to the war.

Elmer convalesced for a short while in Le Havre on the coast of France, and in early November 1918, he was sent back to America. By mid-November, the Eighty-Ninth and the American army had crossed the Meuse River into Belgium, and the war was over. Elmer convalesced further at Camp Zachary and was discharged early in February of 1919. In Louisville, he caught the train going to Clarkson—his parents, Ben and Ida

Newton, were there to greet him. Elmer had survived World War I with his life and a shrapnel wound to his arm.

Then in May 1919, Elmer bid his parents good-bye and boarded the Union Pacific Railway on his way to Denver. In Denver, he would take the UP Omaha-Chicago Line to Sterling. Elmer would be in Colorado just in time for the wheat harvest, and there he would see Johnnie once again.

Homestead house of Ernest and Lydia Heist Dreier built in 1889 near LeRoy, CO, circa 1905. *Newton Family Album*

Ernest and Lydia Heist Dreier, 1894. *Newton Family Album*

Laura Celia Dreier, 1910. *Newton Family Album*

Laura Celia Dreier, 1902. *Newton Family Album*

Laura Celia Dreier, 1918. *Newton Family Album*

Homestead barn of Ernest and Lydia Heist Dreier built in 1901 near LeRoy, CO, circa 1905. *Newton Family Album*

LeRoy Evangelical Church, circa 1900. *Newton Family Album*

CHAPTER 4

The Twenties

Johnnie realized she was pregnant with Elmer's child in the late spring of 1920. She was then living with her mother, Lydia Dreier, and two sisters in Sterling and was sales-clerking at the Glass and Bryant Dry Goods Store. (Lydia had moved off the LeRoy farm so her son and his new wife could move into the home place and take over the farming operation.) Elmer was working and living on the farm of Johnnie's sister Mikie and her husband, Harry Loos.

In those days, the acceptable procedure in this circumstance was to get the two involved to marry, and thus, plans for the wedding immediately began. However, Lydia Dreier was concerned that her daughter of eighteen was now being encouraged to marry a man twelve years her senior. Lydia knew she had well prepared her daughter to be a homemaker, but Johnnie had had few other experiences off the farm. The furthest away from home she had been was Nebraska, while her husband-to-be had traveled to each of the forty-eight states and had fought in a war on another continent.

And what about their faith and cultural differences?

James Elmer Newton's Catholic heritage dated back to the late 1600s, when Thomas Newton left England to avoid the rule of the Protestant monarch. Settling in the English colony of Maryland, Thomas's son, Ignatius, experienced religious persecution himself, so he moved his family to Kentucky in the 1700s. In Kentucky, the family's Catholicism flourished from one generation to the next, handed down to James Newton, to James Irvin Newton, to Benedict Newton, and then to James Elmer Newton. Each generation was taught to marry within the faith tradition. When someone "outside" married into the devout Catholic family, the external partner had to agree to convert to Catholicism and to raise any children as Catholic. All of Elmer's brothers and his one married sister had chosen Catholic spouses—he would be the first and only one to do otherwise.

Similarly, members of the Evangelical Free Church were encouraged to choose a mate of their same faith. All of Johnnie's married sisters had done this. The Evangelical faith was strongly adhered to by members of the LeRoy farming community. Responding to the beckoning of the German Evangelical Association, many Evangelicals had homesteaded in Colorado and settled in LeRoy, joining a community of like believers. Lydia and her late husband, Ernest, had answered that call right after their marriage. Raised as Evangelicals in the Canadian homes of their parents, Lydia and Ernest continued to carry the Evangelical torch. Lydia tended to the sick and sewed garments for members of her church community. As a church elder and as a skilled stonemason, Ernest led the way in building the church, a steepled limestone symbol of their faith. The rich tradition of Evangelical Protestantism had been instilled in the lives of their nine children, including Johnnie.

The immediate concern for Lydia Dreier was to help Johnnie decide where and how the wedding ceremony should take place. Lydia arranged for Samuel Beese, minister of the LeRoy Evangelical Church, to preside. The wedding was scheduled for August in the LeRoy farm home of her daughter, Mikie, and her husband, Harry Loos. Mikie and Harry would witness the wedding. Johnnie's two younger sisters and those with husbands and children were invited.

Johnnie was radiant that day in the dress she had made from multicolored rayon she had purchased from Sterling's Glass and Bryant. Collared and with elbow-length sleeves, the dress was low-waisted with several layers of cloth ruffled downward from her right hip, cascading to fullness at the hemline on her right side and dropping unevenly three or four inches below the knee. Flat chested and slender despite her enlarged stomach, Johnnie's boyish figure still resembled that of a flapper. Her long black hair, pulled tightly into a bun, was laced with daisies from Lydia's garden.

Elmer's handsome appearance matched the elegant style of his fiancée. He must have spent all his monthly disability check on the stylish tweed suit and cap he wore. His jacket was short and high-waisted with narrow lapels, and it buttoned high like the uniform of a World War I army officer. His trousers were narrow and straight with no cuffs. His white club-cut shirt collar, adorned with a black bow tie, stood high around his neck. The chain of his watch draped from one pocket, and a black silk handkerchief peeked out from the other. He wore two-toned, high-topped shoes, laced halfway up, with the remainder fastened with loop and hooks. His cap matched his suit and its wide brim saucered flatly around his head.

In the living room of the Looses' home, Elmer stood with Johnnie before Reverend Beese as they recited their vows and listened to the minister's brief sermon on the virtues of marriage. Guests sat on sofas and chairs listening and watching as Elmer and Johnnie promised to love each other for eternity. Afterward, Mr. and Mrs. James Elmer Newton and guests went to the kitchen, where a buffet lay before them. While the ladies convened in the living room to chat as they ate, the men

Light of Her Children

congregated outside underneath a large elm tree to enjoy the repast and light up their cigars.

Some folks around LeRoy say that Elmer wanted a Catholic wedding as well, reporting that he and Johnnie went to St. Peter's in nearby St. Petersburg to be married by a priest. Was Elmer doing what he knew his mother would have wanted—receiving the sacrament of matrimony in the same church as his forbearers? Learning that her wanderlust son had finally married, Elmer's mother, Ida Carrico Newton, sent a family Bible, published with the sanction of the Roman Catholic Church, to the newlyweds.

Elmer and Johnnie did not stay in LeRoy—they moved to Mead, where Elmer was promised work in the sugar-beet harvest on farms rented by his married brothers, Spaulding and Robert, and the farm of his brother-in-law, Zack Horrell. Two younger single brothers, Claude and Joseph, had already been hired on. The Newton families would work together on the myriad tasks required to get the fall crop to the Longmont refinery before Thanksgiving and before the heavy snows came.

Elmer had left Kentucky to take up farming in Colorado. Like thousands of others all over the nation and the world, Colorado provided that great opportunity for them to start a new life. It was understood that Elmer and his ten siblings would all have to leave their father's small Kentucky farm one day—it was hardly big enough for the family's meager subsistence. On their father's farm, they grew most of their own food, using the corn crop to feed the livestock. Their cash crop was tobacco, and they sold an occasional mule or two. Benedict Newton taught his children all he knew about farming: they learned how to grow corn and tobacco, to raise pigs and chickens, to milk cows, and to plow and plant with a team of mules. They learned even more working on their neighbors' farms, planting and threshing grain, cutting and stacking hay, planting and picking cotton, and raising horses.

The physical challenges of farm work were no obstacle to the Newtons. Farming had been their only way of life, and they were certain that Colorado was where they could make their living doing what they knew how to do best. Colorado farmers were still enjoying the economic prosperity of the post–World War I years, buying cars, tractors, trucks, and threshing machines. Farmers were plowing up marginal lands and planting more seed—they were getting more dollars for their crops. The optimism of this generation of Newton siblings was buoyed by what they saw all around them. In their minds, farming in Colorado promised to be a good life.

It was November 16, 1920, when Elmer and Johnnie's first child was born in the bedroom of their rented house, 3½ miles east of Mead. With Elmer's sister-in-law Mary present along with Dr. Clymer from Mead, Johnnie gave birth to a son. Mother and child did exceptionally well; Johnnie's robust, conditioned body had produced a hardy six-pound infant—a sturdy copy of his mother; mother and son were ready to continue their lives with strength and vitality, hallmarks of both the Newton and Dreier clans. Elmer proudly recorded their firstborn's name, Urban, and Urban's birth date in the family Bible.

Before long, members of Johnnie's adopted Catholic family in Mead began to inquire about Urban's baptism. Father Luther of Guardian Angel Church said Urban was a fine Catholic name and was a good choice. He told them that St. Urban was a second-century pope and that, throughout the ages, Catholics prayed to him when they sought help from a severe storm; Father Luther said praying to St. Urban would keep Urban Newton safe from being struck by lightning.

All of Elmer's siblings and their families attended Guardian Angel, the Roman Catholic mission church in Mead, served by Benedictine priests from Longmont's St. John's Catholic Church who traveled to Mead to say Mass. In January 1921, Father Luther baptized Urban in the holy water font at the church entrance. Elmer's brother-in-law, Zack, and his sister,

Roberta, recited vows as godparents. Firstborn Urban was now a full member of the Catholic community, the faith community of Elmer and his forefathers. Father Luther recorded the event on the church's baptismal rolls. He wrote down Elmer's first name, James, in the Latin form: Jacobus.

Elmer and Johnnie returned to LeRoy in 1921. Elmer would work once again in the summer wheat harvest on Lydia Dreier's farm. The previous war years had been good to Lydia, and she had accumulated a sizeable bank account. Decreased grain production in Europe had caused a greater dependence on America for wheat, and prices shot up; Lydia sold her wheat for a whopping two dollars a bushel. In addition, Lydia's dry land had received abundant rainfall throughout the war, and wheat yields on her farm reached record levels of twenty-five bushels per acre. The war and postwar years had been so good that Lydia had saved enough money to buy her house in Sterling, with a lot left over in the bank.

However, the good times on Lydia's farm would not last. By 1921, Europe had resumed its prewar production of wheat, and the demand for American wheat lessened. Lydia sold her wheat at seventy-five cents a bushel. The whole economy of the LeRoy farming community was seriously depressed. Farmers who sold milk and eggs to supplement their income saw that Sterling milk and produce wholesalers were paying them much less for their products—more than 30 percent less than the year before. Many soldiers, like Elmer, had returned to Northeastern Colorado and were seeking employment—all were willing to work for the reduced wage that LeRoy farmers were paying.

Elmer and Johnnie moved into a small, wood-sided house, a mile east of the Dreier home place and across the road from the LeRoy Cemetery. While Elmer worked in the fields, Johnnie took care of Urban, baked bread, canned fruits and vegetables, weeded the garden, washed and sewed clothes, and chopped wood. Work was plentiful on the farms of Elmer's brothers-in-law, and they compensated for his low pay by sharing their resources. Milk was always available for Urban, and Johnnie's sisters always sent Elmer home with food—apples, potatoes, butter, jelly, cakes, and bread. Johnnie reciprocated with lettuce, beans, cabbage, and carrots from her garden, and in the summer months, Johnnie gathered with her sisters to make jelly and to can vegetables and fruits that were stored in cellars beneath their homes.

When the harvests were over, Elmer and his brothers-in-law butchered hogs and cut the carcasses into hams, shoulders, side meat, ribs, and chops. Johnnie and her sisters put hams and bacon and shoulder chunks into stone jars filled with brine. They scraped and cleaned gut casings and filled them with ground meat, making large tubes of pork sausage, also preserved in brine. The women rendered hog fat in large kettles, adding lye and water and cooking the mixture into soap.

When snow fell and winter time set in, Elmer spent less time in the fields, and he and Johnnie shared more intimacy in the warmth of their home. As the fall of the year came, Johnnie gave birth to a son, Raymond Lee, in September of '22; a daughter, Eunice Elaine, in September of '23; and twins, Robert and Georgia Roberta, in October of '25. All were born at home with midwife Carrie Sonnenberg and Dr. McCormick from Fleming present. The name "Eunice" (the mother of Timothy, the spiritual son of Christ's apostle, Paul, and a name favored by those in the Evangelical faith community) was selected by Johnnie. Referring to the names of Elmer's siblings and following the Catholic tradition of using the names of saints, Elmer and Johnnie settled on "Raymond," "Robert," and "Roberta" for the other three.

Even into the mid-1920s, farmers on the Colorado plains were still suffering. Prices continued to drop as more and more wheat was produced. The economic woes of LeRoy farmers were compounded by the challenges they faced in warding off sickness and disease. Infants, especially, were susceptible to bacterial infections, and without antibiotics, once an infection set in, it was usually fatal.

In early October of '26, one-year-old Robert Newton became listless and cranky and developed a fever. He began to vomit and wouldn't eat. Chills and shaking set in, and a red rash erupted around his eyes, soon spreading to his cheek and puffing it up like an orange peel. Dr. Latta diagnosed it as erysipelas, and Elmer called it St. Anthony's Fire. He knew that back in Kentucky, when folks saw a swollen red rash on the cheek of a baby, they knew right away that the only way an infant could be saved from death was by prayer to St. Anthony. By October 23, 1926, the infection had reached Robert's liver and kidneys, and he died. His funeral was held in the LeRoy Evangelical Church, where his grandfather Ernest's funeral had been held twenty years before.

They buried Robert in Sterling. His young male cousins carried his tiny body in a small coffin into the church and to the grave site. Reverend Beese said a farewell prayer. When it was all over, Johnnie went to her bedroom and wept. It was several months before Elmer could bring himself to record Robert's death in the family Bible; Johnnie had saved a curled lock of Robert's hair, tucked in between two of the Bible's back pages.

As a child, I asked my mother, "Was Bobby baptized before he died?"

She shook her head from side to side."

"Then he's not in heaven—he's in limbo," I conjectured. "Sister Marjorie told our catechism class that's where a kid goes when he dies if he hasn't reached 'the age of reason' and hasn't been baptized. She said they stay there till the 'end of the world' or until someone says enough prayers to get 'em out. I guess we should be prayin' for Bobby—we need to get 'im to heaven."

Rosemary, Elmer and Johnnie's sixth child, was born in the summer of 1927. By then, wheat prices had tumbled to fifty cents a bushel—one-fourth the price during the war a decade earlier. With the harvest over and with little prospect for work in the fall and winter in LeRoy, Elmer decided to move back to Mead.

"Your dad always thought he could get into farming for himself," said my mother, "but he didn't want to farm on dry land. It was easier to make a go of it if you irrigated. So we left Leroy and moved back to Mead."

With the help of his two young sons and his brother-in-law Harry Loos, Elmer loaded beds, chests of drawers, and crates of clothes and toys on to the side-boarded flatbed of Harry's truck. Johnnie sat in front in the cab with her new baby and next to Harry as he drove, and Elmer rode in the back of the truck with his other children. Heaped around them were all their material possessions. Elmer was starting anew. He was hopeful that life would be better on Colorado's irrigated plains in the shadow of the Rockies.

Elmer found a vacant house on the north side of Mead's town park; it had four rooms, barely large enough to accommodate his family of seven. Brightly painted, "the orange house" rented for thirteen dollars a month.

Now back in the Mead community, Elmer and Johnnie reconnected with Elmer's brother Spaulding and his wife, Mary, who lived on a rented farm near Mead and whom they frequently saw at Sunday Mass at Guardian Angel Church. Johnnie wanted herself and her five children to attend a religious service on Sunday, and she and Elmer agreed that it was most convenient for the family to worship at Guardian Angel.

Knowing that Urban had already been baptized into the Catholic faith and the other four children had not, Johnnie's sister-in-law Mary Newton said to her, "Johnnie—ya better get all those kids baptized—if ya don't—ya know—they ain't goin' to git to heaven."

Light of Her Children

The following spring, on April 28, 1928, Raymond, Eunice, Roberta, and Rosemary were all baptized with their uncle Spaulding and aunt Mary as godparents.

In February 1929, Johnnie, now pregnant with her seventh child, and Mary Newton, fearing that complications were about to occur, drove to the Longmont Hospital, where Johnnie's son Jack was born.

"Jack is not a good name for a Catholic boy," said the new pastor, Father Rose, as the baptism was about to take place at Guardian Angel Church. "I think we should name him John."

Father Rose recorded "John Eugene Newton" on the baptismal certificate and the church roll. His godparents, William and Martha Redmond, and Elmer and Johnnie obediently signed their own names in agreement. Such was the power of the Catholic Church.

Crop prices continued to decline through the 1920s, and Mead's economic fabric began to disintegrate. *Mead Gazette* publisher Connie Brust sold his presses and began printing his paper in nearby Johnstown. Dr. Clymer closed his medical office and moved to Greeley to practice. With fewer houses to build, contractor Bill Howard left town, seeking other work, and George Clark shut down his bowling alley. The stock market crashed in October '29, and shortly thereafter, the Mead National Bank closed.

In the following summer, crops around Mead and across the state were invaded by grasshoppers. With crop prices getting lower and lower and farmers' incomes dropping precipitously, Elmer soon found himself making just a little over a dollar a day—even with his monthly disability check, he could not provide for his family. His economic struggles were intensified when his eighth child, Helen Celia, was born in August 1930. Helen was given the same middle name as that of her mother. At her baptism, new Benedictine priest Father Roger decreed that she be christened as Cecelia. After all, he said, "It was

Cecelia, not Celia, who was the venerated saint of the Catholic Church."

Finally, Johnnie concluded that it was best for her and her family to officially accept the Catholic faith. In May 1932, she was baptized, and the next day, she received her First Communion and was confirmed. Her good friends and confidants, William and Martha Redmond, stood with her as sponsors. Laura Celia Dreier Newton received all three sacraments of the Church as Laura Cecelia, as dictated by the new Benedictine pastor, Father Nicholas. Thereafter, Johnnie would become an exemplary Catholic—she accepted a role that she wanted her children to emulate—now a convert, she was more Catholic than the Catholics.

James Elmer and Laura Dreier Newton with son Urban, 1921. *Newton Family Album*

First home of James Elmer and Laura Dreier Newton, located 3.5 miles east of Mead, CO, circa 1920. *Newton Family Album*

Robert and Roberta Newton, 1926. *Newton Family Album*

Urban, Eunice, and Raymond Newton, 1927. *Newton Family Album*

Spaulding Newton, James Newton, Mary Newton, and Spaulding Jr., circa 1920. *Newton Family Album*

CHAPTER 5

The Depression

As Colorado and the nation entered into the Great Depression, Johnnie's and Elmer's family numbers continued to increase: daughter Patricia Ann was born in 1932, and a son, Thomas James, arrived in 1933. It was now becoming apparent that Elmer and Johnnie needed help in the care of their nine children. Elmer and Johnnie, like millions all over the nation, were faced with a depressed economy, the worst in America's history, and they found help with a charity-supported orphanage. For many in this difficult period, orphanages were regarded as places where parents could leave their children temporarily until family circumstances improved. Orphanages were places where children could get a good education and receive far better medical care, nutrition, and hygiene than those available in their own homes, and orphanages had playgrounds, libraries, athletic facilities, musical training, recreation, and vocational education. Most importantly, orphanages of the period generally worked not to break up families—they encouraged connections with families, and they kept siblings together, with the children returning to their homes when the family situation improved.

Elmer and Johnnie sought the advice of William and Martha Redmond. The Redmonds owned a small farm on the north edge of town, about a half mile down the road from the "orange house" where Elmer and Johnnie lived. Devout Catholics, the Redmonds had raised their two girls likewise—both had joined the Sisters of Loretto, and both taught at Loretto Heights College in Denver. The Redmonds encouraged Elmer and Johnnie to send their oldest children to a Catholic orphanage (the one recommended by their daughters). In the summer of 1933, William Redmond transported Urban, Raymond, Eunice, Roberta, and Rosemary to Denver's St. Clara's Orphanage, administered by the Franciscan Sisters, daughters of the Sacred Hearts of Jesus and Mary.

When the Newton children arrived at the orphanage in 1933, there were more than three hundred other children and forty nuns on the premises. Rosemary, at six years of age, flourished with her new academic environment and the gentle and warm treatment she received from the Franciscan Sisters. Eight-year-old Roberta and ten-year-old Eunice were taught sewing and sent numerous gifts home. The girls read Nancy Drew and Bobbsey Twins books and relentlessly tackled their arithmetic assignments. Ray, at eleven, enjoyed singing in the choir and thrived on the challenges of his English and civics classes. But at thirteen, Urban was a belligerent early adolescent who rebelled against the regimented discipline imposed by the nuns. Urban excelled on the basketball court but performed poorly in the classroom. Furthermore, by then Urban had already grown to dislike his given name, and he insisted that everyone, including the nuns, call him Orbin, a name he himself created.

"I ran away a couple of times," Orbin said to us many years later. "I tried to hitchhike back home, but the nuns sent the cops after me—they brought me back."

Orbin communicated with his siblings daily, and as the oldest, he was fiercely protective of them.

"There were a couple of bullies there always pickin' on Ray," he said. "I had to fight 'em and keep 'em away from 'im.

Also, there was this weird guy who was always hangin' around Eunice—she didn't like 'im—so I had to tell 'im to keep away from her. Betty [Roberta] didn't like it there—she was cryin' all the time and wanted to go back home. It didn't seem to bother Rosemary—she's always been the resilient type."

The children wrote letters to Elmer and Johnnie and enclosed "spiritual bouquet" cards. On one, Betty, Eunice, and Raymond attested that they had made four visits to the Blessed Sacrament, performed six special devotions to the Virgin Mary and two Ways of the Cross, received ten Holy Communions, said five rosaries, and attended eight masses. They signed their names on the card, and Johnnie saved each one, placing them between the back pages of the family Bible.

At Easter, Roberta sent a postcard with a note in her cursive handwriting:

Dear Father and Mother,

How are you? Unice, Raymond, and I am just fine. Dear father and mother, I wish you a very happy Easter. From Roberta Newton

On one, a novena to the Sacred Heart of Jesus, they promised to say the Our Father nine days in a row, just for their parents. On another, a novena to the Immaculate Heart of Mary, they promised to say the Hail Mary prayer for nine consecutive days. On all five of the cards, they signed their names, and Johnnie saved each one, placing the mementos between the back pages of the family Bible.

By 1933, the Great Depression had fully descended upon Colorado and the nation. Elmer could only find work in the summer. He thinned and weeded sugar beets until the grain harvest began. Like wheat, the glutted international sugar market was depressed, and the Great Western Sugar Company paid a minimum price for beets hauled to the Mead beet dump.

Some farmers left their crops in the ground and plowed them under the following spring. For the next two years, Elmer often found himself unemployed. He was not alone—one out of every six workers in Colorado was without a job.

In January 1935, Johnnie gave birth to her sixth daughter, whom they named Martha, after Martha Redmond, who had become Johnnie's confidante and best friend. However, Martha's intestinal tract was malformed and obstructed. After one week, she hemorrhaged. Dr. Jones from Johnstown was called in but unable to do anything; Elmer and Johnnie watched helplessly as Martha died.

"Dad had tears in his eyes when he lifted both Pat and me up to see her in her basket," said my sister Helen. "I was five years old then. I knew that something bad was happening because every time Mom changed Martha's diaper, it had blood on it."

Martha had been baptized only days before, and her godparents, the Redmonds, provided a grave site in the Longmont Cemetery. Martha would lie alongside the Redmonds when they were finally laid to rest. She would lie in the wood coffin constructed by her cousin Spaulding Newton Jr. Devastated, Elmer could not bring himself to record her death in the family Bible.

Two weeks later, Johnnie received a condolence card from her mother, Lydia, now residing in Naperville, Illinois. Lydia managed a boarding house in Naperville, making enough money to support her two youngest daughters, who were there attending North Central College. The poem on the card read,

> Over your pathway, daughter of mine,
> A grievous shadow has rested.
> And I know that you feel that every line
> Of your life and your faith has been tested.

> Then sorrowful heart look up through the night
> Of mourning and doubting and catch the bright day.
> As what we call Death but heralds the light
> Of the dawn of the morning of God's Perfect Day.
>
> (Author unknown)

Lydia wrote,

> We are all very sorry for you, and how I wish I could have come to spend a few hours with you and your family. Our concern is about you and how you are faring. Write and let me know all about it as soon as you are able.
>
> Lovingly,
> Mother

As the Depression deepened, the United States Congress passed the Aid to Dependent Children act (ADC) in 1935. This provided cash payments for needy children whose parents were incapacitated or unemployed. Elmer, unemployed, was eligible to receive seven dollars a month for each dependent child. Now with this help, Elmer and Johnnie could bring their five children back from the orphanage—they and all their nine children could now be reunited.

At first, Colorado politicians were reluctant to provide the required matching funds for the ADCA. Then-governor Edmund Johnson ideologically opposed the imposition of the federal government's will upon the state, and he considered the welfare program for needy children to be a waste of state dollars. Critics argued that the program was an incentive for women to have children—encouraged them to live amorously, yield to their passions, and get money. It was said that parents like Elmer and Johnnie should not be rewarded for "excessive" carnal behavior—they should not be receiving cash payments while others with more restrained habits received none. In fact,

Light of Her Children

cynical critics in the Mead community were prone to perceive an unemployed father with numerous hungry children to be worthless and shiftless—a real "deadbeat"—a label Elmer lived with for the rest of his life.

Needing a larger house to accommodate his family, Elmer moved to the community of Highlandlake, a mile northwest of Mead. All the family's belongings were loaded this time into his brother Spaulding's truck and hauled to a vacant house on the east side of the lake.

In 1936 and for the second time, Johnnie gave birth to twins, Agnes Maureen and Mary Kathleen, their first names meeting the Catholic requirement for saintly nomenclature, although Elmer and Johnnie preferred to call them Maureen and Kathleen.

By the mid-1930s, crop prices had dropped so low that growers couldn't pay workers to help with the harvest of fruits and vegetables. Rather than let the produce rot while children starved, the federal government provided price support to growers so crops could be harvested and transported to the homes of needy families. Trucks loaded with boxes, baskets, buckets, and barrels of fruits and vegetables arrived in the communities of Mead and Highlandlake. Drivers drove right up to the kitchen door of the Newtons' Highlandlake house. Known affectionately as the "welfare wagon," the truck carried cantaloupes and watermelons from Rocky Ford, apples and peaches from Durango, cherries from Loveland and Fort Collins, sweet corn from Olathe, cucumbers and potatoes from Platteville, and pinto beans from Fort Lupton. There were even oranges from faraway California. Sacks of flour, sugar, oatmeal, and salt were also delivered to needy families, as well as jars of jams and jellies and peanut butter.

By 1938, Elmer and his siblings had different perspectives on farming in Colorado. Brother Carl returned to Kentucky, and brother Robert quit farming to sell cars in Longmont. Brother Joseph moved his family to New Mexico to take a gardener's job at a veterans hospital. Elmer, burdened with supporting his large family, no longer thought about operating a farm on his own—his concern now was finding work and earning a daily wage. Only brother Spaulding and sister Minnie and their spouses stayed with farming, hanging on as tenants on farms south of Mead.

With the birth of Gerald Anthony in May of 1938, Elmer and Johnnie had twelve children at home with the oldest, Orbin, now eighteen years old. Orbin had just graduated from Mead High School and was planning to attend the University of Colorado in Boulder. Like his father and younger brother, he was constantly looking for work, hoping to save enough for tuition and board for his first semester in the fall. Sixteen-year-old Raymond worked as a part-time janitor after school, sweeping floors at Snider's Drugstore.

In spring of 1939, Elmer was informed by Malcom Mead that he and his large family would have to vacate the Highlandlake house. Mr. Mead had just hired a new "ditch rider," Edward Brossman, to monitor the flow of water in and out of the Highland Ditch that carried water from the Saint Vrain River to Highland Lake. Mr. Brossman was promised that he could move into the house where the Newton family lived.

Elmer commandeered his brother Spaulding to move his family back to Mead, where the only place available was the abandoned Farmers Union Town Hall. The hall was no longer used for public or school functions, having been replaced with a Works Progress Administration project, a new gymnasium that was built adjacent to the school. The town fathers loaned the hall space to two families and charged no rent. The Newtons and the other family were separated by a curtain down the middle. Johnnie was pregnant for the thirteenth time when she moved in with her twelve children. Gaining weight rapidly, Johnnie was convinced that she was going to have another set of twins come September.

Newton children in Highlandlake, CO. *Front row, L–R*: Helen, Rosemary, Jack, Thomas, Patricia, Urban (Orbin), Raymond; *Back row, L–R*: Mary Ellen Newton (cousin), Eunice holding Kathleen, Roberta (Betty) holding Maureen, 1936. *Newton Family Album*

Newton children in Mead, CO. *Back row, L–R*: Thomas, Patricia with Tippy, Helen, Jack holding Kathleen, Rosemary, Roberta (Betty) holding Maureen, Eunice holding Jerry [Raymond and Urban (Orbin) absent], 1939. *Newton Family Album*

CHAPTER 6

Surprise Threesome

It was late in the evening on September 28, 1939, when Elmer left the town hall in Mead, where he and his family were living and walked twenty yards to use the phone booth located next to Snider's Drugstore. He made a hurried phone call to the home of Louis Roman, who farmed a quarter-mile east of Mead. Certain that his wife in labor was about to have twins, Elmer knew he needed the help of Mr. Roman's wife, Hulda. He trusted and valued the expertise of Hulda—she had assisted Dr. Glen Jones when he delivered Elmer's twin daughters just three years before and son Gerald a little more than a year ago. Elmer called information to get the phone number of Dr. Jones, who lived and practiced in Johnstown, twenty miles northeast of Mead. Both Hulda and Dr. Jones said they were on their way.

Elmer was relieved when he heard Hulda knock on the double doors of the old hall. Hulda could hear Elmer's footsteps as he walked across the wooden floor. He unlatched one of the doors to greet her and let her in. She stepped inside into the large meeting room, where aligned against the wall she saw two double beds and a cot where Elmer's five boys slumbered. Elmer and Hulda walked quietly past the cloakroom and storage room, not wanting to awaken any of Elmer's seven daughters who were sleeping there. They passed through a curtain stretched across the meeting room, which once separated Elmer's family from another family in the hall. That family had gone, and Elmer and Johnnie quickly appropriated the space where Johnnie now lay. Two basketball goals hung on each end of the meeting room, which once served as a gymnasium, and faint traces of the keyhole, center circle, and out-of-bound lines could be seen on the floor in between and around beds, bureaus, tables, and chairs scattered across the room. Elmer's oldest son, Orbin, had played basketball on this very floor, and so had Elmer's nephews, Jim, Merle, and Mike Newton.

Like any dutiful husband whose wife was about to bear a child at home, Elmer had placed a pot of water to boil on the wood-burning stove in the kitchen.

Dr. Jones drove to Mead from his Johnstown home right after Elmer's phone call. He recalled that just three years before, he had delivered Johnnie's twin girls. He knew the girls were the second multiple birth for Johnnie, and now she was about to have a third. He thought about all the other Newton children he had delivered and was reminded of the physical toughness that Johnnie demonstrated each time. He admired her casual, self-deprecating manner and her mental tenacity. He remembered what was taught in medical school—humans are genetically endowed with physical and mental strengths, but the environment allows them to learn behaviors that enhance their ability to cope with the challenges of life. In his mind, Johnnie had benefitted from both nature and nurture—he wondered about her ancestral heritage and her upbringing. In his mind, Johnnie was an extraordinary human being. He reminded himself that Johnnie's deliveries had always been easy ones—quick and with no complications. He took comfort in knowing he would be home in bed before midmorning.

Shortly before midnight, the first child emerged and corkscrewed its body outward through the birth canal.

"It's a boy!" exclaimed Hulda.

As the infant gasped with its first breath, Dr. Jones swatted his butt, inducing a loud cry that awakened Elmer's older sons. Elmer went to them quickly and told them to go back to sleep—it would have to be morning before they could see their new baby brother. Dr. Jones cut the cord, and Hulda placed cotton dipped in olive oil on the protruding naval stub. She wiped him clean around the nose, mouth, ears, and anus and dried him with a towel and sprinkled him with talcum powder that Dr. Jones brought with him. Hulda then wrapped him in a blanket and placed him in a bassinet—one used by an older twin sister three years before.

It was several minutes past midnight, into the next day, when the second child arrived—also a boy. He was smaller than the first. Hulda placed his blanket-swaddled body into the second twin bassinet.

Now while deep into the birth of the second child, Johnnie had become acutely aware that there was a third child. Only minutes after the second was born, Johnnie gave the final push to release the third, the smallest of the three—another boy. Hulda wiped him dry and placed him in the same bassinet as the second born.

In less than an hour, Johnnie had given birth to triplet boys. Hulda's eyes watered as she presented a pair to Johnnie to be nursed. Like most midwives, Hulda had never witnessed the birth of triplets—only one out of every eight thousand midwives would observe such a rarity. She and Dr. Jones had just delivered the second set of triplets born in Colorado, and the first all-male.

Hulda saw that each had unique physical features, and she immediately began to differentiate in her own mind one from another. She grew concerned about the last born, much smaller than the other two. In the next days to come, she would make sure that he was always first to receive his mother's milk.

Dr. Jones recorded the times of birth in his ledger: 11:45 p.m. first, 12:30 a.m. for the second, and 12:35 a.m. for the third.

Light of Her Children

Hulda took each child and placed him on the small platform balance of Johnnie's kitchen scale. Dr. Jones recorded: seven pounds two ounces for the first, six pounds eight ounces for the second, and five pounds four ounces for the third. Johnnie had given birth to a mass of humanity totaling more than eighteen pounds!

Johnnie was comforted knowing that, once again, she had endured the rigor of childbirth with no lasting effects. She knew she would be up and out of bed the next day, tending not only to her new threesome but also to twelve other children needing her care. This being her third multiple birth, she herself attached no special significance to the event. She paid little attention to the praise thrust upon her by Hulda and Dr. Jones. Although gracious in receiving their congratulations, she did not consider herself or her three children as deserving of any special adulation.

However, relatives, friends, neighbors, and visitors from everywhere thought otherwise. Johnnie's triplets were a sensation, and she was not prepared for what was about to happen. People came from all over: Frederick, Longmont, Loveland, Windsor, Greeley, LeRoy, Denver, and Boulder. Two-year-old triplets, the first born in Colorado—Roland, Kate, and Raymond Roberts from Littleton—came held in the arms of their parents. The Redmonds and their daughters, Sisters Pancraitius and Martha, were there, and so was Sister Marjorie from Longmont's St. John's School. (Sister Marjorie would be preparing the threesome for their First Communion seven years later.)

The throngs brought gifts of pillowcases, diapers, bottles, blankets, baskets, nightgowns, ropers, wash pans, plates, high chairs, stockings, slippers, shoes, and flowers for Johnnie—some even left money. Elmer constructed three upright support structures to which each basket was attached and suspended above the floor.

Johnnie and Elmer had not named the boys when the multitudes started to knock on their door. All who came to see the nameless triplets left Johnnie and Elmer with suggestions. Their daughter Rosemary wanted to call one Roland—she had read about this historic figure in her literature class—a Christian soldier who helped Charlemagne defeat the pagans.

She said, "I'm sure he was a saint—he went right to heaven when he died."

Elmer suggested names of his own brothers, Joseph and John, and his sister Minnie thought the third should be called James.

"Everyone liked the idea of them all starting with *J* and with them bearing the names of brothers from the previous Newton generation," Rosemary told the three of us later. "But Uncle Spaulding and Aunt Mary had named our cousin Jim after Dad, and Mom didn't want to use 'James' again. Also, she didn't like the name 'John'—she thought he would be called Johnny, and she didn't want that either. We didn't have you guys named until we got around to your baptism."

So there it was—the firstborn just before midnight on September 28, 1939, became Ronald James. The two brothers, born shortly thereafter on September 29, became Richard John and Roland Joseph. As a result, each would have the acronym moniker of RJN.

"How much did we weigh when we were born?" I asked my mother six years later while sitting around the breakfast table.

"You were seven pounds, Richie was six, and Rollie was five," she said.

"Then since I weighed the most, I must've been born first and Richie was second and Rollie was third," I said, rationally concluding that was the way the birthing process worked.

My mother, with no hesitation, nodded and said, "Yes, that was the way it happened."

However, official birth certificates show that Ronald was the second born with Roland first and Richard third. Was Dr.

Light of Her Children

Jones exhausted and confused, or had his memory faded when he completed the birth certificates a month later? Did he get the order wrong, or was it the county clerk who mistakenly mixed up the names? Had our mother confused the order and weights of the three?

A representative of the Pet Milk Company came to see the triplets. His company offered to provide a three-year supply of Pet Milk—the evaporated milk product that had saved the lives of thousands of hungry babies since the Depression began. Babies throughout the nation were transitioned to Pet Milk poured into a bottle just as soon as their mother's nursing ceased. The company had developed technology to sterilize milk through heated evaporation, sealing the liquid in a can that could be shipped anywhere.

As a soldier in World War I on the German front of the Allies, Elmer had drunk Pet Milk. He recalled how the mess sergeant made cocoa with it and fed it to him the morning after he was wounded. He knew Pet Milk was nutritious, and that a source of milk would be needed when the three babies could no longer breast-feed. Reluctantly, Elmer signed the agreement to receive the milk and allow the company to publicize the transaction. Twice a month, a dozen five-ounce cans with the image of a cow on the label were delivered by rail to the Mead train depot and hauled home in a wagon. Each night, the triplets were bedded down with a bottle of the creamy yellow liquid, and occasionally, Johnnie used the "tin cow" contents for cooking.

Father James Maher, pastor of Guardian Angel Catholic Church, went to the Newton home in the town hall for the baptism. He enthusiastically endorsed their saintly middle names and was delighted to hear that one of them was called James. Their aunt Mary and their uncle Spaulding presided as godparents and recited vows to take care of the trio if something happened to Elmer and Johnnie. Dressed in matching gowns that Mrs. Christine Gust had made for them, their sisters Eunice, Rosemary, and Roberta held the babies while Father

James prayed, "Amen, amen I say to thee, unless a man be born again of water and the Holy Ghost, he cannot enter into the kingdom of God."

Together, Mary and Johnnie held each one as Father James poured holy water from a small pitcher on each head and said, "I baptize you in the name of the Father, the Son, and Holy Ghost."

After pouring water over their heads, they were anointed with a chrism, symbolizing the uniting of the three infants with the Holy Spirit. From the lighted Easter candle that Father Maher had set on the table, he lit three more candles and gave one each to Eunice, Rosemary, and Roberta to hold. He turned to Johnnie and Elmer and Mary and Spaulding and said, "The light of these candles are entrusted to you to keep burning bright."

Then Father Maher placed his palm, one by one, on the heads of the triplets. He stepped back, paused for a moment, and said to them, "Receive the light of Christ."

Father Maher opened his bible and read from the Epistle of St. Paul to the Ephesians, chapter 5, verse 8: "For you were once darkness, but now you are light in the world. Walk, then, as children of light."

With Orbin and Raymond away from home working, nine brothers and sisters stood on the hall floor eagerly watching. One-and-a-half-year-old Gerald, perched in the arms of his brother Jack, looked on with puzzling wonder. His life had changed—in fact, the lives of all the Newton children had changed. They all had three new brothers—the triplets had taken the center stage in the Newton household. But there was a special continuity that began with the birth and baptism of these three brothers: the Newton triplets, born on the basketball court of the Mead Town Hall, would as teenagers take center stage on the basketball court of the Mead Consolidated School gymnasium, and Gerald would join them.

Father James was stricken with concern about this family of seventeen, all under one roof and in need. As their pastor, he wanted his own Guardian Angel Church to help, but he also sought help from others. He conferred with the Weld County Sheriff, who asked the Welfare Committee of the Greeley Elks Club to find a way to help the Newtons, particularly their new trio. Elks Exalted Ruler, D. A. Tarra, and Sheriff Anderson visited Elmer and Johnnie and determined that they could help by providing a crib for each of the three. A week later, they came back with the cribs and a photographer. A picture was taken of the three lying in their new beds with their brother Gerald looking on, and it appeared the next day in the *Greeley Tribune* for all of Weld County to see. The Newton triplets were gaining notoriety that Johnnie never thought of or wanted. But like it or not, from here on, the media hounds would be perched on her doorstep. Quoting Father James, the *Tribune* article said, "The family still needs dental care, furniture, and a better place to live."

Elmer and Johnnie hoped that their next house would be one they could own. After twenty years, they had lived only in rentals, never able to save enough money to make a down payment on a home. Try as they might with their growing family, they, like the nation, had not overcome the economic setbacks they had experienced in the last decade. The 1930s had not only devastated America's economy, but it had also thwarted the economic engines of Europe, the Soviet Union, China, and Japan and other countries of the world.

On the world stage, economic discontent had supported Adolph Hitler's power grab in Germany and Benito Mussolini's in Italy. Both dictators abolished democratic rule, established fascist governments, rearmed their countries, and began their conquests of other nations. Italy invaded Ethiopia, and Japan invaded China and later attacked the Soviet Union and Mongolia. In September 1939, Germany and the Soviet Union both invaded Poland—Hitler and Stalin then split the country between them. Economic depression and power aggression had turned the world against itself—now it was clear that the world was on the brink of another war.

Elmer and Johnnie were disturbed about what they heard on their tabletop Philco radio and what they read in the *Denver Post*. Hitler continued his conquest of Europe by annexing Austria and invading Czechoslovakia. Elmer was personally chagrined that Germany had risen to superpower status once again. He thought that his World War I efforts and those of the United States had stymied the Germans once and for all. How could he ever forget the horrors of war he had experienced because of the Germans? Now he hated "those bastards" more than ever. Johnnie found it hard to reconcile that Germans—people of her own ethnicity—were now killing thousands. It was difficult for her to imagine that any of her Dreier or Heist relatives, as Germans, were committing atrocities.

Despite the bleakness across the world, Elmer and Johnnie's fortune on the domestic front had taken a turn for the better. They learned that a nine-room house in Mead that had been vacant for several years. The previous owners, Henry and Mary Mathews, had purchased the land from town founder Paul Mead in 1907 for $200 with the stipulation that they would build a house costing $600 or more within a year. By 1931, elderly and with no children and with back taxes owed, the Mathews transferred ownership to Weld County. In 1945, the county put the property up for sale, and Laura Dreier Newton bid $600, approximately one-third the appraised value.

Johnnie asked her mother, Lydia Dreier, for a loan of $600. When the check arrived, Johnnie arranged to ride with Mary Johnson in her '34 Plymouth to the Weld County Courthouse in Greeley and obtain the deed. Johnnie's fifteen-year-old daughter Helen went with them.

"I remember that both of them were smiling and very happy when we left the courthouse," said Helen later. "The deed said that the house was built in 1903. That summer of 1940 we moved out of the town hall. That was a big day for all of us. Dad and Orbin painted all the bedrooms and the kitchen, and Mom and us girls wallpapered the dining and living rooms. I don't know how long it took for Mom and Dad to pay it off—but I know Grandma got it all back—she didn't charge 'em any interest."

"Grandma was a shrewd business woman," Helen added. "She didn't give her money away—not even to her own children."

By 1941, the war had truly become global, and the draft age was lowered to eighteen. Worldwide events would now directly impact the Newtons. Elmer and Johnnie's eldest son, Orbin, after one year in the army, reenlisted in the marines, and the next oldest, Raymond, joined the navy. As they stepped out the door of their home in Mead, Johnnie pecked them on the cheek with a good-bye kiss and then retired to her bedroom to weep. Elmer looked them in the eye, shook their hand firmly, and said, "Be careful, Captain."

Each night, as Johnnie lay in bed saying the rosary, she prayed for all her children, particularly for the safety of her two oldest sons. Not ever knowing where they were or what they were doing, Johnnie would pray with constant fear the next two years.

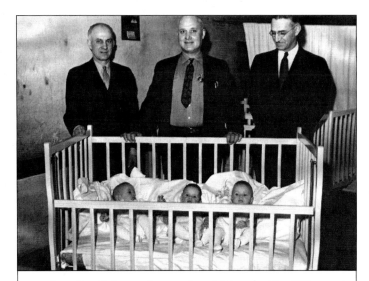

Greeley Elks Club Members and Weld County Sheriff (center) present cribs to Newton triplets, 1939. L–R: Rollie, Ronnie, and Richie. *Newton Family Album*

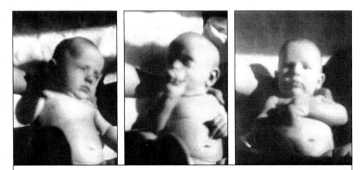

Newton triplets, 1939. L–R: Richie, Rollie, and Ronnie. *Newton Family Album*

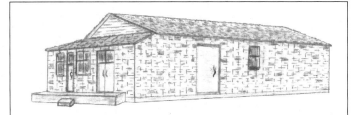

Illustration of Farmer's Union Town Hall, Mead, Colorado. 2015. Ronald Newton.

Chapter 7

Sons of War

Raymond Lee Newton, the second oldest son of James Elmer and Laura Dreier Newton, graduated from Mead High School in 1940. He was drafted into the army in late 1940 but opted to enlist in the navy in March 1941. With eight months of training in San Diego, Seaman Second Class Newton was assigned to serve on the *Tippecanoe*, a fleet replenishment oiler ship that operated between the West Coast and the Hawaiian Islands. In late November 1941, Seaman Newton was transferred to the aircraft carrier, USS *Lexington*, which had just arrived at Pearl Harbor. The *Lexington* had joined an assemblage of carriers, destroyers, cruisers, and tankers, all making up the United States Pacific Fleet. Seaman Newton loved naval ship duty, particularly on a carrier. He liked working in a group—working together to accomplish a common objective of launching aircraft. He liked watching the *Lexington*'s pilots bring their planes to the launch line, rev their engines, release the brakes, and rush down the narrow deck to lift off. Seaman Newton was proud to be one of nearly two thousand men who made sure that the *Lexington*'s dozen fighters, three dozen dive bombers, twelve torpedo bombers, and all their pilots were ready for combat.

Seaman Newton, valedictorian of his high school class, was well equipped with thinking, writing, and typing skills of great use to the operations unit of the carrier. As an operations specialist, his reports, prepared after careful analysis of radar, navigation, and combat information, both of enemy and US warships, were essential for officers of the fleet. Seaman Newton also had been trained to assume special-alert-status duties should the *Lexington* be attacked.

On the day after the Japanese aerial attack on Pearl Harbor, Elmer and Johnnie listened to President Roosevelt's address to the US Congress and to one hundred million US citizens listening on their radios. Their son Orbin, just released from a one-year stint with the US Army, was with them as they listened to their Philco to hear the President say,

> I ask that the Congress declare that since the unprovoked and dastardly attack on Sunday, December 7, 1941, a state of war has existed between the United States and the Japanese Empire.

Elmer, Johnnie, and Orbin had no knowledge of Raymond's whereabouts. They did not know that on the day of the bombing, Raymond was then serving on the *Lexington*. Fortuitous for Raymond and his crew, the *Lexington* had left Pearl Harbor several days before and was in the vicinity of Midway Island when the Japanese attack occurred.

However, Elmer and Johnnie were shaken with the alarming news that Orbin was drafted for the second time. Orbin, now influenced with the post-Pearl Harbor fever of fighting to defend his country on the beaches of the South Pacific, decided to join the Marine Corps. He entered as a private in February 1942. However, his year of prior military service did not go unnoticed, and the corps assigned him to an instructional training unit at the recruiting depot installation in San Diego, California.

In April 1942, Seaman Newton's naval life was to be significantly changed when US admiral Chester Nimitz sent four carriers, including the *Yorktown* and the *Lexington*, and their support ships to the Coral Sea, northeast of Australia. On May 3, Seaman Newton experienced his first naval combat when aircraft from the *Lexington* and the *Yorktown* surprised Japanese forces and damaged enemy support warships anchored in the Solomon Islands. In May 7, aircraft from both carriers sank the Japanese carrier, *Shoho*.

In May 8, *Lexington* pilots made the first search for the other Japanese carriers that had been so close the night before. At 5:30 a.m., the clanging of the carrier's bell announced the take-off of the search aircraft and the call to general quarters. Since Seaman Newton's work shift had begun at midnight, he was already at his battle station. Three hours later, the *Lexington* received word that the Japanese had been sighted about 120 miles away. By 9:30 a.m., the *Lexington* had launched its bombers, fighters, and torpedo planes, keeping a small contingent of protective fighter aircraft on deck.

Captain Frederick Sherman warned the crew to prepare for a Japanese assault sometime around 11:00 a.m.—the *Lexington*'s radiomen had intercepted a Japanese transmission. Captain Sherman followed with the order to "button up" the ship. The watertight door of the operations room was closed, and now in a "blind compartment," Seaman Newton and his fellow sailors had no visibility of the deck or the outside.

At 10:55 a.m., a voice over the loudspeaker crackled: "Now hear this—now hear this—enemy planes are approaching the ship."

Twenty minutes later, Seaman Newton heard a rumbling explosion, followed by a violent shaking of the ship. A minute later, he felt the shock of a second explosion. Unbeknownst to him, the *Lexington* had been punctured by two torpedoes, the first buckling fuel storage tanks and the second rupturing the water main leading to the ship's boilers. Moments later, he felt another reverberating shock, which seemed to roll the *Lexington* forward and upward out of the water. The ship had been hit by a bomb in the gun gallery, setting off ammunition and starting a fire that spread rapidly into rooms below deck. For the next few minutes, Seaman Newton sensed repeated rattling through his compartment as more bombs hit the *Lexington*.

When smoke came through the ventilator shaft into the room, Seaman Newton and his shipmates put on gas masks, opened the watertight door, and ascended ladders to the deck above. There was an eerie silence—flying aircraft and artillery could no longer be heard—the enemy was gone—all that Seaman Newton heard were the shouts of men scrambling to put out the fire and tend to the wounded.

He ran to help shipmates carry wounded onto the deck. Many were severely burned, and he assisted in removing their clothes so tannic acid jelly could be applied to their scorched skin. He gave them water as the chaplain and medics injected morphine to alleviate pain. The wounded kept coming, some of their own accord, while others were brought by shipmates. Some had their clothes blown off, leaving shreds of skin hanging from their flesh. Others were wounded with powder burns and shrapnel from exploding ammunition. Seaman Newton struggled to find words of consolation—he knew that many of his wounded comrades were in their final moments.

The battle lasted only ten minutes, and by noon, the crew began to feel relieved. The *Lexington* seemed pretty much intact—the fires had been extinguished—the damaged engine room could still provide full power—and the flight deck was undamaged. Seaman Newton, aware that there were still important tasks to be done, searched for his operations shipmate to determine who would return below deck to continue. Since the operations room had caught fire, their tasks would take place in the radio repair room. It was agreed that Seaman Newton's shipmate would assume those responsibilities and that Seaman Newton would remain on deck to tend to the wounded and dying. Seaman Newton also hoped he might get an hour or two of much needed sleep.

Meanwhile, the *Lexington*'s airborne planes landed and were refueled and replenished with bombs and ammunition in anticipation of being sent back into the air. All ship compartments appeared to be holding, and progress had been made with damage control. The seven-degree list of the ship had been corrected—everything seemed to be all right.

However, at 12:45 p.m., the *Lexington* was shaken by a loud and violent rumble. Smoke emerged from the elevator and onto the flight deck. Fire broke out from ruptured vents and risers; undetected vapors from broken fuel tanks ruptured by the torpedo had ignited. Seaman Newton was ordered to help move fire hoses from the far aft part of the ship. Small explosions of ammunition occurred all around him, and he could feel the heat coming through his shoes. The elevator surface began to glow red. Then the water pressure became so low, there was no way to contain the fire, and it spread to the engine room. Sherman ordered the crew to shut down the engines. The mighty *Lexington* lay dead in the water with no power.

At 5:00 p.m., Sherman reluctantly gave the order to abandon ship. Seaman Newton helped place the wounded on stretchers and into rope-tethered life rafts and then gently lower the rafts of the wounded into the churning water. At the same time, sailors began to throw life rafts overboard. Seaman Newton removed his shirt and shoes, slipped into a life jacket, and climbed fifty feet down a knotted rope into the warm sea. Fighting five-foot waves, he swam to the nearest raft, where a dozen sailors were already on board. Too exhausted to climb in, a sailor grabbed him by the seat of his trousers and pulled him onto the raft.

A whaleboat came alongside, and the coxswain threw a line to the raft. The whaleboat towed the raft to a nearby cruiser, the USS *Minneapolis*. As the coxswain maneuvered close to the *Minneapolis*, Seaman Newton and his companions clambered up a cargo net to the bow. Seaman Newton grabbed on to a bowline loop at the end of a rope line, and a sailor lifted him on board. Seaman Newton did not see the *Lexington* sink—he was below deck. Later the *Lexington* survivors were all transferred to a large cruiser, the USS *Portland*, where they were clothed, fed, and bedded and the wounded received medical care.

Under cover of night, the US task force of carriers, cruisers, and destroyers headed southwest, attempting to avoid Japanese warships. Early the next morning, the *Portland*, with Seaman Newton on board and accompanied by several destroyers, separated itself from the rest of the fleet and directed its course toward the US military installation on the island of Tongatabu. There the one thousand seven hundred survivors were heroically welcomed by the Polynesian ruler of Tonga, Queen Salote Tupou, and were treated to copious quantities of delicious pineapple. Two days later, the survivors boarded the USAT *Barnett* for transport to San Diego.

As the army vessel entered the San Diego harbor, all one thousand seven hundred survivors were ordered to remain below deck. The sinking of the *Lexington* had not been made public by the US government; the Battle of Midway was being planned, and it was important that the Japanese not know that the *Lexington* would not be available for battle.

A month later, in mid-June, the US Navy announced to the world that the *Lexington* had been sunk. Elmer and Johnnie knew their son Raymond was on the *Lexington* when they heard on their Philco that the ship had been sunk and that three hundred US sailors had been killed. But their worry was quickly assuaged when they received a phone call from Longmont's Western Union office. The caller read a telegram to Johnnie that had been received from the navy: "Raymond had been safely rescued."

However, Seaman Newton's shipmate who volunteered to assume operational duties below deck while Seaman Newton stayed on top that fateful May 8 day was not as fortunate. His parents had been informed that their son was killed when gas vapors in the ship's hull exploded.

Later in 1942, and now on board the USS *Monticello*, Seaman Newton sent a letter to the Sisters of Denver's St. Clara's Orphanage, where he had spent two years of his teenage life:

> It seems that one has to be a long time away from a good thing before he realizes just how lucky he was to have it. I am afraid that, at times, while I was with you at St. Clara's, I behaved in a manner that was very unbecoming to anyone. But time changes everything. I pride myself now on possessing a certain "something" that can only be obtained in a Catholic school—something I can readily see lacking in many of the Catholic fellows here—a knowledge of religion and, aside from that, a certain training that is obtainable in no other place.

* * *

On the evening of July 28, 1943, Elmer sat near his Philco, listening to President Roosevelt's radio address to the nation on the status of the war. Johnnie, at her sewing machine in the adjacent dining room, asked Elmer to turn up the volume so she could also hear what the president had to say:

> In the Pacific, we are pushing the Japs around—from the Aleutians to New Guinea. Thereto we have taken the initiative, and we are not going to let go of it. It becomes clearer and clearer that the attrition—the whittling-down process against the Japanese—is working. The Japs have lost more planes and more ships than they have been able to replace. The continuous and energetic prosecution

of the "war of attrition" will drive the Japs back from their overextended lines. Their shipping and airpower cannot support such outposts. Our naval, land, and air strength in the Pacific is constantly growing. And if the Japanese are basing their future plans in the Pacific on a long period in which they will be permitted to consolidate and exploit their conquered resources—they better start revising their plans now—I GIVE THAT TO THEM—MERELY AS A HELPFUL SUGGESTION!

Tonight, we are able to terminate the rationing of coffee, and we also expect within a short time, we shall get greatly increased allowances of sugar. Those few Americans who grouse and complain about the inconveniences of life here in the United States should learn some lessons from the civilian populations of our Allies.

At that time, Elmer and Johnnie were drinking only two cups of diluted coffee each day without the customary sugar. Before Roosevelt's pronouncement, coffee had been rationed to one pound per person every five weeks, and each family member was restricted to a half pound of sugar per week. With German U-boat attacks on US merchant ships, the supplies of coffee and sugar had been significantly limited. But now that was to change—the United States had successfully thwarted the German attacks. Johnnie and Elmer soon were able to enjoy their accustomed amounts of sweetened coffee. However, supplies of lard, butter, and meat were still limited, and their rationing continued—American and Allied troops in Europe and the Pacific received first priority.

By March 1944, the Japanese were in retreat in the Pacific, and US forces occupied the islands of Guadalcanal, New Georgia, and New Britain, as well as the Marshall and Gilbert Islands, and the marines had just begun the invasion of New Guinea. Johnnie and Elmer suspected that their marine and navy sons had most likely been involved in one or more of these engagements, but they had no knowledge of their sons' whereabouts.

In that same March, Gunnery Sergeant Orbin Newton arrived on Guadalcanal to serve first with the Fourth Base Depot and later with the Sixteenth Field Depot (Sixteenth FD) Company. Gunny Newton had previously been with the Eleventh and Fourteenth Replacement Battalions operating out of Camp Elliott in San Diego. Now he was assigned to the Guadalcanal units that, over the past year, had provided supplies and ammunition to marine infantry as they hopped from island to island, successfully invading and occupying each one and moving toward an invasion of Japan. Palau, just east of the Philippines, were next in line with the first objective of taking an airstrip on Peliliu Island. The First Marine Division was designated to carry out the invasion, and Gunny Newton's Sixteenth FD Company was selected as one of the ammunition and supply units to accompany the division. On September 4, 1944, Gunny Newton and his fellow marines shipped out of Pavavu, a small island north of Guadalcanal, for a two-thousand-one-hundred-mile trip across the Pacific to Peliliu.

At Peliliu, the US Navy's underwater demolition team went in first to clear the beaches of obstacles, and in September 12, naval warships began pre-invasion bombardment. Although shelling damaged Japanese planes on the airstrip, the bombing did little harm to the eleven thousand Japanese troops who held well-fortified positions on the elevated, volcanic terrain of the island.

The First, Fifth, and Seventh Marine Regiments landed on Peliliu in the morning of September 15. As their landing craft approached the beaches, they were caught in the crossfire of enemy gun and cannon artillery. Steep coral ridges that rose up a quarter mile from the beach were swarming with Japanese, firing artillery and guns on the narrow beachhead below. Amtracs, loaded with marines, took direct hits and burst into flames, killing all on board. Other amphibious vehicles were knocked out, forcing the onboard marines to abandon them and wade the coral reef in chest-high water while facing devastating machine-gun fire. Casualties were high, and many who did reach shore lost their rifles and gear.

The marines were bogged down through the morning. By midafternoon, a shallow beachhead had been established, and the Sixteenth FD's one thousand two hundred marines loaded materiel from the cargo ship's holds onto landing craft. Directing and coordinating cargo traffic, Gunny Newton looked across the reef to see Sixteenth FD marines stumbling and falling into the shallow water as they were hit by artillery and sniper fire. He saw familiar faces as boats carrying the wounded passed on their way to the nearby hospital ship. He saw marine comrades struggling to gain foothold on the slippery coral and frantically working to move cargo inland, despite mortar and artillery fire all around them.

By dusk, the Sixteenth FD had stockpiled its ammunition and supplies immediately to the rear of the battlefront, but the frontline marines were out of ammunition and suffering from heat prostration. The temperature had reached 105 degrees on Peliliu, and the infantrymen had exhausted their drinking water.

That night, Sixteenth FD troops rushed ammunition and water to the front line, and Gunny Newton had little time for sleep as he coordinated distribution. He and Sixteenth FD troops also helped evacuate the wounded. Under security of rifle teams looking for snipers, they loaded casualties aboard landing craft boats and then onto hospital ships.

Although remote from the front of battle, the Sixteenth FD was not spared from enemy attack. A small group of Japanese wearing helmets of dead marines infiltrated behind the front line where they encountered a Sixteenth FD guard detail—a furious hand-to-hand struggle occurred using Ka-Bar knives, rifle butts, and bare fists. The entire enemy group was killed but not before the Sixteenth FD sustained several casualties.

At 3:00 a.m. under cover of darkness, Gunny Newton lay in a shallow foxhole he had carved out of the coral crust. His M-1 and Ka-Bar were at his side. He hoped to get an hour or two of sleep before sunrise. He wondered what might happen in the next couple of hours. Would the Japs pull off one of their banzai charges and wipe them all out? What about infiltrators? He knew he wouldn't hear those sneaky sons of bitches comin'—all he could do was be ready and bash their heads against the coral if he had to. It was quiet except for the occasional rustling noise of a marine in a foxhole. As he relaxed into sleep, Gunny Newton contemplated what the Franciscan Sisters of St. Clara's Orphanage always told him at a time of need:

> You are not alone. We are praying with you and for you.

Gunny Newton hoped that the sisters back in Denver were praying in that September 15. He said an Act of Contrition and fell asleep.

Gunny Newton and his company remained as the central supply unit for both the marines and the army until mid-November when Peliliu was finally secured. They were proud of their contribution to success on Peliliu; other than limited water early in the invasion, the seventy-three-day operation had no major supply difficulties.

For Gunny Newton, the blazing sun, stifling heat, jagged coral, rugged terrain, and lack of readily available water all combined to make Peliliu a living hell. The sickening stench of decaying bodies, human excrement, and swarming flies were unforgettable and nauseating. The savagery of the enemy, especially at night in hand-to-hand combat, haunted his memory. The merciless sniper killing of marines wading in the surf as they carried the wounded and dying to hospital ships angered him uncontrollably. He was exuberant that he and the marines, with the help of the army, had wiped out those chicken-shit bastards—more than ten thousand of them.

Gunnery Sergeant Orbin Newton remained on Peliliu through January 1945 when he boarded a ship back to Pavuvu Island and Guadalcanal. There he received orders to report to the Basic School in Quantico, Virginia. On his way across the United States by train from California, Orbin disembarked in Denver. He was going home to Mead to see Elmer and Johnnie and his fifteen brothers and sisters. For the first time, Orbin would see his brother Marc, now 1½ years old. His triplet brothers had been only 1½ years old when he enlisted in the Marine Corps four years ago, and the 5½-year-olds could now see for real their oldest brother—a fighting marine they had grown to idolize.

Elmer and Johnnie were ecstatic with Orbin's arrival. Their two eldest sons had survived the battles of the South Pacific, and now the Japanese were in retreat. The Japanese had been whipped soundly—US troops had taken over the island of Iwo Jima and now were on Okinawa, the last stop before Japan. US bombs were already landing on Tokyo—there was great optimism that the Japanese would surrender before the United States invaded their homeland.

Gunny Newton was participating in a training session in Virginia when he heard the news that the United States had dropped an atomic bomb on the Japanese city of Hiroshima. He knew then that the marines had been spared the deadly task of invading Japan.

Johnnie and Elmer knew that their two eldest sons had escaped World War II with their lives, and Johnnie knew that her nightly rosary prayers had been answered.

Orbin Dreier Newton, 1938. *Newton Family Album*

Raymond Lee Newton, 1940. *Newton Family Album*

Orbin Newton, US Army, 1941. *Newton Family Album*

Raymond Newton, US Navy, 1942. *Newton Family Album*

CHAPTER 8

War Home Front

Richie, Rollie, and I were two years old when another brother, David Allen, was born in March of 1941. David was number 18 for Mom, and in that same year and one month before the Japanese bombed Pearl Harbor, our oldest sister, Eunice, married Byron "Wilbur" Thornton in Mead's Guardian Angel Church. Father Martin Arno presided, and brother Raymond sang the "Ave Maria" while Margaret Dempewolf played the organ. Raymond was home on leave from the navy, and brother Orbin, Wilbur's groomsman, was now at home, having just finished his one year of military service at Fort Hood, Texas. (Right after the Japanese bombing of Pearl Harbor in December '41, Orbin enlisted in the Marine Corps.)

In the meantime, life on the home front for us Newtons continued with as much normalcy as could be expected. Our sister Betty (Roberta) graduated from high school and moved to Denver to attend beauty school. Sisters Rosemary, Helen, and Pat remained at home, cooking the evening meals, washing and drying dishes, scrubbing floors and windows, and washing clothes. In summer and with canning season started, they peeled apples and pears, pitted cherries and plums, sliced carrots and beets, boiled cabbage and tomatoes, and sterilized jars and lids. With Mom's instruction and using her sewing machine, they made their own blouses and skirts, and they helped Mom make blankets and comforters to winterize our beds. The three girls made dish towels and potholders out of flour sacks and embroidered them with elegant designs, entering their sewing handiwork and canned goods in Weld County 4-H Club competitions and bringing home red and blue ribbons.

Each Sunday, with organist Margaret Dempewolf, my three sisters sang in the Guardian Angel Church choir. After Mass, they assisted Mom with preparation of the Sunday afternoon dinner. With us triplets and David now on the scene, my sisters acquired new responsibilities. Each night, one of them could be depended on to read us stories from the *Tales of Mother Goose*. Another would put the four of us to bed with bottles containing warmed evaporated milk, our gift from the Pet Milk Co. On Saturday night, one of my sisters heated water on the wood-burning stove and bathed each one of us in the galvanized washtub. Each day they made our beds, helped us dress, prepared our meals, and emptied our chamber pot.

My fourteen-year-old brother Jack worked after school at Baker's IGA grocery, and he earned enough money to have Mead blacksmith Fred Peterson construct a basketball hoop, which he attached to the side of our two-story barn just east of the house. Mom gave Jack and my brother Tom a basketball for Christmas, and the two of them played one-on-one and horse on the backyard court. Each night Tom chopped scrap wood for kindling, and he brought it into the house along with a bucket of coal so Mom could cook and heat the house in winter. Mom had a few chickens and a rooster that Tom fed and watered daily.

On the afternoon of March 23, 1944, with Dad away working and my older brothers and sisters still at school, Mom suddenly "was sick," and she told us triplets and David that she was going to bed. "You boys sit tight here in the house," Mom said. "The girls will be home soon."

She then went in to her bedroom and shut the door. Rosemary was the first one home, and she entered Mom's bedroom to inquire about her status. When she emerged, Rosemary said, "You kids go upstairs, and don't come down until I tell you."

Unbeknownst to us, Rosemary then called Dr. Jones and midwife Hulda Roman, asking them to come right away—Mom was about to have her nineteenth child.

For two hours, the three of us remained upstairs, oblivious to the events unfolding downstairs. Sisters Helen and Pat brought dry cereal and milk up to us for our supper and sat with us while we finished. An hour later, Rosemary came upstairs to tell us that we had a new baby brother.

"Where do babies come from?" I asked her.

"The doctor brings 'em in his bag," Rosemary answered emphatically.

"What are we going to name him?" Rollie asked.

"We don't know yet," said Rosemary. "Mom and Dad will decide that later."

"Dr. Jones is still here, and you can't come down until he leaves," she added as she walked down the stairs.

Sitting on the upstairs beds, we triplets began our own intense discussion of what name should be given to our new brother. Somehow, we agreed that we wanted to call him Joseph. We liked the idea of calling him Joe for short, and we wanted them all downstairs to know what our decision was. We started yelling, hoping someone downstairs would come to the stairwell door and listen to us.

"Hey down there! We want ta call him Joe!" I screamed.

"Yal—we want him to be Joe!" said Richie in a loud voice.

"Hey, all of you down there," Rollie cried out, "his name's gotta be Joe!"

"Joe—Joe—Joe!" yelled Rollie, loud enough for the whole town to hear.

Suddenly, the stairwell door opened, and we heard Dr. Jones's booming voice. "Okay—okay," he said as he walked halfway up the stairs. "The boy's name is Joe—we'll call 'im Joe—now please keep it quiet so he can sleep—Joe's tired, and he needs to rest."

Two weeks later, Father Martin Arno came to our house and baptized our new brother as Marcus Emerit Newton, taking the names of Dad's younger brother, Marcus, and Mom's only brother, Emerit. Father Martin accepted the name Marcus as adhering to the tradition of naming a son after a saint—in his mind, the name Marcus was as close to the name Mark, a Gospel author and a canonized saint, as one needed to get.

Mom was forty-three when Marc was born. Like Dad, she had lost all her teeth and had them replaced with a poorly made set of dentures. Her black hair now had streaks of gray, and her forehead was creased. Time might have widened her five-foot-eight frame, but it had not diminished her strength. Her walk was still brisk and purposeful. Stooping over for hours at a time, she had no trouble pulling weeds from her strawberry patch or picking green beans from her garden. She could still split a piece of kindling with an axe and dig a hole with a spade. She had not forgotten how to milk a cow and did so when Dad was gone. On her hands and knees, she scrubbed her wood and linoleum floors. The sweltering summer day did not keep her from standing over a hot wood-burning stove canning jar after jar of fruits and vegetables. Twice a week, she washed clothes in her secondhand electric washer, cranking each piece through rollers by hand before she or my sisters hung the laundry outdoors to dry.

With summer upon us in '44, Mom directed Tom to collect scrap metal from neighbors and storeowners in Mead and from our own trash barrel. America had been fighting a war for more than two years, and there was a shortage of metals of all sorts. The government asked Americans to gather iron, copper, brass, zinc, and tin objects so they could be recycled into guns, ships, tanks, and bullets. Mom, fervently loyal, made sure that her family did its fair share.

In these situations when Mom directed Tom to get it done, it was implied that he would be "ordering" one or more of his younger brothers to help. Eleven-year-old Tom, with the wisdom of his six years beyond mine, depicted himself as "the boss." If recruited, I would have to obey Tom's orders or suffer the consequences—i.e., Mom's wrath as well as his—Tom was in charge.

For this metal gathering, Tom drafted Richie and me. However, in this case, Richie and I knew that helping Tom with this chore was going to be an enjoyable experience. Looking to see what "trash treasures" could be found along the main alleyway of Mead was one of our favorite pastimes. When Mom sent me downtown to pick up something from the grocery store, I often took the main alley rather than that of Main Street. In the alley, I could sort through the trash barrels, boxes, and junk heaps looking to find discarded items that were no longer of use to the owner. When I stumbled on a "precious find," I would wonder in amazement why anyone would throw away something that in my mind still had so much value. As I walked along the tire-worn and fine-graveled alley path, I kept my eyes pointed downward, looking for things of worth that might have been dropped by a previous traveler: a buffalo nickel or an Indian head penny, a pendant or medal, a food-ration token, or even a silver or gold ring.

Tom, Richie, and I walked south down the alley, a distance of five short blocks. Richie and I took turns pulling our Radio Flyer wagon as we loaded metal objects. We sorted through the refuse from businesses and households. We collected tin cans of all sizes, steel rods, sprockets, copper tubes, rusted wrenches, and faucets. With the wagon full, we placed all the cans in cardboard boxes, and Richie and I carried them home.

After flattening the cans with a hammer, we placed them back in the boxes and hauled them and all the metal pieces downtown to the train depot. There, they were loaded onto railcars and transported to foundries in Denver. We kept one

Light of Her Children

object we had found for ourselves—it was not to be melted down into a deadly weapon. A metal toy truck that young David Baker had discarded remained with us.

Local representatives distributed food-rationing books at Mead Consolidated Schools building. Mom received a stamp book for each of us. A stamp had to accompany every purchase of sugar, coffee, meat, canned goods, butter, and lard. Mom was allowed extra sugar rations for canning. A butter substitute, margarine, was purchased when we ran out of "real" butter that we made from cream derived from the milk of Dad's cow. When the coffee supply was low, Mom and Dad switched to Lipton tea. Rosemary and Betty could no longer buy nylon stockings. They were not being manufactured; instead, all nylon material was converted into parachutes, ropes, cords, tents, and other military items.

However, by 1944, there was a positive side to the war for the Mead farming community. Spurred on by the war's material needs, America's depressed economy of the '30s had been reversed by the increased industrial and agricultural output in the early '40s. US military forces were now major consumers of flour and meat, and the British were importing great quantities of agricultural commodities from America for their servicemen. Wheat, corn, sugar, and beef were in great demand, so Mead farmers increased their output and production. They planted more seed, raised more livestock, and worked longer days. The federal government established policies controlling market prices, and farmers were guaranteed reasonable returns when selling their crops. The war was dramatically increasing Mead farmers' incomes—some were making more than $5,000 a year.

But although their annual income was on the rise, Mead farmers experienced a labor shortage as their sons and hired hands joined the military. Thus, there was plenty of opportunity for Dad to work, particularly with the harvests. The alfalfa crop produced hay three times that summer, and Dad's job was to arrange the hay into a tall stack with a pitchfork after it was raised up from below with a large cradle. Pitchfork in hand and working alone, Dad spread it neatly and tightly, creating square corners to a rectangular stack approximately thirty yards long and twenty yards wide. By the end of a day's work, Dad had created a stack that was five or six yards high. He stacked hay for Sander Adler, Ted Rademacher, and Frank Schell for five dollars a day—the highest wage he had ever received. During grain harvest on Rademacher's farm, Dad stacked barley bundles into standing clusters, and later, riding on top of a bundle wagon, he pitched bundles into the thresher.

All his life Dad had been a laborer—first as a locomotive fireman and now as a farmhand. Although he had learned to drive, he had no driver's license and did not own a car. He drove no tractors or trucks. Dad had earned his living from the sheer strength of his muscle. He no longer thought about trying to rent or own his farm—those goals were beyond his reach. Now in his late fifties, he had developed a slight midriff bulge, with his weight approaching 190 pounds. The long strands of his graying hair were combed back from his receding hairline, but one could see kinked, curled strands underneath and next to his balding scalp. Town barber Grover Roberts kept the sides trimmed close to Dad's head, and Dad's face, now furled with wrinkles, was always shaven. His dentures had yellowed somewhat, and one tooth had chipped out on the right side. At night, he placed them in a white mug of baking-soda water beside his bed. He smoked Lucky Strikes, rolled his own with Prince Albert tobacco, and enjoyed an occasional Roi-Tan cigar. When not working, Dad spent his spare time at the Mead Pool Hall; his skill was good enough for him to earn a few dollars from his farmer-friend opponents in a game of roun' the world.

Eunice Elaine Newton, 1941. *Newton Family Album*

Georgia Roberta Newton, 1943. *Newton Family Album*

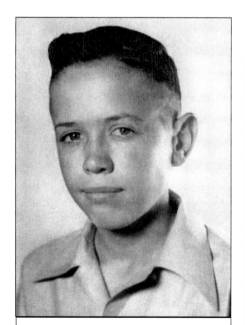

Thomas James Newton, 1945. *Newton Family Album*

James Elmer and Laura Dreier Newton, 1945. *Newton Family Album*

CHAPTER 9

War's End

By the end of the Great Depression and the start of World War II, Mead had undergone many changes. In the 1920s, Mead had three blacksmiths—now there was only one, Fred Peterson. Mr. Peterson made a good living repairing timeworn farm implements in his shop on Main Street. New farm machinery was not available for purchase—America's iron and steel was now converted into tanks and ships.

The Mead Bank had shut its doors, and townspeople and farmers took their banking business to Longmont. Longmont was where people also bought clothes and groceries and where they went to the picture show on Saturday night. Burger Bros. closed the Texaco service station (managed by Tony Dempewolf) on the south end of Main Street; now Tony was using the old service station for storage of gasoline that he delivered to Mead farmers in his Texaco truck. John Gust shut down his Conoco Service Station on the county roads intersection and retired to live with his wife, Christina, in their small bungalow next to Guardian Angel Church. Isaac Doke passed away, and his widow, Grace, now ran Isaac's electrical appliance store. Charles and Eva Dempsey moved into the Mead Hotel; they painted out the HOTEL sign above their front door and no longer boarded travelers for the night. The library was closed, and all the books had been sent back to the Weld County Library in Greeley or transferred to the public school.

With the increased industrial and agricultural output of the nation's war effort, America's Great Depression ended by the mid-'40s, and a few hardy souls in Mead managed to keep their businesses alive. There were still two grain elevators—both owned by Denver Elevators and run by our neighbor Vernon "Bub" Howlett. Their tall silos stored the summer harvests of wheat, oats, and barley, and in the fall, each crop was carried away in railcars.

Gas could be bought from one service station, Redland White's Mead Garage. Although gas was rationed and its use was monitored for work-related purposes and not for leisure, stops at the station for a gallon or two were still frequent. And with no new cars and trucks being built, Joe Jones, the garage's new mechanic, had plenty of work repairing broken-down vehicles and overhauling worn-out engines.

When Dad needed hammers, nails, and lumber to repair his cow pen or needed a shovel, hoe, or rake to work his garden, he went to the Clark Lumber Co. Proprietor Ansel Clark also sold Dad paint to refurbish rooms in our house and to cover the exteriors of barns and sheds that Dad contracted with farmers to paint when he was not working in their fields.

Bunton's Red & White Grocery opened early in the morning and stayed open late at night. If Mom could not hitch a ride to Longmont to shop for groceries, she would send me or my brothers downtown to buy an item she urgently needed. If it was not available at Red & White Grocery, we went to Dale Baker's IGA (Independent Grocery Association) Grocery.

Across the road from the abandoned Conoco Station was the Mead Inn and Liquor Store. Sardonically called the "beer joint" by Mom, it was a favorite meeting place at night for Mexican migrant workers, who came to town from fields afar and stopped over for a drink after buying groceries. On a summer's night, one could hear Mexican music coming from the jukebox inside. Dad played poker with Sandy Adler and other farmers at the Mead Inn, but he didn't drink their beer or whiskey—alcohol was never a part of his life.

Barber Ed Norene left town, so Grover Roberts, owner of the Mead Pool Hall and Barbershop, took over the hair-cutting tasks. He cut Dad's hair and the hair of many of the farmers who also came to town to play pool between settings of water as they irrigated their crops or to pass the time of day in the cold of winter when they could not work in their fields.

The Mead Drugstore, owned by George and Elizabeth Snider, was still prospering. Not having any money, I seldom went in there. It was rare that I was given a nickel to buy an ice-cream cone or a bottle of soda or handed a dime for a chocolate-covered ice-cream bar on a stick. For me, a malt or milk shake for a quarter was out of the question—only my brother Jack, who was earning his own money, could afford such luxury. Post-office boxes for all the Mead residents were in the back of the drugstore—druggist George Snider was also the postmaster.

The canning company, Kuner-Empson, had large wooden tanks next to the railroad tracks where pickles and cucumbers were stored in brine, brought there by growers farming the sandy soils east of Mead. Later, the cucurbits were hauled in railcars to the Kuner-Empson Cannery in Longmont, where they were jarred and sold in grocery stores all over Colorado.

A Kuner-Empson pea huller was located on the northeast corner of town, and it bustled with activity for three weeks in the early summer. Truckloads of pea vines were dumped onto large conveyer belts, moving on rollers into shafts, rising upward into the belly of the corrugated metal building; inside, the peas were separated from the hulls and gathered into large metal tubs to be trucked to Longmont and then canned. Dad, along with local farmhands, Mexican laborers, and summer-vacationing high school students, signed on to work at the huller.

Tom brought home armloads of pea vines that he grabbed off stalled trucks waiting to be unloaded outside the huller. My sisters shelled the peas from the pods, and Mom canned them. At other times, my brothers, sisters, and I hunkered around the vines, pulling off the pods and putting the shelled peas into our mouths—a delectable treat.

There was no activity in the old Farmer's Union Town Hall—it was no longer a meeting place for farmers or townspeople. Instead, folks met in rural schoolhouses and churches or in the Mead Consolidated Schools building. We Newtons had been the last ones to occupy the hall. Now the doors were permanently locked, and tall ironweeds were growing outside along its walls. Holes in its broken windowpanes were stuffed with rags, and tar shingles were missing from the roof. Each time I walked by it on my way to church, I wondered what it was like inside. One day, I kept telling myself, I would crawl through a window and look in. I wanted to see where Orbin, my cousins, the Howlett boys, the Adler and the Mudd brothers, and the Mead Merchants once played basketball. I was proud that the town hall had been my birthplace. I always relished the surprised look on the faces of people when I told them that the hall was where we triplets were born.

Next to the town hall was a slender thirty-foot-high pyramid-like tower of wood, on top of which was hung a cast-iron bell. The wooden structure had never seen a coat of paint, and its pine crossbars and studs had grown gray and brown with age. A long rope hung from the bell, accessible to any citizen who had cause to warn townsfolk of a fire.

The gravel-covered streets of Mead had names, but no one knew what they were—there were no street signs. The streets were laced with potholes and washboard ruts. Buried beneath them were the water mains, constructed of wood and prone to leak. Town marshal Wilse Lamberson was responsible for their repair, and he solicited the help of the Union Pacific Railway station hand, Johnny Maestos. Johnny spent his leisure time at the bars of the Mead Pool Hall and the Mead Inn and arrived at the scene of a spouting water main all red- and bleary-eyed, telltale signs of a hangover.

Our house was on the northwest corner of town at the tail end of a street running north and south. From our backyard and to the west, I had a panoramic view of summer fields of sugar beets, hay, wheat, and corn and the towering Rocky Mountains, majestically overlooking the crops. Penetrating the sky, nearly nine thousand feet above me, were the tips of Mount Meeker and Long's Peak, always clad with patches of snow. In summer, I could smell the fragrant odor of freshly mown hay from Fred Gettman's alfalfa field to the west. To the north, I could hear the loud clacking and clanking noises of a steam-generated threshing machine, coming from the barley field of the Redmond farm a quarter mile away. At Mom's request, I frequently delivered a jar of buttermilk or a loaf of fresh bread to Mamie Akers, the spinster niece of the deceased Redmonds who was now living in their farmhouse.

* * *

On many nights, I heard broadcaster Gabriel Heatter comment on the war as Dad listened intently on his Philco. Although I did not understand the text of his commentary, Heatter's high-pitched, emotional delivery was alarming to me, and it heightened my fears about the war, the Japanese, and the Germans. For Dad, Heatter's words were ones of optimism and encouragement, and they provided him a sound and thoughtful analysis of the war's progress. However, to me, the elevated pitch of Heatter's voice seemed to indicate a man who was himself scared and stressed, and it seemed that he was telling listeners that they needed to be fearful as well. I was afraid that the Japanese were coming to America to take over. I was concerned that one would stick me in the stomach with a bayonet, then twist and turn it and watch me squirm until I died. I told myself, "If they did invade the United States, I would hide in the mountains—I know I'd be safe there."

I had learned to hate and fear the Japanese, and so did nearly everyone else in Mead and across America. We referred disparagingly to them as the Japs. When I was in a heated argument and I wanted to demean the character of another brother, I called him a dirty Jap. One day I expressed my fear of the Japs to my sister Kathleen. She was not consoling—she only confirmed and heightened my fears.

Kathleen said, "The Japs are dumb. They don't care if they live or die. Sometimes their pilots crash their airplanes on purpose into our ships, just to set them on fire and cause them to explode and sink. They call 'em kamikazes. They believe they'll go to heaven if they die for their country. The marines have killed thousands of them on islands in the Pacific Ocean. Their generals don't seem to care—they just send in more to fight."

Kathleen went on to say, "We're not like them—we treat our prisoners well—we give 'em good food and houses to live in—they starve their prisoners and make 'em sleep out in the open. Aunt Mary told me that the Japs made our cousin Robert drink his own pee when he was captured. They're bad people."

With the war having gone on for three years, the United States military had suffered many casualties, and infantry replacements were needed—now young fathers were called up to serve. My brother-in-law Wilbur was drafted into the army, and on Christmas Eve of 1944, he left for Fort Hood, Texas, leaving his wife, Eunice, at home with one child and expecting another.

By December '44, my family and the Mead community had grown weary of war, and everyone turned their attention to Christmas. Town marshal Wilse Lamberson placed a twenty-foot ponderosa pine in the middle of Main Street and decorated it with a string of colored lights plugged into the socket of the overhead streetlight. In Snider's Drugstore, Mrs. Snider displayed Santa's elves skating on a mirror of ice surrounded by a layer of cotton snow, and Mrs. Bunton pasted giant images of Coca-Cola Santas in the Red & White Grocery windows. At work, my brother Jack helped Dale Baker decorate a small blue spruce that they placed on a table in the IGA grocery. Colored bulbs around the perimeter of the Mead Motor Company window blinked on and off, and a twelve-foot lighted spruce tree stood majestically next to the outside white wall of the Clark Lumber Co. Silver bells hanging on the doorknob of the pool hall rang as each patron entered, and bright lights on Christmas trees could be seen in the windows of most Mead households.

With his IGA grocery-store earnings, my brother Jack bought a six-foot blue spruce from Clark Lumber, and he stood it inside in front of our living-room window. After Jack attached the electric lights, Helen parceled out colored glass ornaments for the twins, Jerry, and us triplets to hang. To Jerry, she gave her very favorite one, molded into the shape of a bell. "Put that in a special place on the tree where everyone can see it," she said.

Tom distributed strands of tinsel and instructed us, "Hang them by their ends and make sure they hang straight down—they're supposed to look like icicles." Rosemary put an angel on top, and on a small end table next to the tree, Helen placed a baby Jesus figurine on a bed of cellophane straw in a box-shaped wooden manger.

Through the fall and into the winter, Mom had been sewing and making clothes for all of us. Rosemary wrapped them and piled them under the tree. In the school Christmas play, Pat played the part of Mary, while Rosemary and Helen sang in the chorus. In a mixed quartet, Rosemary sang "Oh, Holy Night," and in a girls' trio, she sang "Ring Out, Sweet Bells of Christmas." Music at church, school, and home was always an important part of the Newton Christmas celebration.

Mom and Dad had established a tradition of opening our gifts on Christmas Eve, starting off with an early evening supper. Betty came, and Eunice and her daughter Diane were there. Mom cooked pinto beans and baked rolls that she served with "real" butter, made with cream that Tom had churned. Mom gave us triplets and Jerry plaid sport shirts, and Betty gave each of us a pair of socks. On Christmas morning, Santa left us a game of Chinese checkers, a rubber ball, a book of *Arabian Nights* stories, and a brown paper sack containing an orange, a popcorn ball, hard candy, and assorted nuts. My brothers and I were hopeful that Santa would bring us a magnificent gift such as a bicycle, but of course, it never happened.

At Christmas Day Mass at Guardian Angel Church, Rosemary again sang "Oh, Holy Night," accompanied by organist Margaret Dempewolf. Her solo performance made the Christmas Mass a very special occasion for me—I was proud of her skill and the beauty of her voice.

"'Oh, Holy Night' is one of the purtiest Christmas carols I've ever heard," said Jerry as the two of us walked home from church. "I heard it the other night on the radio—God, it sounded good!"

Our breakfast that Christmas morning was just as special as the Mass—Mom had our sister Patricia make cocoa with Bossie's milk—a rare breakfast treat for us boys. We toasted slices of her homemade bread, spread freshly churned butter on them, and dunked broken pieces of toast into our hot beverage. We repeated the same thing with the cinnamon rolls she had made. A special breakfast was only the beginning of the food fest that Mom conducted on Christmas Day for her large family. In the oven was a pan of ham and potatoes she had started cooking early that morning, and four cooked banana pies set on the kitchen counter—we all would be eating once again in just a few hours.

* * *

In early afternoon on May 8, 1945, I was on my way down the alley to Bunton's Red & White to pick up a cake of yeast for Mom—she was making bread, and she needed it right away. I suddenly began to hear car horns and the motors of moving cars, and I heard an incessant ringing of the town bell. I saw Ardith Jones about fifty yards away, running hurriedly toward me down the alley, carrying a lunch pail in her hand. Ardith, a year older than me, was Jerry's classmate, and she had moved to Mead two years before with her mother, Lila, and her father, Joe Jones, the mechanic at the Mead Motor Company.

When just a few yards away from me, Ardith yelled out, "Ronnie—Ronnie—the war's over—the war's over!" She ran up to me and threw both arms around my shoulders, hugging me tightly. Startled and surprised, I remained speechless.

"Gotta find my dad and give 'im his lunch," she said. "It's past lunchtime, and I know he's hungry. It's two o'clock, and that's the time the war's s'pposed to be over. That's what my mom said—she heard it on the radio. She said Hitler killed 'imself and the Germans surrendered."

I followed Ardith through the back door of Mead Motor, using the passageway from the alley that led to the garage front door on Main Street. This was the shortcut I always took when I went downtown. Walking through the garage, I expected to see Joe Jones bent over the fender of a car or sitting at his workbench, but he wasn't there. Passing by the garage office, I could see that the manager, Bernard "Duck" Newman, wasn't there either. As Ardith and I walked through the large open door of the garage and onto Main Street, I saw Joe and Duck standing there, laughing and yelling to others on the street. They each had a Coors beer bottle, and they held them up in the air as they acknowledged drivers in passing vehicles. Normally, they each had a beer or two together at six in the evening before they went home. But today was different—their workday ended at two o'clock. Today, Joe and Duck would celebrate late into the night. The war was now over.

Light of Her Children

Further down on Main, I saw Grover Roberts standing in front of his pool hall. Dale Baker had stepped out of his IGA grocery, and the Sniders had left their soda fountain to join the celebration. They were all standing out on the sidewalk, talking to each other and to customers, and waving vigorously to passing drivers. Finally, Ansel Clark emerged from his lumberyard and stood out in the street. I could still hear the repetitive ringing of the town bell—it did not stop—a joyous town person, unknown to me, was relentlessly pulling the rope, sending the celebratory sound to all of Mead's townspeople.

Next to the garage, Bill and Alice Bunton, hands on their hips, stood in front of the Red & White Grocery, smiling and watching. The Buntons, in their sixties, lived in rooms above and behind their store. They had moved to Colorado from Kansas in the 1920s, and had bought the store from the previous owner who had moved it from Highlandlake. Mrs. Bunton, the opposite of her grumpy husband, was warmhearted, cheerful, and friendly. Standing only five feet tall, her white hair with streaks of black, was parted, shortened, and slicked down, resembling a teenage boy who had sprinkled Vitalis over his head. Her face was round, and her chin receded. Her wire-rimmed glasses sat daintily on her small nose, and she always wore a white apron that was starched and neatly pressed.

I waited outside on the street until Mr. and Mrs. Bunton went back into their grocery store before I entered. Seeing me, Mrs. Bunton smiled and said, "Hello there, Mr. Newton. How are you today?"

"I'm fine," I answered.

"What can I do for ya?" she asked.

"My mom needs some yeast—she's bakin' bread," I answered. "She says to charge it and put it on our bill."

Hearing our conversation, Bill Bunton said nothing, but his scowl told me he did not approve of me not paying. He knew Mom had not paid on her account for a couple of months and that she was running up a gigantic bill. Mr. Bunton did not want to add any more to it—no matter how small the amount might be. I was glad that Mrs. Bunton was the one who waited on me and that it was not her "bulldog-jowled" husband—I didn't want to hear Mr. Bunton ask me, "When are ya goin' ta pay?" because I knew I would have no answer.

Mrs. Bunton ignored her husband's look of disdain and walked over to the refrigerated showcase to fetch the yeast. She placed it into a small brown paper sack and set it on the table next to her as she recorded the charge to our account. She walked over to the candy counter and placed the bag on top for me to take. Standing behind enclosed glass shelves of one-cent candies of every description, she asked me, "What kinda candy do you want, young man?"

Pointing to it with no hesitation and trying to avoid the scrutinizing eye of Mr. Bunton, I stuttered, "A—a—peanut-butter log." I knew Mr. Button did not approve of his wife giving things to people.

She opened the sliding glass door, reached in to get the piece of one-cent candy, and handed it to me.

"Thank you," I said.

I unpeeled the cellophane wrapper while Mrs. Bunton carried on the conversation. She said, "I bet cher mom and dad are happy now that your brothers will be coming home soon. Mrs. Newman was in here a few days ago, and she said your mother told her that your navy-man brother survived after his ship was sunk. She said that he was rescued—I'm happy to hear that. I just can't imagine the worry the war has caused your parents. I know if I had kids and they were off fightin' a war, I'd be worried sick."

I said, "My sister Kathleen told me that our brother Ray had to swim to another ship when the Japs torpedoed his. And she told me that our brother Orbin had to kill some Japs with his bayonet."

"Oh my, my," said Mrs. Bunton. "I know they'll be glad to be home—but that probably won't be for a while—we still have to beat the Japs—they say our soldiers will be goin' in to Japan real soon."

I stuffed the candy into my mouth, and still afraid to look at Mr. Bunton, I grabbed the paper sack and left. With yeast in hand, I ran home as fast as I could to tell Mom the news about the war. Of course, she already knew—she and about a hundred million Americans had been listening to the radio.

Then it was August 15, 1941, when the town bell rang once again and Mead townsfolk had another celebration—two atomic bombs had been dropped in Japan, and the Japanese had finally surrendered.

Mead Motor Company, Mead CO, 1954. *Mead Consolidated Schools Yearbook*

Bunton's Red & White, Mead CO, 1954. *Mead Consolidated Schools Yearbook*

Clark Lumber Company, Mead CO, 1938. *Historic Highlandlake, Inc.*

Chapter 10

Expanding Family

I never really knew my older brothers, Orbin and Raymond. They were nineteen and seventeen years older than me, respectively, and had left home to fight the Japanese right after I was born. The first time I met Orbin was when he was home on leave at the tail end of the war.

"Here," he said, "take these and put them in your piggy bank."

He handed me a small jar of forty or fifty pennies he had stashed away in his duffel bag. I was so happy to receive them it was like he had given me all of Fort Knox.

What I knew about Orbin was what I heard from others.

"Orbin played for Mead in the AAU basketball tournament in Denver one year," said Mom.

"Did his team win?" I asked.

"Of course not," said Mom.

"Your brother was a good basketball player," said Hap Howlett. "He could jump like hell and dunk the ball right in the basket—so we started callin' 'im Dunk."

"Orbin always liked to write," said Mom. "Went to CU for a year to study journalism before he had to quit and fight in the war."

Said Mom, "Ray was a good singer—sang at Eunice's wedding—he always won when he sang in the high school contests over in Greeley. He made a record when he was in high school—it's around here somewhere—I'll try to find it and play it for you—Mrs. Dempewolf played the piano for him."

"Did Ray play basketball?" I asked.

"No, he didn't," said Mom. "He liked 4-H and singin'. He raised chickens for 4-H. When he showed 'em, he gave 'em a bath and painted their claws with nail polish. He won a blue ribbon with one of 'em."

Right after the war, I met Ray—he came home for Christmas. By that time, he was living in New York City. Postwar manufacturing of nylon stockings started once again, and Ray gave a pair to each of my older sisters. He bought shirts for six of us brothers. After that, Ray never came home, and I never saw him again until I was an adult. Before that, though, he sent home several large boxes with wrapped Christmas presents inside them for all of us brothers and sisters. For Dave, Jerry, and us triplets, he gave each of us a parka—the inside label on them read: Saks Fifth Avenue. That really impressed us!

As the European war drew to a close in May of '45, my sister Rosemary graduated from high school. An earnest student, she loved reading English literature and English novels, and she could type faster and more accurately than anyone else in her class. Schoolwork had been easy for her, and she had taken on the extra activities of editing and publishing the school's first yearbook and singing lead parts in the high school choir.

After graduation, Rosemary was ready to move on. At five foot ten inches tall, she playfully said, "I'm tired of dancing with boys shorter than I am," and she moved to Denver to take a job with American Telephone & Telegraph Company. AT&T was advancing the use of new technology with high-volume cables capable of handling television signals and was installing automatic dialing systems to replace switchboard operations. (Our next-door neighbor and former telephone operator, Mamie

Light of Her Children

Howlett, had retired when AT&T closed the Mead switchboard.) Now women were no longer needed as operators, and AT&T's parent company, the Bell System, was hiring them to manage the affairs of their expanding workforce. The "Ma Bell" folks quickly recognized Rosemary's keen writing and management talents and assigned her to oversee a personnel unit. Thereafter, I saw Rosemary only on occasional visits on weekends and on holidays, but when she came home, the Sunday church choir always sounded better.

My oldest sister, Eunice, married Wilbur Thornton a year after I was born. And in 1944, he was drafted into the army, leaving pregnant Eunice and their daughter behind. In April of '46, he was discharged after almost a year in Japan, where he assisted with the reconversion of Japanese industries back to peacetime operations. Separated from service at Fort Douglas in Utah, Wilbur took the train to Denver, and Eunice, with their two children, Diane and Dennis, drove to meet him at the Denver Union Station. On their back from Denver, they stopped at our house in Mead. Still in uniform, Wilbur brought in a suitcase and set it on the dining-room table. He opened it and proceeded to hand out gifts. He had a Japanese sword for Tom and several yards of silk cloth for Mom. Jerry got a cloth soldier's hat, and Dave received a brass military button. He gave Japanese fans to Maureen and Kathleen and to Rollie. To Richie and me, he gave each of us a white silk flag with the large orange sun on it—the familiar symbol of the once-mighty Empire of the Rising Sun, which had just fallen.

During the Depression, Wilbur had been separated from his California family as a young boy and was sent to live with his uncle who farmed near Johnstown—not far from Mead. Wilbur's interest was tending with livestock, and he chose to make his living milking cows. My brothers and I saw him and my sister Eunice and their children quite frequently—they were often our dinner guests for Sunday dinner. Wilbur was generous with us and shared much of his time with his expanded family—especially Mom; he bought cherry chocolates for her for no special reason, and he and my sister Eunice picked fruit for her to can. Wilbur took Mom shopping, repaired our leaking toilet, and butchered our pig. He took us kids fishing, to drive-in movies, to the mountains for picnics, and to watch evening softball games.

In 1947, my second oldest sister, Betty, married Jack Curran, a Longmont native and a veteran of the navy. My triplet brothers and I did not attend the ceremony, but I remember for the wedding, Mom made Betty's dress out of nylon fabric from a parachute that Jack had saved from his time in the military. They honeymooned in California, and when they came back, Mom asked how they liked it out there.

"I wouldn't take it if they gave me the whole damned state," said Jack, who was quick to share his opinion.

"We saw Monica and Lynn [a cousin and her husband] out there," said Betty. "They like California—say they wouldn't come back to Colorado—he's got a good job there with the telephone company, and she's sellin' real estate."

"Things are helluva lot more expensive out there," said Jack. "That's why they call it the Golden State. Also, there's too damn much traffic on those freeways to suit me."

All their wedding gifts had been stored in one of our upstairs bedroom, and they came to retrieve them one day. I had no understanding as how two newlyweds could truly love one another and felt the need to express it in their speech. I was amused when I heard them calling each other honey—to me it was baby talk and seemed out of character for grown-ups. I'd never heard Mom and Dad talk like that.

Betty and Jack would often have dinner with us on Saturday night to eat our customary meal of pinto beans and Mom's fresh-baked bread. One evening, a discussion ensued about popular songs, and we started telling each other what our favorites were.

Light of Her Children

"I like Western songs, like 'Cool Water'," I said. "That group that sings it really sounds good."

"Me too," said Richie. "I like Western singers—I like Ernest Tubb—I can sing like him."

"Why are most songs always about love?" I asked innocently. "Why don't they write 'bout somethin' else? It shouldn't be just about love all the time—that's all you hear on the radio."

"What do you think is the most popular song today?" I asked Jack.

"'Stardust'," said Jack immediately.

"'Stardust'?" I blurted out quizzically. "I've never heard of it."

"You ask anybody," said Jack. "They'll tell you the same thing—written by Hoagy Carmichael."

Then in his baritone voice, Jack started to sing:

> Sometimes I wonder why I spend
> The lonely nights dreaming of a song
> The melody haunts my reverie
> And I am once again with you

"There it is again," I said. "That song's about kissin' and all that lovin' stuff. I don't know why people think that's so great."

"That's what makes the world go round," said Betty. "They'll be singin' about it until the world ends."

Talking about love embarrassed me; I hated it when Rosemary sang a popular love song and looked at me as if she was singing to her long-lost lover—I wanted to crawl into a hole and bury my head.

Jack told us about his life in the navy. He had been an airplane gunner in the navy during World War II, and he and a pilot were lost one night on a navigational training flight about a hundred miles off the Florida coast. Their single-engined plane was downed by a rain squall south of the Florida Keys. The plane sank immediately, and he and the pilot battled heavy seas on a life raft till they reached a tiny island. Marooned for six days, they were finally rescued by a coast guard patrol boat after being sighted by a navy plane.

Jack said, "We were like Robinson Crusoes—we ate snails and crabs. We hung our shirts out to collect rainwater."

"I bet you were happy to see that rescue boat, were'n' cha?" I asked.

"You damned right I was," said Jack. "I spent every night prayin'. My dad and mom were told that I was missin'—my dad said he stopped off every evening after work at St. John's to pray for me. It was a week before the navy sent the telegram to 'em sayin' I was okay."

Betty, like all my older sisters, took on an advising role when they came to see us. "Mom really worries about you kids when you go swimming," she said one day when I complained to her that Mom wouldn't let us go swimming with our friends.

"When she was growing up, one of her cousins drowned while swimming in the Platte River. You can see why she doesn't want you kids to go by yourselves without adults around," Betty explained.

Our brother Jack was spending more of his free time working at Baker's IGA grocery, and he saved enough money to buy Mom and Dad a new radio. He brought home a Philco with an automatic record changer from the Mead Appliance Store, paying more than a hundred dollars for it. It was the first automatic phonograph model built by Philco, and it had a louvered reddish-brown walnut case that sat on top of a matching table, making it the most elegant piece of furniture in our living room.

Mom and Dad listened to the morning news and the weather reports. Dad had easy accessibility to the front dials as he sat in his green plastic-covered chair right next to it. Dad still listened to Gabriel Heater in the evenings, keeping abreast of the events of the ending war, and in the afternoons, he heard the "recreated" broadcasts of the St. Louis Cardinals baseball games. On Saturday nights, he and Mom listened to the comedy of Minnie Pearl and songs of country crooners on the *Grand Ole Opry*. I listened along with them, and I soon learned the familiar phrases of Eddy Arnold's "Cattle Call" and the lines from Woody Guthrie's "Oklahoma Hills."

Jack bought the seventy-eight-revolutions-per-minute record of Vaughn Monroe's "Ballerina," and with her babysitting money, Helen bought Monroe's "There! I Said It Again," as well as the recording by Bing Crosby and the Andrews Sisters of the song "Don't Fence Me In." Dad's old Philco had migrated to the upstairs bedroom of my brothers Jack and Tom.

Jack graduated from high school in spring of '47, and one night at supper, he told us all that he was going to work for a while at IGA grocery and save his money so he could then go to New York City.

"I called Ray, and he told me I could live with him and he would get me a job," said Jack. "He's got an apartment there—said I could sleep on the couch."

Turning to Mom, I asked, "What's Ray workin' at there in New York?" I asked.

"He sells import stuff that they get from Italy," Mom answered. "His boss goes over there every year and picks out what he wants. I guess Ray went with him a couple of times."

"New York's the biggest city in the United States," said Kathleen. "It has seven million people livin' there."

"Do ya think you'll get to watch the Yankees play?" I asked Jack. "Probably so—maybe even the Giants," Jack replied. "I'd like to see the Dodgers too—Brooklyn's right there near New York."

"Boy, you're really lucky," said Rollie. "I hope someday I'll get to see the Dodgers—I'd go see them before I'd go watch the Yankees."

By the time I was twelve years old, I was well indoctrinated with the teachings of the Catholic Church. Church dogma had been ingrained into me by what I was told by the nuns at Saturday catechism classes and by the priest on Sunday mornings. In fact, I was so accepting of what they said I had the notion that practices such as meatless Fridays and fasting before receiving Holy Communion had been etched in stone by God, just like the Ten Commandments. Because of the church's powerful influence, my own opinions weren't really mine, and the perspective I had of others and their behavior was clouded and biased.

"Why doesn't Orbin go to church?" I asked Mom. "He just sleeps in on Sunday when he comes home. Sister Marjorie says you're committin' a sin if ya don't go." (I also knew that Dad didn't go sometimes, but I didn't want to bring that up.)

Mom said nothing—she just looked at me, not knowing how to respond—she gave me no answer. When Orbin brought his divorced girlfriend, Ferne, and her daughter Kathy home for us to meet one Sunday and when I heard later that they were to marry, I said to Kathleen, "Orbin's not supposed to marry her—Catholics don't believe in divorce—if he marries her, he's committin' a mortal sin. He'll go to hell for sure!"

"Don't worry about it, Ronnie—don't be so high and mighty—it's none of your business."

Later I talked to Sister Laurance. She said, "Well, Ronnie, the Lord tells us not to be so quick to judge others about what they do—maybe you should just not think about it anymore and let your brother live his life the way he wants to—I think you should just live your life the way you've been taught—don't worry about someone else."

Orbin had become a career marine, and while he was on assignment in Korea, Ferne, Kathy, and their two other kids, Lynne and Patrick, came to live with us. This disrupted the established social routine in our household and invoked jealousy on my part. From my perspective, Mom seemed to favor Ferne over the rest of us, and Mom appeared to give more of her attention to her grandchildren. One day Ferne, perceiving this, saw me in one of my sulking moods and sat down next to me and attempted to put her arm around me and console me. Not wanting her sympathy and not used to having anyone providing me comfort with physical contact, I threw her arm away, and I jumped up from where we were sitting. I angrily walked away to another room. I was too proud to admit that my envious feelings had gotten the best of me.

During the summer and after school, Mom wanted me to watch over four-year-old Patrick while Ferne helped prepare supper. Patrick and I developed a special bond. He greeted me like I was his father when I came home, and he always wanted to play. I gave him rides in the wagon, played catch, pushed him on our bag swing, and ran races with him down our back alley. He was a happy and playful kid, and I enjoyed being with him, and when he and his family left for Virginia, I missed him a lot. Surprisingly, I also missed Ferne—her presence and humor had added greatly to our mealtime conversations.

Three years later, Mom told us that Patrick and Orbin were coming back to Colorado for a visit—I was looking forward to seeing Patrick once again and renewing the bond we had established. I expected him to flash his dimpled smile and recognize me with a shake of the hand. To my dismay and disappointment, he did not even acknowledge me and appeared to have no memory of me—to him, I was just one of many uncles whom his dad had told him about. I had innocently expected too much from the memory of a four-year-old.

It was not long before I overheard conversations that our fifth oldest sister, Pat, was also planning to spend her life married to her steady boyfriend. Since we had no cafeteria at school, my brothers and sisters and I went home for lunch if we had not fixed sack lunches that morning. One noon hour, Pat, with sandwich in hand and standing next to Mom, hovering over the kitchen sink, casually asked her, "Can I get engaged?"

It seemed like a curious question to be asked in the middle of the day at lunch and in the presence of many of us. But it appeared to me that Pat was determined to get the issue placed on Mom's radar screen, knowing full well that the answer would be a negative. Mom, not expecting such a question and particularly during lunch, abruptly turned to face her and forcefully said, "No, you cannot. You're not even out of school yet and you're talking like that."

I still had not fathomed the "concept of love" and had no understanding or appreciation of the commitment that Pat was making to her fiancé, Dale French. I was awkwardly perplexed when I saw them kissing one night as I sat undetected in our tree house twenty yards away. I was always uneasy when I saw people outwardly showing affection for one another, and now with my sister, I felt like an intruder. Pat wisely waited to get engaged until she had moved into an apartment in Longmont with our sister Helen and was working as a dental assistant. Now on her own, Pat would no longer need Mom's permission.

While they were courting, we kids knew that Dale was going to be a good brother-in-law, when he volunteered to take us to see the Denver Bears play baseball. Dad went with us—there were eight of us packed into Dale's new Pontiac as we drove to Bears Stadium.

And the community beyond that of our family had an opinion about Pat's announcement of marriage. "Patty's pretty young to be gettin' married," said Mrs. Snider when I went to her house to collect for their month's *Rocky Mountain News* subscription.

"She's not as young as Mrs. Thompson was," I said. "Her son Allen told me she got married when she was fifteen."

"Well, maybe so, but even nineteen is still pretty young," said Mrs. Snider.

Pat and Dale French were married in Mead's Guardian Angel Catholic Church, and it was the first and only wedding of my siblings that I attended. My triplet brothers, Jerry, Dave, and I sat in the choir loft while Pat and Dale repeated their vows in front of Father Martin Arno. Since Dale was not Catholic, they could not have the traditional nuptial mass, and the short ceremony was conducted with the whole wedding party standing outside the rail that surrounded the altar. Helen was the maid of honor, and Rosemary was a bridesmaid. Pat had been home several times prior to try on her wedding gown, making sure that Mom had precisely fitted it to her liking. Pat was always particular with how she looked to others—not a strand of her hair was ever out of place—she was always looking into the mirror to reassure herself.

My brothers and I listened intently as a tenor, standing right next to where we were sitting, sang the "Ave Maria" while Pat placed a rose at the feet of the Blessed Virgin Mary and knelt to pray. Weeks later, I overheard a conversation between Pat and Helen: "You should've seen what Father Martin made Dale sign before he married us," said Pat. "He had to sign that he would raise our kids Catholic no matter what—even if I died before they grew up. He also had to sign that he'd never approve the taking of an unborn baby's life, no matter what the circumstances might be with me. He told Dale that the baby's life was more important than mine."

It was evident that the powerful hand of the Catholic Church had a wide reach. Pat and now her new husband were caught in its authoritarian web of control. I, still a young boy and a true believer, was entangled in it as well.

Rosemary Newton, 1945. *Newton Family Album*

Wilbur Thornton, US Army, 1944. *Newton Family Album*

Patricia (Newton) and Dale French, 1951. *Newton Family Album*

Patricia Newton, 1949. *Newton Family Album*

Roberta (Newton) and Jack Curran, 1947. *Newton Family Album*

Ferne, Patrick, Kathy, and Lynne Newton, 1951. *Newton Family Album*

Chapter 11

Come Spring

It was March 9, 1946, and I had just gotten home from school when I saw that Mom was "sick" again. She was carrying our flat, oval scrub pan from her bedroom—in the bottom there was water that looked like it was tinged with blood.

She said to me, "Go get your dad—he's down at the pool hall—tell him to come home right away."

I ran down Main Street to the pool hall and entered the door into the pool room where Dad was playing roun' the world with Joe Jones, Bill Schell, Ed Dempewolf, and Jack Pierce. Dad, with his fedora on, had a cigarette in one hand and was holding the cue stick upright in the other. I walked up to him and said, "Mom says she needs you right away—she's real sick and wants you to come home."

Dad took one last shot and said to everyone, "I gotta go—the missus needs me at the house." He hung the cue stick on the wall rack and placed a quarter on the table for proprietor Grover Roberts. He put on his rubber boots and his coat, and the two of us walked home.

Dad, with coat open and hands in his pockets, kept his usual casual pace—his calf-high rubber boots unbuckled and rattling as he took each step. As we passed Bunton's Red & White, I said to him, "Mom's really sick—she lost a lotta blood. I saw it in the scrub pan."

Dad said nothing; he just listened as I jabbered away.

James Elmer Newton was not worried—he had seen his wife this way many times before—Laura Dreier Newton was about to have her twentieth child.

Dad called in midwife Hulda Roman and Dr. Jones to help with the birth. That evening, my youngest brother was born. He was given the name Forrest Benedict, his middle name from our paternal grandfather. Although there is no Catholic saint with the name Forrest, Benedictine priest Father Martin Arno readily accepted his name of Forrest Benedict as "Catholic and saintly enough" at the time of Forrest's baptism. (A year later, Forrest was given the nickname "Frosty" by sister Rosemary.)

"I especially like the name Benedict," said Father Martin, pointing to the Benedictine symbol on his ring. "We Benedictines pray to St. Benedict every day—he started our order more than five hundred years ago."

Forrest was baptized in April, the month usually ushering in spring in Mead, Colorado. We always looked forward to April because it marked the end of the cold winter nights in our upstairs bedrooms, and it meant that the cold, blustery days of March had passed. The arrival of spring told us that the school year was coming to an end and summer vacation was imminent. With spring, the lilac bush in our front yard bloomed with fragrant purple flowers, and we heard red-winged blackbirds twittering in the reeds and cottonwoods on the nearby Redmond farm. However, the arrival of spring also marked the beginning of the wet season in Colorado, a time when a significant portion of the state's annual eighteen inches of precipitation fell from warm fronts moving across Colorado's arid eastern plains.

Every year come spring, warm, moist air from the Southern United States moved into Colorado from the Southeast and moved northward and westward toward the Rockies. As the moisture-laden air rose to higher elevations, frequent and heavy rainfalls occurred on the eastern side of the Rockies, deluging Mead and Weld County, sometimes for two or three days at a time. In May, the rains were frequent and predictable; in fact, they were so predictable we could almost count on having our annual last-day-of-school picnic in the town park washed out. When that happened, we resorted to eating our lunch indoors in the gymnasium before we were bussed to Longmont to see a picture show.

Anticipating the rains, Mead farmers, in their annual spring ritual, worked hurriedly to have the soil ready to capture and store the moisture and to germinate the crop seed they had just planted. Likewise, each spring, Dad got his garden and pasture soils ready.

Dad hired Cotton Johnson to plow up the soil on two vacant lots on the north and south sides of our house. Mr. Johnson had quit farming, and now he and his wife, Gladys, lived in town, but he still did custom threshing, plowing, and disking. Our parents did not own these two lots, but Dad asserted "squatter's rights" and used one to pasture his cow, "Bossie," and the other for his garden. Just days before, Dad had carried twenty or more wheelbarrow loads of manure from his cow pen and had deposited it on his garden land, and my brothers and I had dumped as many loads from our Radio Flyer wagon. With shovel and rake, we took turns in spreading Bossie's dung all over the half-acre area in front of our house.

Cotton Johnson used four tall, muscular workhorses to plow. He walked behind them, holding on to the two plow handles and guiding his horses with a long strap looped around his neck and right shoulder. The shiny silver blades of the plow cut sharply through the soil, turning over the upper layer, bringing fresh nutrients to the surface, and burying weeds and manure below. The odor of the freshly turned soil was new to me, and its distinct earthy fragrance was pleasing and satisfying.

As Mr. Johnson's plow swept by us, my brothers and I pulled earthworms from the furled rows of soil he left behind, and we carried them to the pen holding Mom's chickens and tossed them over the fence. We watched with delight as the hungry chickens scrambled and scurried, competing with one another, pouncing upon and capturing the delectable, wriggly treats suddenly presented to them. The next day, Mr. Johnson returned with his horses and a harrow and smoothed the furrows over, leveling the surface for planting.

My brothers and I helped Dad and Mom with the planting. As a guide to laying down straight rows, Dad tied a long string between two stakes driven into the ground at each end of the garden. For sweet corn, he dug deep holes with a spade, spacing them approximately a foot apart. We followed behind him, dropping three water-soaked kernels into each hole and then covering them up with soil. For vegetable plantings, Dad used a hoe to make shallow furrows parallel to the string, and Mom sprinkled small seeds of carrot, radish, turnip, red beet, and lettuce into them while we followed, crawling on our hands and knees, covering the furrow with soil. For pumpkins, squash, and green beans, she placed two seeds every six inches along the furrow, which we promptly covered.

On the pastureland, with a burlap bag carried at his side, Dad spread tall-fescue grass seed by the handfuls as he walked over the plowed and harrowed surface. He raked the seeds into the soil and then waited for the rains to germinate them.

When the garden's seedlings emerged, our brother Tom hoed furrows between the rows and began irrigating with water carried by a hose from the faucet attached to the outside of our house. The pasture and began to green up and soon started to look like a freshly cut backyard lawn, and soon we would be eating and canning our garden produce.

Newton family. *Front row, L–R*: Diane Thornton, Rollie, Richie, Ronnie, Dave. *Second row, L–R*: Jerry, Kathleen, Maureen, Tom, Laura Dreier holding Frosty. *Third row, L–R*: Helen, Pat. *Fourth row, L–R*: James Elmer holding Marc, Eunice Newton Thornton, Wilbur Thornton holding Dennis Thornton, Roberta. 1946. *Newton Family Album*

Laura Dreier Newton (arrow) in garden, 1942. *Newton Family Album*

CHAPTER 12

Communion Prayer

May was the Month of Mary and was the month when Catholics expressed their devotion to the Blessed Mother of Jesus. Each Sunday in May, the Guardian Angel Church choir sang hymns about Mary. With Mom at the organ and with our sisters Kathleen, Maureen, Pat, and Helen in the choir, they sang, "O Mary, O Mother Mary, we crown thee today, Queen of the Angels, Queen of the May."

From the pulpit, Father Martin said families should pray the rosary. He said, "A family that prays together stays together." Mom, convinced by this advice of Father Martin, assigned Kathleen with the responsibility of making sure this was done.

We had a ritual that we followed. Kathleen created an altar on top of the dresser in the bedroom of my brothers and mine. She put a statue of Mary on it and placed a candle beside her. Using construction paper, Kathleen created a backdrop of three Gothic-arched stained-glass windows and placed it behind Mary. Every day Kathleen placed fresh lilacs in a vase on the altar—blossoms she picked from the bush in our front yard.

Each night in darkness with only the one candle for light, we knelt over our beds, and Kathleen led us in prayer. Kathleen recited the first half of the Hail Mary; in unison, we recited the second half, repeating the prayer fifty-three times.

One night the reverence of the prayer service was shattered when Rollie and Dave got into a fight and started punching one another. Mom, hearing the ruckus, abruptly opened the door and ushered them both out of the room. There was a long pause with our prayer service—we heard Mom say to them, "Okay, you birds—there'll be no play for you tomorrow—I'll find plenty else for you to do. Now upstairs to bed with both of you, and you finish your own rosary—if I hear another peep out of either one of you, I'll come up there with a belt."

Twice a month on Saturday mornings throughout our second-grade school year, we triplets, along with our classmates Shirley Hepp, Joseph Smith, and Josephine Rademacher, attended catechism instruction at Guardian Angel Church. These lessons prepared us to receive the sacrament of Holy Communion. For this event, Mom made white sport shirts and white pants for us and bought us clear plastic belts. Our sisters Rosemary and Betty (Roberta) came home for the occasion and sang in the choir. As we triplets and our classmates gathered in the back of the church, Sister Marjorie smiled radiantly, proud that she had prepared us well with knowledge of God and our faith.

A woman in her forties, Sister Marjorie had a smiling face, surrounded by the traditional white cloth covering her ears, hair, and neck. A white starched crown set over her forehead, elevating the black shroud that hung over her head and shoulders. She wore the traditional white collar up to her chin with the "plastic-like" circular white bib draped down her front. The long ends of the white cincture wrapped around her waist hung down along with a rosary on one side of her long black pleated tunic. The flat head on the gold ring on her finger bore the inscription IHS. When she smiled, a dark-gray spot in her upper gums showed above her teeth. She told us that as a child, she was accidentally stabbed by a classmate with a lead pencil that left its mark forever with her warm and friendly smile.

Sister Marjorie encouraged us to bring small bottles to class, and she would fill them with "holy" water. I cleaned an empty Jergens lotion bottle discarded by my sister Pat, and gave it to Sister Marjorie, who brought it back two weeks later filled with water she obtained from Longmont's St. John's Church. She had pasted a picture of the Holy Family to the bottle. I sprinkled it on my fingers before I made the sign of the cross as I said my prayers. The concept of "holy water" had a magical meaning to me—to me its genesis was sacred and mysterious—I was certain that it came from a very holy place—from where, I did not know. I had no understanding that its "holiness" resulted simply from the sign of the cross wave of the priest's hand over a vessel of tap water accompanied by recitation of a short prayer.

In our preparation for First Communion, Sister Marjorie said, "You are seven years old, and you have reached the age of reason—now you know the difference between what is right and what is wrong, and you must confess your sins before you receive the Lord for the first time." Sister Marjorie rehearsed and walked us through the process in the confessional, having us kneel down on one side of the screen while she sat on the other.

"Tell your sins to the priest," she said. "If you missed your prayers, sassed your mother, lied, swore, or said bad things about others, tell him."

"Remember," Sister Marjorie added, "When you confess your sins, you are receiving the Church's sacrament of penance. This cleanses you so you can receive the Lord's body in the form of the host. In so doing, you receive the sacrament of the Holy Eucharist."

"Do we chew the host?" I asked Mom.

"No—you just let it rest on the roof of your mouth, and it will dissolve away," Mom answered.

To mark the occasion, Rosemary gave each of us a prayer book, and Sister Marjorie told us to hold it between our folded hands as we marched to the front of the church to take our seats. Toward the end of the Mass, all the class approached the altar to receive the host for the first time.

Kneeling at the altar, Sister Marjorie led us in prayer with the words, "Lord, I am not worthy that you should enter under my roof, but only say the Word, and my soul shall be healed."

We knelt at the railing while Father Martin placed the host on our tongues with our brother Tom, an altar boy, holding the brass paten below our chins in case the wafer was inadvertently dropped.

Helen commemorated the event by taking our picture in our white suits with her Brownie box camera.

Summer went by, and when fall arrived and it was time for us to go to school, Mom had no money with which to buy us new clothes.

"What are we goin' to do?" I asked Mom. "All our jeans are too small and have holes in them."

"I guess you'll just have to wear your First Communion outfits," said Mom.

We triplets wore our white shirts and white pants—we wore them every day, and we played football during our two recess periods on the grass area right next to the gym. Our outfits became stained and wrinkled and were not washed until Saturday. One day, a parent of one of my classmates was outside her car as she helped her invalid son get in, and as I walked by, she said, "My gosh, Mr. Newton! You boys are always dressed up in those white suits—how do you keep them clean?"

"We don't," I said. "But we don't have anything else to wear."

Ronnie, Rollie, and Richie Newton, 1947. *Newton Family Album*

Kathleen and Maureen Newton, 1948. *Newton Family Album*

Guardian Angel Church, Mead, CO, 1954. *Mead Consolidated Schools Yearbook*

CHAPTER 13

Chickens

In the spring of '47, Mom and Dad decided to dismantle the old two-story barn that sat forty yards east from our house in the far backyard. The barn had been used to shelter Dad's cow, Bossie. Now Mom wanted to tear down the old chicken coop and build a larger one. She wanted chickens that could provide both eggs and meat for the family table. The plan was to take down the existing barn and use the studs and siding to build a combined chicken coop and cow barn. It would be a one-story structure and would be located northeast of the house.

Our brothers Jack and Tom helped Dad in the afternoons after school and on weekends. After school, I fetched things for them: hammers, nails, wood, a level, a shovel, an axe, a crowbar, buckets, and whatever else they needed. Dad borrowed a cement mixer, bought bags of cement from Clark Lumber, and had Jake Amen haul in a load of sand and a load of gravel from pits near the Saint Vrain River. After Dad and my older brothers built the foundation forms, they mixed the sand, gravel, and cement together with water, loaded the mixture into a wheelbarrow, and carried it to a point where it was poured into the foundation forms. As the cement started to set, Dad and my brothers inserted the heads of long bolts into the fresh mixture with the threads and nuts exposed. These would be used to bolt two-by-fours to the foundation to which the studs could be attached.

When the building was framed, they attached the time-worn, tongue-and-groove pine siding pieces to the studs and made the roof out of long one-by-twelves resurrected from the hayloft floor of the old barn. The slanting roof was covered with sheets of tarred paper with the seams sealed with liquid tar. The chicken coop, with its cement floor, made up two-thirds of the new building, and on the other end, Bossie's dirt floor would be covered with a bed of straw.

Using scavenged railroad ties as posts, Dad and my older brothers built a cow pen with one-by-twelves placed vertically side-by-side, which Dad whitewashed. The chicken pen was constructed with lodgepole-pine posts and a galvanized steel network of chicken-wire. By the middle of May, the building and pens were completed and ready for Bossie and Mom's chickens—she wanted Rhode Island Whites. On a Saturday morning in late May, we triplets, our sister Eunice, brother-in-law Wilbur, and Mom piled into Wilbur's '38 Ford to go to Denver to get Mom's baby chicks. This was our—we triplets'—first trip to Denver—only thirty miles away from our home.

We stopped to have breakfast with our sister Rosemary in her Denver apartment, and then Wilbur took the three of us to the top of the clock tower of Daniels and Fisher Store Co., while Mom and Eunice shopped in the floors below. We saw the broad expanse of the city and the mountains to the west as well as the undulating plains to the east, but we could not see Mead because of the rolling hills to the north.

We had grilled cheese sandwiches and chocolate shakes for lunch in Richard's Restaurant and then headed to Robinson's Chicken Hatchery. Eunice and the three of us waited in the car while Mom and Wilbur went inside. Shortly, they came out of the hatchery each carrying three flat boxes. Each box contained twenty or more chicks, all wildly cheeping—each chick confused by the confined compartment where it now found itself.

At home, we placed the boxes in the kitchen next to the stove. The next day, Mom transferred them to the back porch, where she had laid newspapers down on the floor and put out small containers of water and cracked corn. Electric cords attached to sockets with lighted bulbs provided heat to keep the chicks warm. They soon started to grow and were ready to be transferred to the new coop.

Mom wanted straw on the floor of her chicken coop, and Dad needed straw for Bossie's barn floor. They determined that the best source of straw was the stack on the Redmond farm, where Mamie Akers lived in the old farmhouse a quarter mile from our house. One afternoon, Mom told Richie and me to take gunnysacks with us and walk to the straw stack, fill the sacks, carry them back, and place their contents in the barn for the chickens and Bossie. Before we went, Mom and Dad warned us (many times actually) that we shouldn't crawl on to the top of a freshly made straw stack.

"You could sink down into it and not get out," Dad said. "You could suffocate."

"Don't ever play on a straw stack," said Mom. "I don't ever want to hear about you doing it."

Now the Redmond farm straw stack had been made the year before, and I was certain that it had plenty of time to settle and would provide no danger to Richie and me. Nevertheless, I was not going to take any chances, and I was certain that Richie felt the same way. Richie and I walked across Fred Gettman's hayfield just north of our house. On the north side of the field, we crossed over the road and entered the Redmond farm. We walked to the base of the stack and helped ourselves to handfuls of straw, which we stuffed into the sacks.

Unexpectedly, we heard a "Yoo-hoo" coming from someone standing outside the farmhouse nearby. It was Mamie Akers. I stopped what I was doing immediately and ran over to talk to her. I had visited with Mamie many times before and had enjoyed her interesting conversations. Living by herself, she was lonely and was always glad to have someone to talk to. Mom spent many hours visiting with her on the phone.

"What are you boys doing?" Mamie asked.

"We're getting straw for Mom's chicken coop," I answered. "Didn't Mom talk to you about it?"

"No, she didn't," said Mamie. "But I guess it's okay—just don't spread it all over Christendom!"

Mom had been kind to Mamie through the years—providing Mamie with food and sending us to bring in wood and coal for her when the snow was too deep and when it was too cold for her to go out. She knew that Mamie would be glad for us to take the straw—after all, the amount we needed was very small. Furthermore, Mom knew that Mamie's two cousins, the Redmond sisters (owners of the farm) and now nuns in the Order of the Sisters of Loretto, would generously consent to giving the straw to us. The Redmonds had always been at Mom's side when she was in need.

I ran back to the stack to catch up with Richie, who was well on his way in loading his four sacks. I quickly became engrossed in getting the task done. Standing on the ground, I moved around the stack base perimeter, stuffing bunches into my sacks as fast as I could. Suddenly, I heard Richie yelling frantically, "Help! Hel-p! Hel-p!"

A state of panic came over me. I dropped the hold on my sack and ran around the stack, looking for Richie. Not seeing him, I yelled out, "Where are you? Where are you?"

Hearing nothing, I began to look at pocket-holes in the straw about five feet above ground, where I surmised Richie had sunk. I jumped into the spot of the pocket and began to frantically pull the straw away with both hands. I did not see or feel him, so I turned to another pocket and began to dig ferociously again. Still, there was no trace of Richie, and then I began sobbing. I was certain Richie had succumbed and was dying somewhere in the stack. I cried openly and bellowed as I moved from spot to spot, hoping to find him.

Just then, I heard Richie laughing from above. There he was, lying on top of the stack, laughing and waving to me as if nothing had happened. He was delighted at the fun he was having at my expense.

Angry as a cornered cow, I swore at him, "You—you—son of a-a-a bitch! Richie laughed all the more.

"You dirty bastard!" I yelled.

Then repeating a phrase that my mother always used, I said, "I oughta wring your neck."

Richie kept laughing and said nothing.

"You scared the holy shit right outta me," I said. "I thought you were a goner!"

When Richie came down from his perch, I tackled him and pinned him down into the straw at the base of the pile. I punched him a couple of time in the ribs, but Richie gave no resistance. He just lay there and kept laughing. He showed no inclination to fight back—he was having too good of a time.

We filled our sacks and carried them back across Mr. Gettman's field to the chicken coop and emptied them. Without incident, we went back twice for eight more bags—finally, we had enough straw for both Mom's Rhode Island Whites and Dad's Bossie. It would not be long before Mom would have several chickens frying in pans on her wood-burning stove, ready for Sunday afternoon dinner.

Richie, Rollie, and Ronnie Newton and original chicken house and barn, 1943. *Newton Family Album*

Richie, Ronnie, and Rollie Newton, 1949. *Newton Family Album*

CHAPTER 14

Occasions of Summer

When summer vacation came around, Mead townsfolk would call our home and ask for one of my brothers and me to mow their lawn, weed their garden or do other odd jobs. We used the money to buy our sports equipment and occasional treats at the pool hall or drugstore. We ourselves did not have a lawn to mow, but Mom made sure that we helped weed her strawberry patch, cut down tall weeds that grew in the back alleyway, and keep the yard clean. When not working or playing softball, we spent a lot of our free time building and creating things.

We boys made tents out of gunnysacks that we split in two, and we fabricated a fort out of scrap wood and rusted corrugated tin siding that had been discarded in the downtown alleyway. We built a cart out of orange crates, and we carved out a square hole in a vacant lot for a "dugout," constructed of wood for our softball diamond. We made rubber guns out of wood lathe pieces, clothespins, and tire inner tubes. We made slingshots out of crotched branches from the four-trunked silver poplar tree in our front yard. In that same tree, we erected a tree house, ten feet above the ground in between the four trunks where our brother Jack had built a similar house in the same tree a decade earlier. The same iron chains that Jack had used as railings between the trunks still remained; in Jack's time, the chains must've been five or six feet above the ground, but in our time, they were twelve feet from ground level.

The four-part silver poplar tree was magnificent, towering over the northwest corner of our house. Each trunk was forty or fifty feet tall, and their canopies provided much needed shade to the yard below during the hot summer months. The ledge where these four trunks were fused together was where many of us Newton siblings stood when we had our picture taken. Our family album has many photos showing my brothers and sisters individually perched among the four trunks, including one where all three of us triplets are standing among them.

Our brother Jack brought home a long twined rope that he bought at the lumberyard. He had his high school friend Albert Yakel climb high into the tree and tie it to a limb twenty or so feet above the ground. Jack filled a gunnysack with rags and tied it to the end of the rope, onto which we could sit as he pushed us. The arced path of the swing carried the bag right next to a small elm tree, into which we climbed so that we could jump onto the bag and swing under our own power. It was added fun when one of us jumped from the tiny elm onto the suspended swing while it was occupied by another one of us.

One afternoon as my brothers and I were swinging, Mom came out to the front yard to tell us that Hulda Roman called and wanted to know if one of us could go to her house to play with her grandson, Gary Hearvy.

"I don't want to," said Rollie.

"Me neither," said Richie.

Seeing that Mom was in a dilemma, and before she would order one of us to go, I volunteered, "I'll go."

Hulda Roman was the midwife who had helped deliver many of my siblings and me, and she lived with her husband, Louis, on a farmhouse a quarter of mile east of Mead. Her daughter, Ethel, the mother of Gary, had been a classmate of our brother Raymond. I had been in Hulda's home several times when I delivered milk that Mom sold to her. In winter, Hulda served me coffee and sugar-coated pastry she had made.

"Her coffee tastes really good," I said to my sister Kathleen. "It has a gold color to it—I wonder how she makes it."

"She puts a raw egg yolk in it," says Kathleen. "I like it too."

I knew why Rollie and Richie did not want to go and play with Gary Hearvy. It was always a boring afternoon—Gary, a couple of years younger than us, wanted to play house and dress his stuffed animals as his children. He preferred to dress up in his grandmother's dresses and wear her high-heeled shoes. I knew his behavior was different, but I did not think much about it, finding it bearable when he served me tea, cupcakes, and cookies—I enjoyed the sweet morsels that Hulda made for us. However, I was always relieved when Hulda came to tell me that it was time to go home—then I could resume the playground activities of softball and basketball with my brothers.

Each summer, Kuner-Empson's pea huller in town opened for three weeks to process all the peas that were grown on farms surrounding Mead, and this became an opportunity for my brothers and me to earn money selling soda pop to the workers. We purchased bottles of Nehi from Grover Roberts at the Mead Pool Hall for a nickel apiece, and we sold them for a dime. Mr. Roberts lent us a wood crate holding twenty-four bottles, and we had an empty chocolate-candy box that we used for a cashbox. We carried the crate inside the huller, walking on platforms and up and down the stairs in between conveyer belts and machines, offering pop for sale to thirsty workers.

Seeing us, Mike Sekich Sr. motioned for us to come over where he was working. We knew Mr. Sekich—he was a retired farmer whom we had seen often in the pool hall drinking a beer as the two of us watched men play. Mike was standing over a large tub of shelled peas, and there were loud clattering and clanging sounds coming from all directions around us.

"What'd kind would you like?" I shouted.

"Root beer!" he shouted back.

He handed Jerry a quarter, and Jerry gave him back his change while I opened the bottle and handed it up to him. Jerry and I stood and watched with amazement as the dehydrated Mr. Sekich lifted the bottle to his lips and guzzled all its contents down without removing it once from his mouth. Every day we knew we would have one sale we could count on—Mr. Sekich was always a dependable, thirsty customer.

As Jerry and I walked through the corrugated tin structure, we scooped handfuls of the tasty legumes from the open tubs and popped them into our mouths. We stopped to talk to our friend Loe Hernandez, who was loading tubs of peas into a truck for transport to the Longmont cannery. We sold sodas to Mexican nationals who had been imported by Kuner-Empson to harvest vegetables and work in canneries. At one stop, Jerry turned around to make change only to realize that our money box he had laid down was gone. He ran back to the location of our previous stop—it was not there—the two of us then realized that because of our own carelessness, someone had stolen our money.

"Who do you think took it?" I asked Loe Hernandez that evening when he came into our yard to play kick-the-can.

"I think it was that national," said Loe. "You know who he is—he's that good-lookin' guy with a mustache and is always smilin'. I know it was him because he didn't have any money this morning when he came to work, and this afternoon he had a pocketful of change."

"I know which one you're talkin' about," I said. "I know exactly who he is—he seems like such a nice guy—real friendly—I never would have thought he was the one who did it."

"We had sold fifteen bottles this morning when it happened," I said. "We had almost three dollars in the box that that dirty son of a gun took! Now for tomorrow, we're goin' to have to borrow from Mom and pay her back after we sell it—we'll have to sell for a couple of days before we earn back our money."

The next day I told Grover Roberts what happened.

Light of Her Children

"Loe Hernandez said he thought it was a Mexican national who took it," I said.

"Well, they're a tough bunch of hombres," said Grover. "Last summer, they found a dead Mexican in one of Kuner-Empson's pickle tanks over there by the park. He'd been stabbed to death. I don't know if they ever found out who did it—probably another Mexican. Ya gotta be careful when you're around some of those guys—'specially when they're drunk—you don't know what they're goin' to do."

Sadly, the prejudices of the times were expressed openly in our Mead community—the Mexican nationals were subjected to our biased opinions of those whose lives were foreign to our own. We often spoke disparagingly of them and ridiculed their unfamiliar, rapid speech.

Later that same summer, I went into the Handy Corner to buy a Butterfinger candy bar—I had withheld a nickel from the subscription monies for the *Rocky Mountain News* that I had collected before I turned it in to Mom for safekeeping.

"That'll be five cents," said Sandy Adler as he handed me the candy.

Sandy and his wife had taken over the drugstore from the Georges, who had bought it from the Sniders and renamed it the Handy Corner. The Adlers also had moved off their farm and had bought the vacant Amen house located across from the school.

"Could one of you boys work for me this week?" Sandy asked.

"Yes—I-I can—what a ya need done?"

"I need my lawn mowed and the yard cleaned up," said Sandy. "I'll pay ya fifty cents an hour."

"I can do it tomorrow—Mom wants me to work at home this afternoon."

"Okay," said Sandy. "I'll leave the shed unlocked so you can get to the lawn mower and shovels and rakes—there's a wheelbarrow in there also—you can just dump all the weeds an' stuff back near the alley—I'll haul it off myself when I get time."

I showed up to work the next day at eight o'clock. Sandy and his wife had already gone to open the drugstore. Since the house had remained vacant for several months, the yard had not been tended to. Leaves from the previous fall still remained around the shrubbery, and the grass was now six inches high. It was so tall I could not push the mower through it, and I had to cut it first with a swinging scythe before trimming it with the push mower. Ironweeds had grown tall around the edges of the outhouse, the shed, and the house, and they dominated the garden area that had not been planted that year. Refuse from overflowing garbage cans was strewn over the backyard and into the alley.

I went about my task ferociously, only stopping to get a drink of water and run home for lunch. Finally, at 5:30 p.m., I put all the equipment back into the shed and went home for supper. The next day, I walked into the Handy Corner to collect my earnings.

"What do I owe you, Mr. Newton?" asked Sandy.

"Four dollars, Mr. Adler," I answered. "It took me eight hours to get it all done."

"Eight hours!" exclaimed Sandy. "I could have had it done in a lot less time by the Markham kids."

"May be so—but the Markhams won't do as good a job as I did," I retorted.

"I ain't payin' you for no eight hours," growled Sandy. "You should've had it done in half the time."

Sandy reached into his cash drawer and threw two paper dollars on the counter in front of me.

"Here," he said. "That's all I'm payin' ya."

He slammed the drawer back in to the register and stared at me.

I stared back at him, turned away, and left the two bills on the counter. I walked out the door and slammed the screen door behind me. As I headed for home, I said to myself using a phrase I'd learned from Glen Keller in the pool hall, "That big, fat Sandy Adler can take his two dollars and put it where the sun doesn't shine."

After that, I never went into the Handy Corner unless I really had to, and then I always waited until Mrs. Adler could help me. I never looked Sandy straight in the eye ever again—I shunned him like a snake.

I wondered if Sandy had ever cheated my dad when he worked for him. Probably not, I said to myself—my dad just wouldn't put up with his hogwash.

Silver poplar tree in front yard of Rademacher house (former home of Newton family), 2013. *Sheila Koenig*

Jerry Newton, 1949. *Newton Family Album*

Ronnie Newton, 1949. *Newton Family Album*

L–R: Rollie, Ronnie, and Richie Newton, 1942. *Newton Family Album*

Jack Newton, 1947. *Newton Family Album*

CHAPTER 15

Halloween

When the autumn rolled around in our small-town Mead community, it meant that it was time to begin the football season once again at home and at school and for farmers to harvest the ever-precious sugar-beet crop and gather corn and hay for winter storage and feed for their cattle. For us kids, it was also the time for us to celebrate Halloween—a tradition of trick or treat that was enjoyed by the old as well as the young. Harvest, football, and Halloween were the simple and normal activities that we carried out every autumn in Mead.

When the school year began in Mead Consolidated Schools, the sugar-beet harvest was taking place throughout Weld County. Beet harvesters, pulled by either John Deere or Farmall tractors, were moving from row to row and up and down the fields. Trucks coming from all points around Mead were carrying beets to "the dump" beside the railroad tracks that ran through town. Trucks lined up two and three at a time, waiting to be weighed before their beds were tilted hydraulically and their payloads dumped onto a conveyor belt to be transferred to the top of an ever-enlarging beet pile. Farmers kept their sons out of school to work in the fields to drive trucks and tractors. Some kids would not be seen in the school yard until

Friday afternoon, when they returned to play football, and my brother Tom, who had been working on Wilbert Peppler's farm all summer, missed school, working two weeks during the beet harvest.

In the sandier soil near the South Platte River, the pinto bean and potato crops had already been harvested. Throughout Weld County, green stalks and ears of corn had been sliced into small pieces for ensilage and had been deposited in large earthen openings chiseled out of hillsides, where the silage was stored until it was needed as feed for cattle during the winter months. Some farmers had left their field corn still standing with stalks and leaves turning brown and dry, the ears now ready to be harvested mechanically.

With the grain crops safely stored in elevators, barley and oat stubble had been disked under, and barren fields alternated checkerboard style with patches of pumpkins and squash in the countryside surrounding Mead and in the gardens of townsfolk. In the half-acre garden plot in front of our house, there were rows of vines that were now heavy with large pumpkins and squash, ready for Mom to can. Dried brown cornstalks, already picked clean of their ears, were still standing, and short green-bean stems, barren of leaves, stood diminutively next to them. Strawberries were hanging on, now dormant, ready to last through the winter and to produce next year's crop; adjacent to them, withered stalks of Mom's daisies chattered in the wind. Next to the road and furthest from the house, large rhubarb clumps, their leaves and stems still green and succulent, were thriving in the barrow pit at the southern edge of the garden. Leaves that had fallen from the large elm in our front yard had been raked into large piles, waiting there for Dad to set them on fire.

The grass of the town park had gone dormant, its blue-green hue now brown. Trees of elm, poplar, and maple, growing on the park's perimeter, had shed their leaves, and their naked branches thrust prominently silhouetted in the sky.

Light of Her Children

The days were growing shorter, and the harvest moon began to wax at twilight, appearing as a bright-orange sphere in the eastern sky just above the leafless tree horizons of our Mead community. Just before sundown, Venus blazed in the west above the Rockies. Sparrows, searching for insects, flitted from limb to limb in the leafless elm in our front yard and then flew away to take respite in our barn or in the barns and garages of our Mead neighbors. As darkness fell, bats could be heard flapping their wings as they darted through the sky gobbling unwary mosquitoes and moths. Male crickets, stroking the toothed comb on their wings, chirped loudly as they searched for female companions in their nightly courtship ritual.

Our dog Skeeks returned home for the night after roaming with other dogs from the neighborhood, chasing rabbits in the adjacent farm fields and barking at blackbirds perched on the swamp cattails of Mamie Akers's swamp. Now exhausted from his unsuccessful stalking of prey, Skeeks was on our porch doorstep, waiting to be let into the house for his meal of table scraps.

Cloudless and unpolluted by terrestrial light, the autumn night sky above Mead was clear and transparent and was a stage for the familiar display of the Milky Way, the Big and Little Dippers, and countless galactic stars. Cool and pleasant, the autumn evenings invited Mead families to linger outside their homes after their suppers, gathering final glimpses of the red-and-orange sunset hovering over the mountains to the west.

For me, at age 12, the fall season was still about Halloween, and the usual pleasant weather of October was conducive to an exciting holiday evening with all the Mead townspeople participating. Widows and widowers, spinsters and bachelors, and the married couples all had treats for us kids. Many housewives provided homemade goodies of cookies, cupcakes, and popcorn balls—while others treated us with candies purchased at the grocery store.

Button's Red & White, Snider's Drugstore, the pool hall, and the Mead Motor Company all stayed open late on Halloween night. They gave us trick or treats, a variety of candies from their store counters: peanut-butter logs, bubble gum, jaw breakers, suckers, gum drops, and licorice. Store patrons stayed late and lingered with the proprietors so they could see the variety of costumes and listen and watch us kids squirm with anxiety when asked to "do a trick."

For my brothers and me, our costumes consisted of my dad's or older brothers' discarded shirts hanging loosely on our small frames with our faces covered with masks that each of us had made of either construction or brown wrapping paper and tied around our heads with string. One or two of us would wear Dad's worn-out fedoras, while others wore stocking caps. When an adult asked whom we were trying to portray, we would always answer, "We're hobos."

For several years, Mrs. Margaret Olson brought her son Gary, a classmate of us triplets, into town to trick-or-treat with us. On Halloween of '51, Gary dressed as a ghost farmer. Over his head, he threw a large sheet covering his whole body. He cut two holes for his eyes and then placed a straw hat on his head to anchor the sheet. Gary had grown much taller than us triplets, and as our group went from door to door, his tall, ghostly white figure was most prominent. With all of us collected together on the front porch of Jake Amen's house, Jake was startled when he opened the door and saw the towering apparition—he blurted out, "My god, you're a damn big ghost in the back there, young man—you should be in here watching TV with me." Gary chuckled loudly but still held his sack open to receive a Tootsie Pop from Mr. Amen.

Our good friend Ronald Weber, five years older than us triplets, joined our group when we arrived at his house. Weber's only costume was the commercially made mask covering his face—he had on his plaid coat and baseball cap that he always wore to school. With all of us on the front porch of Coach Edwin

Spencer's house, Coach's daughter Janet came to the door with a sack of candy. Recognizing Weber immediately, she announced, "If there is anybody here above the eighth grade, they will not get any candy." Weber started laughing and descended the steps and walked across the street to wait for us.

At Rodney Markham's house, Hester Markham responded to our trick-or-treat request with "Show me a trick." In unison, we sang the Christmas song "Jingle Bells." Mrs. Markham rewarded us with giant popcorn balls and oatmeal cookies. Mrs. George Snider also demanded a trick from us—so we responded likewise by singing—this time it was "Silent Night." Mrs. Snider dropped a chocolate cupcake into our sacks. We saw a light on in Loe Hernandez's house—we knocked on the door, but no one ever answered. Gary, "the ghost," brought a bar of soap with him, and along our way, he soaped the windows of folks who were not at home and those of unwary shop owners.

But for us Newtons, Halloween revels could not last too far into the night; we had to get home early because we all had to get up at six the next morning to attend Mass at Guardian Angel Church. November 1 was All Saints' Day, a holy day of obligation on which Catholics were expected to attend Mass.

When I got home, I hid my sack of candy in the attic. There, I knew it was safe from my brothers who might be tempted to "sample" my loot. I decided to eat Mrs. Snider's cupcake that night, keeping the rest of the treats for several weeks, eating them sparingly—wanting them to last for a long time.

But later that evening, there was some extra Halloween drama. We Newtons and all the rest of the Mead townsfolk were awakened just before midnight. The town fire siren was set off by Mead High students who had been roaming the streets in their cars and looking for ways to create mischief and test the patience of businessmen and homeowners. Everyone in town knew it was a false alarm—but the noise lasted a long time before Marshal Wilse Lamberson arrived to turn it off. Our brother Tom was not yet at home, and we Newtons all knew that he and his friends were the culprits.

The next morning, I got up immediately when Mom roused us with her usual wake-up call from downstairs. I put my school clothes on, washed up, and combed my hair, and by six fifteen, my four brothers and I were out the door and walking down Main Street toward Guardian Angel Church on the far south side of town. The sun was just rising, and the faint light of dawn was spreading across our tiny Colorado burg of Mead. Passing by the town park, we saw that the green double-seated toilet had been removed from its foundation and was now lying on its side. Hoping to obstruct traffic, perpetrators had removed rusted garbage barrels from the alleyways and had placed them in the middle of Main Street. The large windows of the old library and the Mead Motor Company had been soaped with scribbles and graffiti by the hand of Gary Olson. Seeds and flesh of ripened tomatoes were splattered on Button's Red & White front window, thrown by high schoolers driving by in their cars. The center streetlight on Main Street was not lit as a result of high school student vandals knocking out the bulb with rocks they hurled from the backs of farm trucks. Mr. Roberts's Pool Hall toilet had been severed from its foundation and lay prone on the ground—so had Mary Johnson's.

Walking by the post office, Rollie said, "Boy, Hap Howlett's goin' to be mad when he sees that we soaped his windows."

"Yal, it'll take 'im a week to get all of that off," I said. "But maybe he'll pay one of us to do it."

Approaching the church, we saw Father Martin's Ford already parked near the sacristy door. Because it was a weekday Mass, the service would be short—the choir would not be singing, and the homily would be brief.

Explaining the meaning of this special day of the liturgical year, Father Martin said, "This day, All Saints' Day, commemorates all those who have attained beatific vision in heaven. Beatific vision is the eternal and direct visual perception of God enjoyed by those who are in heaven, thus imparting to them supreme happiness. St. Thomas Aquinas defined the beatific vision as the ultimate end of human existence after physical death. The church teaches us that the saints that have died in the faith are with God in heaven, where they enjoy beatific vision."

Father Martin paused for a moment while he removed his handkerchief tucked into the sleeve of his tunic. He then paused again as he wiped his nose.

He resumed his remarks with "Today we pray to the saints for them to intercede with God on our behalf for we know that they are with Him in heaven."

Continuing, he said, "You know, sixteenth-century writers tell us that this day is also called All Hallows or Hallowmas. Last night we all celebrated Halloween, a tradition that also goes back to the sixteenth century when the Scottish celebrated the festival they called All Hallows Eve, that is, the night before All Hallows Day. In their celebration that evening, they reconnected with their dead saints—visiting their graves and praying to them. So today, All Hallows Eve is now known as Halloween."

"Finally," he said, "I want to remind you that we will celebrate another holy day of obligation tomorrow, All Souls' Day. Tomorrow we will pray for the faithful departed whose souls have not been cleansed and who cannot attain beatific vision without our prayers and the celebration of the holy sacrifice of the Mass."

I sighed with regret, thinking about having to go to church once again, making it three times that week.

* * *

By the time early November arrived, Mom was preparing to can pumpkins, the last food crop she would be puttin' up for storage in our cellar. One year Mom had harvested all her pumpkins except one—it was unusually large. It had not maintained the traditional elliptical-spherical shape of a small pumpkin but, instead, had developed vertically into a large cylinder that was nearly three-feet tall. Because it was almost impossible to move, she had left it in the garden for all to see, and my brothers and I were proud to display this garden curiosity. Drivers in cars passing by looked with wonderment when they noticed the large orange object sitting majestically upright in Mom's garden.

One morning as I walked by the garden on my way to school, I noticed that the large pumpkin was missing—it was not sitting in the place where Mom had grown it, and it could not be seen anywhere.

"I wonder who took our pumpkin," Kathleen asked that night at supper.

"What are you talkin' about?" asked Mom.

"It's not out there in the garden anymore," Kathleen answered.

"Well, for heaven's sake!" exclaimed Mom. "That thing is so big and heavy I didn't think anybody could carry it off. It was starting to soften, and I knew I needed to get out there and cut it up into pieces so I could can it—but I just haven't gotten around to it."

That following Saturday morning, Mrs. Newman knocked on our porch screen door and proceeded to enter into the kitchen, where several of us were still seated at the table, eating breakfast. Mom was reading the *Rocky Mountain News* and drinking her coffee. Standing with her hands on her hips and a big smile on her face, Mrs. Newman said, "I was out in my garden this morning, and I saw your large pumpkin sitting between two rows of my corn."

"Oh my Lord," Mom said laughingly. "I can't imagine who would have put it there."

"Well," said Mrs. Newman emphatically, "if you still want it, you better send somebody real quick to get it—I'm getting ready to clear the garden area before the winter sets in." "I'll get Tom and the other boys to get over there right away," said Mom.

Several days later and in the evening, Weber rode his bike into the yard for a short visit with my brothers and me. He sat on his bicycle seat with both feet on the ground as he chatted.

I said, "Ya know, that big pumpkin in our garden—you've seen it—well, it was missing for 'bout a week—and guess where we found it!"

Before Weber could answer, I said, "It was in Mrs. Newman's garden hidden in her rows of corn!"

Weber roared with laughter. I, sensing a mischievous tenor to Weber's laugh, said, "I knew it—I knew it—Richie and I were talkin' 'bout it the other night—we thought you might know where it was."

Weber then said, "There were three of us, Herb [Newman], Loe [Hernandez], and me. We were going to take it further away than that, but all that the three of us could do was to roll it as far as the Newman's garden."

Halloween was over, but Weber and our neighborhood friends were still playing their tricks.

L–R: David Newton, Jerry Newton, and Gary Olson, 1947. *Newton Family Album*

L–R: Ronnie Newton, Rollie Newton, and Richie Newton, 1947. *Newton Family Album*

Skeeks and Rosemary Newton, 1947. *Newton Family Album*

Ronald Weber, 1950. *Mead Consolidated Schools Yearbook*

Tom Newton, 1950. *Mead Consolidated Schools Yearbook*

Chapter 16

Wheels

Like most young boys, I had a fascination with movement of my body in a wheeled vehicle. I'd seen pictures in the family album of my triplet brothers and me at three years of age, which showed us sitting in a Road Tester wagon. I was led to presume that we were pulled in that wagon by an older sibling many times and that it provided us with great enjoyment as we sensed movement and observed the objects of the world passing by us. Later on, we received a Radio Flyer wagon at Christmas, and I used to guide it around on our narrow sidewalk with one knee kneeling in the bed with the other leg and foot moving back and forth and providing the power for movement. I envied our neighbor Charles Markham, who had a small metal cart—with a steering wheel and powered by the driver pedaling with both feet. Knowing that Mom and Dad would not have the wherewithal to buy us a toy car or even a bicycle, my brothers and I decided to build a cart.

In the summer of '47, Mom brought home two large crates of oranges from Longmont's Safeway Grocery Store. With twelve of us at home, it was not long before all the oranges had been eaten, and Mom said that my brothers and I could have the crates. We decided to build a truck cart with a design where one of the crates would be placed upside down as the "engine" and the other would remain upright as the "box bed."

"Can we take the two hind wheels off of Marc and Dave's tricycle and use them just for a while for our cart?" I asked Mom.

"I don't think so," said Mom. "Maybe you should make something else."

Jerry and I walked down the town alleys searching for wheels in the trash of our neighbors. From the west town alley next to the Gettman farm, we saw a pair of wagon wheels hanging on the wall of an open garage that belonged to Mr. LaFollette, the father of my classmate Joan.

Mr. LaFollette was standing in his garage when I asked him, "Do you think we could borrow those two wheels for a while? We're building a cart. We'll bring 'em back when we finish with 'em."

He pulled the wheels down from the wall and handed them to us saying, "I don't think my kids are going to need these anymore—you can just <u>have</u> them."

"Thanks a million," I said to him, using the phrase Mom always uttered when she received a favor.

Mr. Lafollette's generous gift was totally unexpected—we were as delighted as a dog discovering a bone. Mr. LaFollette was the first person in our Mead community to help us with our project but not the last; the generous help of several more folks was needed before our cart was built.

We took our new possessions home and told Mom about our sudden fortune; we pleaded once again for permission to use tricycle wheels.

"Can't we just have them for just a while?" I asked. "Ple-e-ease? Dave and Marc won't care—we'll put them back on when we're through."

"Okay, I guess it's all right," she said, finally giving in and knowing that we were never going to stop asking until she said yes.

Jerry and I went downtown to the Clark Lumber Company to see if Mr. Ansel Clark could help us with our need for axles. Mr. Clark was not in when we entered into the store, but his

Light of Her Children

son, Robert "Cork" Clark, was. Holding one of Mr. Lafollette's wheels in my hand, I pointed to the hole in the center and said, "We need an axle to fit through this wheel—we're building a cart—do you have anything we can use?"

Cork took the wheel and looked at it. "I think I have something," he said.

He came back with a ten-inch spike in his hand—it was the biggest "nail" I'd ever seen.

"It fits into the wheel hole," he said. "How many wheels do you need axles for?"

"We have four," said Jerry. "What are you going to attach them to?" Cork asked.

"I guess a two-by-four," I said. "I think we could fasten them with big staples."

Cork took a scoop of staples and dropped them one by one onto a tray on top of a scale. When he had dropped fifty, he dropped in just a few more and said, "That's a quarter of a pound—will that be enough for you?"

"I think that's enough," I said. "They're a dollar a pound," said Cork.

"How much are the spikes?" I asked.

"Five cents apiece," said Cork. "With the staples, you owe me twenty-five cents plus twenty cents for the spikes—it totals forty-five cents."

"We're goin' to need some nails too," I said, pointing to the size we needed. Cork took a handful and put them into a paper sack. "I'll just charge ya five cents for these—that'll make it fifty cents that cha owe me."

Jerry pulled two quarters from his pocket that he had earned from mowing Peppler's lawn and placed them on the table. We found two two-by-fours in the woodpile that Dad had hauled in for us to burn in our stove. With Dad's handsaw, we cut one piece to a six-foot length for the chassis and the other into two three-foot pieces for the wheel axles. We took the chassis piece and the front wheel-axis piece down to Joe Jones's auto-mechanics shop in the Mead Garage.

"Mr. Jones—can ya you put holes in these two-by-fours for us with your electric drill?"

"What're you boys buildin'?" he asked.

"A cart—we need these holes so we can put a bolt in them and steer the front axle," I answered.

Joe drilled a half-inch hole in the middle of the wheel axis and the same-size hole on the end of the chassis piece. We stopped at the lumberyard, and Cork Clark fitted us with a single bolt that inserted into each hole and that was long enough to hold them together while at the same time allowing the front axle to swivel. Then with the wheels attached to the front wood axle, we could turn and guide the cart.

"What do we owe you?" I asked.

"Nothin'," said Cork. "Glad I could help you."

We placed the smaller, spoked tricycle wheels on the front of the cart and the solid metal wagon wheels on back. We nailed two tuna-fish cans on each side of the front crate for headlights.

"How are we going to drive it?" I asked Jerry.

"Let's just tie a wire to each end of the front axle and wire the ends to a wood bar that is in front with the driver's seat. We can then pull on the bar with either the left or right hand to turn it."

As we moved along with our project, my brothers and I got some help from another community member, a new kid on the block: Billy Walker, the same age as our brother Jerry, came to Mead to stay with his grandmother Grace Doke. Billy's grandfather, Isaac Doke, an attorney and former owner of the Mead Appliance Store, had died, and Grace had sold it to R. E. White. As we built our cart, Billy Walker got interested in what we were doing, and he rode his new bicycle into our yard to watch. Billy parted his hair in the middle and wore glasses. He dressed like Dick from Dick and Jane, with a collared shirt, shorts, long socks, and shined brown shoes. In Mead and with us Newtons, he looked as out of place as a bug in a bean soup bowl.

Billy talked about his sophisticated living in the big city back East, Louisville, Kentucky, where they had street cars, trains, zoos, and movies. I never knew or saw his mother, Phoebe, but Billy described her by comparing her with Mom. "My mother always wears fine dresses, not like the tattered rags your mother wears," he bragged. She's always dressed-up—your mother never is."

Billy had total control of his grandmother; she seemed to do whatever he wanted. He always had money in his pocket, and so I always persuaded him to buy candy for me whenever I could. One morning Billy showed up with a dozen doughnuts he had bought at Bunton's Red & White—a rare treat for us Newton boys—it was wonderful to have an acquaintance with some discretionary cash.

"Are you goin' to paint it?" Billy asked.

"We don't have any money to buy paint," I said.

"I think you should paint it silver," he said. "I'm sure my grandmother will buy the paint.

"Get some red too for the wheels," I said. "And we'll need a couple of brushes and some paint thinner to clean 'em with."

One afternoon, Billy and I took the cart downtown, taking turns pushing. We got on to the smooth sidewalk in front of the Howlett house and headed downtown. We stopped off at Bunton's Red & White, where Billy bought candy. On the way back, we took a rest in the shade of a large catalpa tree in front of the Alexanders' house, and the two of us began a casual conversation on many topics. When we started to talk about how babies were born, I said to Billy, "My sister Rosemary says that the doctor brings the baby in his bag, but I don't think that is how it is, do you?"

"No, it's not," said Billie. "It comes out of the mother's body. My mother told me it is like planting a garden. She said the father plants a 'seed' in the mother's body and the seed grows into a baby inside her. When it's big enough, it comes out of the mother, just like a plant grows from a seed and comes out of the dirt."

I said, "My sister Eunice told me that a stork brings it—she was laughing when she said it—I don't think she was serious about it."

"You can tell when a mother is about to have a baby," said Billy. "She gets real fat in the stomach."

"Well, my mom has a baby whenever she gets sick," I said.

Billy's understanding of the world was much more advanced than mine, and being the only child, he clearly communicated one-on-one with his mother much more than I did with mine. When it came to the birds and the bees, my knowledge was equivalent to that of a dead chicken. Interestingly, in the Newton family, the whole process of human procreation was never discussed by Mom or Dad in our presence. Neither one of them felt it was necessary to explain to us why our cow Bossie suddenly "went dry" and was taken to Louie Roman's farm and was subsequently brought back later to have a calf in our own barn. We had no idea that ole Bossie sojourned with a lustful bull somewhere on the pasture meadows of Louie's farm. The "mystery" of livestock reproduction had to be explained to me by my farming friends, the sons of farmers whose firsthand knowledge they were most willing to share. It took me awhile before I even made the connection with the similarity of animal reproduction with that of humans.

When the summer ended, Mom told us that we had to put the wheels back on Marc and Dave's tricycle. After removing the wheels, we tore apart the wood crates and two-by-fours, and with an axe, we chopped them into kindling. In the Newton household, nothing was ever wasted—not even our toys.

However, I still hoped for the day when I would have a mode of transportation that I could pedal myself. I saw a picture of tricycle in the Sears catalogue; what impressed me about it was that although it had three wheels, it had pedals connected to a sprocket and chain mechanism—just like a bicycle. In my mind it was a bicycle, even it did have three wheels. I showed the picture to my triplet brothers and to Mom, and I told her that we were going to write to Santa Claus and ask him to bring it to us for Christmas. I wrote the letter and asked Mom to mail it to the North Pole. Mom wisely said to me, "Why don't you give it to Rosemary when she comes home—she'll mail it for you in Denver—it'll get there quicker. "I, a gullible believer in Santa Claus, swallowed Mom's advice like a famished fish on a fly. Right before Christmas, we received a typewritten letter from "Santa Claus":

Dear Newton triplets:

I'm sorry that I won't be able to bring you a bicycle on Christmas morning. You see, up here in the North Pole, it snows so badly I can't get outside to the shed where my rubber tires are stored. So my elves and I can't build bicycles like we usually do. However, I know that you will like very much all of the things that I will have for all three of you on Christmas morning.

Please be good boys to your mom so that you will not be disappointed if there is nothing under the tree.

A merry Christmas and a mighty ho-ho to all three of you.

Cheers,
Santa Claus

My friend, Loe Hernandez, taught me how to ride a bicycle using the new one he had bought. Thereafter, I rode my brother Tom's bike, but only when he wasn't home—he forbade my triplet brothers and me to ride it. I was in the eighth grade before I got my own bicycle—a used one that looked like new. I bought it for fifteen dollars with the money I had earned weeding gardens and mowing lawns, and this was my mode of self-transport until I was a junior in high school.

Clark Lumber Company, Mead, CO, circa 1950. *Historic Highlandlake Inc.*

James Thornton and Marc Newton, 1948. *Newton Family Album*

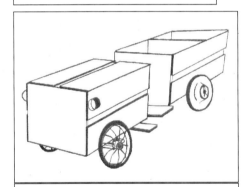

Illustration of cart constructed by Newton brothers. 2015. Ronald Newton

Billy Walker, 1947. *Mead Consolidated Schools Yearbook*

Rosemary Newton, 1948. *Newton Family Album*

Chapter 17

Church Picnic

During summer, the park in Mead was the center of activity for the Newtons as well as other townspeople. The park took up one whole "Mead-size" block and was surrounded by a hay mill to the east, a blacksmith shop to the south, a vacant lot to the north, and the Alexander, Hernandez, and Howlett houses to the west. The perimeter of the park contained large blue spruce, elm, mountain maple, and silver poplar trees with smaller trees of dog-apple and Russian olive and bushes of lilac and currant scattered among them. The central area of the park was planted with a thin-bladed Kentucky bluegrass—very comfortable for bare feet and for children's play.

Teenage visitors to the park often carved their initials and those they loved into the smooth white bark of the silver poplar. With age, the carving wounds healed into black scars, leaving a visible lasting memory. A two-holed outhouse, with explicit graffiti on the unpainted pine boards inside, and a water fountain were located at the south end. Because the fountain was a source of so many water fights during the summer, Town Marshal Wilse Lamberson finally turned it off. Benches and tables constructed of pine and painted dark green were there for picnicking.

The park was maintained by Mr. Lamberson, a man in his sixties, who had several dark birthmarks on his face and who wore suspenders to hold up his pants around his thick waist. He wore a soiled and tattered fedora and smoked a curved-stem pipe. The town had furnished him a gasoline-powered mower with four cylindrical sets of blades that he used to regularly trim the grass. He watered the grass with long hoses attached to sprinklers, which also became instruments of water fighting. His constant mowing was disruptive to afternoon softball games, so he often became a target for a hit softball when his back was facing the batter.

Besides being a playground and a trysting place, the park was where Guardian Angel Church held its annual picnic fundraiser for the whole congregation, an activity that my family looked forward to every summer.

It was "church picnic" Sunday in the summer of '49, and I was sleeping in my upstairs bedroom when Mom opened the door down at the foot of the stairwell and yelled, "Hey, you birds! It's seven thirty and it's time to get movin' and get ready for church." Remembering that it was the day of the church picnic, I quickly got out of bed. I wanted the day to begin. I had taken my weekly bath the night before, and I was enjoying my normal Sunday morning cleanliness after the accumulated grime and dirt of the previous week was gone.

I took off my pajamas and walked to the attic closet where my Sunday pants of corduroy hung with all the rest of my clothes and those of my three brothers. I could tell which pants were mine because mine were dyed a little darker than those of my two brothers. Mom had made pants and jackets for the three of us from brown, white, and orange adult corduroy garments that she dismantled and then dyed a brown color. I found my white shirt with RJN monogrammed on the pocket and my name, Ron, written with a pen inside the collar. I slipped on the shirt and looped my clear plastic belt through the pant loops.

Light of Her Children

I grabbed clean socks out of the bureau drawer and went downstairs to the kitchen. I was hungry, and my mouth was parched with thirst. It was only a week before when I had forgotten about the need to abstain from food and water and was bringing a dipper of water to my lips when Mom walked into the kitchen and yelled, "Unh—unh, don't you dare." Had I drunk the water, I would have forfeited my privilege to receive the host at Communion.

The rule of abstention from food and water before taking Communion was such that it was considered a sin if violated, and the transgressor would have to confess to the priest. But Violet Sekich, a classmate of our brother Jack and the organist for the church choir, had an interesting interpretation of the rule. She said, "I heard if you drink or eat and then take Communion, it was no sin unless you threw up."

I was feeling very good on that picnic Sunday morning, because I had been "reconciled." The day before, I had gone to confession, and Father Martin Arno had absolved me of my sins—talking back to Mom, stealing plums from Mrs. Howlett's tree, not saying my daily prayers for two nights, and fighting with Rollie. I was feeling assured that reciting two Hail Marys and two Our Fathers as penance had redeemed me, and it gave me great satisfaction with my renewed spiritual well-being.

I put on my socks and shoes, and it was now 8:15 a.m., as I waited for my brothers to get ready. Mom and our sisters had already gone, and so had our brothers Jerry and Tom. The four of us walked hurriedly down the alley past the Robertses' and headed south five blocks through downtown. We crossed over the railroad tracks to the southernmost end of town and then to Guardian Angel Church. We saw Father Martin's car parked next to the sacristy. Father was inside putting on his vestments, and Mass servers, our brother Tom and Louis Lee, were lighting the altar candles and placing small goblets of wine and water on the credence table to the left of the altar.

Entering the rear of the church, we could hear the organ played by Violet Sekich, and we heard the choir singing "Salve Regina." Mrs. Lucy Lee's voice could be heard above all the others, including Mom and my sisters. The four of us walked down the right aisle and slipped into the front pew that was always reserved for youngsters.

Just then, bells from inside the sacristy rang, and Tom and Louis Lee, dressed in black cassocks and white surplices, emerged from the side door of the altar, followed by Father Martin. Father Martin was dressed with an emerald-green chasuble trimmed with intricate gold embroidery and which draped over his long-sleeved, full-length white linen cassock alb. He carried a chalice covered by a napkin-size cloth of the same emerald-green color of his knee-length vestment, and the chalice appeared to be perched on top of his protruding stomach. A long stole, also of a green color, bordered with gold, hung around his neck. This was the first time that Father had worn these outer vestments, and they were noticed by the whole congregation, particularly us Newtons, because we all knew that Mom had made them for him. That spring, Father had come to our house, bringing with him several yards of different colored fabrics along with vestment and accessory garment patterns, and he "solicited" Mom's help in making these new garments for Guardian Angel Church. Of course, Mom couldn't refuse his request.

After he left, Mom said to us, "I really don't want to do it, but he came in here and flopped all those rolls of material and stuff on the table before I could say anything. And you know he's not goin' to pay me anything for it—he expects me to do it for nothin'—he knows that we don't give very much to the church."

Our family contributions to the Sunday church collection basket were sporadic and almost nonexistent. To help "pay our way" and contribute our fair share, we Newtons provided "in-kind" services of cleaning the church on Saturdays for one month in the year, cutting down the tall ironweeds that grew up next to the church, and now making the priest's vestments. And Mom always volunteered our services when an altar boy was needed for a funeral or wedding Mass.

Father Martin Arno of the Order of St. Benedict (OSB) lived in Frederick, an Italian community twenty-five miles southeast of Mead, and served two parishes, St. Theresa in Frederick and Guardian Angel in Mead. With two parish collections each Sunday, there was enough money to furnish Father Martin a car, a Ford, which he traded every three or four years. "Father," a portly man of six feet, with a bulging stomach and a broad, ruddy, and shiny face, was in his forties. He combed his receding grayish-black hair straight back, and he stuffed his wadded handkerchief up the long left sleeve of his linen cassock alb. Father, smiling and ever happy, never missed a Sunday Mass in Mead, no matter how severe the weather.

Father began the Mass reciting in Latin, and kneeling servers Tom and Louis bowed their heads toward him as they recited the Latin version of the Confiteor, which they had memorized.

Then Father intoned the Kyrie, drawing out the syllables, "Keeeee-reeeee-ay ay-lehhhh-eeeee-zawn." The congregation responded in unison with "Keeeee-reeeee-ay ay-lehhhhh-eeee-e zawn."

Father continued with "Kreeees-tay ay-lehhhh-eeeee-zawn," and the parishioners echoed with "Kreeees-tay ay-lehhhh-eeeee-zawn."

Father dispensed with the sermon that Sunday and began his remarks to the parishioners with "I want to thank Mrs. Elmer Newton for making all new vestments for Guardian Angel Church. I have one on today that she has sewn, and throughout the year, I will be wearing several others that she has made. These new garments will add greatly to the beauty of Mass here at Guardian Angel Church."

"Please join me in thanking Mrs. Newton," he said as he put his hands together to clap, encouraging everyone to join in.

"This is a beautiful Sunday," he said. "It's a great day for our church picnic. But this event is more than just a picnic—it's an event of fund-raising that helps us meet the needs of the Guardian Angel parish. It's also a day of fun and games and socializing for all our parishioners."

Father went on to thank all the women of the Ladies Altar and Rosary Society for organizing the event.

"I especially want to thank Mrs. Nick Sekich," said Father. "As president of the society, Mrs. Sekich has provided great leadership these past several months, leading to this special day."

Father concluded by saying, "Let's all bow our heads and give thanks to Almighty God for giving us this fine sunny day and this beautiful weather." Finally, he said, "Now let us recite the Our Father together and ask God to bless us and to make our picnic a very successful venture for our parish."

The Mass was over by nine twenty, and my brothers and I hurried home to get ready for the picnic. As we passed the park, Bill Schell was already arranging the green tables and benches in the shade of the silver poplar and elm trees. We triplets changed into our matching polo knit shirts of gray with stripes of different colors across the chest: green for me, blue for Richie, and maroon for Rollie. Each of us put on a new pair of dark-blue, JC Penney's Foremost jeans.

We gulped down a breakfast of cereal and toast and quickly washed and dried the dishes. By ten thirty, we could wait no longer, and we begged Mom to let us go to the park. She finally consented and went for her purse to get change for each of us.

As she parceled out her coins, she said, "I have already paid for your lunch, and here is forty cents for each one of you. Now don't spend it on a lot of junk."

At the park, male parishioners wearing new bib overalls and new long-sleeved shirts and sweat-stained straw hats were making preparations. Louie Rademacher was unloading large galvanized tubs of ice and wooden crates of bottled Nehi soda pop of every variety from his truck. He placed the tubs on the ground beneath a tall elm, added water from the irrigation hose to the ice, and placed the bottles in the tubs to cool. Glen Keller drove up in his pickup with two large padded, cold-keeping containers of vanilla ice cream that he picked up from Snider's Drugstore. Frank Schell unloaded lead pipes, two-by-fours and two-by-twelves, wooden dolls, a box of baseballs, braided cotton ropes, and swaths of canvasses from his truck. He and Glen Keller constructed the doll-baby-ball-throwing game apparatus. Women of the Altar and Rosary Society, with husbands and families, began to arrive with tablecloths and food, and soon the park tables were covered with dishes of fried chicken, potato salad, Jell-O, macaroni casseroles, baked beans, potato chips, slaw, cookies, sheet cakes, and a variety of fruit pies.

As the crowd assembled, I noticed a beautiful lady with long black hair, about thirty-five years old, a woman I had never seen before. She was sitting with Vera and Nick Sekich Sr. and their two sons, Nicky and Freddie. Sitting next to this stunning lady was a young girl about my age, who appeared to be her daughter. She had on a white dress and white shoes. Like her mother, her skin was dark olive, and her cheeks and coal-black hair shone like they had been polished. She was the prettiest girl I had ever seen.

Standing next to Nicky Sekich as I approached Louie Rademacher to buy a Nehi root beer, I asked Nicky, "Who's the girl in the white dress?"

"That's my cousin Ginger," he said. "She lives in Denver with her mother. Her dad was killed while drivin' at the Lakeside Racetrack—her mother is my aunt."

I quickly made the connection of likeness between Ginger's mother and Nicky's mother, Vera. Both were beautiful women whose age was concealed behind their youthful and striking appearances, and both had olive skin like Ginger's. They were the daughters of an Italian immigrant who came to the United Sates and settled in Frederick, where he found work in the coal mines.

I saw Ginger playing catch with one of the new softballs that Vera Sekich had brought for the ball-throwing contest, so I stepped up next to Nicky and asked, "Can I play too?"

"Sure," said Nicky, and soon I was playing catch with Ginger while Nicky stood by and watched. I threw it gently back to her. She was smiling constantly and giggled gleefully with pride when she made a good catch. Soon Nicky wanted back into the game, but Ginger would not throw to him. He began to chase after her into the center of the park as she ran away from him holding the ball. I followed them, and she threw the ball to me as Nicky tried to grab her arms.

As we ran in circles with the ball exchanging hands between us, Father Martin summoned the children to eat. "Lunch is ready to be served," he said. "Will all of the children come over here and get in line?"

I ran to line up with Ginger and Nicky and my brothers and our school and church friends. Barbara Graham, our classmate since the first grade, was there with her mother, Mary Sekich Graham, Vera's sister-in-law.

Father Martin bellowed, "Let's all bow our heads and recite our grace together!" The adult men shed their hats, and all those present said, "Bless us, O Lord, and these thy gifts, which we are about to receive from thy bounty, through Christ, our Lord. Amen."

Ginger ate lunch with her mother and the Sekich family. My brothers and I sat on the grass with Ronald Weber, eating fried chicken, baked beans, Jell-O, and chocolate cake. Rollie made sure he got a plate of potato chips, his favorite food, something he never had at home. I spent one of my dimes on a vanilla ice-cream cone—I wanted to buy another for Ginger, but I was afraid to ask her if she wanted one.

After lunch, the adults played bingo, with Father Martin calling out the numbers. The prizes were dish towels, doilies, potholders, and blankets that the women had made and boxes of chocolates.

Light of Her Children

"Now look under 'I' for number 32: I 32—I 32!'" Father shouted as he twisted the handle of the cage containing the wooden balls with the numbers painted on them. One ball would fall into a small receptacle at the base of the cage, and Father would remove it and call out the next number that was written on it. When Father needed to rest his voice, he turned over the calling to faithful parishioner John Gust.

Bub Howlett, manager of the Denver Elevators, lived across the street from the park with his mother, Mamie, and his brother, Hap, and he attended our church picnic every year. His deceased father had studied to be a priest before he married, and I presumed that he and his brother were raised as Catholics. If so, the three of them no longer practiced the faith, but Bub could always be counted on to attend our church picnic and to contribute to the cause by eating lunch and playing bingo. I stood behind him and looked over his shoulder to watch him play with one bingo card on his lap and two others lying on the seat of the bench beside him. He had one toothpick in his mouth and another in his hand, which he used to slide the black shield over the pocket of the number he had just heard from the caller. Bub had already won several boxes of candy, and he opened up one and offered me a chocolate.

"Take two," he said. "I've got plenty of 'em."

"Thank you, Mr. Howlett," I said as I used both hands to grab two chocolates from the box.

While the adults tested their luck at bingo, we kids drank soda, ate ice cream, played catch, and tried our luck at the wooden doll game. I was very confident that I could win at this game with the six dolls stacked on a two-by-twelve board just ten feet away. For a quarter, adults were allowed four throws with a baseball to knock three dolls off the board for the prize of a box of chocolates, while children, at a cost of a dime, were given five tries to remove three dolls for the same prize. It was a requirement that the doll be completely removed from the board and knocked to the ground—therefore, a forceful, fast throw was needed. A sharply aimed ball made a distinct pinging sound when it made contact with the wood-doll bodies, but a dull thud could be heard when the ball missed the doll completely and hit the canvas behind it. I spent two of my dimes trying to win the chocolates, but both times came away with no prize. My disappointment was augmented with jealousy when I watched Richie, with his accurate throwing arm and fastball, win the coveted prize by knocking three dolls from their perch with his five tries. Richie gave the candy to Mom for safekeeping—he would eat the chocolates later—and when he did, I knew I would be at his side to mooch.

With my allotted forty cents squandered, I approached Dad, who was playing bingo, to get another dime so I could play more games. To my surprise, he reached into his pocket, pulled out a quarter, and gave it to me.

I tried the coin-toss game run by Eddie Rademacher. Standing behind a two-by-four barricade, the challenge was to toss a penny into glass saucers floating in a tub of water a few feet away. For the cost of one dime, Eddie gave me five pennies, and with each, I gently tossed them in the vicinity of the saucers. Several hit the saucer but bounced into the water—all five coins ended up in the bottom of the tub. With the fifteen cents I had left, I used a dime to buy another ice-cream cone, and I kept the remaining nickel in my pocket.

At four o'clock, Father Martin conducted games for all age groups with the winners awarded either a box of chocolates or a fifty-cent piece. Rollie won fifty cents for coming in first in the fifty-yard dash, and Father presented a fifty-cent piece to Richie when he won the softball throw. I participated in both events, but I knew before I started that I would not win. Rollie had already demonstrated his superior speed when he won a blue ribbon for the fifty-yard dash at the grade-school track meet last spring, and I had seen Richie throw a small rock a hundred yards. I teamed up with Dave in the three-legged race, but the Richie-Rollie duo won, and each got a box of chocolates.

There were egg-toss competitions for the teenage girls and boys and the adult men and women. There was egg splattered all over our sister Kathleen's dress when she and our sister Pat were eliminated from the competition. Eddie and Louie Rademacher were teenage winners, and Frank and Bill Schell won the men's. Vera Sekich and Ginger's mother had hardly gotten started when the egg broke in Vera's hands. However, Vera won the slipper-kicking contest handily with her shoe going ten or fifteen yards beyond those of her two sisters-in-law, Violet Sekich and Mary Sekich Graham. Rather than forward, the shoe of Ginger's mother went behind her, drawing a hearty laugh from the crowd.

At five o'clock, the picnic was over, and everyone started to leave. I watched Ginger as she obediently followed her mother's request to get into the backseat of the Sekich Plymouth. She looked out the window and waved to Barbara and Mary Graham as Freddie Sekich steered the sleek vehicle around the corner of the park and sped away with a cloud of dust.

I was very disheartened that late afternoon—the prettiest girl I had just met had gone, and I would not see her again for a long time, perhaps never. Furthermore, I had not won any prizes that day, and the feelings of inadequacy and self-pity were settling in my mind. Also, the church picnic, my most favorite summer activity, was over, a thing of the past. I thought I had nothing to look forward to for the rest of the summer, and it would be two long months before school started and I could see my friends again. I felt abandoned, insecure, and sad. My unhappiness worsened when Mom told my brothers and me to clean up the paper plates, napkins, and cups that had been strewn on the grass. We helped the men put all the chairs, tubs, planks, canvases, and bingo cards into their trucks and carry the park picnic tables and benches back to their prescribed places.

At six o'clock, when the cleanup was finished, Father Martin got into his Ford, holding the canvas bags of the monies collected. I asked Mom, "How much do you think the church made on this?"

"Probably over $200," Mom said.

I knew that Father would count the proceeds and tally the expenses before next Sunday—then he would announce to the parishioners how much money was earned. I was proud that our church was so successful at its fund-raising—to me, $200 was a vast sum.

The rest of the summer went by, and in September, I was back in school. I asked Barbara Graham to see if she could get Ginger's address so I could write. Barbara could always be depended upon, and this time was no exception. By the next week, I had obtained an envelope from my sister Kathleen, and on a piece of three-holed notebook paper, I had composed a letter to Ginger that read as follows:

> October 5, 1951
> Mead, Colorado
>
> Dear Ginger,
>
> I was glad to meet you last summer at our church picnic. You have a very beautiful mother. Your aunt Vera is also really pretty. I hope you can come and visit your aunt Vera and your uncle Nick sometime and come to our church here in Mead.
>
> I am back in school now with Barbara Graham. She gave me your address so I could write to you. I hope you like your school. I like mine very much. Our sixth-grade teacher is also our coach. We're playing flag football now.
>
> Please write when you get time.
>
> Love,
> Ronald

I signed it with "Love," because that is the closing that Mom taught my brothers and me to use when we were writing letters to brothers Orbin and Ray serving in the military. I folded the

Light of Her Children

letter into four quadrants and inserted it in the large square envelope that Kathleen had given me. I sealed it and printed Ginger's Denver address on it. I gave it to Helen, who worked at the post office in the afternoon after school. Helen paid for the stamp and placed the letter in the outgoing mail.

Several weeks later, a small square envelope arrived at the post office. It was among the many other parcels of mail that Helen brought home with her after closing the post office at five o'clock. She gave the letter to me, and I was stunned and speechless when I realized it was from Ginger. I was too embarrassed to open it in front of any of my family, for I could not bear to hear the teasing comments, particularly those of my triplet brothers. I put the letter in my pocket and waited until after supper to read it.

I went outside where I was certain to be alone, and with the light coming from the kitchen window, I tore off one end of the envelope. As I removed two small sheets from inside, Ginger's school picture fell out and dropped to the ground. I picked it up and glanced at her image for just a moment—I was struck once again by her pretty face.

I unfolded one of the small sheets, where upon it was a heart diagram, and within the heart were the words "I love you." I had never had anyone tell me that, and I was embarrassed at reading it.

On the other small sheet was a letter she had written:

Dear Ronald,

Thank you for your letter. I think my mom is pretty too. I had a good time at the picnic. My aunt Vera said that I could come back and visit her and my cousins and my uncle. I like being on a farm.

Love,
Ginger

Somehow, Helen knew how important this letter was to me, and the next day, she asked, "Are you going to let me read your letter?"

I trusted Helen, and I handed the envelope to her and awaited her response. After reading its contents, she placed it back in the envelope and stated, "A very nice letter." I always knew that I could confide in Helen about my true feelings and that she would always have a gentle and understanding response that would provide comfort during any time of uncertainty. This was the case now, and her positive comment of approval provided me a sense of satisfaction and confidence and erased my doubt and embarrassment.

I did not know where I could keep the letter for safekeeping, where it would not be read by anyone else. There was no one dresser drawer that I could call my own, and if there had been, there would have been no way that it could be locked. There was no private space that I could call my own—a place that was definitely off-limits to others. Privacy was a luxury that none of us Newton children had. I decided to find a place where I thought no one would look. I found it in the bedroom I shared with my three brothers. I placed the letter in a tiny space between the north wall and the one-inch-by-twelve-inch baseboard next to the floor of the bedroom. I was certain the letter would never be found or read by anyone.

As the months went by, I thought about Ginger a lot, and I inquired of Barbara to see if she had recently seen her—she said she hadn't. Several times I took the letter out from its hiding place to read it again and to look at Ginger's picture. I put it back each time with confident satisfaction that no one else would know of its contents. One winter Saturday morning, Mom was cleaning, and she emerged from our bedroom with the letter in her hand. My face was red with embarrassment as she asked me, "Do you still want this?"

I said nothing in response and took it from her hand and placed it in my pocket. I would have to find another place for safekeeping. I was sure that Mom had opened the envelope and was aware of its contents. I now was more embarrassed than before. From then on, I never talked to anyone but Barbara Graham about Ginger, but I always hoped I would see her again—perhaps some Sunday morning at Guardian Angel Church sitting next to her aunt Vera and her mother.

Guardian Angel Church, Mead, CO, 2011. Sheila Koenig

Helen Newton, 1948. *Mead Consolidated Schools Yearbook*

Town park in winter, Mead, CO, 1954. *Mead Consolidated Schools Yearbook*

Father Martin Arno, OSB, pastor, Guardian Angel Church, 1951. *Newton Family Album*

Chapter 18

Feeding the Family

The responsibility of providing our large family with ample amounts of nutritious food was a huge challenge to my parents, particularly Mom. Mom's principle approach for this challenge was to can as much produce as possible in the summer to sustain us through the fall, winter, and spring. Mom canned everything—no matter where it came from. If it grew on a stalk or tree—Mom canned it. Stems and roots of every kind, below and above ground, were always potential food sources for the Newtons. Even the repugnant, seldom-eaten parsnip did not escape Mom's preservation. Mom and my sisters put fruits and vegetables of every sort into Kerr jars, covered them with lids and rings, pressure-cooked and sealed them from contamination, and stored them in our cellar.

Friends, neighbors, farmers, and townspeople were always dropping off produce for us. If we couldn't can it, we ate it right away—nothing went to waste. There were peas from vines we yanked from trucks on their way to the pea huller and pickles and cucumbers we picked from neighbor Dulcinea Gallegos's garden. Mr. Gallegos paid us a dime a row to pick them for him, and he gave Mom all she wanted for canning, making dill, sweet and bread and butter pickles.

At night, we "swiped" and devoured ripe plums from Mrs. Howlett's tree; she called Mom and offered the crop for her to can. She said, "You better get at 'em soon before your boys eat all of 'em."

My brother Tom picked apples from the Dempewolfs' and Mary Johnson's trees. The finer apples were cut into thin slices for pies, and smaller usable pieces from around wormholes or partially rotted sections were crushed into sauce with a colander. Others were used for apple butter.

My brother-in-law Wilbur picked chokecherries from mountain bushes in the Big Thompson Canyon and brought them to Mom for making jelly. Mom bought bushel baskets of peaches, pears, apricots, plums, and tomatoes at Longmont grocery stores. The fruits were cut into half sections, the pits removed, and the halves placed into quart jars along with a sugar-sweetened juice. She made prunes out of the large plums and sieved the tomatoes into juice. My sister Betty took Mom, my sisters Helen and Pat, and me to pick cherries in the foothills near Loveland. The women stood on ladders, picking and dropping cherries into buckets that they handed to me for pouring into wood crates.

At home, Mom had us pit cherries, but we brutalized them so much there was very little juice left in them, so she assigned that task only to our older sisters. In a later summer, we learned of a cherry-pitting device that we could buy at Clark Lumber. It consisted of a tiny rod that could be plunged into a single cherry, pushing the pit out and leaving the fruit intact. Mom was happy with the gadget because the cherries retained their round and plump shape and their juice; we kids liked it because it was quick and easy.

Throughout summer, our garden was in perpetual production of vegetables to can—string beans, sweet corn, cabbage, red beets, carrots, and rhubarb. Mom picked the string beans and then had us remove the tips from the ends of the pod and break the pods into three pieces. Mom and Tom picked the sweet corn as it ripened, and we shucked it. Our sisters used butcher knives to sheer the kernels from the cob and then scooped them into quart jars. We threw the shucks and cobs into the chicken pen for the chickens. Our sisters cut the cabbage, carrots, and rhubarb into small chunks and sliced the red beets. Mom worked all day pressurizing quart jars in her cooker on the stove, making sure that we boys provided plenty of coal and wood to keep the stove going.

Garden lettuce, tomatoes, carrots, and radishes were eaten as soon as they were ready. We ate fresh peas we scavenged from the pea huller. For several weeks, we ate fresh sweet corn almost every day. Sometimes corn on the cob was all we ate for lunch; by the end of that summer, I had eaten so much of it the odor made me want to throw up. Unable to eat corn, I filled up with numerous slices of buttered bread and several glasses of milk. Mom's large strawberry patch produced berries for shortcake and for preserves to be eaten with biscuits or toast. As the acorn squash ripened in late summer, Mom baked some for supper and canned some for future use in casserole dishes. The ripened pumpkins were canned for later conversion into pies.

Because I was very selective about what I ate, I was described as "persnickety" by my brothers and sisters. Mom maintained that my fastidious food selection was why my weight lagged behind my triplet brothers and my brother Dave. A matter a fact, I was so selective and unwilling to eat, in today's world, my mother might have thought I was bulimic and might have been afraid I'd commit suicide.

I could not stand to eat canned apricots, peaches, and pears—I wouldn't eat them even raw. Their texture combined with their abhorrent taste was unbearable, particularly the fleshy grit of a pear—it was like chewing on sandpaper. My favorite fruit was apple, and when served as a sauce with Mom's oatmeal cookies, they were an excellent dessert combination for my taste buds.

There was always a large supply of milk that we got from our cow, Bossie, and when nothing else served at mealtime was palatable, I obtained a full-stomach feeling by drinking copious amounts. Mom made soups out of the milk. She took a jar of her canned tomato juice and diluted it with milk, heated it on the stove, and served it—everyone in the family devoured it except me. The same with potato soup—it was simply made with boiled potatoes in heated milk; hot milk had had no appeal to my palate—I wouldn't even drink warm milk—it had to be cold—eating hot milk with potatoes swimming around in it made me vomit. Furthermore, I had a hard time understanding how my brothers and sisters could eat tomato and potato soup with broken soda crackers immersed in it. The texture of a soggy cracker in my mouth was grotesque.

I barely tolerated navy beans in soup, but I loved pinto beans. Brown-bean soup, as we called it, made with pinto beans was the staple protein source that Mom provided at our dinner table. She purchased the pintos in one-hundred-pound sacks and served them often to us. Her brown-bean soup was flavored by a ham bone she had saved from a previous Sunday's dinner or with a slab of bacon. Sometimes she added hamburger and made chili—my favorite bean soup. Mom always cooked beans in a pressure cooker, making them soft and mushy. She baked bread on the same day and served bean soup with hot rolls on which we smeared large amounts of freshly churned butter. Some of us added chopped onions to it. Bean soup with fresh bread and butter was a delightful meal that was enjoyed by all the family, even picky me.

I hated stuffed peppers and rice meatballs. I hated tomatoes—cooked or raw, and I thought that adding chunks of tomato was an excellent way to ruin a good pot of chili. I could barely endure the tastes of red beets and string beans, but I could handle sauerkraut if links of sausage were included. And there was something about a raw carrot that I liked, but I despised it when it was cooked.

When I did not eat Mom's specific entree, it was Mom's practice to have me sit at the table until I did so, sometimes long after others had finished. One summer night, I refused to eat a meat dish that Mom prepared from beef that my sister Pat had canned for an entry into a 4-H competition.

"Com'on, eat this—it's really good," said Mom. "The carrots Pat added to it make it better than the hash I make."

Everyone else had eaten it except me. Mom made me take some, and I gagged trying to swallow it. I sat at the table for thirty or forty minutes, hoping Mom would give in and let me go to bed. She did not—she simply looked my way as she moved in and out of the kitchen and said nothing. Finally, after an hour, I saw my way out—the kitchen window was wide open—I thrust the plate through the open window and scraped the food to the ground. I sat for a few minutes more until Mom came into the kitchen and saw my empty plate. "Okay, you can go now," she said—now relieved just as much as I was.

* * *

Besides a milk cow and chickens, we also raised a pig, which Dad fed table scraps, garden vegetable refuse, and cracked corn in a triangular trough he had made. Watching it feed confirmed what Mom told us when we consumed our food too fast, "You're eating like a hog." We didn't have it too long before it was decided that it was time to butcher it, and it was deemed by Dad and my brother-in-law Wilbur that the pig should be killed with a bullet to the head with a deer rifle.

One day while I was playing in our backyard, I heard a gunshot coming from inside our barn, followed by a screeching squeal. I heard the squeal come louder as I saw the wounded pig emerge through the barn door and run into the outside pen; there was blood streaming from its mouth as it ran in circles trying to find cover. Wilbur emerged after him with the rifle in his arm and forced the squealing pig back into the barn. I heard a second gunshot, followed by the third, and suddenly the squealing stopped. Although I had compassion for the pig as I saw it running and squealing for mercy from its assailant, I likened it to hunting for deer, and I accepted this as a normal behavior of the huntsman stalking the hunted.

The killing of that pig was the first and last time I ever saw a human being down a large animal with a gun. I never went deer hunting, although it was something I always wanted to do. Although my older brothers possessed a .22 rifle, neither I nor my younger brothers were allowed to shoot it, neither by them nor Mom and Dad, and I have never experienced what it was like to gun down an animal. However, I still found it thrilling to hunt for birds or cottontails with a slingshot, and my brother Richie and I were continuously on that quest. For me, the exciting thing about hunting was trekking through the woods and fields hoping to gain sight of an animal—killing them was secondary. However, Richie and I did kill a helpless barn owl with rocks we peppered at him with our slingshots—an act for which I still have remorse and regret.

Chickens were another source of meat for us, and my brothers and I helped Mom raise them as well as kill them in preparation of our Sunday dinner. Mom took great pride in raising her chickens. She had us scavenge the barrow pits and vacant lots to pull greens for her chickens. She was convinced that plant leaves, no matter the source, provided special nutrients to her chicken brood and contributed to the chickens' health and the flavor when we ate them. In summer, a couple of us were required us to pull gunnysacks of greens every day before suppertime.

About every six weeks, my three brothers and I had to clean the chicken coop. At night, the chickens roosted on one-by-two planks suspended a foot above rows of one-by-twelve boards that caught their droppings. We removed this accumulation with a hoe, scraping it into a wheelbarrow and carrying it out to be spread on the garden. We also scraped the droppings off the cement floor, swept it, and then covered it with new straw we got from Mamie Akers's Redmond farm.

One Saturday afternoon, Mom summoned Jerry, Richie, Rollie, and me to help her kill four chickens—she had a large number of folks to feed the next day. We went into the chicken pen with her and followed her until she pointed at an unwary bird and said, "Let's take that one."

I ran after it, grabbed it, and pulled the squawking chicken up to my chest, and Richie, Rollie, and Jerry did likewise. We carried them outside the pen, where each of us held onto a chicken while Mom held its head and stretched its neck so that she could sever the head with a butcher knife. The beheaded chicken shook violently, and it took all my strength to hold it down next to the ground among the tall ironweeds as its shaking tremors resonated throughout its whole body. Blood splattered onto my face and arms—I looked like a speckled trout.

One afternoon, I had a conversation with Robert Humphrey, our school janitor's son, and I asked him, "When you kill chickens, do you cut their heads off with a knife like we do? Or do you use a hatchet?"

"Neither one," answered Robert. "We just grab them by the head and swing them around until their bodies twist and fly off, leaving them to flop on the ground."

When I suggested that technique to Mom, thinking it would rid me from blood splattering all over me, Mom said, "Oh, heavens no—we can't do that—it would bruise the meat."

Each beheaded chicken was immersed in a pot of boiling water for thirty or forty seconds, and the feathers were removed. If I was the last one to have my chicken immersed, and with the water substantially cooled, plucking was much more difficult.

For the next hour, Mom stood over the kitchen sink, scraping the skin to remove pinfeathers, removing entrails, saving the liver and gizzard for eating, and then cutting the carcass into pieces for frying. She wrapped the eight chicken feet in several sheets of the *Denver Post*, and told me to deliver them to widow Mary Johnson, who used them as a meat supplement for her vegetable soup.

Our sister Eunice and her husband, Wilbur, and their two children, Diane and Dennis, were our guests that next day for our Sunday afternoon dinner. Mom also invited Mary Johnson. Wilbur had just bought a new fishing rod and reel, and he opened the trunk of his Ford to show it to Tom and me. I asked him, "Can you take us fishin' today?"

Wilbur responded by asking, "Where would you go around here?"

Tom said, "You can go to Mulligan Lake or Highland Lake. Highland Lake is closer and easier to get to. If you stay away from the boat shop, they won't bother you, and you won't have to pay."

Wilbur said to me, "Go ask your mom."

Hearing that Mom had given her consent for my brothers and me to go, Wilbur asked, "Can you kids dig some worms for us?"

"Sure," I said, "we can dig them from the ditch that carries the wastewater from the kitchen. We can make fishin' poles from the silver poplar in the front yard. Where do we get the hooks?"

"I have some that I'll let cha use," said Wilbur. "I also have some fishin' line you can have."

"What'll we use for a bobber?"

"You can just tie a stick to the line," said Tom. "I've used them before, and they work."

Mom had started frying chickens right after Sunday Mass was over. She made gravy from the rendered chicken fat and the crusted pieces of flour remaining in the frying pan. The day before, she had baked four apple pies and kneaded dough for hot rolls that were being taken out of the oven. Our sisters Helen and Pat peeled, boiled, and mashed the potatoes, cooked the corn, and prepared the salad. The coffee had been made, and iced tea had been poured into tall glasses on the table. Our sisters Maureen and Kathleen had set the large dining-room table with a white tablecloth, cloth napkins, and Mom's new china, which Rosemary had bought for her from the May Company of Denver.

With heads bowed and hands folded beneath the table, we all repeated in unison, "Bless us, O Lord, and these thy gifts, which we are about to receive from thy bounty, through Christ, our Lord. Amen."

As was customary, Mom made sure that Dad got the chicken platter first to choose the pieces he wanted. The wishbone and the gizzard pieces went to him. Dave, remembering how chickens were killed and still seeing their entrails, had no stomach for them; instead, he filled his plate with mashed potatoes and gravy and corn. I preferred wings and thighs and could hardly wait till everyone else was finished so that Mom would give me permission to eat my apple pie.

Mom would not excuse any of us from the table until both Tom and Wilbur had finished.

"Okay, you birds," said Mom, "catch us a mess of fish—we can fry them for tomorrow's supper. It's been a while since we've had some."

With worms and poles in the trunk, we all climbed into Wilbur's Ford and drove a mile and a half to Highland Lake.

"Let's park the car on the west side, where they won't notice us," said Tom.

Wilbur cut pieces of fishing line and gave them to my brothers and me to tie to the ends of our poplar branch poles. He gave each of us a snelled hook to attach on the end of the line and showed us how to thread a worm through the hook.

"Go to the edge of the water, and find a small floating stick—you can use it as a bobber," said Tom. Wrap your fishin' line around it, and tie it so that the worm is about two feet below the stick floating on the surface of the water."

When all were ready, Wilbur said, "Ronnie, Dave, and Richie, you come with me, and Jerry and Rollie, you go with Tom. We'll go on the south side, and Tom, you can take the west side."

To accommodate more water coming in from the Highland Ditch, the lake had been enlarged, and a dike built on the south side. A row of outlets embedded in concrete in the dike were used to let water out to irrigate farms around Mead. Wilbur decided that the four of us would fish from the dike. He had plenty of room between trees to cast his line with his spinning reel, and with Dave and me on his left and Richie on his right, he could keep an eye on us as he fished.

In a short time, Wilbur hooked a fish, and his line tightened as the fish fought underwater, struggling to loosen itself. The three of us laid down our poles and ran to his side, eager and excited to see it as he pulled it from the water.

Seeing the gold fringe on its belly, Richie asked, "What kind is it?"

"It's a sunfish," said Wilbur. "It's too small to keep, so I'm throwin' it back."

He dipped his left hand into the water to wet it and then wrapped his palm around the fish to hold it while he removed the hook. He then gently laid the fish in the water, and we watched it swim away. Seeing a fish caught was an exciting event for us, and we scurried back to resume our fishing, hoping we would catch one on our own. In a few minutes, Wilbur caught another one.

"It's a crappie," he said. "I think we can keep this one."

I saw my bobber stick move slightly below the surface, and I instinctively moved my pole upward hoping to see a hooked fish, but there was none there. Wilbur glanced over at me and asked, "Didja have a bite?"

"I sure thought I did," I said. "But I guess it was just the waves that were movin' my bobber." I desperately wanted to catch one—it would be my first.

Light of Her Children

For a moment we said nothing, and all we heard was the lapping of waves of water against the dike. Suddenly we heard a splash. I looked left, and there was Dave flailing in the water. Wilbur ran over and jumped in right next to him. He grabbed Dave by the arm with one hand and lifted him into his arms, standing in water up to his crotch. Dave was shivering and his teeth were chattering as Wilbur carried him to the car. Wilbur took an old blanket from the trunk and wrapped it around him.

"Go get our poles." He said to me. "Richie," he said, "get Tom and the rest of them. We need to get Dave home before he catches cold."

Wilbur drove into our driveway all the way to the back door of the house. He carried Dave in to our bedroom and laid him on the bed. Mom, sitting in her rocking chair and crocheting, got up immediately to help. It was obvious to her what happened.

She said to Wilbur, "Get those wet clothes off him, and I'll get a towel and his pajamas."

"Dave was never in any real danger," said Wilbur. The water was not very deep, and I got to 'im right away."

"Thanks," said Mom. "I always worry when the kids are around water. I just can't help it. But I always know that I can trust you in taking care of them. I know that I can always depend on you."

Mom and Dad had distrust for lakes and rivers. My brothers and I were not permitted to go swimming, not even in the public pool in Sunset Park in Longmont. Mom and Dad remembered that brother Jack's high school classmate, Charles Malchow, drowned at Sunset while swimming with Jack and other high school friends. Mom also remembered that one of her Heist cousins had drowned in the South Platte River near Sterling.

We did not bring home that "mess of fish" that day for Mom, but that would happen at another time—besides athletics, fishing was a favorite pastime, and we would have plenty of opportunities later. However, Mrs. Mike Sekich Sr. one day dropped off a basket of sunfish she and her husband had caught in Lake Mulligan; Mom had my brothers and I put newspaper down on the porch floor, and we cut off their heads and scraped off their scales. Fish bathed in cornmeal and fried in hot Crisco in iron skillets was our meal that night. A mess of fish was always an opportunity for Mom to expand her repertoire of entrées that she would offer her hungry family— for her, fish were another source of protein for which she didn't have to pay.

L–R: Ronnie, Richie, and Rollie Newton, 1949. *Newton Family Album*

Wilbur Thornton, 1947. *Newton Family Album*

Dave Newton, 1948. *Newton Family Album*

Jerry Newton, 1948. *Newton Family Album*

Tom Newton, 1949. *Mead Consolidated Schools Yearbook*

James Elmer Newton and *Bossie*, 1942. *Newton Family Album*

CHAPTER 19

Way it Bounces

Ever since I took my first shot at a basket at five years of age with my brother Jack holding me up within four feet of the rim, I was consumed by the game of basketball. There was something about a ball filled with air and bouncing on a hard, smooth surface with me controlling it with either hand that excited me. I loved holding a basketball and flipping it up and in and out of my hands. I loved how the ball felt when I held it with the tiny protrusions on its rough leather surface, stimulating the nerve endings of my fingertips. I loved how the indentions of its seams found their way to mold around my fingertips whenever I took a deliberate shot at the foul line. I loved how the ball rolled from my fingertips, making its trajectory toward and over the top of the rim. It was that familiar sensory feeling of touch, coupled with confidence in my mind and knowing as soon as it left my hands, the ball was going into the basket. I always felt that I was in complete control—no matter whether it was shooting, dribbling, or passing.

Mom just about went insane with the fixation that my brothers and I had with basketball. In the house, we were always feigning a jump shot to an imaginary hoop or dribbling a basketball on our upstairs bedroom floor—a very annoying sound.

"Cut that racket out," she would yell up the stairs to us, "or I'll take that ball away from you, and you won't be playing with it for a week!"

We would cease, and then resort to passing the ball to each other across the room, sometimes with a bounce pass, hoping that she wouldn't hear one bounce. At other times, we would toss the ball into a wastebasket in the corner, banking the ball off the wall. We saved empty cylindrical boxes of Mother's Oats and used them as the basket for a tennis ball or a rolled-up pair of socks. Any object that could be tossed and any receptacle that could receive it became an opportunity for a "basketball shot."

It was always amazing to Mom how one ball and one hoop could keep her young boys occupied for hours at a time—my brothers and I needed nothing more—our backyard basketball court was the place we wanted to be—it was there where we had our most fun. Our first basketball goal had been constructed by our brother Jack, who was ten years older than we triplets—it consisted of a pinewood backboard attached to a single pole. Jack had the local blacksmith handcraft a rim out of a thin ribbon of iron and then attached a net to it with electrical tape. It was on this backyard court where my brothers and I played our first game of basketball together. After school, we triplets teamed up with either our older brother Jerry or our younger brother Dave to play a game of two-on-two.

When Jack walked home in the late afternoon after working at the local IGA grocery, he would pause to play a game of horse with us before we all went in to the house to eat supper. Jack, being more experienced and more physically developed than we younger brothers, always moved one or two yards back from the prescribed spot to make it more challenging for him and to level the playing field for us younger opponents.

At supper one evening, Jack said to us, "I scored thirty-seven points in a game against Frederick when I was in junior high."

"Didja beat 'em?" I asked.

"No, we didn't," said Jack. "They had a guy on their team named LaBrei, and he scored forty-three points."

Jack also played on Mead High School's basketball team, but I never saw him play. In 1946, Mead High won the conference crown and the district tournament and made it to the state playoffs—they were defeated in the first round and then went into the consolation bracket, where they won two games and came home with the consolation prize. Whenever I went into the gym foyer where the trophy cases for Mead were, I always looked for Jack's name on the trophy.

We younger brothers were not always able to attend school games. Mead High School's basketball-game admission costs for four or five of us were always a stretch. However, this issue was resolved when my sister Helen began to purchase season tickets for the home games and present them to us as our annual Christmas present. I saw my first high school basketball game as a third-grader, and this experience ignited my fascination with basketball. By that time, Jack had graduated, and my sisters Helen and Pat were cheerleading. These three siblings continued the tradition of basketball participation established by our oldest brother, Orbin.

My triplet brothers and I played our first competitive basketball game as third-graders. Our third-grade team competed against the fourth-grade team, of which our brother Jerry, a year older than us, was a member. We played during the lunch hour with nearly two hundred students—grade-schoolers and high schoolers screaming with their support as we dribbled and passed our way back and forth on the court. Playing before a large crowd was a thrilling experience and only heightened my obsession with basketball. Surprisingly, we third-graders beat the fourth-graders that day—it was the first win on a basketball floor that we triplets experienced. However, my joy of winning was bittersweet; our victory was at the expense of my brother Jerry. I took no joy in defeating Jerry—he was family.

"I didn't like beatin' Jerry," I said to Richie. "They just don't have a very good team."

"Yal," said Richie. "Besides Jerry, the only other good player they have is Marvin Blazon. George Ulibarri is tall, but he's never played basketball before. Same way with Darrel Gettman and Kenneth Heil—they're all taller than us, but they haven't played very much—they don't know how to dribble or shoot."

Several weeks before, I had seen Jerry's team get walloped by the fifth-graders—I had compassion for him each time I saw him step out of bounds to toss the ball in after his opponents had scored once again—the tired forlorn look on his face told me that he was thinking: "What's the use? They're just goin' to take the ball away from my teammates and score!"

However, I was quick to learn that in the spirit of a competition such as basketball and with the goal of winning, family association was going to become secondary—in basketball, the team is more important than the individual. In the game of basketball, I had to play better than any opponent, even if the opponent was my brother. This had been my mantra when I faced my brothers on our backyard court, and they shared this belief.

It was our fourth-grade teacher, Mrs. Jepperson, who first understood how important basketball was in the lives of us triplets.

"I'm going to have Mr. Carlson [superintendent] buy a basketball for you boys," she said. "You need one of your own—just for our class."

Mr. Carlson wisely provided us with a soccer ball that was much smaller than a regulation basketball—one that our class could play with at lunch hour and during recess periods. Our play consisted of eight or ten of us boys standing underneath the basket fighting for the rebound when someone shot the ball. It was then that I learned how one had to be clever and maneuver under the basket and anticipate where the ball caroming off the rim or backboard would go. I learned I had to be aggressive against my classmates. Without that combative play for position—physically maintaining my space with bodily contact—I would have little opportunity to gain possession of the ball so that I too could take a shot.

My brother Tom was the first sibling I saw play when he was a member of both the junior varsity and varsity teams at both guard and forward positions. During his senior year, he averaged nearly twenty points a game and was one of the leading scorers in the conference.

"Tom's also a good defender," said our friend Loe Hernandez. "When he blocks a shot, he comes from the side and knocks the ball out of play—that way he doesn't get a foul called on him."

"Yal, that's when he plays center," I said. "But I like it better when he brings the ball down the floor—then he gets to shoot his jump shot, and he's more fun to watch. I'm tryin' to shoot a jump shot like his, but I can't get the ball over my head to shoot—it's too heavy."

In attending Tom's games as fifth-graders, my triplet brothers, and I proudly wore white sweatshirts we had received as Christmas presents from our brother Jack and on which our sister Helen stenciled the Mead mascot, the bulldog. We younger brothers marveled at the orange jersey and the coal-black warm-up jacket with the large *M* on the left side that Tom wore, and we looked forward to the day when we ourselves might be wearing the same uniforms on Mead High's team.

Brother Jack joined the marines, and one Christmas while on military leave, he constructed a new basketball goal for us. The backboard of the one he had built nearly a decade earlier had disintegrated, and the hoop had rusted and broken. As the basketball season approached, my brothers and I had assembled scrap wood for a new backboard and obtained a stout new rim from a neighbor.

Light of Her Children

Mom said, "Why don't you birds wait until Jack gets home and have him build it for you?" As soon as Christmas was over, Jack began his project—it was unique—it was not the typical backboard and rim attached to a single pole. No, Jack's backboard extended three feet out from two upright posts. This allowed us to maneuver underneath the basket, eliminating all obstruction of the support posts. My brothers and I could drive to the basket at a brisk speed and lay up the ball with a glance off the backboard, without being worried about injury. Jack's basketball goal was tight and rigid—there was no shaking or vibration of the backboard when the ball glanced off it. Assembled with bolts and screws—Jack had built it for sturdiness and longevity. Our new basketball goal was the envy of our neighborhood friends, and they came to play with us.

In the sixth grade, our teacher C. H. Clark served as our coach. He scheduled competitions with two large schools from Longmont—a town of twelve thousand population and just ten miles southwest from Mead. We went to play on their courts.

"I bet they're going to have some real good players since their schools are much bigger than ours," I said to Mr. Clark.

"Well, I'm not so sure about that," said Mr. Clark, "but I know they have 'fan' backboards—they may give you a little trouble with your bank shots."

However, much to our surprise and joy, neither their suspected superior talent nor their backboards provided any problem to us, and we beat both teams soundly. With his and our confidence now building, Mr. Clark entered our team into a peewee tournament that was held in Mead's gym with eight teams from the North Central League participating. The requirement to be a peewee was not age but was size. All the players were small, around a hundred pounds, but their ages varied from twelve to fifteen. We lost the first game to an experienced opposition, and we were eliminated from the tournament. That was the first loss that my triplet brothers and I experienced as basketball players, and I sobbed openly over the outcome. I had played poorly, missing two easy layups, one in which the ball did not even touch the rim. It was also disappointing to me because I felt we had been shortchanged by the referee, a Mead high school teacher.

"Maurer called a foul on me when all I was doing was grabbing for the ball with both hands," I said to my nineteen-year-old neighbor, John Roberts, as we sat on stools at the bar of his dad's pool hall a week later. "Then he called another on me—he said I fouled when one of Johnstown's players tripped over my leg as he tried to dribble around me. There's no way that I fouled him—if anything, he should have been called for chargin'. Maurer doesn't know anything about basketball."

"Well," said John, "Maurer shouldn't have been reffin' in the first place—he doesn't seem to me to have been an athlete—I bet he hasn't played much basketball, or any other sport for that matter."

"It's not fair when you have a referee who doesn't know what he's doin'," I said to John.

Although I received some comfort in my conversation with John, I received very little from others when I placed part of the blame for our loss on the referee. I was beginning to learn that in any competition, things are not always fair, and referees, just like players make mistakes. I had to learn to roll with it and accept it—that was the way life was.

Like all those who engage in competitive sports, winning was important for my brothers and me. Particularly for me, losing was disappointing and most difficult to face—I always ended up crying. I coped with loss by credulously saying to myself, "That's the way God wanted it." In my child's mind, God operated like a bouncing ball—sometimes his favor bounced in your direction, and sometimes it didn't.

Jack Newton, 1947. *Mead Consolidated Schools Yearbook*

Jack Newton, US Marine Corps, 1953. *Newton Family Album*

C. H. Clark, 1953. *Mead Consolidated Schools Yearbook*

Tom Newton (middle), 1951. *Mead Consolidated Schools Yearbook*

Chapter 20

Warriors

Every two weeks on Saturday, Father Martin Arno would travel to Longmont to pick up Sisters Marjorie and Laurance, who were teachers at St. John's Catholic School. He would then bring them to Mead to teach catechism to the lower- and upper-grade students in the Guardian Angel Church. Father would hear adult confessions while classes were conducted in the back pews downstairs and the choir-loft pews upstairs.

The confessional door, located to the right of the altar, opened into a small four-foot-by four-foot cubicle with a wooden kneeler facing a wood grid covered by a thin curtain. On the other side of the curtain was the sacristy where Father sat in an armchair "saying the rosary" while he waited for a transgressor to enter and recount his or her sins. Although I never understood what he said, I and all the other students downstairs could always hear the garbled sounds of Mr. Gust's voice as he spoke.

Sister Marjorie dismissed the class fifteen minutes early so that all of us could go to confession and so she could have some time to help us triplets and David learn the Latin prayers that altar boys needed to recite as servers of the Mass.

Pronouncing the Latin words of the priest, Sister Marjorie would say, "In nomine Patris, et Fílii, et Spiritus Sancti."

The four of us responded in unison with "Amen."

Sister Marjorie then said, "Introibo ad altare Dei" (I will go to the altar of God).

The four of us recited the response together, "Ad Deum qui laetíficat juventutem meam" (To God, the joy of my youth).

"Judica me, Deus, et discerne causam meam de gente non sancta: ab homine iniquo et doloso erue me" (Judge me, O God, and distinguish my fight from unjust causes. Rescue me from the wicked and deceitful man), said Sister Marjorie.

We four brothers followed, "Quia tu es Deus, fortitudo mea: quare me repulisti, et quare tristis incedo dum afflígit me inimicus?" (For Thou, O God, art my strength, why hast Thou forsaken me? And why do I go about in sadness, while the enemy afflicts me?).

She recited all the many Latin prayers of the Mass thereafter. Whenever she said, "Dominus vobiscum" (May the Lord be with you), we responded with the obligatory, "Et cum spiritu tuo" (And with thy spirit).

After several months and when we could recite them verbatim, Sister Marjorie said we were ready; she took us to the altar to teach us the help functions performed by us altar boys. As she led us around to the various stations, she would say, "Now when you bow at the altar or to Father Martin, you bend at the neck—not at the waist—only your head should go downward. And remember as you move, keep your hands together with all of your fingers pointing upward at an angle."

Attending Saturday catechism class took precedence over any sporting event if both happened to be scheduled at the same time. If a basketball game was played on Saturday during our scheduled catechism, we were not at the game to watch. During the state six-man football playoffs, Coach Spencer asked us to help chalk the dirt field on Saturday morning before catechism. We triplets were disappointed that we would not be watching Mead win its way to the state championship that afternoon—we were just half a block away learning our catechism lesson.

Intensive study of the Baltimore Catechism began on Friday afternoons after school or Friday evenings. We only had one book from which to prepare, so my brothers and I had to take turns studying, or we worked together in pairs, listening to each other recite the answers to the questions posed for each lesson. We were not allowed to attend a Friday night basketball game unless we had studied our catechism.

When it was time for us to be confirmed, Sister Laurance was our teacher. She was from the Midwest and had been in Colorado for only a year. We liked her because she told funny stories about herself and laughed a lot. She prepared us for the sacrament of Confirmation and explained that an archbishop or the bishop, not a priest, administered it.

"Now when you kneel before the archbishop, he will anoint you on your forehead with the oil of chrism and then give you a slap on the cheek," said Sister Laurance. "Don't worry—it won't be that hard—just a gentle pat."

Then with a smile and a wink, she said, "When I was your age and about to be confirmed, my older brother told me to duck when the bishop started to slap me in the face."

She said, "In receiving Confirmation, you are becoming a soldier—a warrior—for Jesus Christ. The slight blow is meant to remind you that you are ready to suffer anything, even death, for the sake of Christ."

On an April Thursday afternoon, my triplet brothers and I hurriedly walked through the door into our house—school had just been let out. Mom had told us to get home as soon as we could, because Uncle Spaulding and Aunt Mary would be there to pick us up at 6:30 p.m. That night we were to be confirmed, and we had chosen Uncle Spaulding, Dad's brother, to be our sponsor. Uncle Spaulding was our godfather—he was our sponsor at baptism, and I was proud that he would also stand for us at Confirmation. He was the only uncle whom we ever knew—all the others were too remote from us or had died. Uncle Spaulding had experienced modest success with farming, and he had saved enough money to buy a small acreage near Longmont, where he raised New Hampshire hogs.

Wanting to tell everybody that I was going to be confirmed, I mentioned it to my teacher Mrs. Newman as I left the classroom that afternoon.

"You're kinda young, aren' cha?" she said. "In the Swedish Lutheran Church, you aren't confirmed till you're much older. I don't see how you'd have any understanding of what you're doin'."

"Well, we've been goin' to catechism for five years—we've learned a lot about our religion—so I guess they think were ready," I said. "Josephine and Betty are being confirmed with us. Urban J. Vehr, the archbishop from Denver, will confirm us tonight over in Frederick."

Frederick's St. Theresa's Church could seat more than two hundred people, and since the archbishop would be confirming members from the catechism classes of both Mead and Frederick, St. Theresa's was selected for the event—a large crowd of parents, brothers and sisters, uncles and aunts, grandparents, and friends was expected to be there.

Sitting at her sewing machine in the dining room as the three of us entered the house, Mom said, "Get your chores done, and take your baths—we'll hafta eat supper early since they will be here to take us to Frederick at six thirty. Be sure your shoes are polished. I've ironed your white shirts and church pants—they're hangin' here over the bedroom door. Your ski sweaters have been washed, and I just finished pressin' them—they're lying on the bed."

I polished my shoes while I waited my turn to bathe. After my bath, I picked up my dress clothes to take upstairs. I would wear the green ski sweater, while Richie would wear the blue one and Rollie the maroon one. Mom knew that ski sweaters were mostly worn during the winter, but she knew that a sweater was a good substitute for a sports jacket, which we triplets did not have and which most of the other young males would be wearing. Her three boys had to look their best for the archbishop. Mom had attended this ritual many times before—perhaps a dozen times—each one was significant to her. However, this one would be special—tonight three of her boys would be receiving the "Warriors of Christ" sacrament.

Uncle Spaulding and Aunt Mary drove into the front yard of the house a few minutes past 6:30 p.m. I sat up in front between Aunt Mary and Uncle Spaulding while all the rest climbed into the backseat. My aunt and uncle had purchased a new '49 Chevrolet just a year ago. It was a vanilla six-cylinder model with fabric-covered seats and rubber on the floor. They had gone to Detroit, where their son Jim lived, bought it, and drove it back to Colorado.

"We saved a $1,000 on it," said Aunt Mary. "We could get it a lot cheaper than buying it in Longmont."

As we pulled out on the Washington Highway and headed south, I asked, "How far is it to Frederick?"

"It's about ten or 'leven miles southeast of here," said Uncle Spaulding. "We should get there in twenty or twenty-five minutes."

"We've been there before," I said. "Our Mead junior high team played them in basketball in their gym—they're called the Warriors—Mrs. Newman took us to the game. Kathleen says they have a lot of Italian kids goin' to school there. She says that their ancestors came from Italy and are Catholic. So there will probably be a lot of Italian kids there tonight to be confirmed."

"We call them dagos,'" said Aunt Mary. "I guess the people in Frederick, Firestone, and Dacono are all mostly dagos."

"What's a dago?" I innocently asked.

"That's what they call the Italians here in the United States," answered Aunt Mary. "I think they started callin' the early ones that because they came from a place in Italy that sounded like 'dago' when they pronounced it. You know your cousin Red [Aunt Mary's son] married a dago—her name was Helen Tisone—she's from Lafayette. You boys know her—she's been in Mead at your house a couple of times. She's a dark-complected gal—just the opposite of Red, who's white as snow. I think her grandfather came from Italy to work in the coal mines around Lafayette. She's Catholic. She and Red got married at St. John's in Longmont. Their son Joey just made his First Communion last year at St. John's."

Then Mom interjected, "But you kids don't want to call them that to their face—they won't like it. It's like calling a Mexican a spic—they don't like it either. They think that you think you're better than they are. You better be careful about what your sayin' when you're around those people."

"Where does 'spic' come from?" asked Richie.

"I think it comes from 'Hispanic,'" said Mom. "Many of the Mexicans from Mexico have Spanish ancestors. I think a Hispanic is someone from Mexico or Spain."

However, Aunt Mary was not so careful when she talked. Laughing as she spoke, she said, "I think we'll have a lot of dagos and spics there tonight." She winked at me and chuckled.

But to me, referring to people in such a way was not a laughing matter. I was uncomfortable joking about others at their expense. Although these ethnic terms were commonly used and Aunt Mary meant no harm, it sounded to me like she was making fun of them. I did not think that was fair or right. I knew that many of my Mexican classmates did not have some of the advantages that I did. Oftentimes, their parents could not speak English, and they could not teach their children to be American. I thought about Ginger. Her dark complexion came from her Italian mother—and perhaps her father. I wouldn't think of calling her a dago. I knew she wouldn't like it.

Then quickly changing the subject, Aunt Mary said, "Hey, you boys—your uncle Spaulding and I bought you something for your Confirmation." She reached into her purse and pulled out three tiny plastic boxes and handed one to each of us.

I opened mine and took out a silver medal with the three figures of the Holy family etched on one side of it and attached to a heavy chain. Looking around to see that Rollie and Richie had received the same thing, I said, "Thank you, Aunt Mary, I've been wanting one of these for a long time."

"Can we put them on?" I asked Mom.

"Well, I don't know why not—that's what they're for."

Aunt Mary said, "I picked these up from St. John's in Longmont. The Ladies Altar and Rosary Society is always selling religious stuff after church."

A large crowd was starting to gather when we pulled into the parking lot of St. Theresa's. Men dressed in double-breasted suits ushered my brothers and me and Uncle Spaulding to our assigned seats. Josephine Rademacher and Betty Lee and their sponsors were already seated.

As we waited for the archbishop and his entourage of priests to appear, I became anxious and worried. Sister Laurance told us that he would ask questions of those of us to be confirmed—questions about our religion and the meaning of Confirmation.

She said, "If he calls on you, stand up and give him your answer."

I hoped that he wouldn't call on me. I had studied my catechism, but I had forgotten much of it. Besides that, I was terrified when I had to stand up in front of a group and say something. We Newtons had been taught that "children are to be seen and not heard"—what we had to say was not important—it was only the conversation of adults that mattered. Now all of sudden, the archbishop might be interested in what I knew—and I knew I wouldn't be able to speak if he called on me.

Everyone in the church stood when Archbishop Vehr, with crosier in hand, emerged at the altar with Father Martin and Father James Maher from Longmont on each side of him. He blessed all those present, told them to be seated, and began to speak to his young audience of confirmands.

"You know," he said, "St. Paul was persecuted for his belief in and promotion of Christianity. Paul spent time in prison and eventually was killed by his captors. By receiving the sacrament of Confirmation, you are telling the world that you will do what Paul did if it comes down to it. You must be prepared to die if death is required in defending your Roman Catholic faith."

Archbishop Vehr then asked us, "Do you all believe in God?"

We all nodded.

"Who is God?" asked the archbishop. "Who can tell me who God is?" He looked around at us. I did not look at him, and I stared down at the floor—I didn't want the archbishop to even think that I might have an answer.

A hand rose up in the front row. It was Jimmy Sekich, Vera Sekich's nephew and Ginger Staffeiri's cousin.

Jimmy stood up and faced the congregation of kids and families.

"Who is God?" the archbishop asked again.

"God is the creator of all things and heaven and earth," said Jimmy.

"That's right," said the archbishop. "But why did God make you?" he asked.

"Well, I think he needs us to serve him in the world, and if we do a good job, he will reward us in heaven," responded Jimmy.

"Very good, Jimmy," said the archbishop.

The archbishop then asked a few other questions, and when finished, he said to Father Martin, "Father, you and the sisters have taught these young people well—they know their faith and their religion—they are well prepared to receive the sacrament of Confirmation—they are ready to become Warriors of Jesus Christ."

I felt a great relief when the archbishop proceeded to confirm each one of us. We knelt before him, and Uncle Spaulding placed his hand on our shoulder while Archbishop Vehr patted us on the cheek and said, "Peace be with you."

Then with his right thumb, he anointed our forehead with the oil in the form of a cross, and said, "I sign thee with the sign of the cross, and I confirm thee with the chrism of salvation, in the name of the Father and of the Son and of the Holy Ghost."

When all of us were confirmed, the archbishop asked all the family members and friends attending to give the newly confirmed a round of applause. I felt energized with a renewed spirituality—I was determined that I would die if I had to, defending my Catholic beliefs.

As we walked back to the car, Aunt Mary said, "Boy, it was hot in that church—I'm thirsty—let's stop and get something to drink."

Driving down Main Street in Frederick, we saw that all the restaurants and stores were closed, but the neon OPEN sign was on at LePore's Tavern. Uncle Spaulding cut a U and swung the car into a parking spot in front of the tavern. All seven of us walked cautiously and slowly into the dimly lit tavern room with booths and tables. Off to one side were a couple of teenagers playing pool. Aunt Mary and Mom slid into a booth facing each other. Uncle Spaulding and Dad sat down at the table next to the booth, and Richie and Rollie joined them. I sat next to Mom, facing Aunt Mary. The bartender brought each of us ice water in Coca-Cola glasses and asked for our order.

After drinking her water, Aunt Mary said, "I think I'm going to have a little glass of brandy to celebrate this Confirmation tonight. How about you, Johnnie? What're you goin' to have?"

"I guess I'll have the same," said Mom.

"Mom, can I have a Coke?" Rollie asked.

"Oh, I guess so," said Mom. "Richie and Ronnie, do you want one also?"

"I'll have orange," I said.

"I'll take root beer," said Richie.

"I want red wine," said Uncle Spaulding.

Then looking at Dad, the bartender asked, "How about you, sir?"

"Captain," said Dad. "I'll have the same."

When we all had our drinks, Uncle Spaulding raised his glass of wine, and looking toward us triplets, he said, "Here's to the three of you—may this night be one that makes you strong Catholic soldiers for the rest of your life."

"And remember to be like your Catholic ancestors," said Aunt Mary. "They were run out of England and run out of Maryland, and when they got to Kentucky—they still weren't liked. They've had to stick up for Catholicism—they're real religious warriors."

Mom and Dad said nothing—they simply smiled and raised their glasses. We triplets held our pop bottles up also. Then everybody took a drink.

That night was the first and the last time I saw Mom and Dad take a drink of alcohol. This appeared to be a special occasion for them, as well as for the three of us. Never before had I seen my parents so content and happy. Mom had applied rouge to her cheeks and lipstick to her lips—she looked pretty and special to me. The tone of her voice seemed more gentle than ever before. I wanted her to always be that way—why couldn't Mom every day be like she was that night?

Dad's talking was livelier, and his short conversations were more engaging and expressive.

Looking at Uncle Spaulding, Dad said, "I remember when our brother Marcus was confirmed back in Kentucky—he was the last one in our family to be confirmed—our mom was feeling a little bit sad that he was the last one and that there would be no more. She felt that way about everything Marcus did—him bein' the youngest—there was none after 'im."

That night, there was a distinct kinship that was evident between Dad and my brothers and me—there was a bonding with him that I had never before experienced. Other than Dad, none of the rest of us there that night really knew what it was like to be a true warrior—only Dad had been a soldier—a warrior who had risked his life fighting for principles as noble as those of the Catholic faith.

We triplets were happy too that evening. We were proud of the medals that we received from our aunt and uncle. I vowed that I would never take mine off. I knew that I would wear it on the basketball court. I knew that each time I stepped up to the free-throw line, I would briefly hold on to it and say, "Jesus, Mary, and Joseph, help me."

L–R: Richie, Ronnie, and Rollie Newton, 1950. *Newton Family Album*

Spaulding Newton family. *Back row, L–R*: Jim, Tex (Shively) (Spaulding Jr.), Mike, Spaulding, Bill, Red. *Front row, L–R*: Nell, Marie, Mary, Mary Ellen, Monica. 1950. *Newton Family Album*

CHAPTER 21

Winter's Children

One February evening, I went to bed with the snow falling and the wind howling through the crevices around the window of my upstairs bedroom. I heard the whistling sounds of the wind sweeping around the corners of our house and the rattling of the attic door on the north side of my bedroom, confirmations to me of what Mom had said at suppertime, "We're supposed to have a blizzard tonight." I was really hoping that she was right—then in all likelihood—we would not be having school the next day.

With the room temperature just above freezing, I dispensed with kneeling at my bedside to say my prayers and climbed into bed with a quart jar of hot water I had boiled on the kitchen stove—that jar of water was the only external source of heat I would have that night. Sliding in between the two sheets, I felt the weight of two large comforters that Mom had made and that soon would be sealing in what little heat was left in my body.

I was not the only one of us siblings experiencing the discomfort of the blizzard-cold weather—none of the three upstairs bedrooms where my sisters and my brothers slept was heated. In my bedroom, there were two large twin beds, one I shared with my brother Dave and the other where my triplet brothers, Richie and Rollie, slept. Our twin sisters, Maureen and Kathleen, slept in a second bedroom on the west side of us, and brothers Tom and Jerry slept in single beds in the east-side bedroom. By our bedtime, the house's only source of heat was the coal-burning stove in the dining room on the first floor, and before midnight, its blazing coals would be only embers. Then there would be no heat either for the downstairs bedrooms, one occupied by my younger brothers Marc and Frosty and one by Mom and Dad.

I was awakened by Mom the next morning as she opened the door leading to the upstairs and yelled, "Hey, you birds. Ya better get up right now and get ready for school. It's still snowin'."

I turned over in bed and rolled against the jar of water beside me—next to my skin, it was so cold I opened my eyes to see if it had turned to ice during the night. I jumped out of bed, my feet landing on the cold linoleum. From a heaped pile on the floor, I grabbed the same clothes that I had worn the day before, and I ran down the stairs to dress next to the coal-burning heater that Dad had fired up a half-hour earlier.

As I dressed, I heard weatherman Bowman on KOA Radio attribute the blizzard conditions to the jet stream. He said, "It's all because of the jet stream—the high altitude jet stream dipped south and allowed dry polar air from the north to move southward across the Great Plains and into Colorado. This cold polar air clashed with cold moist air from the Pacific Ocean that was moving eastward over the Rockies and was simultaneously clashing with warm, humid air from the gulf."

Weatherman Bowman added, "When these three air masses meet head-on over the Great Plains, a blizzard is bound to happen."

Bowman said that winds of fifty-five miles per hour were clocked and that snow was expected to continue throughout the day. He also reported that the Western Slope town of Frazier was the coldest spot in the state with a temperature of eighteen degrees below zero.

Newscaster, Carl Akers, followed with a report that hundreds of head of cattle in Southern Colorado were stranded on the plains and might perish if the blizzard continued and if ranchers were unable to get food and water to the animals. He also reported that tall snowdrifts on the Washington Highway (US 87) north of Fort Collins prevented motorists from traveling to Cheyenne; they had to stop and seek shelter in Fort Collins and Loveland. Flights in and out of Denver's Stapleton Airport were cancelled, and schools all over the eastern part of the state were closed.

"Do you think we'll have school?" I asked Mom.

"I don't think so," she answered. "I called Emily Newman a few minutes ago, and she said she'd call back as soon as she heard from Mr. Carlson."

Soon after, and with clothes in hand, Dave stumbled down the stairs, followed by Richie and then Rollie. One by one, my brothers and sisters and I collected downstairs, dressing by the warm stove and eating our breakfast of dry cereal and milk and buttered toast. Brother Tom was last to appear, and Mom told him to bring in enough coal and kindling to keep the house warm for the day and to clear the snow away to make a path to the outhouse located twenty yards from the house.

Each school-day morning, the kitchen sink area was a busy place because each of us had to wash our face, comb our hair, and brush our teeth. All this took place while we were simultaneously washing the breakfast dishes, also in the kitchen sink. Mom had started the fire in the kitchen stove and had boiled a pot of water for use in washing the dishes as well as ourselves. Taking the drinking dipper, I removed a small portion of hot water from the pot and poured it into the white-and-gray–speckled, galvanized wash pan in the sink. Then I cooled it down with several dippers of cold water from the tap. I immersed a washcloth cut from a worn-out shirt into the water, rubbed a bar of Palmolive soap onto it, and proceeded to wash my face and arms. I rinsed the soap from the cloth, washed my ears and neck, and then wiped over my head to wet my hair.

As I poured the soapy water out of the wash pan into the sink, I noticed that the sink was not draining properly.

"Mom," I said. "I think the sink's stopped up."

"Oh, for heaven's sake, not again!" exclaimed Mom.

Lacking a sewer system, our wastewater from the kitchen sink was drained through a lead pipe that extended four feet from the house and then was spewed out onto the open ground. Because of the drain pipe's exposure to the cold night air, the water inside it had frozen.

"Tom," Mom commanded, "go light a fire under that pipe."

Our brother Tom had addressed this problem before. After locating several pages of yesterday's *Denver Post*, he went to the metal match dispenser hanging above the kitchen sink and removed a handful of wooden matches. Putting on his boots, plaid coat, and earmuffs, he went out into the cold once again. Soon the newspaper sheets were ablaze, the flames rising around the frozen pipe to melt the enclosed ice. Through the kitchen window, I saw Tom standing comfortably over the fire warming his hands as he watched the melted ice drip from the outer tip of the pipe.

Suddenly, the phone rang—it was Mrs. Newman on the other end of the line—we would not be having school today. My eight siblings and I would be spending the day in the house, taking warm refuge from the blizzard.

The nineteen copies of the *Rocky Mountain News* that my brothers and I delivered every morning to Mead townspeople had not yet been dropped off by our house. It was Dave's and my turn to deliver the papers, and it was Richie's and Rollie's turn to wash and dry the breakfast and supper dishes. Every other day, the two pairs of us alternated these chores. Because all the roadways into Mead were blocked with drifts of snow, I was certain that the news would not be brought to our house until the next day, if then. I was happy—there was no need for me to leave a warm house—I planned for my whole day to be spent indoors—doing whatever I wanted.

With pencil and lined notebook paper, I drew a picture of General Douglas MacArthur that I copied from a *Reader's Digest*. My brothers and I read Donald Duck and Superman comic books and *Popular Mechanics* magazines we had received from Margaret Olson—her son (and our classmate) Gary had finished reading them. David, Marc, and Frosty, riding "horses" of broom and mop handles and with silver toy pistols in their holsters and cowboy hats on their heads, maneuvered in and out of rooms—shooting at one another—hiding behind couches and chairs and feigning death when an imaginary bullet found its mark. With the Erector set we had received for Christmas, Jerry and Richie built a tall crane that they hooked up to the electric motor and then lifted objects off the floor by winding an attached string around a spinning axle. Our sisters Kathleen and Maureen embroidered designs on pillowcases for their beds, and they read the latest issues of the *Denver Catholic Register* and the *Capper's Weekly*; they helped Mom prepare the lunch and supper meals. Outdoors, Tom removed the snow, cleared a walkway from the house to the coal shed, and then at Mom's request, went downtown to Bunton's Red & White to buy bread and cereal.

With bucket in hand, Dad waded through snowdrifts to reach Bossie in her barn, waiting patiently to be milked, and he threw a couple of coffee cans of cracked oats into her trough—the drifts were stacked so high around the haystack outside the barn it would be a day or two before Dad could get to the hay for Bossie to munch on. With his pitchfork handle, Dad broke the ice on the surface of Bossie's water tank so she could have drinking water. And before leaving the house that morning, Mom had reminded Dad, "Don't forget to take care of my chickens." Dad fed them cracked corn and carried them a bucket of water.

Becoming restless and wanting more physical activity, Rollie challenged me to a friendly wrestling match on the bed of our upstairs bedroom—it was no contest for him, winning easily, and he then went on to defeat Richie. I played a game of horse with Richie, shooting a tennis ball into a cylindrical Mother's Oats box that we placed on the floor in the bedroom corner. Then we dribbled our regulation-size basketball on the linoleum-covered floor of the bedroom, but it made so much noise for those downstairs that Mom made us stop.

Later I got into a fracas with Rollie while playing tackle football in our living room using a small pillow. Rollie was carrying the pillow toward the designated "goal line," marked by Mom's couch on the west side of the room, when I tackled him; the two of us fell against the wooden arm of the couch—shearing the arm off, which fell in two pieces to the floor.

"Look what you did," said Rollie, pointing at me. "Wait till Mom finds out—she is really goin' to be mad."

"What do you mean 'I did it'?" I yelled. "It wasn't my fault."

"It was too—you're the one that hit it," said Rollie.

I threw myself at him and began to wrestle him to the floor. Rollie, taken by surprise and finding himself suddenly on his back, started to slug me with his closed fists—aiming at my stomach and back. I turned him over on the floor, and as we rose up, grappling at each other, we hit against the couch with the force of our two bodies and thrust the couch against the wall, making a thudding sound that Mom, in the kitchen, could hear. She came running into the living room.

"What's goin' on here?" she asked.

Seeing us still skirmishing on the floor, she yelled, "Stop it—stop it right now!"

Then peering over at the corner of the room, she saw the broken arm pieces of the couch lying on the floor. She grabbed us forcefully and swatted both of us on the back and butt several times.

"You go sit in the corner, and don't get up until I tell you to," she said angrily.

The next day, there was still no school—many of the country roads had not been cleared, and the school buses could not be driven. At noon, the phone rang—it was Mamie Akers on the other end of the line.

"Mamie wants one of you birds to pick up some groceries for her at Bunton's," said Mom after she hung up.

"I'll go," I said.

I wanted to get out of the house in the worst way. The blizzard had kept us out of school for two days—cooped up in a small space for that long was all that a family of twelve could take—if it lasted any longer, there was sure to be an assassination—and I was afraid that I'd be the one with the murder weapon in my hand.

"Take this quart of buttermilk and this loaf of bread with you," said Mom. "She also wants you to bring in some coal and wood for her."

Mamie greeted me at the door when I arrived. She flashed a smile, revealing her yellowed and decayed teeth. Her long gray hair was tied into a bun and was tinged a dirty yellow with age. A faded brown cape, threadbare and tattered around the edges, swirled around her neck and shoulders. She shivered with the sudden cold and escorted me into her kitchen, where she had been living for the last two days—a small cot was placed next to her table.

"Put all those groceries over there on that chair," she said. There was no room on the table for any additional items—it was cluttered with jars, bottles, stacks of newspapers, folded paper sacks, plates, and piles of opened envelopes.

"I'm about to have some tea, Mr. Newton," she said. "Would you like some too?"

"Yes, I would," I said. "Mom says it's okay for us to drink it—she says it not bad for you like coffee is. She always gives it to us when we're sick."

"I ordered some cinnamon rolls from Bunton's," she said. "Would you like one?"

"I sure would—we don't get store-bought rolls very often—I really like 'em."

Mamie cleared a small area on the table for my cup of tea and roll.

"Pull up a chair," she said. "By the way, which Newton are you?" she asked.

"I'm Ronald—everybody calls me Ronnie."

"Are you one of the triplets?

"Yes, I am."

"I remember when you were born—I went to the town hall to see the three of you. My cousins who are nuns, Sister Pancraitius and Sister Mary Martha, went with me. You kids attracted a lot of attention, you know—triplets just aren't born every day. I was in church when the three of you received your First Communion—that seems just like yesterday—but you must be in your teens now."

"No, I'm only twelve and in the sixth grade.

"Mom says you want me to bring in some coal and wood for you—is that right?" I said.

"Yes, please. But finish your tea and roll first," she said. "Could you also clear a path to the coal house and toilet for me before you go?" she asked.

"I sure can," I said. "I've been in the house for the last couple of days—I like bein' outside and workin'. I like walkin' in the snow as long as my feet stay dry."

"Be sure to tell your mother thank you for the milk and bread," said Mamie. "I'll make toast in the oven tomorrow morning and drink the milk with my supper tonight."

On the way home, I took the shortcut through Gettman's snow-covered field, plowing through knee-high snowdrifts. When I arrived home, Richie and Rollie were clearing the snow from our backyard basketball court. Tomorrow, my brothers and I would no longer be in a crowded household and held hostage by the blizzard—we would be playing a game of two-on-two on the ground surface dried by the warm Chinook winds that descended down the eastern slope of the Rockies.

Interior of upstairs bedroom of Dave, Ronnie, Rollie, and Richie. *L–R*: stairwell, attic closet door, south window, 2012. Sheila Koenig

L–R: Richie, Rollie, Dave, Jerry, and Ronnie Newton, 1949. *Newton Family Album*

Chapter 22

Picture Show

The phone rang just as our family sat down for supper at our kitchen table. My sister Kathleen, sitting the closest to the phone located in the adjacent dining room, got up from her chair to answer it. She came back in to the kitchen and said, "Ronnie—it's Freddie Sekich—he wants to talk to you."

Freddie, the son of Vera and Nick Sekich Sr., was the classmate of my twin sisters, Maureen and Kathleen. I wondered—why would Freddie want to speak to me?

At supper, sitting on the bench next to the kitchen wall with my brothers sitting on both sides of me, the only way I could leave the table was to crawl under it and emerge on the other side.

I was nervous as I picked up the receiver—speaking on the phone was not an easy thing for me to do, and now I had to talk to somebody I had never spoken with before on an unknown topic. Until this time, Mom discouraged us from using the phone; she would not let us younger boys answer its ring—this was a responsibility she had given only to her older daughters. I was glad that my whole family was in the kitchen and that no one would hear my conversation.

"H-hello," I said.

"Hi, Ronnie, this is Freddie Sekich. My cousin, Ginger Staffieri, is visiting us and my girlfriend, Donna, and I want to take her to the show on Saturday night. Ginger wants to know if you can go with us. Do you think you can?" Freddie asked.

"I-I don't know for sure—I-I'll have to ask my mom."

"Okay," said Freddie, "I'll call ya back tomorrow to find out."

I was overwhelmed by this sudden turn of events. I had not seen Ginger for almost two years, and I was flattered that she was still thinking about me. I wondered if she was as pretty as I had remembered. Had she changed? How did she look now? I was excited and apprehensive with the prospect of "double-dating" with Freddie and his fiancée, Donna Clark.

At the phone call's end, I did not return to the table, even though I had not finished my supper. I did not want to explain to Mom about my phone conversation in the midst of all my brothers and sisters. Furthermore, I knew that this would be a request for which it would be difficult to receive her permission, and I decided to postpone the pain until the next day.

It was apparent to me that Freddie wanted to provide his cousin with a pleasant experience during her summer stay at the Sekich farm, and a Saturday night outing with him and his fiancée was a good thing to do. And perhaps, it would make the evening even better if a double-date arrangement was made. I, being the only one in the Mead community who knew Ginger, was the logical one to include. In my mind, I was needed, and I needed to go. The feelings I still had for her were complex and intriguing, and knowing that she had asked for me heightened the need and my desire to go even more.

The next day, with Mom alone in the dining room and sitting at her sewing machine, I finally mustered up the courage to ask her permission. I explained to her that the caller the night before was Freddie Sekich, and I said, "H-he wants me to go with Ginger Staffieri and Donna Clark and him to the show on Saturday night."

"Absolutely not," Mom replied. Knowing that Freddie and Donna were planning their wedding right after graduation, Mom added, "You're too young to be going with them."

"But I'm in the eighth grade, and Barbara Graham and Allen Thompson have gone out together," I retorted. "Why can't I?" I asked. "It can't hurt nothin'," I blurted out.

"I don't care what anybody else has done," Mom said. "Let Freddie find someone else—it doesn't need to be you."

Mom responded no further and proceeded to start up her sewing machine. As far as she was concerned, the matter was closed, and the conversation was over. However, I had hopes that if I "nagged" her again, she might reconsider—I was determined that I would try again.

On Friday evening, again while the family was eating, the phone rang. I knew right away that it was Freddie. This time my sister Maureen answered, and she came into the kitchen to announce it was for me. I shuddered with the thought of conveying the negative news to Freddie. I crawled under the supper table and out the other side and walked to the phone.

"Did you ask your mother if you can go tomorrow night?" Freddie asked.

Giving myself another chance to ask, I lied and said, "Not yet. Hang on just a minute, and I'll go ask her."

I set the receiver down and walked back into the kitchen where my nine siblings were babbling furiously as they slurped their potato soup and bit into giant ears of corn. I looked directly at Mom and said, "It's Freddie, and he wants to know if I can go."

"No, you cannot. I told you once before," said Mom emphatically as she laid her corn down and positioned her elbows on the table and folded her hands in front her mouth.

"Why not?" I argued. "It won't hurt nothin'."

"You know exactly why," she said. "I've already told you."

"I'm old enough—nothin's goin' to happen," I contended.

I persisted. I did not want to tell Freddie I couldn't; the thought of his asking someone else to take my place was unthinkable.

"It's not fair—everyone else my age gets to," I whimpered.

By now the whole family had stopped talking and was listening. Kathleen, exasperated by it all, suddenly stood up from the table and said, "Oh for heaven's sake—go ahead and tell him you can go! My-y-y god! We are tired of listening to you whine," she said. "Tell him you can and shut up. We don't want to hear about it anymore."

Stunned with Kathleen's remarks and her unexpected entry into the discussion, Mom said nothing more and continued eating. I interpreted her silence to mean that she had granted her consent, and I hurried back to the phone to tell Freddie.

With Kathleen's help, I knew that I had won this "battle" with Mom, but I also knew that I would have to work more and work harder to earn this privilege. I did not say another word to Mom about it for fear that she would reverse the decision. Not wanting to face my brothers and sisters again, I did not go back to the table to finish my supper—besides I never liked potato soup. When I finished with washing the dishes, I quietly went upstairs to bed.

The next morning, I was out of bed earlier than usual. I knew that the only way I could earn the right to the special privilege that had been given to me was to work extra hard and efficiently on all the tasks that Mom assigned to me. It was Saturday, and I knew that Mom would have a long list of jobs for us to do.

Mom got Dave up early also—it was our turn to deliver the *Rocky Mountain News*. We finished at seven, ate our breakfast, and began weeding Mom's strawberry patch, something my brothers and I did every year. Richie and Rollie joined Dave and me a half hour later; we worked rapidly—breaking only to drink water—we needed to get one-third of the patch completed by noon.

Light of Her Children

After lunch, Mom ordered us to clean up the yard. She said, "I want the yard cleaned before Betty and Jack [my sister and brother-in-law] get here tonight for supper—I don't wanna see any junk layin' around."

While Richie and Rollie washed and dried the lunch dishes, Dave and I began clearing the yard area of cans, papers, boards, gunnysacks, and just plain junk that we had strewn about while playing over several weeks. Richie and Rollie helped, and by three o'clock, we had all the debris removed, the exposed soil of the yard raked, and the sidewalk swept.

Dave and I began cleaning the porch while Rollie and Richie chopped wood into kindling and brought in a bucket of coal for Mom's cook stove. Dave and I washed down the dual sinks, washed the windows, and swept and scrubbed the wooden floor. The four of us gathered gunnysacks of greens for the chickens and also gave them grain and water. We shucked a half bushel of corn that Mom had picked for supper. While Rollie and Richie swept and cleaned the outdoor toilet, Dave and I changed the sheets on all the upstairs beds.

Finished with my work at five thirty, I took my bath, put on a pair of jeans and a knit shirt, and polished my shoes. At six fifteen, I went outside to wait for Freddie and the two girls to arrive. Even though I was hungry, I took no time to eat. I did not want to see Mom or interact with her any more than I had to. I was glad that she was occupied in conversation with our supper guests, my sister and brother-in-law, who had already arrived. I was standing beneath the large elm in front of the house when Freddie arrived in his '52 hard-top, two-door Plymouth.

"Hi, Ronnie," he said as he stepped out of the car.

Freddie folded his front seat forward, and I stooped to climb into the rear seat, where Ginger was sitting. Her pink-and-white pinafore dress with the starched multilayer petticoat underneath covered three-quarters of the backseat, and she took her hand and pulled it to her left side to make room for me to sit. The mass of fabric mounded between us, covering her left arm.

Ginger's face and brown skin were just as pretty as I had remembered. She shyly smiled and said, "Hi."

"Hello," I said. "Barbara [her cousin] told me that I'd be surprised to see that you'd grown much taller—it's been two summers ago since I last saw you."

"Hi, Ronnie—how are you tonight?" Donna asked.

"Fine," I said. "It's nice to meet you, Donna—my sisters Maureen and Kathleen have told me all about you—they told me you guys are engaged."

"That's right—it happened two months ago," she said as she reached back to show me her ring.

With my youngest brothers, Marc and Frosty, standing in the yard curiously watching and wondering what was going on, Freddie backed out of our driveway and drove south toward the school. At the Stop sign, he turned west toward the mountains, where the sun was setting just to the left of Mount Meeker. The direct rays penetrated the front car window with great intensity and shone on Ginger's olive skin. Again, for a moment, I pondered her youthful beauty.

Freddie, going at his usual high speed down the gravel road, broke the silence that prevailed and asked me, "What are your twin sisters doin' this summer?"

"They're helping Mom with canning and doin' a lot of babysittin'—a lot of farmer's wives call them up wantin' them to help with cleanin' their houses," I said. "Kathleen entered some of her canned stuff in the 4-H competition at the fair—and Maureen's been drawin' and paintin' some pictures."

As Freddie slowed down to turn south onto the county-line road, I said to Ginger, "Barbara told me that your mother has remarried and you now have a stepdad. When did that happen?" I asked.

"Last year," she said. "Now he and my mom keep saying that they would like to get out of Denver and live closer to the

Sekiches. Last week they looked at a restaurant in Longmont that they'd like to buy."

Donna then turned her head toward the backseat and asked Ginger, "What have you been doin' the last week on the farm?"

"I rode on the tractor with Uncle Nick when he was baling hay," said Ginger. "And every morning and at night, I rode in the truck when Freddie fed the cattle."

"What has been your favorite thing?" asked Donna.

"Feedin' milk to the baby calf!" exclaimed Ginger. "He was never finished—he wanted to lick up every last drop left in the bucket. He just kept lickin', and he pushed the bucket right out of my hands.

"I also liked helping Aunt Vera can peaches—we drove over to Brighton to get them—we had four bushels to can. Then Aunt Mary came over to help, and she brought Barbara with her—Barbara and I both helped—we cut the pits out."

"I don't like cannin' very much," I said. "I've been doin' it all summer. My mom's been cannin' everything—peaches, corn, apples, red beets, peas, beans—you name it, we've canned it, and we've got it in a jar in our cellar."

"I'm a city girl," said Donna. "My mother never cans anything."

When we reached US 287, one mile north of Longmont, we turned south and drove into downtown and into Main Street. On our right, we saw the large neon-lit vertical sign of the Trojan Theater with the marquee below saying: *The Half-Breed*—Starring Robert Young.

Now just the week before with all my family at supper, Kathleen had told us that she and Eddie Hetterle had gone to see this movie—a Western that they both liked. She said, "I guess I wasn't s'pposed to see it—but we went anyhow. I read in the *Denver Catholic Register* that the National Legion of Decency rated it as 'morally objectionable in part' and that it is 'for adults only.' But I really didn't see anything wrong with it."

"The only part that I saw that was bad," said Kathleen, "was when they showed a young Indian girl with some of her clothes torn off when she was killed."

As Freddie searched for a parking place on Main Street, I recalled how Father Martin Arno of Mead's Guardian Angel Church asked all of us parishioners to stand and recite the pledge: "I condemn all indecent and immoral motion pictures and those which glorify crime or criminals. I promise to do all that I can to strengthen public opinion against the production of indecent and immoral films and to remain away from motion pictures that endanger our moral life." (I smiled momentarily when I remembered how Father Martin added an extra syllable and accentuated the word "films" to "fil-ums.")

Freddie found a parallel-parking space about a block from the theater. I held Ginger's warm, moist palm for just a moment as I helped her emerge from the backseat. Holding a girl's hand for the first time was exciting for me, but I suspected that Ginger, living her whole life in big-city Denver, had experienced this many times. We walked up to the ticket booth, and I removed two dollars from my billfold, which I slid under the arched opening of the glass shielding the cashier who reciprocated with two quarters and the tickets. Ginger and I then followed Freddie and Donna into the lobby.

Because the teasers on coming attractions had just begun, the theater was darkened, and the usher had to guide us to our seats with a flashlight. Shortly thereafter, the RKO radio tower on-top-of-the-world symbol appeared on the screen, followed by the title words: *The Half-Breed*. The movie began, showing the good guys, with Robert Young playing the part of a gambler who befriends a mixed-blood Apache Indian. As the story progressed, it was easy for us to identify the conspiring villain. He was the crooked town politician who wanted the gold that had been discovered on reservation lands. His plan was to drive the Apaches off the reservation; cleverly, he and his renegade henchman incited a war between the white settlers and the Indians.

As the brutal, violent scenes of war appeared, Ginger flinched in her seat and placed her hands over her face. Both Ginger and Donna gasped when they heard the screams of the young Indian girl, the sister of the half-breed, who was violently attacked and killed.

As the credits zipped by at the final end of the movie, Ginger said, "I'm glad it's over—I don't like all that fightin' and killin'."

"I don't like it either, but I like Westerns," I said. "I like it when they show all that great scenery—it makes me wanna go and see it myself—I think it would be fun to ride a horse in all those places."

With the house lights on, the four of us strode through the lobby entrance and then onto Main Street toward our parked car. Freddie and Donna held each other's hand as they walked, but Ginger and I strolled together behind them with our arms and hands at our sides. Even though I wanted to, I could not bring myself to hold her hand.

We stopped at the A&W Root Beer Drive-In on Main Street. While Ginger ate her hamburger and drank a small root beer, I devoured a cheese sandwich, an order of fries, and a chocolate malt. Freddie paid for all of it.

As we passed Johnson's Corner, leaving town, Ginger said, "I think I would like it in Longmont if my mom and dad moved here."

"My friend Walt Slee says it's a good place to live," I said. "He sez that the porch lights of all the houses are always on because the city pays for the electricity. He's lived in Longmont all his life—he sez he wouldn't live anywhere else."

"I like Longmont," said Donna. "But I'm glad that I'm leavin'—when Freddie and I get married, we're goin' to live on a farm—no more city life for me."

As Freddie turned east onto Highway 66, I moved forward in my seat to ask him, "Do you help with the irrigatin' on your farm?"

"I sure do. We just finished with the sugar beets—we've got over seventy acres. My dad was one of the top-ten growers in Weld County last year. He says he wants to be one of them again this year."

"Are you goin' to have to stay outta school to help with the beet harvest?" I asked him.

"No—but Dad puts me to work as soon as I get home from school. We have lights on our tractor and topper—we can work late at night."

Ginger and Donna continued with their own conversation for the next several miles, Ginger mentioning that she would be going back to Denver the next day.

Freddie stayed on Highway 66 for seven miles and then turned north toward Mead, passing by the Guardian Angel Church on the south edge of town. When Freddie turned west at the northeast corner of the town park, I was reminded of my captivation of two summer years past when I first saw Ginger at her mother's side at the church picnic. That same feeling of that bygone afternoon still prevailed, and I was grateful that I had a chance to experience that excitement once again with her that night.

"Isn't that the park where your church has a picnic every year?" Ginger asked.

"It sure is," I said. "We just had it a couple of weeks ago—your aunt Vera and uncle Nick were there—so were Nicky and Freddie—Freddie brought Donna with him."

As Freddie turned into our driveway, I could see that there were no lights on in our house, but I was certain that Mom noticed the headlights through the window of the dining room just outside her bedroom and that she had noted that eleven o'clock was an unusual, late night for her son.

Light of Her Children

I thanked Freddie for taking me along, and I said good-bye to Donna and Ginger. I was confident that I would see Ginger again, even though I didn't know when that would be. I stood by the back door and watched the car drive out of sight, and then I stepped to the back side of the house to pee. I looked up at the bright stars and the Milky Way through the clear summer sky and reflected on the events of the evening. My thoughts turned to the image of Ginger's beautiful smiling face and her gorgeous olive skin.

I entered the house quietly and walked up the stairs to my bedroom. Kneeling at my bedside, I whispered, "Thanks, God, for getting Mom to let me go."

Then apologetically, I uttered, "Dear God, I'm sorry I went to the movie that I wasn't s'pposed to." I said the Act of Contrition and told Him I wouldn't do it again.

As I lay in bed, I thought of Freddie—I knew he was pleased that I had gone with them that night. I thought of Kathleen—she had stepped in to help me—she was the one who really made it happen. In my mind, without her intercession, I would have suffered humiliation and permanent isolation from Ginger. I remembered Helen's understanding and complimentary words when, two years before, I showed her the letter I received from Ginger. I was feeling lucky that I had big sisters—they had always been there to help me and my brothers. All my sisters, older than me, were my constant source of counsel when I needed someone to talk to—when I was unsure of the next step I must take.

The next morning, I was out of bed at seven—Mom did not have to awaken me. Dave and I had to deliver the news before church. I descended the stairs and entered the kitchen where Mom was reading the paper.

"You're looking mighty spry this early," she said sarcastically. "You got home a little late last night, didn' cha?"

I nodded but said nothing, and I grasped the teakettle from the stove to pour hot water into a wash pan in the sink.

"What show did ja see?" she asked quizzically.

"We went to *The Half-Breed*—that was the only thing that was showin'," I answered. It never occurred to me to attempt to tell a lie.

"Isn't that the one Kathleen saw last week, the one she said was not for kids?" Mom asked. I nodded but said nothing as I proceeded to wash my face.

"You birds!" she said with an annoyed look at me. "You get an inch, and you take a mile. You and Kathleen had no business goin' to that show. I have a mind to ground you both for a week. When you get home from church today, young man, I want you to clean the bathroom. Eunice and Wilbur are comin' over for dinner, and I want that place lookin' spic-and-span."

This was the first, but not the last, serious confrontation I had with Mom. And obviously, mine was not her first—I had witnessed many defiant episodes that my sisters had with Mom, particularly those involving relationships with their boyfriends, how they dressed, and her perception of their fixation on their own self-importance. My sisters and I were growing up at a rapid pace and stepping out into the world—a world that Mom, like all mothers, could not easily control.

Laura Dreier Newton, 1951. *Newton Family Album*

Ronnie Newton, 1952. *Newton Family Album*

Freddie Sekich, 1952. *Mead Consolidated Schools Yearbook*

Kathleen Newton, 1952. *Mead Consolidated Schools Yearbook*

CHAPTER 23

Pool Hall

I got my first bike when I was in the eighth grade—bought it for fifteen dollars with my own money. With this new mode of transportation, I abandoned the scooter I had found in the alleyway and began taking short journeys all over town without Mom realizing it. One summer afternoon, I sneaked downtown to the pool hall and barbershop to drink a soda pop. The sidewalks were still wet from the torrential thunderstorm that smashed through Mead just an hour before, and rainwater lay collected in large potholes on all the streets. I parked my bike against the pool-hall wall, and as I proceeded to the screen-door entrance, I noticed a green GMC pickup coming down Main Street toward me. The vehicle did a quick U-turn at the intersection of the Clark Lumber Company and Effie Markham's house and pulled in directly in front of me to park diagonally against the sidewalk. When the driver got out, I recognized right away that it was Bill Nygren, the husband of my eighth-grade teacher Eva Jane Peters Nygren. Bill and his wife lived on the rental farm one mile west of Mead.

"Hello, Mr. Nygren," I said as I held the screen door open for him.

"Good afternoon, Mr. Newton."

Light of Her Children

I followed him into the pool room and past the pool tables to the far corner bar where proprietor Grover Roberts sold snacks, soda, and 3.2 percent Coors beer, both bottle and draft.

Mr. Roberts had just bought a new snooker table, much larger than the older eight-ball table sitting next to it. He did not permit us kids to play on his new purchase: this was reserved for the men who played round the world for small stakes. However it was okay for us Newtons to play on the eight-ball table as long as Dad was there. If we had a spare dime, my brothers and I would ask for Dad's permission to play our own game of round the world on the eight-ball table. Usually, five or six men could be seen standing around the big table holding their sticks upright and smoking cigarettes while they patiently waited for their turn to shoot, but that afternoon, the pool room was empty.

Bill and I sat down on the red vinyl-covered stools, their chrome cylindrical posts attached to the bare pinewood floor. Sitting behind the bar was Francis Palinkx, a man in his seventies, wearing bifocal glasses and with a hand-rolled cigarette in his mouth. Mr. Palinkx laid his cigarette down and stood up to wait on us. He said nothing and smiled broadly, revealing his cavernous mouth with no teeth.

Across the way to our left, we saw Mr. Roberts in his glassed-in barber cubicle cutting the hair of Joe Jones; Joe had taken an afternoon break from fixing cars at the Mead Motor Company garage. Mr. Roberts had draped Joe with a cloth that was held tight around the neck with a large safety pin. The cloth was made from two one-hundred-pound flour sacks that had been ripped open and sewn together by Mrs. Roberts. The barber chair had a black leather seat and was held upright and anchored to the floor with a flat, round porcelain disc, trimmed with chrome. On the south side of the room below the large horizontal mirror was a marble shelf, sitting on top of several cabinets below. On the shelf were all the tools of a barber's trade: clippers, brushes, combs, scissors, razors, and shaving-cream cups with brushes. Several ashtrays were dispersed among the clutter of objects strewn haphazardly on the marble surface; Mr. Roberts's lighted cigarette lay smoldering in one of them, and smoke filled the tiny room.

Waiting for his turn for a haircut was Louie Roman, who sat on a gray-painted wood bench with his back planted against the wall, vertically paneled with tongue-and-groove pine—it too was painted gray. Louie was taking rapid consecutive swallows from a bottle of Coors that he held in his hand.

Bill took off his straw hat and laid it on the bar, revealing the tan line just below his white forehead, the signature symbol of a hard-working man who earned his living as a farmer.

"I'll take a glass of Coors," Bill said to Mr. Palinkx. "What'll you have, Mr. Newton? I'm buyin'."

"I take an orange pop and a bag of peanuts to go with it," I answered.

With palsied and trembling hands, Mr. Palinkx set the beer glass down in front of Bill—it clattered slightly as he stabilized it on the counter. Bill blew the foam off the top of his beer and took a giant swallow. I took a five-cent bag of Tom's Peanuts from the gallon jar in front of me and began pouring them into my bottle of orange pop.

"What's Mrs. Nygren doin' this summer?" I asked.

"She's home takin' care of Willie D.—Willie's six years old now—just finished the first grade—we started 'im in school early—the missus thought he was ready."

"My best friend, Mike Eckel, told me he's real smart," I said.

"Well-l-l, the damn kid wants to know somethin' about everything," said Bill. "He's readin' all the time—even when he goes to the bathroom—he sits on the pot with a *World Book Encyclopedia* on his lap."

Then turning to Mr. Palinkx, Bill said, "That thunderstorm moving from the south this morning dropped a butt load of hail this side of [Highway] 66 and wiped out my barley. Thank God the missus is teachin'—otherwise, it would be a hard winter for me and her."

"Did it get anybody else?" Mr. Palinkx asked.

"Well, it hit Frank Schell north of me—it got one side of his field as it moved past the county line. I don't think it was east enough to get folks down by the river."

"Ya know, last week, a buncha wheat near Sterling was knocked out by hail."

"Those poor bastards," Bill sighed. "If hail doesn't get 'em, a goddamn tornado will."

"What about sugar beets?" I asked. "Do they ever get damaged by hail?"

"They didn't get hurt—hail never seems to bother 'em."

Abruptly I heard the twang of the stretched spring on the screen door, and Clayton Claus walked into the pool room. I knew Clayton—he was my best friend Mike Eckel's uncle who had graduated from Colorado A&M College, bought a farm one mile northeast of Mead, and married Lois Graham soon after she graduated from Mead High School. Mike told me that Clayton had studied animal husbandry in college.

"Hello, Ronnie," said Clayton, flashing his trademark smile.

Seeing a familiar face, he said, "Hey, Bill—how's it goin'?"

"Not so good—my barley got wiped out by hail this mornin'—knocked every goddamn head to the ground."

"Sorry to hear that," said Clayton. "All I got at my place was a helluva lot a rain. What are you going to do with it?"

"I guess I'll make silage out of it and feed it to the cattle."

"It's a shame—every year somebody in the county gets hit," said Clayton. "As big as it is—somebody's bound to get wiped out."

"How big is Weld County?" I asked.

"I would guess a couple of million acres," said Clayton. "It goes all the way up to the Wyoming border, and as far east as Wiggins. Here in Mead, we're just on the west edge of it. I guess Weld is the third largest county in the state. They told me in college that Weld was one of the best farmin' counties in the whole United States."

"Ya know—it's interestin'," said Bill. "When I was at A&M, I had to take a geology class, and the prof told us that millions of years ago, Weld County was covered with a big lake—matter of fact, he said most of Colorado was underwater. He said it was real hot back then and all kinds of plants were growin'—palm trees—algae and stuff. He said they died and dropped to the bottom of the lake, and after millions of years, they were covered with layers and layers of dirt and sand—the heavy pressure turned them into coal. He said that's what they're minin' over there by Erie and Frederick."

"Wasn't it that silt and sand that settled to the bottom of that big lake that formed the red flagstone that you see up there in the foothills around Lyons?" asked Clayton.

"Yal, in Lyons, you can see where those flagstone layers broke off when the Rocky Mountains came up outta the ground," said Bill.

"I guess all of Colorado was covered with ice too at one time," commented Clayton.

"That's what my professor said," confirmed Bill. "He said big glaciers carved sand and gravel outta the mountains, and when the ice melted, rivers started washing them into the lake down below."

"Was the Saint Vrain one of those rivers?" I asked.

"I guess it could've been," said Bill. "Probably the Poudre, the Big Thompson, and the Platte too."

"The Saint Vrain must have been there back then," said Clayton. "There's a big pile of sand and gravel on this side of it—right next to the highway—they're goin' to use it when they build the new interstate."

Bill ordered another beer, excused himself, and walked out the back door to use the toilet.

Clayton, finally pausing to drink the beer set in front him several minutes ago, said, "Those guys at A&M said that Weld

County has some of the best soil around. They said that all those rivers were runnin' through it and were carrying tons of water—their banks were always overflowin' and droppin' minerals and stuff on their sides. Those wide floodplains are what farmers all over Weld County are now farmin'—they say it's some of the best soil in the whole United States."

"My dad says that our garden has some of the best dirt he's ever seen," I said. "He says it's better than anything he's seen in Kentucky. All we do is put chicken manure on it and plow it under—we have a good garden every year."

"That's all I do too," said Clayton. "I put loads of cow shit on my land—plant it, and when it comes up, I irrigate the hell out it."

"I guess they started farmin' in Weld County back in the 1800s," said Clayton. "Back then, farmers were raisin' crops to feed the gold miners, and railroads were startin' to be put in. Pretty soon, a lot of people were comin' to Colorado—many from Europe and Russia."

Bill, coming back to take his seat at the bar, hearing the tail end of the conversation, said, "Yal, many were Germans—they had lived in Russia for years before they came over here. My dad called 'em German Russians. They settled over near Windsor—they have names like Schottenheimer and Margheim."

"We've played basketball against Windsor," I said. "They had a guy on their team by the name of Grauberger—I bet he's German—don' cha think?"

"I bet he is," said Bill. "My dad says that the German Russians are good farmers. He says they started out as common laborers in the fields, and now many of them own their own farms. Now all of the hard work is done by the nationals that come up from Mexico. Great Western brings them here—we have to pay Great Western fifteen dollars a head to get 'em here. I have a beet shack on the farm where they live while they work."

"Sugar beets need a lot of water and a lot of care labor wise for six or seven months if you're goin' to have a good crop," said Bill.

"You're damn right there," said Clayton. "You've got to plant 'em, thin 'em, hoe 'em, top 'em, dig 'em, and haul 'em. That takes a lot of folks."

"Thinnin' is where the problem is," said Clayton. "Ya gotta separate the seedlings that are growin' close together and get rid of the weeds. You have to hire the Mexican nationals to do it."

"Ted Rademacher hires my brothers and me to do it—he doesn't use Mexicans," I said. "He pays us the same money they get—$13.25 an acre."

"The second hoein' costs 7½ bucks an acre," said Bill. "Is that what you boys get?"

"Yes, and we get three dollars for the third hoein'," I answered.

"How many acres did you guys plant this year?" I asked.

"I only planted thirty-five," said Clayton. "Next year I think I'll rent some land and plant more."

"I got forty-two," said Bill. "My brother Walter's got sixty-some acres. Last year, he was one of the top-ten growers for the Longmont Factory district—he got over twenty-four tons to the acre—planted forty acres. Great Western likes to see them have a lot of sugar in 'em—Walter's beets were 16 percent sugar, and he averaged nearly eight thousand pounds to the acre."

"I saw Walter's picture in the paper," said Clayton. "Joe Seewald and Jake Heil were also in it."

"Great Western makes a lot of money from the beet growers in Weld County," said Clayton. "They've got a lot of factories makin' granulated sugar."

I mentioned, "I saw sugar factories in Windsor and Fort Lupton and in Eaton too when we went there to play 'em in basketball."

"They have a factory in Greeley, and outside the county, they have 'em in Loveland, Fort Collins, and Fort Morgan," said Clayton.

Bill took his last swallow of beer and said, "Ya know, all of us are sittin' right here in Mead because of sugar beets. My dad told me that fifty years ago, Great Western decided to build a feeder line from Johnstown to Longmont to gather and take the sugar-beet harvest to the Longmont factory. The railway passed directly through Paul Mead's property, who decided to plat a new town on his land next to the tracks."

He paused for a moment and then said, "It was no accident that they decided to call the town Mead."

Bill handed Mr. Palinkx a dollar bill and told him to include my Nehi and peanuts. Hands shaking, Mr. Palinkx removed the change from the cash drawer and then spilled several coins on the bar. Bill left them there and stood up to put on his hat. I thanked him for treating me.

Clayton got up from his stool and placed fifty cents on the bar and said, "I gotta go—I'm irrigatin' my beets right now—gotta see how they're doin'."

Barbershop, Mead, CO. *L–R*: Grover Roberts and Joe Jones, 1954. *Mead Consolidated Schools Yearbook*

Clayton Claus, 1957. *Patricia Eckel*

Sugar-beet topper/digger and tractor, 1954. *Mead Consolidated Schools Yearbook*

Chapter 24

Hoedown

I awakened to see a shaft of sunlight penetrating through two open windows in the upstairs bedroom on the east side of the house where my brothers Tom and Jerry were sleeping. My bedroom had only one small south-side window, and even when left open, air movement through its tiny portal into the room where my three brothers and I slept was nil. So the door between my bedroom and theirs was left open during the night to circulate the cooler air coming from outside through their two open windows, which were screened and left open all the time.

 I was facing east when my eyes opened slowly to the direct rays of sunlight coming all the way through the adjacent bedroom. Even this early in the day, I sensed a heat buildup in the room, and I quickly surmised that this was going to be another sweltering day in the beet field. I rolled over to see if Richie, sleeping beside me, was awake and then lifted my head to see if Rollie and Dave in the bed across the room were awake; all were still asleep. I remained reclined on my side and closed my eyes, hoping to get a few more minutes of sleep before Mom would call up the staircase hallway to get us up. I did not know the exact time—there was only one clock in the house, and that was downstairs on the kitchen wall. But I could tell from the angle of the penetrating sun that it was time for me to get out of bed. I dozed off thinking how great it would be if we didn't have to go to work that day, but with the hot sun already baking the roof, I knew there was no chance of a morning thunderstorm keeping us out of the field. I was awakened when I heard the door to the stairs hall open, and I heard Mom saying, "Hey, you birds, it's six thirty—ya better get movin'."

Clad only in my JC Penney briefs, I rolled over, put my feet on the floor, and walked over to the stair railing, where I had piled my clothes. With my white T-shirt and jeans on, I went down the stairs to sit at the kitchen table to put on my socks and shoes.

In the kitchen, Mom was pouring cold milk into four empty, wide-mouthed Skippy peanut-butter jars. Dad had milked Bossie the night before, and Mom had already skimmed off the cream that had risen to the surface and placed it in the churn jar along with several other batches of cream she had accumulated over several days. Since all of us older brothers would be working in the fields, our younger brother Marc would be churning the cream to produce butter that day. Furthermore, Marc and our youngest brother, Frosty, would now be delivering the *Rocky Mountain News* that morning, a role that Dave and we triplets transferred to them a year earlier.

Mom screwed the Skippy lids on the jars and placed them into a flat, rectangular cardboard box that my brothers and I used as our collective "lunch pail," and then she said to me, "As soon as you finish your cereal, you can make the sandwiches."

I poured milk from the pitcher into my bowl of Cheerios, put on two teaspoons of sugar, and ate hastily. I knew that Louie Rademacher would soon be parked in our driveway at seven sharp to pick us up and transport us to the beet field.

Rollie, Richie, and Dave each stumbled down the stairs and sat down at the kitchen table. They shook the boxes of

Light of Her Children

Wheaties, Cheerios, or Grape-Nuts, trying to decide which one had enough remaining in the box for them to choose to eat.

I cut a slice from a loaf of Mom's fresh-baked bread, dropped it in the toaster, and then placed eight slices of store-bought Wonder Bread on a large rectangular breadboard lying on the kitchen counter. I took a jar of Skippy peanut butter from the pantry and spread large amounts on each slice, followed by two tablespoons of Mom's strawberry preserves.

Meanwhile, my toasted bread slice popped up in the toaster; I put churned butter on it and took a large bite and washed it down with a quick gulp of milk. I topped each one of the peanut-butter-laden Wonder Bread slices with a second slice, and Rollie wrapped all eight of the sandwiches individually with waxed paper and placed them into a flat cake pan.

I went to the refrigerator to pull out three trays of cubed ice from the ice compartment. I pulled up the lever to loosen the ice and poured all three trays of ice onto and around the four jars of milk. Mom wrapped eight peanut-butter cookies together with waxed paper, placed them on top of the sandwiches, and placed the cake pan on top of the milk jars.

As Dave filled up a gallon glass jug with water from the faucet at the sink on the porch, he noticed Rademacher's brown Hudson parked in the driveway. He yelled into the kitchen, "Louie's here."

With buttered toast in hand, I went to the porch to pick up my wide-brimmed straw hat sitting on the freezer, ran out the screen door, and climbed into the backseat of the car. Richie emerged from the house holding his hat, and he elected to sit in the front seat. Rollie, hat on his head, carried our lunch to the back door of the car, set our lunch box on the floorboard, and took a seat in the back. Dave was already in the backseat with the jug of water at his feet.

It was seven five when Louie backed out of the driveway. "Well, how are you boys doin'?" he asked.

"I guess okay," said Richie, speaking for the whole group since he was sitting up front.

"It's going to be a hot one today," said Louie. "I looked at the thermometer this morning on the side of the house, and it was already eighty-six. You better have plenty of water," he stated with a chuckle.

Louie's distinctive laugh personified his jovial nature. He always appeared to be happy and content with his life. He had married Longmont's Joann Colburn, and they had set up housekeeping in a small house on a farm that he and his dad, Ted, had purchased, not too far from the river. The year before, my brothers and I had thinned beets on his farm right next to the house, and we grinned and laughed with one another as the two of them passed by in their Chevrolet Fleetline with Joann sitting very close to Louie as if they had just begun dating.

Louie, in his mid-twenties, had a ruddy complexion, which was even more reddened with the summer sun. His infectious smile and his downward arching nose, now scorched by the sun, were prominently featured on his face. Like his brother Eddie, then playing basketball and football for Mead High School, Louie was six feet two or three and weighed a 190 or so pounds. He had played basketball with our brother Jack, and his sister Josephine was a classmate of us triplets. Having taken up farming with his dad, Louie told us that morning, "I've been up since four o'clock—had fifty inches of water comin' from the Highland Ditch—I'm puttin' it on our barley."

It was seven ten when Louie steered off the Washington Highway and turned onto the lane leading into Ted Rademacher's home place, set back about fifty yards. Louie stopped in front of the house long enough for Rollie to put our lunchbox in the shade of the large silver poplars in the front yard. Louie then proceeded further down the lane to the front of the beet field and parked. The four of us slowly and reluctantly emerged from the car.

"See ya at five," said Louie.

Dave placed the water jug in a group of three-foot-tall ironweeds, growing in eminent splendor on the edge of the field. In addition to the cottonwood tree, ironweeds were the dominant native vegetation on farmlands throughout Weld County. They were found everywhere in thriving abundance, eking out their existence in farm yards, on roadsides, near ditch banks, on alkali flats, and in the fields. Their soft, fleshy leaves held erect by stiff branches and a hard stem were constantly replenished with water extracted from the soil by a deep and spread-out root system. Dave tore the stem tops off several of these hardy dark-green weeds and, attempting to keep the water inside cool, placed them around the water jug—thus blocking the sun's rays.

With long-handled hoes in our hands, each of us walked to the beginning of an unthinned beet row. The beet field, comprising a little over eleven acres, began about a half mile from the Washington Highway. Louie had planted this field to sugar beets for his dad in early April. The rows were about a quarter mile long on soil gradually sloping downward toward the east, facilitating easy irrigation flow. They ran perpendicular to the highway, and Louie had planted them twenty inches apart with his dad's tractor-pulled drill. Like all farmers, Louie planted the sugar-beet seed clusters in a dense fashion, with less than one inch between them. Now at end of May, the young seedlings had just emerged to a height of an inch or so above the ground surface. The shoots were surrounded and smothered with weeds of every type, including ironweed, foxtail, bindweed, morning glory, and barnyard grass.

The previous year, Louie had given us a lesson in thinning beets on our first day in the field.

He said, "There are two steps to thinnin'. The first is to leave about eight inches between the seedlings—that's about the width of the blade of your hoe. You need to remove all of the weeds and beet plants in this eight-inch space. Dig your hoe down deep so that you get all of the deep roots. If ya don't, the second hoeing will be a tougher job for ya later."

As Louie talked, he demonstrated with his hoe and moved quickly down the row. He dropped his hoe handle to the ground and bent down to one knee. He hovered over a clump of beet seedlings that he had intentionally left in place.

Louie said, "The second step to thinnin' is to make sure that only one seedling is left between the eight-inch spacing. If you leave more than one, they will be too close together, and the roots won't grow big—they'll be competing with each other for minerals and water."

"The roots are where the sugar is stored," he added. "If they're small, they won't have as much sugar in 'em. We make more money if they are big and have a lotta sugar."

"Come harvest time," Louie said, "we want the beet root to be six or seven inches wide and weigh three or four pounds."

"When I planted these, the seeds were clumped together—sometimes six or seven of them wrapped in a ball. That's the way Great Western gives 'em to us. Some of them separate naturally before planting, but most of them don't," he said.

Louie pulled several seedlings from the clump, leaving only one. I noted that sometimes, instead of bending over to pull out the unwanted seedlings from the clump, Louie would stand upright, placing his hoe precisely and skillfully as he removed extraneous seedlings while leaving one sole survivor. I had tried this procedure myself, but I was not always successful. Often I would inadvertently remove the whole clump with not one seedling left standing. I resorted to stooping with the hoe handle resting on my thigh and thinning the clump to a single seedling with the index finger and thumbs of both hands. With my brothers doing likewise, we found ourselves constantly standing up and bending down as we moved down the row. It was this repetitive up-and-down motion, along with hard digging of the hoe every eight inches down the full length of

Light of Her Children

the row that exhausted us. The tiring and monotonous exercise was eight hours of boredom.

To pass the time, my brothers and I carried on lengthy conversations with one another. With each of us taking a row for ourselves and working at a similar pace, we were all in close proximity.

"Louie said that the goin' rate for thinnin' was still $13.25 an acre," said Richie. "And he told us the other day that there was 'leven an' half acres in this field."

Richie knelt down and began to write the numbers to multiply in the soil between two rows. "That works out to be $152 and thirty-seven cents."

"And we get $7.50 for second hoein'?" I said.

"With three dollars for third hoein'," said Richie, "we should have close to $300 at the end of the summer just from this field."

"Well, ya know Mr. Rademacher wants us to thin another nine acres on down the lane from here," I said. "That'll be some more money for us."

"I hope we can get to 'em soon—it's taken us almost two weeks to get these done—if we wait too long, the weeds will be like small trees down there," I said.

"It could be more than that if we work for Wilbert Peppler," said Rollie. "Las' night he stopped to talk to me when I was coming home from the store, and he wanted to know when we would be finished. I told him by the end of next week. He said he could wait that long and to let him know if we wanted to do it," said Rollie.

Dave said, "Let's don't do it—I want to take some time off before we start the second hoein'. I'm getting tired of doin' this stuff."

Before starting down the row, we each took a giant swig of water. It would be three hours until the next opportunity to take a drink. Doing three rows that morning, we found ourselves on the opposite end of the field, when lunchtime arrived. We had to walk up the lane an additional quarter mile in order to eat in the shade of three large silver poplars in the front yard of the Rademacher home.

We sat on the Rademacher's bluegrass lawn with Long's Peak and Mount Meeker in full view, leaning back against the gray bark of the poplar tree trunks, eating our sandwiches, and taking giant swallows of milk between bites. Although the milk had warmed considerably from the heat of the morning, it still soothed our throats momentarily, and it was a welcome, temporary relief for the constant thirst we experienced throughout the day. The hot, dry air of the morning had literally sucked the moisture from our bodies. Whether in the field or at home, milk and water were our only liquid refreshment. Nehi sodas and Coca-Cola were expensive and were considered to be luxuries in the Newton household. Furthermore, soda was like coffee—it was deemed by Mom not to be fit for youngsters. Rollie, from an early age, had never liked milk, and even though he was thirsty, he gave his jar to Dave after taking only a drink or two.

Dave quickly finished his lunch and then walked along the Washington Highway to see if he could find a cigarette butt or two to smoke. A patrolman stopped to ask him where he was going and offered to give him a ride.

"That's okay," said Dave. "I'm just walkin' up here to go work in the beet field."

Finishing our lunch, we sprawled out on the cool grass of the Rademacher lawn to rest. I laid my head on a large root, elevated at the base of one of three silver poplars surrounding us. I heard the screeching sound of locusts from a location that could not be determined—the sound seemed to be coming from all around me. The intense shrieks were compounded with the droning sound of car and truck tires on the highway pavement just fifty yards away.

High in the silver poplar canopy above me, its maple-like leaves fluttered in the soft breeze, and rays of sunlight shimmered from their silvered undersides. Tiny cotton-like fibers, breaking off from the coats of seeds nestled among the poplar branches, floated softly through the air. There was sudden darkness as an eastward-moving cloud came between the land and the sun, creating the eerie appearance of a blackened landscape scorched by a prairie fire. Toward the mountains and to the west, I saw thunderclouds rising above the croplands, conjuring hope that they perhaps might move in my direction before quitting time.

I was about to doze off when I heard the slam of the screen door on the back of the Rademacher house. Mr. Rademacher was on his way to his pickup—the noon hour was over—it was time for all of us to return to work.

The thinning session that day, long and seemingly never-ending and, like all days in the beet field, was grueling physically and mentally. Scraping and chopping, bending and crouching, and stooping and standing were repeated endlessly. There was always the temptation to rest, but resting was procrastination—resting was allowed only at lunchtime. When one row was finished, we had to immediately start on the next one. If I or my brothers rested at the end of the row, it meant more time in the field and a longer time to complete our chore. Among my brothers and me, resting signified weakness and laziness and was regulated with ridicule and admonishment to "get goin'." If any one of us lagged behind egregiously and did not keep up with the pace established by the others, he was perceived as a slacker and a "deadbeat," and we said so.

"Get off your duff and get goin'," I said to my brothers, taking a rest before starting with a new row.

"Why don't you take a flyin' leap at a rollin' doughnut," said Rollie back to me. "I'm gonna rest here a little bit more—I can catch up with you guys in no time—you're all slower than hell—I can work faster than all of ya."

Our mantra was to work as a team, and all four of us had to carry the load equally. A timely and successful outcome was dependent upon our teamwork. Although two years younger, we triplets expected Dave to perform at the same level as us. Dave was given no special deference as our younger brother; we treated Dave as our equal, both mentally and physically. In the work of hoeing and thinning beets, Dave and we triplets functioned as quadruplets.

At five o'clock, Louie came driving down the lane to take us home. As the four of us climbed into the four-door Hudson, Louie asked, "Well, how many rows did ya get done today?"

Sitting in the front seat, I said, "We all did six—so I guess we got twenty-four done."

"That's a little more than an acre," said Louie. "When I planted that field, I remember that there were nineteen rows to the acre."

That night at the supper table, Mom asked, "Are ya 'bout to get done with that field? Ya been at it for more than a week."

"We still have quite a ways to go," said Richie. "But we got twenty-four rows done today—Louie told us that it's over an acre—matter a fact, it's an acre and a quarter."

"We made about sixteen dollars today," said Rollie.

"That's four dollars apiece for ya," said Mom.

"Yal," said Richie. "We're makin' fifty cents an hour."

"That's more than what Mr. Bunton pays me for weedin' his garden," I said.

That summer, Mr. Rademacher's daughters helped with the thinning. Rita, Theresa, and Josephine, in long-sleeved shirts, jeans, and wide-brimmed straw hats to protect their fair skin from the sun, worked with us for several days.

Moving down the rows, just twenty inches apart, we Newtons and the Rademachers had plenty of opportunities to talk.

I said to Rita one morning, "Our friend Walt Slee took us to the movie last night—we saw the <u>Miracle of Our Lady of Fatima</u>—have you seen it?"

"I saw it last Saturday—I really liked it—those kids were really holy," said Rita.

"Sister Marjorie told us about them in catechism," I said. "She told us that the Virgin Mary appeared to them standin' over a bush. That's exactly how they showed it in the movie."

"I liked it at the end when their friend Hugo saw the vision of Mary, and he too was converted to believing," said Rita.

"In catechism at church, Sister Marjorie told us that we should pray to Mary to convert Russia from Communism. Sister Marjorie said that was what Mary told those kids to do—and that's exactly what they said in the movie."

"They were really scared when she first appeared to 'em," I said. "Boy, I would be too if she appeared to me. When I went to bed last night, I wondered what it would be like if she appeared in the dark in our bedroom. I kept my eyes closed all the time—I was afraid to look."

"I think the oldest girl became a nun in real life," said Rita. "I'd like to be like her—maybe I'll join a convent when I get outta school."

"I think I'd like to be a priest—Sister Marjorie says that nuns and priests come from big families," I said. "You Rademachers have a big family—maybe you're like me."

Unlike our Mexican national counterparts who worked in the beet fields on Sunday, we did not. Sundays were looked forward to with welcome anticipation as a day of relief and escape from the ardors of hoeing beets. On Sunday in early June, we Newtons sat down at our dining-room table to have our customary afternoon dinner. Our guests were Aunt Mary and Uncle Spaulding and their daughter Mary Ellen and son-in-law Dean Maynard. The Maynards were renting a farm near Platteville, where they raised potatoes, corn, tomatoes, and pinto beans.

Sitting all together at our large dining-room table and eating a roast-beef dinner, Dean asked, "I need some help in weeding my tomatoes—would you boys like to hoe them for me?"

"We still have to finish hoein' Mr. Rademacher's sugar beets," I said. "It will probably be a week or so before we get them done."

"We can wait till then," said Dean. "It'll take ya several days—but we can put ya up overnight on the farm."

"Yes," said Mary Ellen. "I've got two sets of bunk beds in the bunkhouse—Dean and I got it all fixed up."

"Sure," said Mom. "They can work for ya—I'm sure Ted Rademacher won't mind if they're a little late startin' with the third hoein'."

This new work assignment was not what my brothers and I wanted to hear. We were looking forward to some time off before we began the third hoeing of Rademacher's beets.

"Mom—call Mary Ellen up, and tell her we can't do it—we need some time off," I said.

"I won't do anything of the kind," said Mom. "You're gonna do it—you owe it to Aunt Mary—it won't hurt you to help Mary Ellen—you don't need to be lyin' around here for a week—if you've got that much time on your hands, I'll put cha to work."

A week and a half later, Dean picked the four of us up in his truck. Rollie rode up in front while Dave, Richie, and I rode in back, sitting in the bed.

"I wish we didn't have to go," said Dave. "I'm tired of workin'."

"Me too," I said. "But Mom says we have to. I don't like stayin' away from home, either—we could be over here for a week."

Dean drove to the tomato field and dropped us off with our hoes. The four of us stood there alone, looking at the expansive growth of weeds spread across the field at least a quarter of a mile in front of us. Giant ironweed and sunflower were standing tall and upright with thistles and clumps of grass in between. Sand burr and bindweed and morning glory were at my feet. Weeds of every type known in Weld County appeared to have invaded Dean's tomato field. Their growth was so tall and so dense I could hardly glimpse a tomato plant.

Light of Her Children

"Goddamn it," said Rollie as Dean drove away, "I don't wanna be here."

"This is a crock a shit," said Dave. "I don't see why Mom's makin' us do it."

"These fuckin' weeds are so big—we're goin' to need a shovel to chop 'em out," said Richie. "We should've brought one with us."

"Dean should'n've waited for us to do this—he could've gotten some Mexicans," I said.

As we looked at the mass of unwanted vegetation that had accumulated over the last two months, unchallenged by machine or by human hands, we were overwhelmed by the task before us. We were certain that this was going to take a lot of work and a lot of time. We knew what it was like to face the challenge of pulling weeds from Mom's strawberry patch, but in our minds, this was worse—this was the most brutal assignment we had ever undertaken.

"This is not fair," said Dave, and he sat down on the sandy ground, put his head in his hands, and sobbed profusely.

Richie started hacking away at the base of a three-foot tall ironweed. "This son-of-a-bitch has roots like a tree," he said.

"Yal, we're goin' to need an axe to chop it down," I said.

"If it were me," said Rollie, "I'd plow this whole thing under—the hell with the goddamn tomatoes."

"I bet Dean makes a lot of money off of these," I said. "Mom says they're expensive at Safeway—she doesn't buy 'em anymore—says she's canned what we need from our garden."

Finally, after a long pause of bitter procrastination, we began to hoe. All four of us worked on the same row. We cussed and chopped, continuing with our complaints to one another about this futile predicament we were in. Suddenly our cursing and whining stopped and changed to outbursts of inane, humorous phrases—we howled with laughter even before the words came out of our mouths.

"Isn't this shittiest mess you've ever seen?" Dave blurted out. "When we finish this, I'm not goin' to eat another fuckin' tomato—these things aren't worth feedin' to the fuckin' pigs." Then he took his hoe and slung it across the field. All four of us could not control ourselves—we wailed and roared, laughing until our eyes watered.

It took us three days to finish that patch of tomatoes. But while there on the Maynard farm, we ate well; our cousin Mary Ellen fed us bacon and eggs and pancakes for breakfast—eggs cooked the way we wanted them. Each day at noon, Dean hauled us back to the house to eat a lunch of soup, sandwiches, potato chips, and soda pop. In the evening, we ate meat and potatoes, corn from the garden, and cake and ice cream. After supper, we watched TV in their living room. We showered in the bunkhouse and slept well every night in its cool confines. Dean paid each of us five dollars a day; we told him to write the check out to Mom—Mom deposited it in Longmont's First National Bank.

The next week, we began the third hoein' of Mr. Rademacher's beets.

Ronnie and Rollie Newton, 1953. *Mead Consolidated Schools Yearbook*

Richie and Dave Newton, 1953. *Mead Consolidated Schools Yearbook*

Frosty Newton, *left*, and Marc Newton, *right*, 1953. *Mead Consolidated Schools Yearbook*

CHAPTER 25

Beet Dividend

My three brothers and I had just finished working in the sugar-beet fields for our employer, Ted Rademacher. We had not been paid all summer long, and we had Mr. Rademacher make out the lump-sum check to Mom. With the school year just about to begin, our neighbor Mrs. Emily Newman gave Mom, Richie, Rollie, Dave, and me a ride to the neighboring town of Longmont so that we could buy new clothes. It was a day that we had looked forward to all summer—a joyful day—we knew we had plenty of money. We had not spent a dime of what we had earned—Mom had deposited it all in Longmont's First National Bank.

Mrs. Newman dropped us off at JC Penney's, the first stop for us. "See you all later," she said. "I'll meet you at four o'clock at the corner of Longmont Drug—we can stop at Safeway for groceries on the way home."

Penney's was the favorite store for all who went to shop in Longmont for clothes. We could be certain if we bought a new shirt at Penney's, a schoolmate would be wearing the same shirt come fall and the start of the school year. I was mesmerized with the newness smell of clothing as the four of us followed Mom to the back of the store where they stacked Penney's Foremost brand of jeans.

Mom made us try on several pairs before she settled on the right size. Mom picked out seven white T-shirts and briefs for each one of us. She pointed to stacks of plaid and striped socks of our size and said, "Pick out which ones you want—get seven pair."

We saw short-sleeved sport shirts made of a fabric that none of us had ever seen; it was crinkled and transparent. See-through sport shirts of every color were hanging on racks everywhere. Mom bought four of them—all of different colors that each of us decided on; I picked a beige one. (When I wore it on the first day of school, Ronald Weber also had on the same shirt of the same color.)

The saleslady wrote out the bill, and Mom wrote the check. The saleslady inserted them both into the cylindrical compartment of the pneumatic transfer tube and pulled the cord. The cylinder zipped along a wire to the cashier sitting in a small cubicle next to the ceiling high above and away from us. While we waited for the receipt to return, the saleslady asked Mom,

"How old are your boys?"

"Three of them will be fourteen next month. The youngest one is twelve."

"So you've got triplets, huh? They all look the same age."

"The youngest one eats more than the other three put together," said Mom. "He eats me out of the house and home."

With sacks of clothes in our arms, the four of us followed Mom to Ralph Miller's Shoe Store. Mom said, "I like going to Miller's—they don't try to sell me shoes that don't fit you birds like the other stores do."

The salesman, Ralph's son, greeted Mom, "Hello, Mrs. Newton—how are you and the boys today?"

"We're all just fine—we want to look at what you have for all four of 'em—we want an oxford in brown."

Measuring Richie's foot, salesman Miller said, "Mrs. Newton, your son's got a narrow foot—looks like he's goin' to need a size 9A."

"They've all got narrow feet," said Mom.

All four of us were intrigued by the x-ray machine that confirmed to Mom that the narrow-width shoes definitely fit us. Mom wrote another check—each pair of shoes cost nine dollars.

We stopped in at Harry O'Lynch's Clothing Store and bought three sport shirts, a green one for me, a blue one for Richie, and a maroon one for Rollie. Dave ended up with a shirt of another completely different design. Mom saw colored T-shirts on sale, so she picked out green, blue, and maroon ones for us triplets and a red one for Dave. She picked up three collared, knit shirts—all of the same color—and placed them on the checkout stand. She said to Dave, "Pick out the color you want—we'll get one for you also."

By now it was three thirty, and the five of us, carrying sacks and boxes, walked to the Longmont Drugstore. Mom bought ice-cream cones for us and a milk shake for herself. At four o'clock, we put all our purchases in the trunk of Mrs. Newman's car, and we headed south on Main Street to Safeway. An hour later, with sacks of groceries and clothes in the backseat with the four of us brothers, Mrs. Newman turned east on to Highway 66.

"Looks like you folks bought a lot of clothes today," said Mrs. Newman.

"Well, enough to keep this bunch goin' till Christmas," said Mom. "The boys have been workin' all summer—saved all their earnings—paid for all the clothes themselves."

"We made $465 this summer," said Richie.

"That's a lotta money," said Mrs. Newman. "Who have you been workin' for?"

"Ted Rademacher," said Richie.

"We also thinned beets for Wilbert Peppler, and we hoed tomatoes for our cousin Mary Ellen," said Dave.

"Yal, we thinned and hoed twenty-three acres of beets," I said. "Took us about two months to get it all done."

"Do you like doin' it?" asked Mrs. Newman.

"Can't say as I do," I responded. "But it's the best-payin' job we've ever had."

"It keeps them busy all summer," said Mom. "If they weren't workin' for Ted and the others, I'd find somethin' for them to do—I could sure keep them busy—and then they wouldn't make anything."

"We still got a lot of money left too," said Rollie. "We didn't spend it all today. It's a good thing too. I still have to buy a pair of cleats for football."

"I don't have to," I said. "I'm not goin' out."

"Me neither," said Richie.

"I gotta buy some new tennis shoes—mine are too small," said Dave.

"You'll all need tennis shoes," said Mom. "You birds are all goin' to have to buy 'em—I don't think Santa Claus is goin' to do it this year," said Mom with a wink and a smile.

"Mrs. Newman—you otta see the new coats that Mom ordered for us triplets from the Denver Dry Goods Co.," I said excitedly. "They're really cool—Mom saw the advertisement in the *Rocky Mountain News*—they're all black and have a thin orange stripe down the side of each sleeve. The inside is lined with orange satin, and we can wear the satin on the outside if we want to. They cost us eleven dollars apiece, which included the mailing charges. We ordered one for Allen Thompson too—his mom gave him eleven dollars, and he gave it to Mom."

"Yal, they're really sharp lookin'," said Richie. "I can hardly wait till it's cold outside so we can wear 'em to school."

"Allen really likes his," said Rollie. "He says he's now one of the Newton quadruplets!"

"I think we could wear them as warm-up jackets for our basketball games," said Richie.

"I think we could too," said Rollie.

"I wish Mike [Eckel] would've bought one," I said. "Then the whole starting five would be wearing 'em."

We saw fields of sugar beets on both sides of us as we moved down the highway. Their large dark-green leaves had grown so large that bare ground could no longer be seen between rows. Only a few tall weeds, missed by the third hoeing workers, were scattered across their leaf canopies. Soon the harvesting machines, pulled and propelled by tractors, would be in these fields. Leafy tops would be severed from roots with spinneret disks as the harvester moved along each row then to be followed by rotating steel claws removing the headless root from the soil. The beets would then be dropped onto conveyer belts and then into the bed of a moving truck. The several-ton loads of beets would then be hauled to the Mead beet dump. I remembered that not long before, my brother Tom was topping beets on Wilbert Peppler's farm, one at time, with a long knife. Now this task was being done with full automation.

I began to think about the upcoming school year as the car sped down Highway 66. I was excited about going back to school with all my new clothes. I was proud that we did not spend all that we had earned and that we would save it to buy school clothes for the following spring. I knew that working in the sugar-beet fields all that summer had made me physically stronger and would help me as a basketball player. For that reason, the physical activity was just as important as the money to me. Although not realizing it back then, there were psychological payoffs for basketball as well. We had learned that we had to be tenacious and steadfast in accomplishing our task—a job not done meant no pay. The work created a mental toughness in us—no work challenge was so great that we could not overcome it, but to get done, we had to work together—teamwork was required. Each day we had to face adversity, and we could not shrink from it.

Later in the year, in the first week of October, the beet harvest began all over Weld County. Truckloads of sugar beets traveled down country roads to Great Western Sugar Co. dumping stations scattered throughout the county; one such station was the Mead dump located on the east side of the Great Western Railway track that ran diagonally across the southeast corner of town and connecting Johnstown with Longmont. Drivers from farms within a ten-mile radius of Mead lined their trucks up, waiting to have their beet loads weighed on the large wood platform scale. With their tonnage recorded by the Great Western attendant, they moved their trucks forward twenty or so yards to stop next to a large metal bin. Another GW attendant unchained the truck sideboard, and while the engine ran, the driver put the hydraulic lift system in gear, tilting the floor of the truck bed to a sixty-degree angle and sliding the load into the live-bottom of the bin, a conveyer belt of chain metal. The beets were conveyed up a tall, silver-painted shoot extending forty or so feet into the sky, at the top of which the beets tumbled off the belt and onto the ever-enlarging pile. By Thanksgiving, the beet pile was enormous, extending to a length of a sixteenth of a mile and to a height of more than three stories.

To my brothers and me, the beet pile was an awesome display of Weld County agriculture, a giant mound of harvest created every year by the efficiently run network of the sugar-beet enterprise. Millions of individual beige-colored, cone-shaped roots, separated from their stems and leaves in the fields of farmers all around Mead, were now piled one on top of the other into a tall mountain—a lofty mound that we wanted to climb.

Richie, Rollie, Dave, and I rode our bikes to the base of the pile. It was a ritual each year for us to climb to the top. Beets slid from underneath our feet and rolled downward a short distance with each step. At the top, we majestically looked eastward across the rolling prairie grassland on Louie Roman's farm, beyond which the land sloped downward toward the Saint Vrain River, several miles away, but which we couldn't see. Eighteen-wheelers, some with the big letters PIE (Pacific Intermountain Express) on their sides rolled down the Washington Highway in north and south directions, with their horns and the sound of their wheels on the pavement singing loudly. We could see fields to the south where sugar beets had once been grown. To the north, we could see a barren beet field next to the highway—beets had already been removed, and the field was now ready to be plowed and converted to next year's planting of a different crop. Cattle were now on the denuded beet fields, feeding on the leftover and wilted greenish-brown leaf tops of sugar beets lying on the ground, from which below the sugared root had been dug. Beyond the horizon and beyond where our eyes could see were hundreds of empty sugar-beet fields spread across Weld County, their crop now being washed, sliced, and fed into the boilers of sugar factories in Windsor, Eaton, Greeley, and Fort Lupton.

"Let's eat one of these things," said Richie.

He took out a rusted pocket knife he had found in the alleyway and split one open. I saw a tiny central ring surrounded by a thick cortex of tissue impregnated with a crystalline substance reflecting the sunlight; I assumed it was the sugar. With happy expectation, we each took slivers of the root flesh and placed a tiny morsel in our mouths.

"God, that's shitty tastin'," said Rollie.

"You got that right," I said. "I was expectin' it to be much sweeter."

"Yal, it's bitter as hell," said Richie, puckered with disappointment.

All of us, except Dave, spit out the pulp.

"It ain't bad," said Dave as he kept chewing. Dave would eat anything—it all tasted good to him.

"Let's take some home to Bossie," said Dave. "Mom sez cows like eating the beets as well as the tops."

We descended the pile, beets sliding from under our feet, forcing us to sit abruptly several times before we could reach the ground. We each took a beet in one hand as we rode home. Bossie seemed contented as she chewed on them—she was experiencing a food she had before never tasted. I wondered if the taste to her was sweet rather than sour, as it was to me.

JC Penney Co., Longmont, CO, circa 1950. *Longmont Museum and Cultural Center*

Sugar beets in five months, Mead, CO, 2014. Sheila Koenig.

Sugar-beet piling, Mead, CO, 2004. Sheila Koenig

Emily Newman, 1953. *Mead Consolidated Schools Yearbook*

Chapter 26

Up the Mountain

It was five thirty on late Saturday afternoon of the Memorial Day weekend, and my two triplet brothers and Dave and I were arriving home in Louie Rademacher's car after working in the beet field. This was the second week that we had been working, and we were looking forward to the two-day weekend. Colorado's trout season had opened the weekend before, and for the first time that year, we were going fly-fishing on Rock Creek and on the North Saint Vrain River. We would be spending the night in the cabin of our friend Walt Slee in Allenspark—high up in the Rocky Mountains. Our brother Jerry would not be going with us—he was working on Wilbert Peppler's farm, and Wilbert wanted him to work on Memorial Day.

    Walt Slee was a generous and trusted friend of my brothers and me. When we triplets were ten years of age, we were introduced to him by our brother-in-law Dale French. Dale had known Walt all his life—both of them grew up in Longmont. Walt had taken Dale and his friends fishing when Dale was in his early teens. Walt was a scoutmaster at heart but did not have the time or the patience for the organized aspects of scouting. Walt's father had introduced him to fly-fishing and to the mountain outdoors at an early age, and Walt received great

Light of Her Children

personal satisfaction in seeing others experience the same joy that he did. Walt had introduced many youngsters to the art of fly-fishing, many who were disadvantaged and who prospered from the experience. One of them was Marv Cinnamon, who grew up in a home with no father.

Walt told us, "Marv was a good fly fisherman—he'd go off by himself—one time he started off at Wild Basin and fished the North all the way down to Rock Creek and then fished it up to Ferncliff."

Walt added, "Marv's goin' to Colorado State College of Education now—sez he wants to teach—but said he might become a doctor if his grades are good enough."

Walt's character and behavior were impeccable—he never swore or judged others. Although he was a spiritual man, he was not conventionally religious. He was brought up in the Congregational Church but did not attend regularly, preferring to spend his weekends in the mountains in his cabin in Allenspark.

Said Walt, "My church each Sunday is the amphitheater of trees, streams, and mountains." However, he respected Mom's dictum that my brothers and I must go to church on Sunday.

Walt had served in the army during World War II, and when he returned to Longmont, he took a job as a salesperson at Lewis Furniture on Main Street. With a strong interest in sports, he started to referee basketball games in the evenings. One night after a ball game, while descending a set of cement steps down to the locker room, he tripped and fell. He landed on his knees and broke both kneecaps. The doctors removed both of them, but his mobility was greatly inhibited thereafter. This mishap caused him constant pain, and it greatly restricted his mountain-hiking and fly-fishing activities.

In his fifties, Walt rented a room from on Longmont's Kimbark Street. With no cooking facilities, he ate every meal during the week at a restaurant. Short—and now rotund—Walt had taken on the build of a Coca-Cola Santa Claus, and inside his compact frame was the same kind and generous heart of the jolly old Christmas elf himself. Walt always shared his resources and was happy and jovial—to Walt, every day was Christmas.

For Christmas, Walt had given each one of us a fly rod and a reel and line, and we were eager to try our new equipment for the first time. Designed for kids, our fly rods were shorter than the standard size. Said Walt, "Chick Clark, the salesman at Longmont Sporting Goods, said that he liked to use the short rod himself. He said that when you're in amongst a lot of willows and brush, it's good to have a short rod.

I told him that I thought that they would be just perfect for fishing on Rock Creek. It'll be easier for you guys when you're fishin' a small stream."

All four of us were well equipped fly fisherman—for our birthdays, Walt had given each of us rubber hip boots and a canvas creel.

Walt told us that he would pick up some flies and leaders for us at Longmont Sporting Goods but we would need some worms.

He said, "It's early in the season, and the stream will be high and muddy. The fish can't see the fly as well, so you might have better luck with worms."

"I don't care what time of the season it is," said Richie. "I'm always going to use worms. I don't like to use flies."

Walt said, "You can dig for worms by the side of the stream, but it would save time to dig some beforehand."

So Richie and I paid our younger brothers Marc and Frosty each a quarter to dig night crawlers for us.

"We'll have to dig them from Mamie Akers's swamp," said Marc. "Or maybe near Mr. Gettman's irrigation ditch."

"I HOPE MARC AND FROSTY DUG THOSE WORMS FOR US," SAID RICHIE AS LOUIE RADEMACHER PULLED INTO OUR YARD.

"Where ya goin' fishin'?" asked Louie.

"We're goin' to fish Rock Creek and the North Saint Vrain up in the mountains," said Richie. "We're goin' to be up there for two days—we're leavin' tonight."

I said good-bye to Louie, and as I opened the car door, I announced to my brothers, "Dibs on being first to take a bath."

"I'm second," said Richie.

I walked into the kitchen, where Mom was taking a pan of chocolate-chip cookies out of the oven.

"What time is Walt pickin' us up?" I asked.

"He just called and said he would be there about seven," answered Mom. "He said he was going to stop by right after work and pick up some groceries first."

Mom had a large pressure cooker of pinto beans cooking on the stove, and that afternoon, she had baked three pans of rolls and eight loaves of bread.

"Hurry and get cleaned up," said Mom. "The beans are ready."

With all the preparations that Mom, my brothers, and I had to do, we had to forego the customary sit-down-together dinner.

At 7:15 p.m., Walt drove into the yard in his four-door '53 Chevrolet. My brothers and I then began carrying clothes, shoes, boots, rods, reels, creels, and night crawlers to Walt's car. Walt had to rearrange two tents he had borrowed as well as some of the groceries in order to make room for all the belongings and fishing gear, including two backpacks that Richie and I had crafted from wood lathes and old leather belts.

"I borrowed a couple a backpacks too," said Walt. "What we can't carry with them, we can put in our creels."

Mom carried a flat cake pan of chocolate-chip cookies, a loaf of her fresh-baked bread, and a jar of her strawberry preserves outside and handed them to Walt.

"Great," said Walt. "Those cookies will be our dessert down on Rock Creek tomorrow, and we'll make some toast out of this bread for breakfast tomorrow morning."

With clothes and gear loaded, Walt said, "We'll be back Monday night about nine or ten o'clock. It will be late when we hike out of Rock Creek."

"I'll just look for you when I see you," said Mom. "You boys behave," she said. "And bring home a big mess of fish."

We drove out of Mead and onto Highway 66 and then headed west toward the foothills and the town of Lyons.

Walt said, "I picked up some potato chips—I know Rollie likes them. I got tuna fish and pickle relish for our sandwiches, and apples and oranges. We'll have pancakes for breakfast tomorrow morning before we go fishin'. We'll take eggs and bacon for breakfast on Monday morning. We'll have them along with the fish we catch. I've got plenty of cornmeal and butter to fry 'em. We'll have hot dogs and beans tomorrow night on the Creek. I bought peanut butter and an extra loaf of bread for lunch sandwiches on Monday. With Hershey candy bars and cookies, we'll have plenty to eat. And oh yes, I also got a couple of rolls of toilet paper."

By the time we left Lyons to head up the South Saint Vrain canyon, Rollie and Dave, who were in the backseat with me, had fallen asleep. I, sandwiched between them, remained awake—I was beginning to experience the backseat syndrome of gettin' sick.

Walt pulled out a cigar from his shirt pocket, pushed the cigarette lighter in to heat up, and as he peeled the cellophane wrapper off his Roi-Tan, he announced, "I'll open my window wing here to let the smoke out so it won't bother you guys."

We followed the South Saint Vrain River on Highway 7, which took us through the rock-walled canyons of the Little and Big Narrows. With Walt's maneuvering and negotiating of the car around abrupt and sharp curves in the highway, my whole body rocked from side to side. Not wanting to bump into my brothers sleeping on both sides of me, I tried to remain stationary, but my torso moved back and forth ever so slightly, rolling my head from side to side as it rested on the seat back.

Adding to my dizzied, light-headed sensation was Walt's cigar smoke which had found its way to the back of the car—suddenly I was unbearably nauseated.

I said to myself, *Hang on, hang on, if you can—don't throw-up—hang on until we stop in Allenspark.* I wanted Walt to stop immediately so that I could get out of the car and walk around for a minute or two. However, I didn't want to admit that I was sick, and I also knew that everyone wanted to get up the mountain as soon as possible—none of them would want to stop. Passing the community of Raymond, I knew that we had at least another fifteen minutes to go before we got to Allenspark. I had experienced this nauseated feeling many times but never before had I thrown up—I hoped that tonight would not be the first time.

It was dark when we arrived in Allenspark and stopped at Crystal Springs to fill a large five-gallon can with water. I immediately got out of the car and walked several yards into the darkness and puked my supper of beans and bread on the side of the road where neither Walt nor my brothers could see me.

Walt left the car lights on so he could see as he held the top opening of the can underneath the pipe carrying the cool water from the spring's aquifer below. The cabin had no running water or indoor plumbing, so Crystal Springs's water would have to serve our needs for drinking and for washing ourselves and the dishes.

With us all back in the car, we drove two miles southeast of Allenspark on an abandoned ski-slide road, and Walt brought his car to a halt to put his standard-shift car into low gear so we could drive up the hill and park right next to his cabin. When parked, my brothers and I emerged from the car and waited while Walt, with flashlight in hand, found the keyhole to the front door. He went inside to the breaker box located in the kitchen, and soon lights inside and outside were on. We then carried our food and belongings in.

"Ronnie, can you and Richie get the fireplace fire started?" Walt asked.

"You betcha," I said. "I'll get some pine needles and twigs from outside—Richie, you can get the newspapers and matches."

I placed the needles and twigs on top of the wadded newspaper that Richie had placed in the iron cradle grate of the native stone fireplace, located in the corner of the small central living room. Richie lit the newspaper, and when the needle and twig tinder was aflame, he placed sticks of dried aspen branches on top—they caught fire immediately. With flames thrusting high up into the chimney, he then put on two shortened pine logs that Walt had gathered from the ski-slide area. In minutes, their bark caught fire, and soon thereafter, their wood was alight. Odors of smoke and pine resin began to fill the room, and the heat of the fire became so intense Richie and I had to step back away from it.

Walt lit two portable kerosene heaters and placed one in the bedroom and another in the living room. Within thirty minutes, the whole cabin was heated, including the small kitchen off to the side of the living room.

As my brothers and I sat next to the fire, enjoying its warmth, Walt came up to us with a sack in his hand and said, "Here's some leader material and some flies I bought for you guys. Each of you ought to tie up a couple of leaders with flies before you go down the creek tomorrow—it will save you lots of time."

"Thanks, Walt," I said. "What kinda flies did you buy?"

"I got Rio Grande Kings, black gnats, mosquitoes, and grasshoppers," said Walt. I also bought several Royal Coachmans, and there's a couple of Gray Hackles with a Yellow Body in there as well. I got some hooks too if you want to fish with worms."

"What are these bead-headed-lookin' flies in here?" asked Dave as he poured the contents of the sack onto the coffee table.

"Those are supposed to look like insect larvae," said Walt. "Chick Clark at Longmont Sporting Goods said they work real well in muddy water. He said you want to fish them on the bottom. So I got some lead shot to weight them down in the water."

"This one looks like an ant," said Dave, holding it up for all to see. "I didn't know that fish ate ants."

"That's called an Adam's Ant," said Walt. "Chick Clark said it worked for him—told me to try it."

Having assembled our leaders and flies together, my brothers and I were ready for bed—the work in the beet field that day had tired us.

"I want to sleep out here in front of the fireplace," I said.

"So do I," said Dave.

"Okay," said Walt. "Richie, you and Rollie can take one bed in the bedroom, and I'll take the other."

Needing to relieve myself, I went outside, walking several yards away from the cabin, glimpsing the stars through the needled branches of ponderosa that huddled around the cabin. Clad in T-shirt and jeans and feeling the cool night air on my arms and shoulders, I shivered momentarily and breathed deeply, taking in the intoxicating fragrances of vanilla, phenol, and butterscotch, volatilized from the trunks and needles of the forty or fifty trees surrounding me. Now wet from the flowing stream of my urine, the sand and rocks at my feet glistened with light from the full moon above me. Below me and thirty feet away, the tall ponderosa cast long shadows down the mountainside onto an incline, sparsely covered with tufts of grass and low-lying shrubs of juniper. There, a small cottontail, nibbling on a tasty tufted morsel and suddenly startled by my appearance, scampered under a branch of juniper for cover. Then I could hear only the soft whisper of wind stirring through the trees—nothing else—I was struck by the profound silence of the forest around me—except for the wind, the mountain world was still.

Dave and I bedded down on the folded-down couch right next to the fireplace in the living room. Walt worked in the kitchen placing all the groceries in the cupboard and in the refrigerator. He yelled to everybody from the kitchen, "Church at Saint Malo's is at eight thirty in the morning, so I will get you up at seven thirty! We only have about eight or ten miles to drive, so we should have plenty of time."

I watched the fire blaze and listened to the crackling of the logs as they burned furiously. I lay on my back with hands joined on my belly and said my prayers. I recited the Our Father, the Act of Contrition, a Hail Mary, and a Glory Be.

"Say your prayers, Dave," I whispered. My words were all for naught—Dave was already asleep.

I lay awake watching the fire and listening to its snapping and crackling as red and white sparks flew up the chimney. I thought how the next two days were going to be great fun for my brothers and me—for two days, we would not be staring down rows of sugar beets under the hot sun—instead, we would be in the forest shade or standing in the cooling waters swirling around our rubber-booted legs and feet. I looked forward once again to reliving that exciting moment when a trout would suddenly strike a fly I had laid on the moving water surface above him. I recalled when I hooked my first fish—I lost it—I had not given that extra jerk that was needed to set the hook into the trout's mouth. I recalled my disappointment. But in just a few minutes, I too was asleep.

On CO 66 with front range of Rocky Mountains and Mount Meeker and Long's Peak in background, 2004. Sheila Koenig

St. Vrain River near Lyons, CO, on CO 7 in Roosevelt National Forest, 2013. Sheila Koenig

L–R: Ronnie, Richie, and Rollie Newton, 1950. *Newton Family Album*

Chapter 27

Down the Creek

My three brothers and I were still asleep when Walt Slee arose Sunday morning to start a fire in the kitchen stove of his cabin. He then started another fire in the fireplace. He made a pot of coffee for himself and put a teakettle of water on the stove to boil. He knew that my brothers and I would not be eating or drinking before we went to church. Beginning at midnight, we were to fast from everything, even water.

At eight ten, we were in the car, descending the hill and taking the sandy road toward Allenspark and Highway 7. As we drove back on to Colorado 7 and headed west—there in front of us was the magnificent view of the bulging cone shape of Copeland Mountain. We drove by a broken-down remnant of a native stone fireplace standing as a monument in a grass flatland park just a couple of miles from Allenspark.

"There's Allen's fireplace," said Richie as we passed by the spot where Alonzo Allen built his cabin. Allen was a miner who came to Colorado during the Gold Rush in the late eighteen hundreds. He was a squatter on the grassy meadow that surrounded his cabin—nevertheless, his home site became known as Allenspark.

Light of Her Children

At the base of Copeland Mountain, we veered north and crossed over Fox Creek, a small stream that merged with Rock Creek about a mile and a half east of the highway.

"I remember catching a fish in that creek way up here," said Richie. "Walt dropped Dave and me off there one Sunday afternoon to fish. It was a brook—'bout six inches long—caught 'im with a worm. I'm goin' to catch another one outta Fox when we fish it this afternoon—you just watch me."

After several miles, we came to the creosoted wood log sign that said Wild Basin in big white block letters. We crossed over the North Saint Vrain River that was hidden from view by willows, which extended thirty or forty yards on either side of it.

"I don't like to fish the North up here in Wild Basin," said Walt. "I don't like fightin' the willows. There's so many of 'em—they're tough to walk through. I like to fish the North, where we're goin' tomorrow—there's fewer willows there—where we're goin' is just a couple of miles down the river from here."

Leaving the Basin, we turned north on Highway 7 and headed northwest toward Estes Park. Several miles further, we saw the sign that said Camp Saint Malo was just ahead of us. As we came around a wide curve of the highway, we saw a white statue of Jesus, standing on a rock on a high hill, arms stretched outward up into the sky—welcoming us to the sacred grounds of Camp Saint Malo. Right below the statue was the small chapel of St. Catherine, built on top of large granite outcropping almost completely surrounded by a pool of water. The pond had resulted from a widening of Cabin Creek, originating in the high elevations of Mount Meeker, which majestically overlooked the camp and chapel directly at its base. The water of Cabin Creek was moving slowly through the pond, exiting as a small stream flowing under the highway. Standing nobly on a large boulder surrounded by water of the reflecting pond, the chapel's walls of granite glistened in the morning sun.

"There it is," said Walt, "right on top of that the rock that the Highway Department wanted to dynamite when they were widening the road. I guess the priest who wanted the chapel built on that rock had to really fight to keep them from blowin' it all to smithereens."

We crossed over Cabin Creek and turned left onto the gravel road taking us through the Camp Saint Malo archway. Walt parked the car in the parking lot in front of the chapel entrance. As I got out of the car and looked to the west, I saw all of Mount Meeker with the morning sunlight gleaming from snow-covered, rocky surfaces high above the timberline. With the light snow that had just fallen, Mount Meeker's familiar midrib chasm separating two rock ridges on each side was now most prominent.

"I'll pick you up about nine fifteen," said Walt. "I'm goin' back to the cabin to get breakfast ready for us and to do some packin' and gettin' things ready for our campout on Rock Creek."

My three brothers and I entered the chapel—it was cool inside, and I was glad that I had put on my sweatshirt. The church floor, like the steps up to the chapel, was covered with red flagstone. I genuflected and knelt down on a wooden kneeler between two pews. As I looked ahead, I saw the familiar carved wood statues on each side of the altar, one of St. Catherine and the other of Jesus Christ. St. Catherine, holding a crucifix, was centered in a stained-glass window just over the altar. Sister Marjorie had told us about St. Catherine in our catechism class. She said that St. Catherine was an Italian woman who experienced stigmata, the "wounds of the crucified Christ" in her own hands and feet.

I had just finished saying the Our Father when the bell from within the sacristy rang, and the presiding priest entered in to the area of the altar, followed by a young man of college age, dressed in his street clothes. The priest introduced himself.

Light of Her Children

"Good morning to all of you," he greeted. "I am Father Edward Baraco from the Catholic Archdiocese of Denver, and I am the religious coordinator here at Camp Saint Malo."

He welcomed all of us visitors and then said, "Tomorrow is Memorial Day, the day when we remember those who have made the ultimate sacrifice for our country—so let's begin the Mass by singing 'America the Beautiful.'"

With more than forty of us in the chapel, we began singing the words, "Oh beautiful for spacious skies." When we had sung all three verses, Father Baraco and the server, with their backs to the congregation, knelt down and began reciting the introductory Latin prayers of the Mass. Shortly thereafter, Father Baraco went to the small podium to read the Gospel and address the congregation with his homily. He focused once again on the memory of the war dead and the greatness of America.

"We are here in Colorado, the location where Katharine Lee Bates was inspired to write the well-known poem 'America the Beautiful' many, many years ago—long before her words were put to music. It was while standing on the top of Pike's Peak," said Father Baraco, "when Ms. Bates was looking out on to the Eastern Colorado plains that she became so inspired and later described that experience with the words to her famous poem."

"There's a beautiful phrase in that poem that is very familiar to you and me," added Father Baraco. "It reminds us in words of what we Coloradoans see each day from our homes all along the Front Range of the Rockies. These words are:

> For purple mountains' majesties
> Above the fruited plain.

"Year after year," said Father Baraco, "we Coloradoans stand on the plains down below amongst the fruits of the farm harvest and see the mountains rising gloriously from the earth in purple magnificence in front of us."

"We Coloradoans stand amongst the amber waves of grain and look with awe at the mountains," added Father Baraco. "The plains where we stand are blessed with the fruits of the farmer's labor, the crops of sugar beets, corn, and wheat. They are the things that end up on our dinner table."

Father Baraco's remarks reminded me that Long's Peak, Mount Meeker, and the Twin Sisters were always in full view for me to see in their violet-colored splendor. They were always there, standing majestically before my brothers and me as we stood on the plains, working on farmlands, helping to produce and harvest the fruits—the crop fruits that were so prevalent all over the northeastern plains of Weld County.

Said Father Baraco, "God has established a unique relationship between the mountains and the plains—he has connected them with rivers and streams, carrying the water that nourishes the sugar beets, the grain, and the corn—the crops now so abundant on the fruited plains."

He said, "Let us remember that God has not only provided us with a harvest of prosperity on the irrigated fruited plain, but he has also provided us with a sense of wonder and awe as we gaze at the beautiful mountains. All of you visitors out there this morning stood on those very plains and looked to the west and marveled. And now this morning, you are here in the midst of those mountains, basking in their beauty and grandeur."

Father Baraco added, "God has given us a special quality of life here in Colorado, here in beautiful America. This weekend, we memorialize those who gave their lives fighting to preserve this life. Those fallen soldiers have preserved a quality of life that all Coloradoans and all Americans today can enjoy and cherish."

"Let us give thanks for the fallen war dead," continued Father Baraco. "They have allowed us each day to continue to see those 'Purple mountain majesties above the fruited plain.'"

My brothers and I and the rest of the congregation received Communion, and when the Mass was finished, we exited rapidly from the chapel to get in Walt's car parked in the same spot where he had dropped us off. Walt was smoking his cigar and reading the *Denver Post*.

"That was quick," he said.

"Yes, it was," I said. "The priest had a short sermon. He talked about Memorial Day and America. At the beginning of the Mass, we sang 'America the Beautiful.'"

"That's a purty song," said Walt. "I really like to hear it when it's sung by the opera star Marian Anderson or the Mormon Tabernacle Choir. It makes the hair stand up on the back of my neck."

"I bet you guys are thirsty and hungry, ain' cha?" stated Walt. "I've got the sausage fried and the pancake batter ready, and with Crystal Springs water, I made a pitcher of orange juice from the can of concentrate."

In fifteen minutes, the four of us were sitting at the kitchen table, each taking a turn to receive a plate of pancakes that Walt cooked for us in a large iron skillet. While waiting for pancakes, we ate sausage and slices of buttered toast made with Mom's fresh bread and topped with her strawberry preserves.

Walt made plenty of pancakes, and he said, "If we don't eat all of 'em, we'll throw them outside so the birds can eat 'em."

Dave ate eight or nine large ones smothered with syrup and then slathered a tenth one in butter and devoured it. When all of us were finished, Rollie and I washed and dried the dishes while Dave and Richie made the tuna-fish and pickle-relish sandwiches. We gathered all the food we were going to take with us on the kitchen table, and from the bottom cupboard, Walt got a large blue-and-white-speckled enameled frying pan that we needed for frying fish and bacon and for scrambling eggs when we were down on Rock Creek.

"Go ahead and load all the food in the car," Walt said. "We'll divide it up to carry in with us when we get to Ferncliff."

Walt said, "Make sure you got all your stuff, because we won't be coming back here tomorrow. We'll head home as soon as we walk out from Rock Creek."

Richie put out the fires in the fireplace and kitchen stove with water. Walt flipped all the circuit breakers, pulled the drapes over the picture window on the front porch, and locked the front door.

It was a short five minute ride down to the small village of Ferncliff. Walt had long-standing permission from Chris Swenson to park his car next to Swenson's Sinclair Gas Station and Garage. Rock Creek ran through Ferncliff, and we would follow its watercourse all the way down to the North Saint Vrain. With short pieces of rope, we attached our boots, sleeping bags, and tents to our backpacks. We attached the frying pan to Dave's pack and the aluminum kettle to Rollie's. Walt packed all his gear into a green canvas backpack that he had used in the army, along with most of our food. We divided the sandwiches, candy, oranges, and cookies and stuffed them into our creels. Walt carried his hip boots, rolled tightly and held with a leather belt in one hand and his rod in the other. Although the loads we carried were heavy and cumbersome, the hike to the camping site along Rock Creek was just a mile, so our physical toil and pain would be short-lived.

We helped each other slip our arms through the shoulder strap loops of our backpacks and mount them on our backs. With our assembled rods and reels in our hands, we walked across Highway 7 to a large grassy meadow area on the other side. Rock Creek, originating south of Allenspark, flowed under the highway and cut its way through the meadow and moved toward a deep, rock-walled canyon about a quarter of a mile away. Constant creek overflows had produced the fertile soil that supported a lush green growth of timothy grass. This triangular meadow, covering several acres, was surrounded on two sides by hills of juniper and sagebrush, with the third bordered by a barbed-wire fence that paralleled the highway.

Across the meadow to its furthermost point and next to the canyon walls was a grove of willows. With hundreds of white blossoms on every branch, the willows stood out in the landscape. Warblers perched momentarily on their tops, the birds' tiny green and yellowish forms moved restlessly from one branch to another, hardly stopping as they moved across the grove, snapping at insects in the open air, and pecking them from leaves and branches when alighting momentarily.

At the edge of the meadow was a barbed-wire fence. I held the barbed-wire strands apart with one foot and one hand and waited while Dave crawled through. Likewise, Dave reciprocated so that I could climb through to the other side. Once across the fence, all five of us walked along the side of the hill for about a quarter of a mile on a sandy trail etched among the juniper and sagebrush. The trail was used by cattle that wandered down the creek to forage and was covered with cow patties. With our pathway elevated above the meadow and willows, we saw Rock Creek making its way to the mouth of the canyon. Among the willows, we could see where the creek widened into large pools of still water. Beaver had constructed dams of aspen trunks and branches, slowing and spreading out the water flow for stretches of thirty to forty yards. The five of us stopped for moment to watch trout coming to the top of the pond, grabbing floating insects, and leaving behind rings of water that rippled outward from the point of the trout's intrusion of the pond's placid surface.

Walt commented, "Some of us will most likely be back here to fish these ponds tonight, and we'll try to catch some of those critters in there."

"Remember to stand below the dam and drop your worm or fly just on the other side," Walt reminded us. "That's where the water will be the deepest, and that's where the fish will be."

"What kinda fish do ya think are biting out there right now?" I asked Walt.

"Those rings on the water look pretty small to me—most likely they're made by tiny brooks," replied Walt. "But there will be some big ones in there as well—most likely browns. Just don't let 'em see you—you'll scare them away."

We resumed our hike down the trail and down the creek. Cattle, chewing on the luxuriant timothy, stared at us as we walked by. Richie took the lead as we walked, and he set the pace. Turning around and yelling back at the others, he said, "I get the first chance to fish the pool when we get to Fox Creek."

Walt yelled back to him, "Are you fishin' with worms or flies? If it's worms, you better let someone with flies go first. With flies, you don't have to get as close to the pool as you do with worms. You don't want the fish to see you, and you scare them away so the next fisherman won't be effective."

"You know me!" Richie yelled back. "I'm fishin' with worms."

"I've got a fly on already," said Dave. "Let me go first."

Passing the grove of willows, we came to the point where the sagebrush hill transitioned into a narrow rock-walled canyon, about two hundred feet high on each side. The hard granite had been sliced open by the moving water of Rock Creek, over thousands and thousands of years of time, and the rock walls were covered with lichens in shades of pink, blue, white, yellow, and gold.

With the canyon narrowing, the sandy trail began to cut through a bed of tall wheatgrass and skyline-blue grass, which stretched from the wall to the creek. The smell of peppermint plants permeated the air. Sedges and rushes were dispersed among the tall grasses along the creek, tucked in between occasional alders and maples. We crossed over broad areas of sand and rock, surrounded by wide-trunked ponderosa and pocket stands of blue spruce and aspen.

Shrubs of antelope brush, raspberry, chokecherry, and kinnikinnick grew profusely over the trail, catching on our clothes, fishnets, and our backpacks and snagging hooks and flies on our rods. Their countless flowers of white, pink, and yellow, along with the brilliantly pink flowers of primrose and mountain ball cactus, indicated that spring had arrived even deep in the canyon. Sometimes the trail took us right next to the creek where we saw water ouzels diving underwater, feeding on mayflies and midges. Black garter snakes glided through and out of silent pockets of water, winding their way into the nearby grass, avoiding us intruders invading their peaceful habitat.

Chickadees and vireos, seemingly advancing ahead of us from bush to bush, kept their distance from our entourage and then suddenly reversed their direction and flew over us, flitting from one aspen tree to another. Sapsuckers and flycatchers maintained refuge in the tall aspens, while blue birds and wrens perched in branches of ponderosa. The chorus of bird calls was like a choir singing to the accompanying musical sounds of the creek as it tumbled rhythmically over rocks and logs and danced down the canyon.

We continued down the trail for another thirty minutes and, by then, had walked just over a mile from the highway and Ferncliff. Suddenly, we heard Richie yell out, "Here's Fox Creek!"

"Okay," said Dave. "Let me try the pool first."

We took our backpacks off and set them down. Walt sat down on a large rock and lit up a cigar. There, about 150 feet above us and highlighted by the clear blue sky behind it was the large V that Fox Creek had carved in the top of the canyon wall and through which the water of Fox Creek descended into a fall of thirty or more feet before splashing into a large pool below. The pool itself had been hewn out in a large rock formation, created by the constant pounding of the water as it dropped from above. The pool, elevated fifty feet above us, could not be seen, but we could see water flowing over the front edge of the sculpted rock dam that temporarily held the water back. Leaving the pool, Fox Creek then flowed another thirty yards before it merged into Rock Creek.

Dave ascended to the right side of the pool and stood back from it about ten yards. He had a wide open space behind where he stood, free of trees and brush, and where he could whip his fly line backward and then move it forward between two ponderosas, growing twenty yards apart. Walt had taught my brothers and me to use two flies separated by eighteen inches and attached to a three-foot leader at the end of our fishing lines. Walt always fished with a Rio Grande King, and he said to place it on the top.

"What cha got on there?" Walt asked Dave.

"A Rio Grande King and a Royal Coachman," said Dave.

Dave's first cast placed the flies in the middle of the pool, and he let them flow downward. He let the flies float over the front ledge of the dam and into the creek below. Dave tried the same location again several times, but nothing stirred any interest from the fish. He then cast to his right and placed both flies at the back of the pool, right next to the splashes of the falling water. The King and Coachman danced and swirled violently as the water dropped from above with a powerful force. For a moment, Dave could not see the flies as they circled about in the white foam of the churning water. Soon they emerged floating gently outward to his right on the surface of calmer water. Suddenly, Dave felt the tug on his line as a small brown lunged through the surface to latch on to the King. Instinctively, Dave yanked and set the hook solidly in the fish's mouth.

He yelled out excitedly, "Hey, I got one!"

The fish fought valiantly as it moved toward the swift-moving water, but Dave quickly shortened his line and guided the fish back to the quiet water on the right side of the pool. Knowing that he could not move into the water to net the fish for fear of disturbing other fish that still might be there, he then quickly yanked the attached fish out of the water and "dry-docked" it in the middle of a tall stand of wheatgrass. He ran over and grabbed the struggling fish with both hands.

"It's a nice one!" Dave exclaimed. "It's a German brown, about eight or nine inches long—caught him on the King. I'll keep him—we can eat 'im tonight."

Dave took the fish into his right hand and slammed its head on the handle of his fly rod several times. He took everything out of his creel and placed several handfuls of moist wheatgrass into it. He placed the fish in the creel and surrounded it with grass.

"Richie," said Walt, "it's now your turn—I bet there's still fish in there. Maybe, they'll take a worm."

Richie walked up to the pool and anchored his right foot on the soil incline right below the rock dam. His head was where he could just peer over the dam and see the pool surface. He had threaded a large night crawler on a hook that was weighted down with several lead beads attached to the leader, just above the snell of the hook. With the end of his rod right in front of him and extending over the rock dam, he swung the bait forward and let it gently down in the water about six feet above the dam. The slow movement of the water carried the night crawler toward him, and he had to lift it gently out of the water so that the hook would not snag on any rock or woody debris that had collected in front of the dam. Richie repeated this several times, and on the next try, the submerged line soon stopped and did not move with the water flow. Richie could feel the tug and saw that the line became taut. He knew he had a fish. He lifted the end of his rod upward and pulled the fish out of the water and swung it back toward him where it landed on the bare soil right at his feet.

"It's a brook," he said. "I knew I could catch one with a worm. They always work." Richie grabbed it and placed it next to the twelve-inch ruler outlined on his creel.

"How about that," he said. "This one is eight inches. I guess we can keep him too."

"It looks like they're going to bite today," confirmed Walt. "Let's move on down the creek and set up camp. Then all of us can fish. We're about halfway to the North now. Let's walk a little further and see if we can find a good place to set up our tents."

Walt Slee's cabin, Allenspark, CO, 1950. *Newton Family Album*

Walt Slee, 1950. *Newton Family Album*

St. Catherine's Chapel with Mount Meeker, 2013. Sheila Koenig

CHAPTER 28

On the Creek

Walt Slee and my three brothers and I walked about halfway down Rock Creek before it met with the North Saint Vrain River. Our group, with backpacks and hands loaded with camping and fishing gear, was looking for a good place to set up camp. The trail had become more rugged, and our pace had slowed as we negotiated around and over rocks.

"Let's look for a nice level place," said Walt. "I don't want to slide down into the creek in the middle of the night."

We came upon a large ponderosa needle bed, about twenty yards from the creek.

"This looks like a good spot," said Richie. "Those pine needles will make a soft place to sleep."

"Yal, this is a good place," I said in agreement. "That overhanging rock ledge over there can keep us dry from the rain, if we need it. We can put our campfire over there as well."

"Let's set up camp before we go fishin'," said Walt. "We'll put the tents up so we don't have to do it tonight. After fishin' all day, we won't want to do it. And it gets dark pretty early here in this canyon."

"Richie and Dave," said Walt, "string those two fish you got on a willow branch and weight them down in the creek with a rock. That'll keep 'em fresh—if luck has it, we'll have a lot more to eat with 'em for supper tonight."

All three tents were small and simple to set up. Aluminum rods in the interior supported a ceiling peak that was tall enough to allow a person to at least kneel inside. We inserted small steel spikes through eyelets in the canvas and pounded them in the ground with a rock to attach the sloping sides of the tent to the ground.

Walt had Rollie blow up his air mattress.

Said Walt, "I'm too old to sleep on the bare ground with my sleepin' bag. It's too doggone hard for me—I know I'll sleep a lot better with a soft mattress under me."

We placed all our gear and food in the tents.

"What if someone comes by an' takes our stuff?" Dave asked.

"They won't take anything," said Walt. "The people you see down here are honest folks—they'll leave it alone."

Walt said to Dave and me, "See if you can gather a few loose rocks from around here so we can use them to surround our campfire tonight."

"Richie and Rollie," he said, "grab some of those dead pine branches from these trees around here, and pile them up for us to start the fire. And yes, take the axe, and go over there in that aspen grove to see if there is a dead log that we can chop up to burn tonight as well. If you stumble onto a piece of pitch pine, bring it over here too. Pitch-pine logs really give off the heat, and they burn for a long time."

In a short time, we had the camp set up, and we were ready to start fishing. In our creels, each of us had two tuna fish and relish sandwiches, five chocolate-chip cookies, and potato chips wrapped in waxed paper, along with an orange. We could drink water right out of the creek when we got thirsty.

Walt told us, "The Giardia bug is not a problem up here. There is not any human waste going into the water from Allenspark or Ferncliff. There aren't enough cattle to cause any problem either. They tell you not to drink the water down lower near Lyons. I guess if you ever get that bug inside you, you are real sick for a long time—it's hard to get rid of."

Walt had an easy-to-carry, collapsible aluminum cup that he used for drinking from the creek. My brothers and I simply cupped our hands together, collected the cool water, and sucked it into our mouths.

Walt liked to chew Doublemint gum when he was fishing, so he gave each of us a stick to chew as well.

"Don't drop the wrappers on the ground," he said. "Put them in your pocket. The rule is that we take out everything we bring in. We don't leave garbage all over and up and down the canyon."

With hip boots on, creels strapped over our shoulders, and rods in hand, we were ready to fish Rock Creek.

"Any of you guys want some worms?" Richie asked. "I've got plenty here if you need 'em."

"I'll take some," I said.

Richie proceeded to take a pinch of the soil and nightcrawler mixture from a half-pound coffee can he had stowed in his creel, and he placed it in the small tobacco snuff can that I had found behind the Mead Pool Hall and was using as a worm container.

"I got what I need," said Dave.

"You better give me some," said Walt, holding out his commercially made container. "But I hope I don't have to use 'em."

"I'll get some later if I need 'em," said Rollie.

"Who wants to walk down the Creek?" Walt asked. "I'll start fishing here, and a couple of you can walk further up to fish."

"I'll go down." I said.

"So will I," said Dave.

"Okay," said Walt. "Richie and Rollie—you two walk up a ways. You can probably hit those beaver ponds about five o'clock. They should be bitin' about then. You all keep everything you catch that is at least seven inches—the little ones are probably the best eatin'."

Dave and I walked further down from the campsite. At first, we made good time winding our way through the level land of the brush understory. We stopped only briefly now and again either to decide which pathway would provide the least resistance or to remove our hooks from the entangling branches. We walked a quarter mile until we came to a vertical rock ledge with the creek running swiftly below us.

"Let's cross the creek to the other side," I said.

We backtracked a few hundred feet to the place where we could again approach the creek, crossing quickly, stepping in and out of the water, and leaping from rock to rock while the water moved swiftly under our feet. We reached the other side east of the creek to where the brush understory was thick once again, and we continued our journey at a faster pace.

As we walked, we surveyed the creek, looking for promising holes where we knew the fish would be. It was late spring, and the snow and ice in the Rockies above Allenspark had begun to melt. There was now a lot of water in the creek, and it was moving rapidly, slowing only to swirl in deep holes dammed by rocks and logs and enclosed next to steep earthen sides overgrown with grass.

"Walt says a good place to fish is near that grass side where the water is slowed down a bit," I said. "He says it's deep there and the fish are hiding under the shadow of the overhanging grass. They come out when they see a floating insect passing by in the swifter moving water. He says the insect is moving fast, and the fish has to move quickly to grab it. Sometimes fish move with such great force that they jump right out of the water when they go after it."

The walk down the creek was almost a sensory overload. The wax currant and chokecherry understory was interspersed with peppermint, wintergreen, sweet-smelling verbena, and lemon sumac. With the resinous scent of ponderosa, the redolent combination of scents was inebriating. The knocking sound of the wood-pecking sapsucker seeking insects from ponderosa bark echoed from the canyon walls. The loud and complex chirps of wrens and blue birds seemed to be cautionary calls, informing mates that humans were invading their habitat. In the background was the constant, hushed sound of splashing and gurgling water, as Rock Creek tumbled over rocks, pebbles, logs, and sand. Moisture on the flickering leaves of aspen trees reflected sparkling flashes of light as we walked beneath their canopies. The beauty of thousands of spring flowers surrounded by tall rock formations, heightened by pleasing aromas and the sudden appearance of birds, made me forget momentarily about fishing and drink in the splendor. At that moment, I knew that Rock Creek was the place where I wanted to be—I did not want to be anywhere else. I thought of myself as a lucky young man.

"Have we gone far enough?" asked Dave.

"I think so," I responded. "It's another three-quarters of a mile before we reach the North. We should have plenty of water to fish before we get back to the campsite."

Dave walked over to the creek to take the first hole, and I walked above him, being careful not to get too close to Dave's hole, while seeking the next available one. We would alternate hole after hole all the way up the creek; both of us were fishing with flies. In a small stream such as Rock Creek, the fly fisherman does not have a lot of space either in front or behind to manipulate a length of fly line. This limitation hampered us in placing a fly in the spot we desired, and in trying to do so, we found our flies often snagging onto the branches of a shrub or tree. It was especially frustrating when the snag occurred over a good hole that we had not yet tried. Whenever that happened, we had to wade into the water, startling the fish as we unhooked the fly. But wasting a good hole was better than losing a good fly.

I fished several holes before I caught a small brook. I wet my hand before I grabbed the fish, gently removed the small hook of the Adam's Ant from its mouth, and then returned it to the water. For a few moments, the fish appeared dazed and motionless at my feet, but then it suddenly revived and swam swiftly away. I wondered if this fish had learned something from his experience—would he be more discerning in going after his next meal? Would he take just a little more time to see that the fly was tethered to a leader string? Couldn't he see that there was a small hook on the fly's underbelly?

Dave passed me on his way to the next hole. "I got one," he said. "It's about eight inches—caught 'im at the beginning of a real long hole. I hooked another one in the same place, but I lost him."

"I hooked one too," I said. "But I threw him back—it looks like they're startin' to bite."

"This next hole looks like a good one," said Dave. "But I'm goin' ta have ta kneel down and flip my fly in there with a real short line."

I walked past Dave, now crouched in the grass on his knees, and I moved to the next hole—it was a beautiful one—long and wide—built up by an aspen log lying diagonally across the creek, slowing and damming the water flow. There were soft ripples on the surface, and there was nothing but grass on both sides of the creek—there was plenty of room for me to cast my line. The log had diverted the water to the left bank, and the flow swept rapidly by where I was standing in two feet of slower-moving water. To the right and downside of the hole, I could easily drop my flies at the top of the hole and let them float the full length to the bottom of the hole, where Walt told us a fish would most likely be.

I watched the white wings of the Rio Grande King float through the ripples and then past the bottom of the hole and on into the swift water. I yanked my line out of the water and flipped the flies once again to the top of the hole. I could still see the King float on the surface, but the Black Gnat that I had just put on at the tail end of the line was indiscernible. With my eyes focused on the King, I was startled by a momentary splash just above the King, and I felt the gentle tug of the fish that had swallowed the Gnat—I jerked, and the line remained submerged with the hooked fish maneuvering and heading for the fast water. I moved the end of my rod to the right, nearly ninety degrees, and tightened my hold on the line with my left hand, keeping the fish in the slow water. I coaxed the fish clear to the right side of the hole and then jerked it out of the water on to the grassy bank. I laid my rod down and crawled up and over the bank's grassy edge. I pounced on the fish like a banty rooster on a bouncing cricket, and I grabbed it with both hands. It was a big brown—at least big to my eyes—I knew it was the largest fish I had ever caught. I knocked its head on the handle of my rod and removed the Gnat from deep down in its throat. I held the fish next to the ruler on my creel—it was 11½ inches long—a record for me.

However, I had no such luck with the next hole I tried, and now while I was attempting to get out of the creek and move to the next spot, my right foot slipped, and I lost my balance and fell into the flowing water. I landed on my left knee on the solid rock bottom of the creek, falling forward with my left hand also hitting the rock bottom and with the upper part of my body now immersed. The sudden sensation of cold water on my chest and back caused me to gasp breathlessly. As I slammed into the water, I lost control of my rod, and I saw it floating downstream. I struggled to regain my balance and to stand in the fast water. My boots, now heavy with water, were difficult to lift as I tried to step toward shore. I felt a sharp pain in my left knee and a numbing throb in the palm of my left hand. I stepped slowly toward the knee-high grass on the bank. I placed my right knee on it and crawled forward to lift my left leg out of the water.

I turned over and lay flat on my back on the grass and held up my right leg to drain the cold water out of my boot then did the same with my left. The water ran down into the seat of my jeans and under my back, and it gave me a sudden chill once again. Never before had I experienced such penetrating coldness. My whole body shivered, and my teeth began to chatter. I stood up and looked to see where my rod was. I spotted it downstream about twenty yards away, caught by several protruding rocks. I stepped back into the creek and walked carefully, cross-grain to the water flow to retrieve it. With rod in hand, I went back to the grass-bank area where I removed my long-sleeved and T-shirts. I wrung the water from them and laid them on a large rock to dry. The intense sunrays hitting my naked back felt good and warmed me.

Luckily, my canvas creel floated and was not immersed. My sandwiches, cookies, and potato chips, still wrapped in waxed paper, had been spared. I sat in the warm sun and began eating my lunch.

Dave, finishing the hole just above, came out of the brush and saw me sitting there and realized what had happened. He sat down to eat his lunch too. We ate quickly, wanting to resume fishing. I concluded that the only way I could really warm up was to get moving and generate more body heat. I knew that my legs would quickly warm up inside the rubber boots. I slipped on my half-dry shirts, and Dave and I walked to our next holes.

Dave and I fished tirelessly all afternoon, going from hole to hole, tossing our lines and flies repeatedly and waiting patiently for some fish to strike. By the time we reached the camp at dusk, Dave had caught five fish, and I had three. We could see smoke from the campfire that Richie had already started.

"Rollie and Walt were fishin' the beaver ponds when I last saw them," explained Richie. "Walt had five fish all over ten inches. He said he caught a lot more but had thrown them all back because they were real small. Rollie had three when I left 'em about fifteen minutes ago. I got four—caught 'em all with worms."

I went over next to the fire and sat down on a rock to remove my boots.

I asked Richie, "Will you pull these boots off for me? I'm wet all over—I need to dry out—I fell in two hours ago, and I've been cold ever since."

With my boots off, I stripped to shorts and socks and held my wet clothes over the warm fire to dry, steam rising as they began to absorb the heat. In a short time, my clothes were dry, and I put them back on—they smelled of campfire smoke. I put on a clean pair of socks and a sweatshirt and slipped on my walking shoes. I then held my rubber boots over the fire to dry them out.

Soon Walt and Rollie arrived—they set their rods down upright, supported by a branch of a nearby ponderosa.

"How'd you guys do?" Walt asked.

"I got three, and Dave got five," I responded. "Richie said he had four. How many did you get?"

"I think I got five, and Rollie has three," said Walt. "We caught three in the beaver dams—one brown and two brooks."

"Why don't you and Dave clean them?" said Walt. "I'll get the cornmeal and frying pan out so we can start cookin' them. Also, remember to clean those two we caught this mornin'."

Dave and I placed all the fish in one creel and carried them to the side of the creek. With Walt's pocketknife, Dave began to slit their undersides all the way to the gills and to lay the fish on the grass next to the creek. Then one by one, I placed my left index finger into the mouth of the cut fish, and with my right index finger, I reached into their gill set and pulled it out—with my continued pulling, the attached gullet entrails came free. I threw the removed parts into the creek, and then holding the fish in my left hand, I took the tip of my thumb and placed the thumbnail next to the backbone, and then running my thumb upward through the body cavity, I scraped away any intestinal portions that remained. I dipped the fish in running water to rinse it and then placed it on the grass. Dave followed with another wash and placed all twenty-two fish on paper plates, which we carried to the campfire for Walt to fry.

I said to Walt as I pointed, "That one there is the one I caught, and I want to eat him myself."

Richie had cut several branches from a willow for us to use for roasting hot dogs. He also had opened a large can of pork and beans and set it on a rock next to the fire. Walt had a paper plate of cornmeal ready to dredge the fish. He put a stick of butter into the frying pan and balanced it on the rocks Richie had carefully placed near the fire. By now, Rollie, who also had fallen into the water, had dried himself, and he had made a kettle of Kool-Aid with cold water from the creek.

I quickly roasted a hot dog and put a spoonful of beans on my plate. When I was finished, I said to Walt, "Let me have that big brown that I caught—I want to eat him first."

Walt placed the brown and two small brooks on my plate. I gently removed the surface meat, leaving the rib and backbones intact. The contrast of the toasted, crisp cornmeal-coated skin and the juicy meat was wonderful, and my eating pleasure was heightened by the warmth of the campfire and the beauty of the mountains. By the time I had stripped and eaten all the meat from the three fish, Walt had two more ready for me. I satisfied my thirst with two cups of Kool-Aid, and then deciding that this was all the supper I could consume, I threw my paper plate and fish bones into the fire, finishing off my delicious meal with two chocolate-chip cookies.

When Walt had finished frying fish, I took the frying pan down to the creek to wash it. I scooped a handful of sand from the side of the creek and began to scour the pan. When all the fish particles and cornmeal had been removed, I rubbed the inside of the pan with wheat and sedge grass and then rubbed it with a bar of soap. I washed off the soap and rinsed the pan several times in the creek and removed the remaining water with dry grass.

Rollie, Richie, and Dave roasted marshmallows and, having already eaten several, roasted some more for Walt and me. Walt lit up a cigar and sat down on a rock that Richie had found especially for him and placed near the campfire.

"We had a pretty good day today," Walt said. "I hope they're hittin' like this tomorrow down on the North, and I hope they're bigger. Most of the ones we caught today were pretty small."

"They sure were," said Richie as he laughed. "I watched Rollie trying to net a brook that he caught in the beaver dam—it was so little and skinny it went right through the mesh of his net."

"God, that was funny," said Richie, shaking with laughter.

"I think we'll catch some bigger ones tomorrow," said Walt. "There'll be some big browns down there—at least fourteen or fifteen inches. That's a pretty good size for fish at this high altitude. At eight thousand feet, they don't seem to be as big as those down lower at five thousand. They say that with the long winters and short summers and low water temperatures, there just isn't that much food available for them to eat. So I guess they don't eat as much as they do in the warmer waters."

"What's the biggest fish you've ever caught up here?" asked Rollie.

"I guess about eighteen inches," answered Walt. "I caught him on the North down by Riverside. It's about two miles from here at about six-thousand-feet elevation. It took me quite awhile to bring 'im in. Luckily, there was not a lot of swift water around for him to go to, or I would probably have lost 'im."

"I'd like to nail a big one like that," said Rollie. "What did you catch him on?" Rollie asked.

"It was a Gray Hackle," replied Walt.

"Do ya think you could catch one that big on a worm?" asked Richie.

"I don't know why not," Walt answered. "It's worth a try."

The night air above us was clear, and the dense blanket of stars was readily visible above us. It was peaceful and quiet—the only sounds were the crackling campfire and the tumbling waters of the creek. The moonlight, bathing the ponderosa grove on the sloping mountain across the creek, created the appearance of fresh fallen snow on needled tree branches. The temperature had dropped considerably to a downright coolness, so the campfire heat was even more comforting as we huddled around.

    Rollie stood up, holding his boots to dry over the fire. With a stick, Richie positioned a small pine log to the center of the fire, hoping to get it to burn more vigorously. The fire began to die down, and then our weary but contented group turned in for the night.

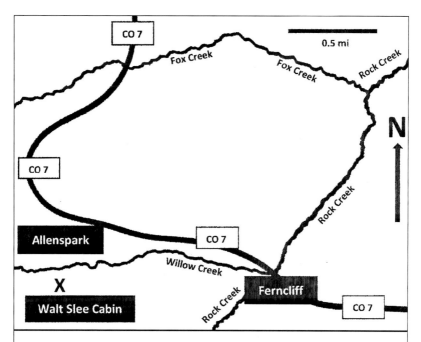

Willow Creek, Rock Creek, and Fox Creek near Allenspark, CO, 2015. Ronald Newton

L–R: Richie, Jerry, Rollie, Dave, and Ronnie Newton, 1952. *Newton Family Album*

CHAPTER 29

On the River

It was daybreak, and I awakened inside my tent that Dave and I had set up along Rock Creek high in the Colorado Rockies, two miles from Allenspark and thirty or forty miles from our Mead home. Richie and Rollie, alongside in another tent, were still sleeping, and Walt Slee was slumbering soundly in another. I unzipped the flap of my tent and stuck my head out to view the morning surroundings. The outside of our tents was wet with dew. I slipped my coat on over my sweatshirt and sat down on the tent floor to put on my hiking shoes, emerging with a roll of toilet paper that I needed to start the fire. I gathered pine twigs and needles and placed them on the paper and used Walt's cigar lighter to light things off. On my knees, I bent over, and with my face next to the smoldering mass, I blew to stimulate its burning. When the needles, twigs, and paper were shooting with flames, I broke dead aspen branches into pieces and placed them crossways over the flames. I now had a vigorous fire that I could use to ignite the small pine branches that I added.

    Walt emerged from his tent and began to assemble the frying pan and food to prepare breakfast. He threw a pound of slab bacon into the hot skillet. The melting fat produced a crackling sound and a pleasant smell that attracted the attention of my brothers, just awakening and still in their tents. In a few minutes, we all were standing around the fire, sipping paper cups of Kool-Aid as we waited for scrambled eggs.

After breakfast, I opened jars of peanut butter and Mom's strawberry preserves. To make sandwiches, I spread paper towels on the pine-needle bed and placed the bread on it. Rollie wrapped the sandwiches in waxed paper and doled out two to each of us, which we placed in our creels. We all then worked to dismantle our tents and collect our belongings into one spot behind a rock for safekeeping. We would pick these up later that evening on the way back from the North.

By seven thirty, we were walking along Rock Creek, heading toward the North Saint Vrain. We came to the rock cliff where Dave and I had been the day before, and just as we did then, we crossed the creek. Soon thereafter, the canyon narrowed with steep cliffs on both sides. The only way for us to continue was to ascend about two hundred feet over the cliff on the left side. Richie led the way with Dave and Walt right behind, followed by me and, finally, Rollie. The climb took us in a snaking route where the path wove in and away from the cliff's edge. Richie and Dave, now about three-quarters of the way up the cliff, were thirty feet away from Walt and me. It was then when Richie unwittingly dislodged a boulder about two feet in diameter that began to tumble down the cliff. As it passed Walt and me, we both yelled out almost in unison with "Look out!"

The boulder rolled directly toward Rollie, bouncing erratically as it descended. Just a few yards in front of Rollie, it took an exceptionally high bounce and flew over Rollie as he ducked and hunkered to the ground. Rollie's instinctive move saved him from being pummeled by the rock broadside in the chest. Rollie stood up and turned to look down the slope as we all observed the rolling rock pick up speed and descend to the creek floor. Rollie then turned back toward us and started laughing—and soon all of us did as well.

"Crimenee," said Richie. "That rock was really movin'."

"Boy, that rock coulda hurt Rollie," I said to Walt, standing nearby. "It coulda knocked him all the way down to the creek."

"Yes, it could've," said Walt. "Last summer, a woman from Ohio was killed by a fallin' rock—she was hikin' up in Rocky Mountain National Park—I read about it in the *Times Call*. It was real sad—she was married and had two young kids with her."

As we continued our climb, I thought about how lucky Rollie had been—if he had not ducked, the impact of the speeding boulder would have sent him backward down the cliff, causing serious injury, perhaps even death. I thought of how sad a task it would have been for us to carry Rollie's body for two miles to get him out of the Rock Creek canyon. I quickly erased the thought and thanked God for saving him from harm and preserving the joy we were all sharing—I recited the Our Father in my mind as my way of offering gratitude.

We continued our journey to the top of the cliff, where we looked down two hundred feet and a quarter mile ahead to see the small valley where Rock Creek merged into the North Saint Vrain. The river was mostly obscured by ponderosas and brush, but from our high vantage point, we could see an occasional ribbon of water as more than a mile stretch of it moved from left to right down the canyon. We could faintly hear the river's distant roar. We stood in awe of the sight before us. We knew this was a view that only a lucky few got to see. There were not many who were willing to journey two miles into the wilderness to fish and see the magnificent splendor of the North Saint Vrain.

From where we were standing, we were just a couple of miles downstream from Wild Basin and the high-altitude lakes that gave genesis to the Saint Vrain River, and with the dense willow growth along its upper part, we were certain we would not be seeing another person following the river from above, even if it was Memorial Day.

Light of Her Children

    I could barely wait to get to the river—Richie, still in the lead, hurriedly led our group down the cliff to the river's edge. Compared to Rock Creek, the Saint Vrain was gigantic and ferocious. When its water was confined to a narrow pathway, it gathered and fell forcefully over large boulders, splashing onto rocks below and then separating into rivulets of splashing waterfalls, producing a collective deafening sound. Glancing high into the air with each splash, the water showered us with cold droplets. The large volume of water moving at such a rapid speed was frightening—I naively wondered how a fish could stand the constant pounding? I imagined their writhing bodies would often be hurled against rocks with a great force.

    "My god," said Richie. "If you fall into this, it would carry you all of the way to Kansas.

    "I think it would be more like Nebraska, wouldn't it?" Rollie asked.

    "Yes, that's right," answered Walt. "The North merges with the South there at Lyons, and from there, the Saint Vrain runs into the South Platte down by Platteville—then the South Platte runs north up into Nebraska where it merges with the North Platte. However, at one time, the South Platte did flow eastward into Kansas. That was when its valley floor was much lower in elevation, perhaps only a few thousand feet above sea level."

    Walt continued explaining, "Rusty Laybourn told me that geologists think millions of years ago, the South Platte River Valley was uplifted to its present mile-high elevation, and the river was then rerouted northward toward Nebraska."

    "That's really interesting," I said. "Lookin' at the map of the United States, you tend to think that all the rivers run south, just like the Mississippi."

    We then walked down to an open grassland area beside the river, where the water was more tranquil and where the river widened to thirty or so yards, flowing more gently with a quiet rippling sound over a bed of small rounded rocks and pebbles.

"Let's all walk down a ways before we start fishing," said Walt. "We can then split up."

After thirty minutes of walking, we stopped. Rollie and Dave decided to begin fishing and move upriver. We checked to make sure that we all had ample leaders, hooks, worms, and flies. Then Walt, Richie, and I walked further down.

After fifteen minutes, Walt said, "I'll start right here. The two of you walk down another half mile before you begin."

Richie and I fished until noon and sat down on a rock beside the river to eat lunch. Richie had caught three browns, all on worms, and I had caught two with flies, both with the Rio Grande King. After lunch, we moved upriver until we caught up with Walt. It was now two o'clock, and Walt had just begun to resume fishing.

Walt said, "I caught seven or eight fish right away from about ten until noon, but then all of sudden, they stopped biting. Finally, at one o'clock, I decided to eat lunch and wait for them to start biting again. I started back up just a few minutes ago. We can fish on up from here until we reach Rock Creek. We'll have to start walkin' out of here about five, if we want to fish a little bit on Rock Creek again and reach the car before it gets dark."

I was the first to reach Rock Creek, and I decided to lay my rod down and go upriver to see if I could find Dave and Rollie. I soon saw Dave but not Rollie.

"Where's Rollie?" I asked.

"I haven't seen him for a while," responded Dave nonchalantly. "He should be above here somewhere."

I proceeded further up the river, but there was no sight of Rollie. I walked further up but still did not see him. I walked upstream some more until I came to a long stretch of fast water—I was certain that Rollie would have concluded this was not good water for fishing, and he would have turned back and resumed fishing downstream. I called out to Rollie as I walked back, but I got no response. At times, I moved closer to the water to look up and down the river to see if I could see him—still Rollie was nowhere to be seen. I was fearful that he might have died and that his body had already been carried far down the river. I conjured up the thought that he had hit his head on a rock when he fell in some fast-moving water.

I hurried back to where Dave was fishing.

"Has Rollie shown up yet?" I asked.

"Haven't seen him," said Dave as he continued to cast his flies into the water.

"I'm gettin' worried that somethin' has happened to him," I said. "I walked up the river a long ways, and I didn't see him. I'm goin' to get Walt and get him to help us look."

Wracked with worry, I became more concerned than ever, and I began to run through the brush and grass to find Walt. I soon came upon Walt, who was standing midstream and casting his line to the other side with his back to me.

I yelled, "W-walt, w-we can't find Rollie! We don't know what has happened to him! We need you to help us find 'im!"

Walt turned to face me, reeled in his line, and walked toward me.

"Where have you looked?" Walt asked.

"I walked a long way up past Rock Creek and called out his name, but I didn't hear him yell back," I said with a shaken voice. "Dave said he hadn't seen 'im either."

Richie then came up to us, and I explained that we didn't know where Rollie was. The three of us walked until we reached Rock Creek. We stood our rods against a pine branch and began walking upriver searching for Rollie. We came to where Dave was fishing.

"Have ya seen Rollie?" Walt asked.

"Haven't seen 'im," said Dave. "He was fishin' up above me."

Now hearing that we were all still looking for Rollie, Dave too became concerned, and he stood his rod upright next to a ponderosa and went with us as we continued walking upriver. Fearing the worst, we looked into the river as we walked, each one thinking that Rollie had drowned and that his body must be lodged somewhere downstream. We walked rapidly and for a long while, not talking to one another, only yelling Rollie's name. I looked at Walt, and I sensed that he too was getting really concerned.

Suddenly we came to a large rock, nearly ten feet in height, and there we saw Rollie standing on it above the river, rod in hand, casually dropping his line and a hooked worm into the pool below him.

Arriving at the rock, I looked up at Rollie and asked in a relieved voice, "How long have you been here?"

"I just got here," Rollie said excitedly. "I had fished a long way up from here, and I decided I better head back down toward Rock Creek. I had hooked a big brown here in this hole 'bout an hour ago on my way up, but I lost 'im. I just stopped here to try again and see if I could get 'im to bite once more. He was a big one, must 'uv been eighteen inches."

With relief and joy at seeing him, we all climbed onto adjacent rocks to see if Rollie could entice the fish once more to take a worm.

When it was apparent that a worm was not effective, Walt said, "Why don't you try a fly? I've got a leader with flies here that you can use."

Walt took a circled leader with two attached flies from his vest and handed it to Rollie. Rollie removed his leader and hook, tied Walt's fly leader to his line, and began to cast it into the giant pool. For more than ten minutes, we watched him attempt many casts all over the pool, hoping the large fish might again bite. But this was to no avail. That fish was not be fooled a second time, neither with worm nor with artificial lure.

"We better get goin'," said Walt. "We've got a long way to go before the sun goes down."

Knowing we were all safe and together once more, we chattered cheerfully as we walked. We described the fish we had caught, the type of water where we caught them, and the degree of difficulty we had in bringing them in. I was thankful that Rollie had not met with serious injury by the falling rock and that he had not drowned. I was feeling very good about the experiences I had over the last forty-eight hours as I recalled them one by one, wishing that I could stay in the mountains for a few more days. I did not want to think that the next day, my brothers and I would be back working in a beet field. For now, all I wanted to do was focus on the next few hours fishing Rock Creek as we made our way out of the canyon. We had a lot of fish in our creels, and there were more fish to catch in Rock Creek. Mom would be happy that we were bringing home a big mess of fish.

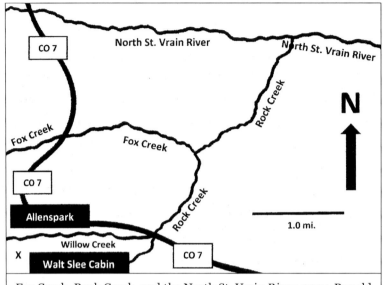

Fox Creek, Rock Creek, and the North St. Vrain River, 2015. Ronald Newton

North St. Vrain River in Wild Basin, Rocky Mountain National Park, 2013. Sheila Koenig

Chapter 30

Highland Lake

I was in Bunton's Red & White Grocery Store in Mead when we triplets' classmate Anita Jensen and her mother, Mary Mead Jensen, entered. Mom was gone for the weekend—my brother Tom had taken her to Fleming to see my grandmother, and my sister Kathleen, who was temporarily in charge of the household, had sent me to the store to buy bread and peanut butter for our lunch.

"Hi, Anita," I said.

"Hello, Ronnie," said Anita.

"Hello, Mrs. Jensen."

"Hello to you, Mr. Newton," said Mrs. Jensen as she went to pick out her groceries.

"What cha doin' this summer, Ronnie?" asked Anita.

"We just finished thinnin' beets for Josephine Rademacher's dad—on Monday we're goin' to start the second hoein'—Josephine's workin' with us. How 'bout you?" I asked.

"I help my mom out rentin' the boats out at the lake and runnin' the concession stand," said Anita. "In the afternoons, we go swimmin'."

"Why don't you and your brothers come an' go swimmin' with us?" added Anita.

"That'd be fun," I said.

"How deep is it where you swim?"

"We take a boat out and dive off of it—I guess it's fifteen or twenty feet deep."

"I didn't know you went swimmin' in Highland Lake," I said. "I thought it was only for fishin'."

"My brothers and I swim in it all the time," said Anita. "The Palinkxes go with us sometimes."

With Mom away, I knew that I would not seek her permission, so I said to Anita, "I think we can come." I said "we" because I knew I'd want one of my brothers with me were I to go swimming without my parent's explicit permission. In disobedience, it was always better to have an accomplice—the punishment was easier to take if it was shared.

"What time are you goin' swimmin'?" I asked.

"Usually about two," said Anita. "We'll wait for ya—we'll be at the house."

Highland Lake, the first irrigation reservoir developed in the Mead area, was situated a mile northwest of the town of Mead. Replenished by water from the Highland Ditch, which carried water from the Saint Vrain River, the lake was owned by the Mead family, who rented boats and sold fishing permits to fishermen—usually from Denver. The lake was an occasional spot where my brothers-in-law took my brothers and me to fish before we were teenagers, and later, it became known to us as a good place to swim. The community of folks around the lake was referred to as Highlandlake, and this was where several of our classmates lived. Highlandlake's close proximity to Mead made it easy for my brothers and me to socialize with our classmates living there, and in the summer, Highland Lake became a frequent walking-distance destination for us.

Not telling my sister Kathleen that Richie and I were going swimming, I convinced her that we were walking to Highland Lake to watch the Jensens catch fish.

"Lawrence and Roland Jensen fish from the dock," I said. "Richie and I are goin' to watch 'em—they catch a lot of sunfish and bluegill—maybe if they catch a lot of 'em, we'll bring some home with us."

With cutoff-jeans "swimming trunks" in our hip pockets, Richie and I slipped out of the house, on our way to Highland Lake, a mile and a half away by road.

"Let's cut across Gettman's field," said Richie. "It'll be shorter."

We crawled through the barbed-wire fence separating Mr. Gettman's field of alfalfa and Dad's cow pasture and followed a small irrigation ditch, running north and south for a quarter of a mile, across the field to the other side and on to the dirt road that would take us west toward Highland Lake. Mamie Akers's cattail slough was on the other, north side of the road, and its level was unusually high with irrigation water draining from John Minch's farm located east of Highland Lake. The slough's flow was silent and slow through Mamie Akers's alfalfa-stubble field, picking up speed through a culvert under Road 7 and continuing for another mile before it was dammed up into a small lake on Louie Roman's farm, on the west side of the Washington Highway.

A mountainous stack of straw from the previous year's harvest stood in a just-cut alfalfa field across the road and north of the slough. My brothers and I had been to this site many times before, getting straw for Mom's chickens and, with homemade slingshots, hurling rocks at birds flitting among the cattails and cottonwoods growing along the sides of the slough stream.

"Remember when we killed that owl sitting up in that tree over there?" Richie asked.

"Yes, I do," I answered. "And I remember, when Walt [Slee] found out about it, he chewed us out for what we had done. He told us that owls were protected by law and that they were good for the environment, feeding on rats and field mice."

"Remember how bad we felt when the owl died, and we felt even worse when Walt told us how wrong we were for doing it," I said.

"It was so easy to do," said Richie. "It was during the day, and the owl seemed to be sleeping. It wouldn't move as we peppered it with rocks. It just perched there, not seeming to know what was going on."

"I remember looking at that beautiful animal lying dead on the ground, and I asked myself, 'What have we done?' After that, I didn't want to kill another living thing. After that, even when we shot at small cottontails hiding in the alfalfa clumps, I hoped that I wouldn't hit 'em."

"I still kill rabbits," said Richie. "I can hit 'em a mile away with my slingshot—it doesn't bother me."

Richie and I walked for another half mile past the Gettman barn and farmhouse, and then we turned north toward Highlandlake. We walked another half mile till we came to the lake's south side, and we followed the road around the east side of the lake for another quarter mile until we came to the house where the Jensens were living with Anita's grandmother in the Mead homestead.

I knocked on the screen door, and immediately, Anita opened the wooden door on the other side. She smiled shyly and said, "Hi, Ronnie—hi, Richie."

"How ya doin'?" I asked.

"Hey, Anita," said Richie. "We're ready to go swimmin'. Where's Lawrence? Is he around?"

"Yes," said Anita. "He and Roland are already out on the lake."

Then suddenly, Ginger Palinkx, coming from another room, walked up behind Anita and looked curiously over Anita's shoulder to see who was at the door. She smiled timidly and said, "Hello."

Both Richie and I said, "Hi," and then moved back as Anita pushed the screen door open and stepped onto the porch and pointed, saying, "You can put your swimmin' trunks on in that bathhouse over there, and we'll meet you at the dock where we can get Lawrence to come and get us and take us out to the middle of the lake. We have to go away from the shoreline to get where it is deep enough for us to dive."

Richie descended the steps and walked toward the bathhouse, but I stayed a moment longer to talk to Ginger, whose striking appearance had gotten my attention. Ginger was the granddaughter of Emil Palinkx, who worked late afternoons and evenings in the Mead Pool Hall.

She was Dave's classmate, two years younger than me—she would be a freshman at Mead High School in the fall. However, her youth was contradicted by her already-womanly figure, obvious in the formfitting Levi's she was wearing and the V-necked white blouse that undulated over her breasts. Her auburn hair, parted in the middle, was cropped short just below her ears, and its sides curled forward, framing her face. Her smile, friendly and charming, was highlighted by her soft milk-like complexion. Knowing that I had taken an interest in her, she shyly glanced downward and did not know what to say.

Trying to make conversation, I asked, "Is Connie around?"

"No," said Ginger. "She and Betty went to Longmont with my mother to shop and buy groceries."

I already knew both Connie Palinkx and Betty Bernhardt. I had become acquainted with them at school when I sat across the table from them during the afternoon study hall. The two of them also attempted to teach me to dance one day in the gym during lunch hour. Connie, three years older than Ginger, was just as pretty.

"Are ya goin' swimmin'?" I asked Ginger.

"Yes, I am," she said. "See ya out there."

Lawrence and Roland, seeing Richie and me on the dock, paddled to shore to pick us up and then took the four of us to the center of the lake. We took turns diving into the clear water, which, on the surface, had been warmed by the sun. But as we descended deeper, the cooling sensation we experienced reminded us once again of the mountainous origin of the icy water that continuously flowed into the lake. However, enough sunlight reached the lake bottom to support the growth of three-foot-long strands of elodea weed, which wrapped around our legs and arms at the bottom of a dive. For a moment, I panicked when it seemed that I might not be released from the clutches of those monstrous weeds clinging tenaciously to my arms and legs and thwarting my attempts to get back to the surface.

Soon Anita and Ginger joined us in another boat. As I floated on the surface, I could see Ginger, standing, ready to dive. The exposed milk-white skin of her legs glistened in the sunlight, and her hair, wetted and straightened by the water, was now swept back, revealing every part of her beautiful face. Her splashing entry into the water and her joyful face upon emerging, accompanied by frantic arm paddling, reminded me of a playful cocker spaniel that had suddenly been thrown into the water and had to fend for itself.

This playful and pretty girl interested me; trying to get her attention, I splashed water into her face. To avoid the onslaught, she dove underwater and then swam for a few seconds, emerging ten yards away, where my splashing spurts could no longer reach her.

"Okay, Mr. Smarty-Pants," she said. "Take this." And she hurled a glob of elodea at me, which she had pulled up from the bottom. It landed in front of me. I picked it up and threw it back at her—hitting her across the face. As she untangled the long strands from her head, I swam toward her and began splashing more water in her face.

"No—no more," she said, and she dove underwater and surfaced on the other side of the boat and then swam up to its side for support and protection. Soon everyone was diving under to grab handfuls of elodea weeds and throwing them at whoever was closest.

During the following school year of '54–'55, I saw Ginger every school day in the cafeteria. She ate lunch with her best friend, Joann Becker, Rollie's girlfriend. Either Ginger or I would somehow manage to walk by each other so that we could exchange a greeting before the lunch hour was over. Both Ginger and I were too timid to show outwardly to any of our classmates how we were beginning to feel about each other. Furthermore, both of us were engrossed with our own separate friends and activities, and we had little opportunity to see each other, except in the cafeteria.

I was focused on my studies and athletics—and with my part-time jobs and my work responsibilities at home—I had little time for anything else. Besides, I prided myself on not being distracted by an intense relationship with a girlfriend. Often, I had heard Ronald Weber say about one of his fellow classmates, "He's pussy-whipped—he could really be a good player, but he doesn't care that much about playin'—his girlfriend's more important than basketball. He'd rather be with her than goin' to practice."

I determined that I would never be that way—sports were my favorite activities—particularly basketball, and I knew I had to be a good student if I wanted to go on to college. I took no time to socialize with Ginger during the lunch hour—but whatever extra free time I had, I used for studying for an upcoming test or for reading assigned texts. And with no car, I had limited mobility and no opportunity to see her except at church or at school.

However, during Lent, I knew I would see Ginger every Wednesday evening at the Lenten service at Guardian Angel Church. I looked forward to seeing her and took comfort knowing that she was there worshipping the same God in the same way that I was by participating in the Stations of the Cross service. I especially looked forward to serving as one of the altar boys because I could readily see Ginger as I walked alongside Father Martin, with one of my triplet brothers on his other side, going from one station to another, fourteen of them, up and down the middle aisle of the church.

Wearing black cassocks hanging to our ankles and covered by wide-sleeved, waist-length white tunics, Rollie, Richie, or I either carried a staff to which a crucifix was attached, or we carried an urn-like censer of burning charcoal upon which we poured white grains of incense, diffusing a white vapor of smoke and a sweet odor of spice and resinous gum throughout the church. When I carried the censer, it dangled below my knees, supported by three gold chains, which I clutched in my hands at my waist and which served as a fulcrum as I swung the vessel from side to side.

At each station, Father Martin would start by saying, "We adore you, O Christ, and we bless you."

Then the congregation would respond by genuflecting and saying, "Because by the holy cross, you have redeemed the world."

The fourth station of the cross, where Jesus meets his sorrowing mother, is the one I especially remember. Father Martin would read a passage from John 19:26–27: "When Jesus therefore saw his mother and the disciple standing by, whom he loved, he said to his mother, 'Woman, behold your son.' Then he said to the disciple, 'Behold your mother.'"

Then Violet Sekich, Lucy Lee, Mom, and the rest of the church choir responded by singing:

> Stunned and stricken, Mary, Mother,
> In your arms was placed our Brother
> Full of grace—now filled with grief.

The fourth station always caused me to think about Mom. Mom was like Mary—both had lost a son. My brother Robert had died when he was one-year-old—although I never heard her express it—I was certain that Mom, like Mary, was saddened by her son's death.

After fourteen stations of prayer, the service concluded with Father Martin taking the smoking censer from me and shaking it in an up-and-down motion as he walked around the church altar. After the service, I took the censer out to the side of the church to pour the burning charcoal onto the ground and to smother it with sand and gravel. I saw the Palinkx's Studebaker leave the churchyard—I would not have the opportunity to see Ginger after the service.

Highland Lake, 2014. Highland Lake Facebook

Ronnie Newton, 1955 *Mead Consolidated Schools Yearbook*

Anita Jensen, 1955. *Mead Consolidated Schools Yearbook*

Richie Newton, 1955. *Mead Consolidated Schools Yearbook*

Ginger Palinkx, 1955. *Mead Consolidated Schools Yearbook*

Chapter 31

Big Band

I heard on the Englewood KGMC radio station that the famous band leader Eddie Howard was coming to Denver and that he and his group would be performing at Denver's Elitch Gardens' outdoor Trocadero Ballroom. I knew about Howard because of conversations I overheard from my older brothers and sisters and when they sang the lyrics of his popular hit tunes. I heard them talking about other big bands as we listened to the music of Tommy Dorsey, Glenn Miller, Benny Goodman, and Woody Herman.

To me, fast-dancing looked like it was almost as much fun as playing basketball, and I wanted to learn how to do it—my sisters were always commenting about boys they knew or dated and whether they were good or poor dancers.

Said my sister Rosemary, "Ronnie boy, if you want to make a hit with the girls—ya better learn how to dance."

I had watched my sister Pat square-dance with other high schoolers in the gym during one noon hour—she was laughing and having a good time hanging on to the shoulders of two male partners on each side of her, her feet off the floor as they swung her around within their dancing square.

I surmised that Ginger Palinkx could teach me to dance if I took her to Elitch Gardens. I was sure that she knew how to—theorizing that she must have learned dancing from her sister, Connie.

I called my friend Mike Eckel and suggested that perhaps he could invite Josephine Rademacher to go with him and the four of us could go in his parents' new Oldsmobile to hear Howard and dance to the music of his orchestra.

I borrowed a sport coat and tie from my brother Jerry, both of which had been handed down to him by our brother Tom. Arriving at the Highlandlake community at six o'clock, we could see several fishing boats still out on the lake. As we circled around the east side of the lake, Mike pointed to the Eckman house on our right and said, "My grandfather used to live in that house—he was the minister for the Highlandlake Church—the house used to be the rectory—my dad lived in that house for a couple of years."

Mike added, "You'd never know the way my dad cusses and drinks that he was once the son of a Congregationalist minister."

"They've closed the church down," I said. "I think they have a service there once a year at Christmastime."

"Ya know, Mike," I said. "Before I was born, my dad and my mom and twelve of my brothers and sisters used to live here in Highlandlake. As a matter of fact, they used to live in the same house where Ginger now lives."

I walked up the steps of the Palinkx house. It was situated at the edge of the lake next to the concession stand, bathhouse, and boathouse complex. The house was small in comparison to our house in Mead, and I asked myself as I knocked on the door, "I wonder where all my twelve brothers and sisters slept? How could they live in this little house?"

"You may have to leave the dance early," said Ginger's mother as we left the Palinkx's house. "I want her home at the latest by midnight."

As I walked behind her to Mike's car, I was struck again by Ginger's beauty. Her auburn hair glistened like gold with the evening sun, and the milk-white skin on her bare back was as smooth as ice. A wide ribbon belt knotted with a bow at her back cinched her tiny waist.

"I'm wearin' Connie's dress," she said as she and I climbed into the backseat. "Mom only had to take it up in the waist a little bit for me to wear."

By six thirty, we had Josephine in the car with us, and we were on our way to Denver.

"Ronnie," Mike asked, "what time does the ballroom open down there at Elitch's?"

"I checked the *Rocky Mountain News*, and it said at seven thirty," I answered. "I bet there's goin' to be a lot of kids there from all over Denver—it'll probably be real crowded."

"Marg sez there will be lotta adults there too," said Mike. "She sez that they remember Howard when he started back during the war."

"Josephine," said Mike, "tonight, you gotta teach me how to dance. I've never done it before—Marg tried to teach me the two-step the other night, so I know a little bit about it. But you're goin' ta have ta help me."

"That goes for me too, Ginger," I said. "I wanna learn."

"I've danced the two-step before," said Ginger. "Connie taught me how to do it. She also taught me how to jitterbug—that's what they do at the Jitney in Longmont."

"I can jitterbug," said Josephine. "My sister Theresa taught me how—she learned it at the Jitney."

"I guess that's the dance that my sisters do too when they go to the Jitney," I said. "They're always talkin' about goin' there—they have lots of fun."

"I asked my sister Rosemary why they called it the Jitney," I said. "She told me it's because it used to only cost five cents to get in to the dance—she said *jitney* is an old slang term that people used when talkin' 'bout a nickel."

"Marg says the Eddie Howard Orchestra is a swing band—whatever that is," said Mike. "She says all the big bands play swing music—she says that even the Western bands have a swing sound these days."

"I guess it has been the craze ever since the war," said Mike.

"I wonder if they play bop music?" I asked.

Then looking over at Ginger, I said, "Your sister, Connie, and Betty Bernhardt were tryin' to teach me how to do it in the gym last year—they called it the dirty bop. They were doin' a lot of hoppin' and gyrating—it reminded me of an Indian war dance—they said that a lot of parents and teachers don't want ya to do it. They said it was a new dance—and it was spreadin' all over the United States. I never did learn how to do it."

"I know how to do it," said Ginger. "Connie taught me—if they play the right music, I'll teach you. It's a different dance—sometimes you dance it alone—you're not hangin' on to a partner like ya are with the jitterbug—but you can jitterbug if you want to. The music is new—so this band may not play it."

"Hey, I know 'bout that music," I said. "I've heard it on KGMC—there's a guy named Bill Haley that sings a song called 'Rock around the Clock'—it's in the top 10—it sure is different—the music is real fast and has loud drums playin' with a steel guitar and a saxophone."

"Mike," I said, "I'll bet you could play it on your saxophone."

With two hundred couples standing on the dance floor, Bob Shriver of KOA Radio announced, "From the beautiful flower-trimmed Trocadero Ballroom at the world-famous Elitch Gardens—in the Mile-High City of Denver, Colorado—at the foot of the towering snowcapped Rockies—this is the music of *Eddy Howard and His Orchestra*."

The four of us joined in with the crowd to welcome the radio-listening audience with a big applause as Howard played his band's theme song, "Careless."

We listened and danced to Howard's *Orchestra* songs, "To Each His Own," "My Adobe Hacienda," "Sin," and more.

Howard and his vocal group sang the familiar Mills Brothers tune:

> You always hurt the one you love
> The one you shouldn't hurt at all
>
> You always take the sweetest rose
> And crush it till the petals fall

These words would stay with me—I heard them many times on the radio and when my sisters and brothers sang along, listening as they did their housework chores. Mom meticulously nurtured one rosebush in front of our house—its pinkish blossoms brightened the barren space below the dining-room windows. In the palm of my hand, the rose had a soft, fragile feel, and I handled it delicately, knowing that it could easily fall apart with the slightest disturbance. In the late summer, I was saddened when I saw petals lying on the ground and the bush then void of its beauty as nature took its course.

Howard concluded the evening with his solo rendition of "Stardust." All the songs I heard that night were familiar. I had listened to them as they were played on KGMC and were sung by my brother Tom and my sisters Pat and Helen. I was transfixed when I heard them performed live. I was also exhilarated that night, because Ginger had helped me with my dancing. In my mind, I had begun to master both the two-step and the jitterbug.

Palinkx family house (formerly the rental house of the Newton family), circa early 1900. *Highland Lake Photo Archives*, Pauli Driver Smith

Josephine Rademacher, 1956. *Mead Consolidated Schools Yearbook*

Ginger Palinkx, 1956. *Mead Consolidated Schools Yearbook*

Mike Eckel, 1956. *Mead Consolidated Schools Yearbook*

Ronnie Newton, 1956. *Mead Consolidated Schools Yearbook*

CHAPTER 32

Independence

The bell rang at 3:30 p.m., and I scurried out the schoolhouse door and quickly ran home, trying to conserve as much daylight time as possible to play basketball in our backyard. As I approached our house, I noticed that a shiny new Pontiac was parked in our driveway. I had seen it there before, and I knew that it belonged to "Mrs. Brown."

Mrs. Brown would come to visit Mom several times a year. When I had previously asked her, "Who's Mrs. Brown?"

Mom answered, "She's just a friend from Greeley—she's a nice lady who wants ta see how we're doin'."

Sometimes with visitors, Mom would let us kids stay in the room and listen to their conversation, but not with Mrs. Brown.

Upon entering the dining room where the two were sitting, Mom introduced me to Mrs. Brown, "This is Ronnie, one of the triplets. They're in the fourth grade now."

Mrs. Brown smiled and said, "Hello, Ronnie, where are your two brothers?"

"They'll be home in just a minute—they walked home with our friend Allen Thompson—they took the long way home—as soon as they get here, we're goin' to play basketball."

"So, Laura," asked Mrs. Brown, "how many children are still home now?"

"Well—with Pat as a junior and Helen ready to graduate, there's twelve kids here."

Before giving Mrs. Brown a chance to respond or ask any more questions, Mom said to me, "Go outside and play your basketball—and remember, you have to bring in the coal and kin'lin' too before supper."

I obediently left the room and went outside to shoot baskets. Ronald Weber rode up on his bicycle and began shooting with me. Weber, as we called him, moved to Mead as an eleven-year-old in the summer of '45. Although five years older than us triplets, he had a passion for sports, and thus he became a close and dear friend.

Rollie and Richie arrived home and went inside to get something to eat. Rollie emerged with a piece of buttered bread in his hand and stood and watched Ronald Weber and me play momentarily and then asked, "Who's that lady in the house anyhow?"

Stopping my play to talk to Rollie, I said, "Mom said her name is Mrs. Brown, but I don't know why she's here."

"I know why she's here," said Weber. "My dad told me—she's the welfare lady. She comes here from Greeley. She's talkin' to your mom about welfare."

"What's welfare?" I asked.

"Welfare is when the government gives you money," said Weber. "My dad says that the money comes from the county. You guys are livin' off the county. I guess your dad doesn't make enough money to take care of all you guys, so the county has to help."

"I've never heard of it," said Rollie.

Richie, eating his bread and now listening to our conversation, said, "Me neither."

Weber interjected, "My dad says that Roosevelt set up the welfare program before the war started—that's a long time ago. He said it was back in the Depression when a lot of people couldn't find work. Mr. Stoddard told us in social studies class that things were really tough in America during the Depression. He said that a lotta of kids were starvin'—so the government had to do somethin'."

"Rosemary told me that she had to be put in an orphanage in the Depression," said Richie. "She an' Betty, Ray, Eunice, and Orbin too—I guess Mom and Dad didn't have enough money to take care of 'em."

"I heard Hap Howlett talkin' about welfare down at the pool hall," said Weber. "He said it was the dumbest thing Roosevelt ever did—he says welfare's no good. He says that when you give money to people, they just have more kids."

"Who was he talkin' to?" I asked.

"Bill Collins," said Weber. "Collins was talkin' 'bout you Newtons. He said your mom and dad are like rabbits—they just keep havin' more kids. He said your dad should be out workin' more instead of stayin' at home havin' all those kids—he was laughin' when he said it."

"But our dad works," I said. "He paints houses and stacks hay and stuff."

"That doesn't matter," said Weber. "Collins says he's not workin' for what the county's givin' 'im. He says it's not fair that your dad doesn't have to work for the money you Newtons get. Collins says he pays taxes to the county—he doesn't like it that they give his tax money to you guys."

"I wonder how much we get," said Rollie.

"I don't know," said Weber. "But Collins says he thinks it's the dumb people that have big families. He says that a lot of US senators in Congress think that—those senators think that those who know how to go out and make money are smarter than those who live off of the government. They think that most of these people can't hold a job—they ain't smart 'nough."

"Well, our dad's smart," said Richie. "He reads the paper all the time—he knows a lot about the wars."

"Collins says that there's a lotta senators who want to change the law and get rid of welfare," said Weber. "Collins says he's all for it—he says he doesn't want this country taken over by dumb people."

"Well, I've heard other kids say stuff like that about our parents," I said. "They say things like, 'They're just stupid—they don't know any better.'"

That night, I chopped some kindling and brought it in the house to lay behind the kitchen stove for Mom to use the next morning. Helen was in the kitchen preparing supper when I asked her, "Are we getting money from the county? Weber said we are."

"Yes, we are," said Helen emphatically. "We were gettin' it before you were born. That was back in the Depression—Dad couldn't find work. Then the war started, and things didn't get any better."

"I never knew that—I thought Weber was just makin' it up," I said. "Weber also said that some people in town think that Dad should be workin' more and not gettin' any money from the county. He said that those people are sayin' that once you get on welfare, you don't want to get off and don't want to work."

"For heaven's sake," said Helen. "I've heard that too, and it may be true for some people but not Dad. Dad works whenever he can. But it's not always easy to find work around here."

"Weber said he heard them talkin' down at the pool hall that it's the dumb people who have big families," I said. "He said that those guys were sayin' that only the smart people know how to go out and actually make money."

"I read that in the paper too," said Helen. "But I don't believe any of it. Mom and Dad are just as smart as any of 'em. Rosemary's smart, and so is Ray—they had to get those brains from someone—it just didn't happen. All us Newtons do pretty well with our schoolwork when we put our minds to it."

"By the way," said Helen, "did Weber say who he heard sayin' this stuff?"

Light of Her Children

"He said it was Hap Howlett and Bill Collins."

"Well," said Helen, "I'm sure there are a lotta other people in town besides them who think we shouldn't be gettin' money from the government."

On Friday of that same week, Mom told me to take our Radio Flyer wagon and go downtown to the Denver Elevators and pick up a one-hundred-pound sack of flour. She said, "Charge it."

I knew that this was going to be a problem for me. The manager of the Elevators, Vernon "Bub" Howlett, shared his brother Hap's opinion about us Newtons and our dependence on others to help us put enough food on our table. Bub, like his brother, did not think it was his responsibility to take care of us. Both Hap and Bub lived with their mother, Mamie, and both knew that she was in total philosophical disagreement with them. Mamie Howlett had adopted the benevolent views of her husband, who had studied for the priesthood before marrying her. Mamie was also a local leader of the Democratic Party and a strong supporter of Roosevelt and his programs. Mamie and Mom were also neighborhood friends and frequently talked on the telephone. Mrs. Howlett let us pick plums from her tree for Mom's use in making jam; Mom reciprocated by having one of us drop off jars of jam to Mrs. Howlett.

It was dusk, at nearly five o'clock, when I entered into the Elevators office, where Bub and Mrs. Margaret Dempewolf, his clerical helper, worked. Mrs. Dempewolf, the wife of Tony, the Texaco gas distributor to the farm community of Mead, was also Mom's friend. She had given Mom rides to Longmont and, as the organist at Guardian Angel Church, had accompanied our brother Ray when he sang at our sister Eunice's wedding. And Mrs. Dempewolf played the piano to accompany him when Ray needed a recording of "God Bless America" for his entry in a Weld County competition.

Bub was standing next to Mrs. Dempewolf's desk and, seeing me, asked, "What brings you in here?"

"We . . . we need a sack of flour," I stammered, cowering and not looking at him.

"Are you gonna pay for it?" Bub asked sarcastically.

"Na . . . no, n-not today—Mu . . . Mom sez to charge it."

Bub did not say anything and turned away and went about his work. I knew that Bub was resisting giving it to me on credit. For the next fifteen minutes, Bub ignored me, and he walked in and out of the office, managing his outside workers and waiting on other customers. But I knew I could not go home and face Mom without the flour. My only alternative was to stand there and wait. Mrs. Dempewolf ignored my presence as well—remaining engrossed in her sorting through papers and bills. I stood there, feeling out of place, much like a bastard child at a family picnic, knowing that they wished I hadn't come in, particularly since it was so close to quitting time.

Finally, I heard Mrs. Dempewolf say as Bub entered the office, "C'mon, Bub, give the boy the flour."

Mrs. Dempewolf knew Mom well and knew of our circumstances. She knew too that Mom would get around to paying for it, when times were better. But in the meantime, Mom needed Bub's help. Mom bought on credit from Mr. Bunton at his Red & White Grocery Store, and like Bub, Mr. Bunton was unhappy about this. I remembered that one time when our charge bill reached eighty dollars, Mr. Bunton was convinced that he would not get his money, and he refused to give Mom any more credit until he was paid in full.

Bub went about his work, pretending that he had not heard what Mrs. Dempewolf said, moving in and out of the warm office. Finally, he stepped in front of me and asked, "What are you haulin' it in?"

"A-a wagon," I answered softly.

"Well, bring it around to the side door here," he growled. "I'll have Mr. Leonard load it up for ya, and get your little butt outta here."

Mrs. Dempewolf said nothing more, keeping her head down, pretending to be oblivious to our conversation. Mrs. Dempewolf knew that she would hear from Bub later—he would remind her once again that he was running a business and not a welfare agency. Mrs. Dempewolf took out her pad of sales slips, wrote out a charge for the flour, and handed the carbon copy to me.

"Here, take this home to your mother."

Then giving me another carbon, she said. "Here's the bill that tells the total that she owes us. Be sure that she gets both of 'em."

My family had been helped many times by many folks in the Mead community, and Mrs. Dempewolf was no exception. Without her, I would have gone home empty-handed and with feelings of cowardice and failure.

As I pulled the wagon down the street toward home, I thought about Bub Howlett. Mom had told me that Bub's dad had studied to be a priest but dropped out of the seminary and later married Mrs. Howlett. In my simple, childish logic, I concluded that since their father was Catholic, Bub and his brother Hap were mostly likely brought up as Catholics. If so, I asked myself, why didn't they attend Guardian Angel Catholic Church? Maybe it was the same reason Dad sometimes did not go to church—whatever that reason might be. I did not know and did not understand. But Sister Marjorie had told us, "It's a mortal sin when you don't go to church." In my juvenile mind, Hap and Bub and Dad were committing a sin of a very serious nature. In my inexperienced and limited way of thinking, Bub's nonparticipation in religion and seemingly unwillingness to help me was a total mystery, particularly when I noted that Bub attended the Guardian Angel Church picnic every year. Why was he so different from his mother? I remembered that Bub's brother, Hap, our postmaster, often acted the same way toward me and my brothers. When Mom sent me downtown to the post office to get the mail, I had to ask Hap to get it out of the box for me—I did not know the combination to box no. 105.

He was reluctant, annoyed, and "put out" that he had to retrieve the mail for me. "If you don't know the damn combination," he would growl, "you shouldn't come down here to get the mail."

With the one-hundred-pound sack of flour now stored in her pantry, Mom began to make bread early on Saturday morning. She prepared the dough in a huge dishpan, kneading with her hands. By noon, the dough would be rising steadily, spilling over the pan's edges. On this day, Mom would use a portion of that expanding dough to feed her hungry brood of children at lunch. The rest would be saved for baking loaves that afternoon when the dough had fully risen.

"Mom, are we going to have 'hot dogs' for lunch?" I asked eagerly.

"Yes, we are, but we're not eating until you get all of your work done."

"Hot dogs" were a special food item in the Newton household. During the Depression, Mom, like many of her mother counterparts in the 1930s, adopted the long-standing practice of frying bread dough in skillets of hot fat and serving this hot bread coated with sugar—a "poor man's doughnut." She always prepared them for lunch. None of Newtons seems certain how the term "hot dogs" became a part of the family lexicon, but with us, they were never confused with a "wiener in a bun."

Soon the smell of fried fresh bread wafted from the kitchen into the rest of the house. Mom was standing over the hot kitchen stove with chunks of dough crackling on the surface of Crisco, bubbling in two large iron skillets. Maureen and Kathleen had set the table with ten plates and ten glasses of milk. Milk and fried bread were all that Mom needed to offer us nine hungry children assembled around a kitchen table on a cold winter day. Hot dogs were one of our favorite meals.

"Marc," Mom said, "go tell everybody to wash up for lunch."

There was a mad dash to get to the kitchen sink to wash hands in cold tap water. Mom attended to the cooking while

Light of Her Children

we bowed our heads, folded our hands, and gave thanks to the Lord with our grace ritual. Hot dogs were supplied piping hot as each of us "hogged" them down as quickly as Mom could take them out of the hot fat. In twenty minutes, all of us had consumed four or five hot dogs apiece, washing them down with milk.

Seeing that most of her brood had enough to eat, Mom asked, "How many more do you want?"

Only Dave replied, "I'll take another one." Mom always knew that Dave would want more.

* * *

Three years later, with all of us children sitting around her at the supper table, Mom said, "Mrs. Howlett called me today—wanted to know if I wanted to help Hap out at the post office. He wants me to work in the afternoons—just like Helen did when she was in high school. I told Mrs. Howlett that I wanted to—I'm goin' down there tomorrow to talk to Hap about it."

"How did Hap get to be postmaster anyhow?" Richie asked.

"Well, when George Snider died, Hap was appointed," Mom answered.

"Who appoints him?" Rollie asked.

"The president does," said Mom. "But it depends on whether you're a Democrat or a Republican. Truman was in office when Hap was appointed. I'm sure Mamie had something to do with it—she's always been active in the Democratic Party—takin' care of the primary elections for the Democrats here in Mead."

"Well, Mom," said Kathleen, "if you keep workin' there, maybe you can become postmaster when Hap retires. But I guess it will depend on who wins the election coming up."

"Right now, they say in the paper that Stevenson is ahead of Eisenhower," said Maureen.

"Is Hap wantin' you to work every afternoon?" Kathleen asked.

"Probably not," said Mom. "But he may want me to work on Saturday mornings sometime. He pays by the hour—I'll find out tomorrow how much he pays."

"This'll be your first job—won't it?" Kathleen asked.

"I guess so," said Mom. "Father Martin had me make new vestments for him—but he didn't pay me anything."

As nine hungry mouths bit into biscuits covered with tuna gravy, Mom continued talking, "You know—this comes at a good time—we need the money. We've been livin' off of Jack's allotment check every month—that's been hard to do since Mrs. Brown stopped the county from sendin' us money over a year ago."

"Why'd she do that?" Kathleen asked.

"Well, she came to the house last summer when we were remodeling the kitchen and puttin' in the bathroom. She started askin' us where the money was comin' from. I told her that Jack was sendin' us a check each month and so was Rosemary."

"Why should that matter?" Kathleen asked.

"She thought we now had other income and didn't have as much need for what the county was giving us—so she cut our check in half. Then this year when your dad started gettin' a Social Security check, she had the county cut us off altogether."

"How much does Jack send us?" I asked.

"It's $250 a month—Jack has the marines send us a check," Mom answered. "The government writes the check on the first day of the month, and it gets here in the mail on about the fifteenth. I don't know what we would do without it. If I can make some more to add to it, then we won't have to keep chargin' and runnin' up big bills."

"It must cost a lot for us with our big family—doesn't it?" asked Dave.

"Sure, it does," said Mom. "Food is gettin' more expensive. The price of milk has gone up—with ole Bossie goin' dry last month and with us now buyin' milk at the store—it takes a lot more money for us to keep up."

Light of Her Children

Kathleen said, "When Rodney Markham dropped his coal bill off, he apologized that it was more now—said that they were chargin' 'im more for coal now at the Washington mine."

"A sack of sugar from Bunton's is now fifteen cents more than it was last summer," said Mom.

"You still have the money we got from thinnin' beets, don' cha?" I asked. "You can use it if you need to."

"Don't kid yourself," said Mom. "You kids are goin' to need that yourselves—you'll be needin' to buy more clothes and Christmas presents—you need winter coats. That money's goin' to run out here real soon—it's a good thing you're all workin' somewhere now—you'll need every penny you can get to last you till next summer."

Mom said, "Thank God you twins have babysittin' and housecleanin' money—and that you, Jerry, have a job at Longmont Drug. You have your own money, and you can buy most of what you need."

"Don't forget, Mom," I said. "I'm workin' for Tony Dempewolf—I gave you some money yesterday."

"Yes, Ronald," she said. "I knew you'd remind me."

"And Helen and Pat are helpin' us whenever we need it," added Mom. "They will give me money whenever I have to ask for it."

Then looking at us all and seeing that she had our strict attention, she said, "You kids need to be grateful for what your older brothers and sisters are doin' for ya."

That was in the year 1952, and that year marked a turning point for us Newtons. Catalyzed by an unsympathetic social worker and supported by a combination of older children with real jobs and lots of us younger children contributing, a marvelous change had taken place. Mom and Dad, at long last, had escaped the dependence bonds and shackles of welfare. Dad was now retired and was drawing the Social Security and disability benefits that he had rightfully earned. My brother Jack's allotment check continued to arrive in the mail. Mom worked in the Mead Post Office until mid-1954, when Hap Howlett died after a long bout with cancer. Robert "Cork" Clark, the son of Ansel Clark, owner of the Clark Lumber Co., was appointed as acting postmaster; Clark had voted for Republican candidate Dwight Eisenhower, who was now our thirty-fourth president. So with the change in local politics, Mom changed jobs—she signed on as a cook in the Mead School Cafeteria.

By 1954, Laura Dreier and James Elmer Newton were no longer in need of the benevolent, helping hand of the government. They and their children were now fueling the family's economic engine with their own resources, earned with perseverance and never-ending toil. Laura Dreier Newton's children had lived by her creed, "Children should be seen and not heard," and for more than thirty years, the diligent work of Laura's children was demonstrated in the yards, in the gardens, in the stores, in the homes, and in the fields of the Mead community; the children's industrious labors had been witnessed by townspeople and farmers alike. Their deeds were visible evidence that the Newtons had not taken the assistance of a generous humanity for granted. The Newtons were now earning their own keep every way they could. Laura was now selling a quart of Bossie's milk each day to Doreen Clark, Postmaster Clark's Irish war-bride wife, a daily transaction that netted Laura another fifty cents.

Jack Newton, US Marine Corps, 1953. *Newton Family Album*

Laura Newton (*second right*), school cafeteria, 1957. *Mead Consolidated Schools Yearbook*

Helen Newton (*right*), United Airlines, 1955. *Newton Family Album*

Rosemary Newton, American Telephone & Telegraph Co., 1957. *Newton Family Album*

CHAPTER 33

Departing

Death frequently arrived at the doorstep of our Mead community. As eight- and ten-year-olds, my sisters Pat and Helen told us triplets the story of when they lived in Mead's Town Hall in 1939, they peaked through a window of the blacksmith shop next door and saw a dead man lying on the floor.

"We were really scared," said Pat. "We told Dad, and he went over, and he got Tony Dempewolf at the gas station—the two of them went inside and saw him. They called the sheriff."

"What'd he look like?" I asked.

"I was so scared I didn't really take a good look at 'em," said Pat. "I didn't see his face—his head was turned away from the window."

I wondered then how it would be for me too to see a dead person. I knew too that I would be frightened. That experience came to me when widow Mary Johnson died; Mom thought that my brothers and I should attend the funeral Mass at Mead's Catholic Church. At the end of the service, her casket was wheeled to the rear of the church and opened for all the mourners to view. I did not want to look at her, but I had no choice as we all exited the tiny church. Fear came over me momentarily as I glanced at her powdered sunken face and the rosary beads in her shriveled hands. Except for her glasses, she was much different looking than the gentle lady whom I remembered sitting at our dinner table and eating with us. As I watched them load the casket into the hearse, my fear abated and turned to bravado—I was proud that I had seen a dead person for the first time—I knew that I had faced one of life's tough realities, and I knew that I could do it again.

Later, my brothers and I went to Bernard Keller's funeral at the same church; Bernard, just out of high school, died after an operation for a brain tumor, and the top of his head was crowned with white bandages. I saw a black limousine leave the churchyard with Bernard's brother Glen, sitting in the backseat, bent and leaning forward with his head down and sobbing uncontrollably. Seeing him grieve, I was so overwhelmed that I too began to cry.

My ten-year old brother, Jerry, was asked to serve at the funeral Mass of a fallen soldier, Max Hernandez. Max was the brother of our good friend Loe, and Max had been our brother Tom's classmate. Jerry told me how Mrs. Molly Hernandez cried when the casket was opened. Earlier and before the Korean conflict had intensified, Loe's other brother, Don, had also died in a training accident. The Hernandez brothers' deaths and the entry of the Chinese into the war frightened the bejesus out of me. Like the fear I had of the Japanese in World War II, I was afraid that Chinese soldiers were coming to America—I was fearful that I would be killed if they did. It wasn't death that I was afraid of—I was afraid of the pain that I would undergo—I had not given much credence to the finality of death—all I knew was that I needed to be spiritually and contritely prepared before it happened.

The sister of my classmate Irene Stotts, eighteen-year-old Nadine died of a blood disease. I saw Nadine at her home shortly before she passed. As I stood at their door collecting payment for delivering them the *Rocky Mountain News*, I saw her sitting at the piano. I heard beautiful sounds coming from across the room as her nimble fingers moved along the keyboard, and she turned and smiled at me as she played. She looked happy and well, and I thought to myself how wonderful it was that she was out of bed and appeared to be on the road to recovery. I was shocked when I heard she had died just weeks later; my innocent perception had always been that death from a prolonged illness always brought on emaciation of the body.

My cousin Bill Newton was killed as a teenager in an automobile accident, and Mom decided that we triplets were too young to attend his funeral. A dozen years later, his father, my uncle Spaulding, died with cancer. I saw him shortly before he died. Mom told my brothers and me to clean up and get ready to go to see Uncle Spaulding. She didn't explain why, but we readily knew—he had been suffering with cancer for a long time. He was on his deathbed in his home near Longmont.

My brothers and I had seen Uncle Spaulding that summer while we hoed potatoes on the farm of his daughter and our cousin Mary Ellen Newton Maynard, who lived with her husband, Dean, on a farm near Platteville. We saw that Uncle Spaulding had lost weight, and his bib overalls hung loosely on his thin body. He walked slowly and bent slightly at the waist, giving me the impression that his stomach was hurting and that he was suffering from abdominal cancer. He still smiled when he greeted us, and he always flashed his false teeth with his characteristic wide grin.

Said our cousin Tex (Shively) when talking about his father, "It makes you sick when you think about the big *C*—no one knows what causes it and how to treat it—Dad didn't smoke or drink—he doesn't deserve to be withering away like this and to be in so much pain."

Despite his pain, Uncle Spaulding was still able to put his weakened body onto the seat of a tractor, and he was cultivating corn for his son-in-law on the Platteville farm. On his way from Longmont traveling to work, Uncle Spaulding stopped at our

Light of Her Children

house to pick us up and take us to the potato field adjacent to the cornfield on the Maynard farm, where he worked.

One afternoon, Uncle Spaulding's tractor came to a standstill. With the loud two-cylinder sound of the John Deere engine still running, he sat in his seat and motioned for me to come over to him. As I arrived near the large rear wheel of the tractor, Uncle Spaulding pointed downward in front of it and began speaking, giving me instructions to do something, but I could not hear his voice over the rat-tat sound of the engine. I looked down to where he was pointing, and I still could not figure out what he wanted me to do.

Finally, he shut the motor off and said, "Damn it, young man—are you blind? Can't you see that that iron claw is about to drop off—my god, kid, anyone can see that it's just hangin' there!"

I was offended by his remark and shot back at him with "I don't care what you think—I couldn't see it and I couldn't hear ya."

I angrily yanked the dangling piece of iron off the cultivator frame, handed it to him, and walked off. As he drove us home that night, I couldn't look at him or talk to him. I was having second thoughts about my spouting off to him, and I was not pleased with what I said—I knew that it was not right for me to talk to my uncle like that—especially when he was sick and not feeling well.

Our brother Tom took my brothers and me in his '49 Ford to Uncle Spaulding's house, where he lay on his deathbed. When we arrived, Aunt Mary was in the kitchen. She told my brothers and me to go into the bedroom—Uncle Spaulding was in his pajamas, lying on his back with his left knee bent, angling his leg up off the bed, showing that there was nothing but bone in his pajama leg. He did not give us his characteristic smile when he saw us.

"Hello, boys," he said. "What cha been doin'?"

"Well," I said, "we just finished helpin' Dean sack potatoes, and next week, we're goin' to finish the third hoein' of Ted Rademacher's sugar beets."

Then Rollie said, "Then we're goin' to take a couple of weeks off before school starts."

"That's good," he said.

We all stood there waiting for him to say something more, but he did not. I could not speak either. My eyes were now starting to water—I knew that he would not live much longer, and I wanted to apologize to him for talking back at him the way I did, but I did not have the courage to do so.

Finally, Uncle Spaulding says, "You boys can go now—with the good Lord willin'—I'll see ya again."

We knew, and he knew that this was the end—we would not see each other ever again on this earth. The only uncle whom my brothers and I ever knew—a courageous warrior—was now fighting his last battle. We left the room, and I walked out of the house and stood under their silver poplar tree and cried.

* * *

In 1955, a catastrophic death event occurred just three miles southeast of Mead—shocking our small sheltered town out of its innocent existence and propelling its citizenry into an area that none of us had ever experienced before. A crime of great and unforgettable proportions was committed—committed for the sake of money and one that involved a tormented family, resulting in the death of two them while, at the same time, taking the lives of many other unwary, innocent victims. The crime directly impacted the lives of Richie, Rollie, Dave, and me, as well as many of our classmates and their families, and it rocked the world with horror and dismay—a never-to-be-forgotten event. No other previous experience of death prepared me for this.

Light of Her Children

It was on the evening of November 1, shortly before 7:00 p.m., and we Newtons had just finished supper. My brother Marc was at the kitchen sink washing dishes while my brother Dave was drying—I was sitting at the kitchen table tending to my history homework. I was feeling unusually tired—I had gotten home late the night before, because that was Halloween. My brothers and I and our friends had roamed the neighborhood and streets of Mead, looking for ways to create mischief and pranks that we thought would rankle the townspeople. Having gone to church that morning to celebrate All Saints' Day, I had been up since 6:00 a.m. I was also unusually tired because Coach Adams had worked us especially hard at football practice that afternoon.

Suddenly, Dave, Marc, and I heard this loud boom. It was the loudest noise I had ever heard. I imagined it to be an explosion that had taken place, and it seemed to have occurred very close to us.

"What the heck was that?" I asked excitedly.

"I dunno," said Dave.

"Sounded like dynamite!" said Marc.

The three of us ran from the kitchen out into the yard. There in the eastern sky was a hovering bright-red light—it did not move—I quickly concluded that it was not the red light that I was accustomed to seeing at night on the wing or tail of an aircraft. It appeared to be just a few miles away and perhaps several hundred feet off the ground.

Soon Richie, Rollie, and Frosty came running out of the house, followed by Mom. Across the street, Mr. and Mrs. Gallegos were standing in their front yard looking at the red phenomenon in the sky. Everyone was perplexed as to what we were seeing and how it related to the loud explosion that we had just heard.

"That sounded like a loud firecracker," said Richie.

"I wonder what that red light is—it's just hangin' up there in the sky," exclaimed Rollie.

Just then, Weber drove into our driveway with the top down on his Buick convertible. "What the hell was that loud noise?" he asked.

"We don't know," I responded. "But that red light up there in the sky has stayed in that same place where it was just a minute ago—it doesn't seem to be moving. It looks like it is just a couple of miles away from us. Let's go see where it is."

"Get in and let's go," said Weber.

Dave and we triplets jumped into the car, and soon Weber was driving east on CR 32, leaving Mead and crossing the Washington Highway—heading toward Platteville at sixty or more miles per hour. Clouds of dust from the gravel road billowed behind us. Weber's car skidded from side to side in a weaving fashion as the tires engaged the piled furrows of gravel and sand built up by previous traffic. With the red light still in our view and to our right, we slowed down abruptly to turn on CR 13 and then continued south at a rapid speed, still on a gravel road. From the top-down Buick, we could see for miles in every direction, and the giant red light we were following seemed to dwarf the millions of stars that were shining all around it. Weber's car moved alone and up and down along the darkened country road carved out among the contours of the eastern plains prairie hills that butted up against the Saint Vrain River Valley. After a mile, we stopped briefly to cross Highway 66 and then continued south on CR 13 as the red light appeared larger and larger to us.

"Just what the heck is that red light?" Weber asked. "It looks like it may be hangin' on a parachute that we can't see."

"It can't be from outer space," I said. "I know it's not a flyin' saucer—I've never believed any of that stuff. I think it is a light attached to a parachute," I said, agreeing with Weber's speculation.

"Look!" said Dave, pointing to his right. "Look over there—there's a lot of light coming from somethin' on the ground."

Suddenly, our car descended into a large ravine, and the light on the ground was no longer visible to us. As we reached the top of a hill, we instantaneously saw a gigantic blazing light emanating from a large ground fire immediately to our right.

"My god!" shouted Weber. "What the hell is that?"

Weber slowed down when he saw a pair of headlights in front of him on his side of the road. We saw that it was a pickup truck parked on the west roadside with the driver's door wide open. Weber swung his car immediately in front of it, slammed on the brakes, and skidded to a stop. We saw Mr. Jake Heil standing near the fence and opening a wire gate. I recognized Mr. Heil right away. I had worked on this very farm for him two summers before, driving a grain truck for his threshing crew. The fire was on the other side of his farm, and it had started in the middle of a sugar-beet field that belonged to his son, Harold. Harold and Jake had just harvested the crop, and the loosened soil was now barren. "What's caused the fire?" Weber asked him.

"It's a star!" said Mr. Heil. "Fell out of the sky just a few minutes ago! It was the loudest sound you've ever heard—it fell right out of the sky—right into Harold's beet field."

Immediately, Weber and my brothers and I jumped from the car, and we ran through the opened gate and toward the burning mass about a half mile away. Just as I was bursting into a long stride, I stopped. There in front of me was a crater about ten feet wide and two feet deep that had been dug in the soft soil of the recently harvested field. Lying right next to it was the contorted body of a woman, her legs twisted and still partially covered by rolled-up and torn nylon stockings. It was then that I realized that I was at the site of a plane crash. I ran no further.

I walked timidly toward the burning debris, looking for others. The bright light produced long shadows from bodies all around me. To my left and to my right, I could plainly see indentions in the soil with human forms nearby, which spread all across the smooth and level surface of the field.

I thought about when I was much younger and watching large aircraft flying over Mead en route to Denver, I had fantasized about saving passengers from a crash. I would be a hero, I thought. I would help the passengers, presumably all alive, taking them way from the mangled metal body of the plane.

But that night, there could be no heroism. The heat and flames of the piled debris were so intense I could go no further. The passengers had been disfigured beyond recognition. How could any of them survive? Shocked with disbelief, I stood riveted, looking at the wreckage from a distance. The burning heap was forty or fifty feet tall and nearly a hundred yards wide. Flames shot high up into the air, and sparkling cinders blew all over Weld County. Increasingly obscured by the smoke, I could still see the dim image of the red light right above me. It then quickly dawned on me; the red light had been a signal, a signal of distress. It was an automatic signal, a sign high in the sky for all in Weld and neighboring Boulder County to see.

I turned from the blaze to walk back to the car and to gather comfort from my brothers and Weber about what I was seeing. We heard sirens from fire trucks and ambulances. We could see rows of headlights moving from all directions toward us. Curious folks, townspeople and rural people, were driving toward the red light in the sky and the fire on the ground. They parked their cars, and some crawled through the strands of barbed wire so that they could walk closer to the burning pile. Others stood outside their cars talking to others, trying to understand what they were seeing and what had happened. They were listening to their radios and talking to one another.

Weber said, "I saw the body of a passenger still strapped and sitting in his seat."

"The bodies I saw were so mangled it was hard to recognize any features on their faces," said Richie.

"I saw a man in a T-shirt and pants—he didn't have any shoes on," said Rollie. "It looked like the explosion blew his shirt and shoes right off of 'im."

"There were pieces of suitcases all over the place," said Dave. "An' when I saw a dead lady on the ground—I didn't wanna go any further—I came back."

My brothers and Weber and I stood next to the car, talking with other observers, who were walking up and down the road, talking with groups of folks trying to find out what had happened. Standing in the road with them, not wanting to leave, we too hoped we would find out more.

Soon we learned that it was a United Airlines plane—one of the bystanders heard on the radio that someone had seen the intact tail section that landed down by the Saint Vrain River about a mile away.

"I hope Helen was not on it," I said to Richie when we both learned that it was a United aircraft. Our sister Helen had been flying for United as a stewardess (as they were called then) for two years.

Richie said, "She'd been assigned to fly in and out of Newark, New Jersey. She wouldn't be flying through Denver—I don't think she was on it."

A car slowly approached us and parked across the road. The driver was Jessie Thompson, Allen's mother. She was with Myrtle Newman, Duck's wife. In explaining to them what they had just seen, I mentioned, "You know our sister Helen is a stewardess for United—we hope she wasn't on this flight."

With anguish, Mrs. Thompson cried, "Oh, I hope not! Oh no, that would be a terrible thing!"

Weber and my brothers and I had not been the first to arrive at the scene: unbeknownst to us, Connie Hopp and his brother Kenneth had arrived there before we did. Months later, Connie, who the year before had been my high school football and basketball teammate and had graduated, told me that he and Kenneth were eating supper when they heard the loud boom.

"Ken and I both ran out of the house and saw the burning plane as it was coming down," said Connie. "It was fallin' fast toward the ground, all on fire, with sparks trailing behind it. We heard a big explosion as it hit, and immediately, fire went straight up into the air."

"How long was it before you got there?" I asked.

"It was just a matter of minutes," said Connie. "We drove our car part of the way, and we walked the rest. We walked all around the wreckage, looking to see if anyone was alive—we didn't hear or see anyone—there were only dead bodies."

"It started to get cold later that night, so Ken sent me back to get our coats," said Connie. "On the way back, I saw a seat with a body still strapped in on it—that really got to me. I still have nightmares about the whole thing."

"Weber and my brothers and I got there about fifteen minutes after the crash, but we didn't see either you or Ken," I said.

"We were driving all over the field looking for bodies," said Connie. "We could see the outline of the bodies in the ground where they hit."

Later that night, my brothers and I were home describing our observations to Mom when the phone rang. It was our sister Helen calling to tell Mom and all of us that she was all right. Helen had received her wings in '55 at a ceremony that most of us Newtons attended. In publicizing this and her large family, United brought in a *Rocky Mountain News* reporter and photographer, and the airline provided the whole family with a plane ride that flew us over Mead—in a plane that was very similar to the one that had just crashed.

Now near midnight, I still had my American history homework assignment to read. It would be a short night's sleep for me. I would be up at 6:00 a.m. to go to church for All Souls' Day. I knew that we would be praying for the repose of the souls of all the passengers and the crew members.

Several weeks later, the FBI determined that John Gilbert Graham had planted a dynamite bomb in his mother's suitcase. The blast, originating from the luggage compartment, severed the tail of the airplane from the fuselage. The paper reported that from an airport vending machine, Mr. Graham had taken out a life insurance policy on his mother worth $37,500. That was a lot of money, but how could a person kill his mother? Graham's motives were impossible for me to fathom. I knew that I was just the opposite of Graham—I loved my mother. If I had $37,500, I would give it all to Mom to make her life better, not end it.

Conrad Hopp, 1955. *Mead Consolidated Schools Yearbook*

Ronald Weber, 1953. *Mead Consolidated Schools Yearbook*

Helen Newton awarded stewardess wings. *Front row, L–R*: Frosty Newton, Laura Dreier Newton, Helen Newton, James Elmer Newton. *Second row, L–R*: Maureen Newton, Patricia Newton French. *Third row, L–R*: Eunice Newton Thornton, Kathleen Newton Hetterle, Marc Newton. *Fourth row, L–R*: Jerry Newton, Richie Newton, Dave Newton. *Fifth row*: Ronnie Newton. *Sixth row*: Rollie Newton. 1955. *Newton Family Album*

Chapter 34

Losing

Playing basketball for Mead High School was a goal to which my triplet brothers and I aspired for most of our young lives. At long last, we matriculated into high school as sophomores and as seasoned players; we were cautiously confident that we would be selected as substitutes for the varsity team. We had gained a lot of experience the year before as starters on Mead's junior high team. Throughout our nine years of playing basketball, we knew what it was like to win, but we also had learned about losing. As sixth-graders, we endured one disappointing loss, and as eighth-graders, our losses had been frequent.

Then as ninth-graders, our junior high team was undefeated in conference play, winning all seven games. We were the heavy favorites to win the postseason tournament because we had defeated most of our opponents by wide margins. Just before that tournament started, our accomplishments as triplets on the basketball team received some acclaim and publicity in the *Denver Post*. Mom, fearing that we were developing a sense of self-importance that was way out of proportion, cautioned the three of us with her proverbial phrase: "Remember, you are not the only star that twinkles."

Although I basked in the publicity and notoriety, I took Mom's admonition seriously, and I readily realized that our team's success had been not only because of us triplets but also because of the other skillful members of our team, namely Allen Thompson, Leonard Smith, and Mike Eckel.

We lost by two points in the quarterfinals and were eliminated from the tournament by a team we had beaten easily several weeks before. I cried openly as I undressed and showered in the locker room.

"What happened?" asked Ronald Weber as we sat in the pool hall drinking soda pop.

"I'm not sure," I said. "We couldn't dribble the ball through them—we couldn't get any good shots—we were just standin' around."

"Did they guard you one-on-one?" asked Weber.

"No, they didn't—they just seemed to stand in one spot—each one of them just moved around in a small space when we had the ball—I couldn't go anywhere when I was dribblin'—they wouldn't let me through."

"How many points did Thompson get?" asked Weber.

"I think only four—we couldn't pass the ball inside to him like we usually do—everything was clogged up at the center round the basket."

"Sounds like they threw a zone defense against you," said Weber.

"What's that?" I asked.

"That's when they don't take you man-to-man—each player just stays in their own little area on the floor, and they follow the ball wherever it goes."

"I've never heard of it."

"There's a way to beat it," said Weber. "I learned how to do it from Coach Peterson when I was playin'—I'll show you guys how to do it sometime."

Nevertheless, many of the town wags and gossipers preferred to think that we triplets were stuck on ourselves and far too confident. That was not the case then, and it never had been. None of the three of us habitually displayed arrogance, boasted about our accomplishments, or took our opponent for granted. As seasoned basketball players and constantly in the limelight as triplets, my brothers and I had to learn to tolerate the opinions of ill-informed critics. Furthermore, I had resigned in my own mind that they had little credibility—after all, I thought, most of them had never played basketball. They, just like my brothers and me, had a lot to learn about the game of round ball.

My triplet brothers and I were elated when Coach Jim Beers selected us to play on both the junior varsity and varsity teams. We played with brother Jerry, who was then a junior. All four of us were junior-varsity starters, and we won twelve games while losing only two. Most of our wins were with overwhelming margins, and had Coach Beers given us Newtons more playing time, the team most likely would have won every game.

Although none of us Newtons started on the varsity team, we did play, and we certainly contributed to the success of the team. Rollie and Jerry filled in when one or more of our starting forward got into foul trouble, and Richie and I were substituted when Coach Beers felt he needed more ball-handling skills at the guard positions. Rollie, an excellent rebounder, a situation in which he was fouled incessantly, scored many of his points at the foul line. Jerry had an excellent hook shot at the center position, and he too protected and coveted his space beneath the boards. As guards, Richie and I brought the ball down the court and got it in to our big men inside. Richie's forte was his jump shot—if left open by an unwary opponent, he could pot it from almost anywhere on the court. I established a role as the floor general—my job was to control the tempo of the game and pass the ball to our top scorers. I also controlled the ball with my dribble when it was time for our team to go into a stall in the final minute or two of the game.

Because of my ball-handling skills, I got to play in all the varsity games, sometimes as much as two quarters and sometimes when my brothers saw very little action. Because of that, I was keenly aware that I could be perceived as becoming too big for my britches, especially by Mom. She had started to attend our home games, and each morning after an evening's game and sitting at the breakfast table, I was reluctant to discuss any details about the game with her. I knew too that she would not shower me with praise, because if she did, she would think that my head would swell bigger than a watermelon. I tried to say very little about the game and my own play for fear of giving her cause to remind me that I was not the only star that twinkled. I didn't want to hear that again—I had heard that phrase too many times before. But deep down, I was proud that my own star was shining, and I knew that in the coming years, those of my brothers would be shining as well.

Mom was always concerned about the amount of playing time each one of her sons received, especially Jerry. Jerry had not been as passionate about basketball as we triplets, and as a consequence, he had not developed comparable skills as a player. After any game that she had not attended, she would ask me the next morning at the breakfast table, "Did Jerry get to play?"

If I answered, "No," she would sigh and shake her head with disappointment.

In Mom's mind, all her sons should get to play—and in her mind, age took precedence over skill, and age took priority when it came to opportunity for participation: that was the rule she had always followed in raising her children. She was reluctant to accept the fact that skill reigned supreme in the arena of competitive sports and that basketball was no exception.

That year our Mead varsity team placed second in the conference, and we were knocked out of the district tournament in the first round. Nevertheless, Mead High had the most successful basketball season it had had in a decade, and we four

Newton brothers experienced a learning season that prepared us well for the upcoming year.

In the next season of '55–'56, we had a new coach. Jack Adams, an athlete in his own right, had played sports in both high school and college and was a man of great integrity and self-discipline. He came into the lives of my four brothers and me at the right time—we needed someone to refine our raw talent and mold us into a competitive unit as a team; it turned out that Jack Adams was the man to do just that, and my brothers and I were equally ready for him to do so.

I admired Coach Adams: he did not smoke, drink, or swear, and he demanded that we follow the same rules. He was physically fit, and he conditioned us with rigorous workouts so that we were fit also. He understood the game of basketball and how to teach it to his players. I idolized Coach Adams, adhering to his rules, following his example, and listening intently whenever he spoke. My brothers and I believed in him, and he motivated us to perform at our very best. In my simple teenage mind as a believer in God, Coach Adams was a blessing from heaven, and his sudden appearance in the midst of my brothers and me was a match made by divine intervention.

As the season began, the county newspaper, the *Greeley Tribune*, picked Mead to win the conference championship; the paper's rationale was that Mead was loaded with talent and had good height with its returning seniors; furthermore, Mead had five Newton brothers playing—Dave Newton, a gifted freshman, was joining the team.

As our first game on our home court was about to begin, Coach Adams said, "Tonight I want to start with all of the Newtons. Richie and Ronnie, you take the guard positions—Rollie and Dave, you two play forwards—Jerry, you start out at center."

We Newtons played together as the starting five for four or five minutes before Coach Adams began substituting with his other ten reserve players. Those several minutes had been a historic moment in the history of Mead High School as well as in the nation's chronicles of high school basketball. No other team had been known to have five brothers as simultaneous starters. However, this historical event was never again repeated. In the following week at practice, Rollie began to sense that the pain he had been feeling in his chest for more than a month was now becoming more intense.

"Son, you have a heart murmur," said Dr. Cooke as he removed his stethoscope from Rollie's chest.

"What's that mean?" asked Rollie.

"Your heart valve isn't workin' right—you probably had strep throat when you were a child, and it scarred some of the tissue. You're goin' to have to quit playin' basketball for a while—I'll write you out a prescription—we'll see if it helps you—I want you to come back and see me in six months."

We five Newton brothers never played again together on Mead High School's basketball team—our phenomenon as a sole team of starring brothers had vanished—the light of our collective basketball star dimmed—a memory to just a few: only Coach Adams and we five Newtons realized the significance of those few minutes in Mead High School's gym.

In that '55–'56 season, Coach Adams guided our team to winning the conference championship—we had only one defeat. After winning our final conference game and riding the bus back to Mead, Richie yelled out, "Hey, Coach—I'm going to ring the siren tonight—the whole town needs to know we've won the conference."

"Well, I guess they need to find out the news somehow," said Coach Adams. "I'm told that Mead hasn't won a league title since the mid-forties."

"Yal, that was when my brother Jack played," I said. "Mead took consolation that year in the state tournament. Maybe we'll go back to state again this year."

"Let's win the district tournament first before we start thinking about state," said Coach Adams. "We still have a long way to go."

We defeated three teams to win the district tournament, and we did make it into the state playoffs for the second time in Mead's forty-year history. We won our first game but lost the second. I had played poorly and had fouled out several minutes before the game ended. My sadness and disappointment were magnified when I saw Coach Adams's wife, Arden, crying, and he, with his arms around her, was trying to comfort her. I had let both my team and my coach down—I too sobbed in the locker room. Brother Marc too was crying. Brother Frosty was back in Mead watching the game on television—he could not hold back his tears.

On a happier note, Richie was the high scorer for Mead for both games, and he was named to the all-state team. Our final record for the '55–'56 season was twenty wins and four losses. We pointed our compass to the next year—perhaps Rollie would be playing with us—if so, we might win the state championship.

Four Newtons on Mead Team

Coach Jack Adams, former Greeley high and Colorado State athletic ace, stands surrounded by Newtons. These four Newton brothers are members of the Mead high basketball team coached by Adams. Left to right are Ron, Jerry, David and Richard. A fifth brother, Roland, was also on the team, but stopped playing to become manager of the team due to a heart condition. Ron, Richard and Roland are triplets. Mead rolled up what is believed to be the highest total by a high school basketball team in the history of the state, 106-40 over Evans two weeks ago in North Central league play.—Tribune photo by Robert Widlund.

Chapter 35

Summer Job

Our spring track season continued right up until the end of the school year, and one night as I was leaving the locker room, Coach Adams asked me, "Are you and your brothers goin' to work in the beet fields again this summer?"

"I'm sure we will," I said. "I don't know what else we could do to earn money. It's goin' to be hard for all of us to find work on a farm—there's so many of us. None of us knows how to drive a tractor or operate farm equipment. I don't know if there is any farmer around here who wants to hire us."

"Workin' in a beet field doesn't sound like very much fun," said Coach Adams. "And you're not learnin' anything when you do it—sure'd be nice if you guys could find work doin' somethin' else."

"It sure would," I said. "But I know Ted Rademacher is counting on us to work again. We only have two weeks of school left—I imagine Mr. Rademacher will want us to start as soon as school's out. He'll be callin' us to see if we wanna work."

School had been out for two days, and I was enjoying the time off with no responsibilities. Sleeping in late to midmorning and now with free time, I went downtown to hang out at the pool hall, where I could watch Dad play with his farmer friends. Bill

Schell's farm was just a half mile south of Mead—he was there. Bill's brother, Frank, was there. Glen Keller was taking some time off from his electrician's job—he was playing. Joe Jones was taking off a few hours from his auto repair shop located next door, and he had slipped over to play. Ed Dempewolf, Tony's brother and retired from the military, was playing.

I was intently watching the rivalry of each individual player in their customary round-the-world game when Coach Adams walked into the pool hall and sat down beside me. He had stopped off at our house, and Mom told him where I was most likely to be.

"Can you come outside for a minute?" he asked. I obediently arose and followed Coach Adams out the pool-hall door and onto the sidewalk of Main Street.

Turning to me, he said, "How 'bout doin' somethin' else this summer other than thinnin' beets? I just came back from Frank Eckel's farm, and they wanted me to work for them—I told them that I couldn't. But I asked Frank, what work did he want done? He said that they were going to get into the milkin' business and that they were going to install milkin' machines in their barn. Frank has already hired a contractor to install them, but the guy said he needed some additional help. Frank wanted me to help him with the construction. After I told him I couldn't, I asked him if he thought you could do it. Frank said he thought that you could, so I told him that I would contact you to see if you wanted to. Frank said he thought it would take most of the summer to build it."

I hesitated for a moment. I knew that my brothers were depending on me to work with them that summer in the beet field. If I left, I would be leaving them shorthanded. On the other hand, this was an opportunity I had been waiting for. My brothers and I all wanted to quit hoeing beets and do other farm work. I was not afraid of the physical labor of thinning beets, but I was dreading the drudgery and boredom that it involved.

"Yes I think I do wanna work for the Eckels!" I said to Coach Adams. "It beats thinnin' beets!"

"Good," said Coach Adams. "Get in my car, and I'll take you out to the Eckel farm to talk to Frank."

Coach drove to the barn and pulled up where Frank Eckel was talking to his contractor, Frank Malevich; they were looking at the installation drawings placed on Malevich's pickup-truck hood.

After we had been introduced, Frank Eckel said, "We've hired Malevich to install this thing for us. He's built a lot of dairy barns all around Weld County.

"Ronnie, do you wanna work for us this summer?" Frank asked. "Coach Adams thought cha might."

"I sure do. Whatta ya want me to do?" I asked.

"Malevich here needs someone to help him out," said Frank. "When he's buildin' this dairy barn, there are lots of things to do where it takes two people—he'll need you to help with those. When you're not workin' with him, we'll have you workin' on the farm with Mike. We'll pay you seven dollars a day—will that be okay?"

"It sure will!" I said excitedly, thinking about the money I was going to make.

"When do you want me to start?" I asked.

"How 'bout tomorrow?" Frank asked. "I'll have Mike [his son] pick you up in the mornin' 'bout seven fifteen. Malevich starts workin' at seven thirty—so he'll tell you what he wants done then."

I was ecstatic. I would be making more money that summer than ever before in my life.

When my three brothers and I finished thinning and hoeing beets in the summer of '55, our brother Jerry was not working with us as he had the year before. Jerry had obtained steady work on Wilbert Peppler's farm, where he made more money and where the tasks were more diverse and less laborious than hoeing beets. Richie, Rollie, and I knew that eventually we too would be working independently on farms as hired hands for the summer and that we would soon be rescued from the drudgery of the sugar-beet field. This was the pattern established by our brother Tom and now continued by Jerry. We triplets looked forward to the day when we would be old enough to operate farm equipment, irrigate a sugar beet or barley crop, or milk a herd of cows. And now in the summer of '56, that opportunity had come to me.

"What's this goin' to do with the others who are still thinnin' beets?" asked Mom when she heard the news. "I know they are still dependin' on you to work with 'em. Ted Rademacher was askin' the other day after church if you all were goin' to work for him again. I told him that I thought you were."

"I don't know what they'll do," I said. "All I know is that I can make more money working for the Eckels than I can thinnin' beets. Mr. Eckel said he would pay me seven dollars a day and that he would keep me on all summer."

"Well, maybe they'll find somethin' else too," said Mom. "With just the three of 'em, they probably won't wanna thin beets."

Mom was seeing that just like her older children, we triplets were becoming independent from one another. Each one would encounter different opportunities, and we could not always function as a threesome. We had ceased dressing alike several years ago, and our differences were becoming more evident to her each day. No longer could we live with her mantra of all being treated the same way. The outside world was not going to function that way, no matter how hard she might have wanted it to.

Installing the dairy in the Eckel's big red barn involved a variety of tasks. First, we laid a concrete foundation for each wall. Then I unloaded cinder blocks from the Eckel truck and hauled them with a wheelbarrow and stacked them in piles—strategically located around the perimeter of the milk barn for Malevich to use. To strengthen my arms as I worked, I grabbed a block in each hand and swung them upward as I loaded and stacked—I wanted to be stronger for the upcoming football season in the fall. I mixed cement and fine sand together for mortar to be deposited between the cinder blocks that Malevich laid as he constructed the walls.

Malevich inserted metal window frames into the spaces he left in the block walls, and I followed by inserting rectangular pieces of glass into the frames and glazing them in with putty. Mike brought in a truckload of dirt and dumped it right next to the barn. I hauled fifty or sixty wheelbarrow loads and then shoveled the dirt into a four-foot-tall brick-walled enclosure—the earthen mound was to become the elevated walkway for the cows as they were lined up to be milked. I dug holes for posts in the holding pens constructed outside the big barn, and Malevich and I attached feeding troughs that we constructed out of pine two-by-twelves and two-by-fours.

Malevich ordered a load of cement to be brought in by truck from Longmont, and Mike Eckel and I helped him pour it onto the elevated walkway and the barn floor and then float the uncured concrete with hand trowels. Inside the milking area, I painted the block wall surfaces with pure-white enamel. Workers from an outside vendor came on-site to install the milking apparatus, which was placed in each of the four stalls and hooked to stainless-steel pipes attached to the walls, which were to carry the warm fresh milk to a large stainless-steel cooling tank.

I cashed my first check at the pool hall—for two weeks' work, I made eighty-four dollars—I stopped at Bunton's Red & White and bought a couple of weeks' supply of food for my lunches: lunch meat, oatmeal cookies, oranges, potato chips, and bread. I put the remainder in a checking account at Longmont's First National Bank.

While I worked with Malevich on the dairy barn, Mike worked for his dad, irrigating and cultivating corn and mowing hay. Mike and I had been best friends since the ninth grade, and he played with my brothers and me on our high school football and basketball teams. Mike drove about their farm on a Vespa motor scooter, and he frequently stopped by to visit with me. Mike also had started dating Linda Miller, a junior from Longmont High School, at the beginning of the summer, and now he was seeing her a couple of times a week.

One day I asked Mike, "Do you think Linda could line me up with one of her friends?"

"I don't know," said Mike. "I'll ask her and see what she says. She's got lots of friends—Longmont's a big school."

Several days later, Mike rode up again on his Vespa as I was eating my lunch.

"I talked to Linda last night," said Mike. "She said one of her best friends just broke up with her boyfriend, and maybe she might be interested in goin' out with someone else. He's on the wrestling team—Linda didn't know what happened between them—they broke up about two weeks ago. Her name is Kathy Nottingham—she and Linda sat next to each other in their typing class. I guess Linda sees her almost every day this summer—she drives her dad's car all over Longmont. Linda's goin' to ask her when she sees her—she'll let me know."

Hearing this, I was ecstatic. I hoped Kathy would consent. I saw Mike riding his Vespa on the road over the next couple of days, but he did not stop to talk. I became worried that Kathy did not want to go out and Mike was having a hard time breaking the news to me. Finally, one morning, Mike gave me the good news, "Linda told me that Nottingham wants to go out with you. Shall we take 'em to a movie in Longmont Saturday night?" he asked.

"That's okay with me," I said casually, trying not to show my excitement.

That Saturday night in July was the beginning of the relationship with Kathy that lasted into our high school senior year. Mike and I double-dated with Linda and Kathy several times using Frank Eckel's Oldsmobile. Soon Kathy and I were going alone as I managed borrowing cars from either Jerry or Tom to get to Longmont.

By the end of the summer, I had deposited more than $500 in my checking account, and I had plenty for new school clothes. Also, I had $200 I could contribute to buying a used car; my triplet brothers and I were ready to buy a '49 Ford; then I would have another choice of car in which to take Kathy out.

Eckel dairy barn and horse, Patsy, 1957. Patricia Eckel

Mike, Pat, and Frank Eckel, 1957. Patricia Eckel

Chapter 36

Agnes

My sixteen-year-old sister Maureen was missing one evening as we sat down for supper. Maureen should have returned home from school by four o'clock that afternoon, but it was now after 6:00 p.m., and her whereabouts was not known.

"Did you see her at school today?" Mom asked Kathleen.

"She was there this morning, but I don't know about this afternoon—we don't have any classes together in the afternoon—so I don't know."

"Maybe she went to Longmont to see Pat or Helen," said Jerry.

"Did she go home with somebody from school and stay overnight with 'em?" I asked.

"Who would that be?" asked Kathleen. "She never runs around with anyone."

Unlike Kathleen, Maureen didn't socialize with her classmates, and she had no close friends. It was doubtful that any of her classmates would know where she was, and if they did, we would not know which one to contact. Not even to her twin sister, Kathleen, had Maureen shared the intent to be away from home that evening. But the non-communication was not just with Kathleen—it was that way with all of us, including Mom and Dad—Maureen was somehow remote. At home, Maureen spent a lot of her time alone—sitting in her chair—staring ahead—occasionally with a grin.

"What are you laughin' about?" I once asked her.

She said nothing, seeming to ignore me and sending a message that I was prying into her private world, where I had no place. It seemed that she was telling me that what she was thinking was that it was "none of my business" and that maybe she had secrets that she did not want me to know anything about.

"Was she laughin' at me?" I asked myself. Twelve-year-olds worry about that sort of thing a lot. "What could have happened that made her smile?"

But sometimes, as Maureen sat alone in the corner of the room, I saw her grimace, and I heard a groan coming through her curled lips. Maureen was aching about something. What might that be? I had no clue—nor did anyone else in the family. She made no effort to tell anyone.

Displays of pleasure and pain by Maureen were regular—so frequent that my siblings and I simply dismissed them as "That's just Maureen," and we came to think of them as ordinary—nothing unusual. When friends and classmates made comments about my sister's unusual ways, I made no apologies.

"That's just the way she is," I said. After all, Maureen was not the only "different" one I knew in Mead. There was Manuel, the grandson of our next-door neighbor, Dulcinea Gallegos—eight-year-old Manuel frequently placed his stretched palms outward in front of his eyes while he squinted behind them—seemingly shielding his eyes from something he really didn't want to see.

In my twelve-year-old mind, there was also another distinctive trait of Maureen's—she was prone to lie. Often Maureen would blatantly deny any wrongdoing. All my siblings and I savored the taste of coffee and when combined with Bossie's fresh cream and a teaspoon of sugar—a delicious elixir. However, we were rarely allowed this treat. Sometimes on Sunday morning after Mass, Mom would let us have coffee—and then it was highly diluted with cream.

Maureen, especially, was always nagging Mom for permission to drink coffee but was constantly denied. One morning as Maureen was washing dishes and I was drying them, I saw her prepare her own cup of coffee, putting in three teaspoons of sugar and a giant pour of cream and then hiding the cup behind the bread box. Mom was cooking beans that day and decided that they needed more water, so she approached the sink to take the drinking dipper and get water from the tap; in so doing, she noticed the coffee cup behind the bread box.

Looking at Maureen and me, she asked, "Whose is this?"

"Not mine," I answered.

"It's not mine," said Maureen.

"Whose is it then?" asked Mom.

"I don't have any idea," said Maureen.

"I don't either," I said, not wanting to tattle on my big sister.

Mom took the cup and poured the coffee into the sink; when she left the kitchen, I confronted Maureen with "You did too do that—I saw you make it."

"I did not," said Maureen. "It wasn't me."

"You did too," I said.

"No, I did not," said Maureen.

Determined to get the last word, I said, "You lie like a rug."

As Maureen grew older, Mom granted her and Kathleen permission to drink as much coffee as they wanted. In addition to drinking coffee, Maureen had embarked upon another forbidden practice: smoking. To satisfy her newly acquired pleasure, Maureen stole packs of cigarettes from cartons purchased by Dad and from our sister-in-law Ferne, who stayed with us for several months. Our brother Tom also noticed that cigarettes were frequently missing from open packs that he had laid on his dresser top. When Mom was informed of the missing smokes, she suspected it was Maureen who had taken them.

"Did you take cigarettes from Ferne?" Mom asked Maureen one day.

"No, I did not," said Maureen. "It must've been Jerry or somebody else—it wasn't me."

On many evenings, Maureen sat alone at the dining-room table, pencil in hand and paper before her, copying a picture of an image she saw in a back issue of *Good Housekeeping* or *Ladies Home Journal*. Short sentences emerged from her mouth as she labored—as if she was carrying on a discussion with someone sitting next to her—but her words made no sense to me. Whom was she talking to? Her monologue seemed childlike—similar to that of a four-year-old playing house with her doll—neither caring nor even aware that anybody was nearby and listening.

One night Maureen sketched a drawing of a smoking cigarette lying in an ashtray. She had copied it from a Camel's ad in the *Denver Post*. She showed it to our sister Rosemary, who had come home for the weekend.

Rosemary asked Maureen, "Can I have this?"

"Sure," said Maureen.

"I want to frame it and hang it up in my apartment," said Rosemary.

But Maureen was physiologically different too. Unlike the rest of us who had ceased wetting the bed in our early years, Maureen, now in her teens, still could not control her urination.

Mom asked her, "My gosh, child—did you go to the toilet before you went to bed last night?"

"I did," Maureen answered.

"Are you usin' those pads I made for ya?"

"Yes, I am," said Maureen.

"You better be," said Mom. "I haven't seen many in the wash lately—I hope you're using 'em."

With a reek of urine on her body, Maureen got herself ready for school wearing a blouse she had worn the day before. Seeing the soiled and wrinkled garment on her unkempt daughter, Mom said, "Young lady—you go right back upstairs and put on somethin' else—you're not wearin' that to school."

At the supper table, Mom would say to Maureen, "I want you to wash your hair tonight before you go to bed—do you understand? You're startin' to look like a real greaseball. Kathleen washes hers two or three times a week—you need to do the same."

On many nights, as my brothers and I lay in bed, we heard Maureen crying in her bedroom, which was right next to ours.

Sleeping in the bed next to Maureen's, Kathleen would ask, "What are you cryin' about?"

But there was no response from Maureen. She just continued to wail. Kathleen had asked Maureen the question that we all asked her whenever we heard her haunting moans, but we never got an answer. We never knew what was troubling Maureen. Was she suffering from a physical ailment? Had she had a confrontation with one of us kids or Mom or Dad? Was it one of her teachers? Was she suffering from mistreatment from another? If so—who was it?

And then, Maureen disobeyed constantly and then lied about her transgressions. Mom was known to discipline all of us children with a slap in the face or on the back or a switch or belt to the bottom and back, and Maureen was no exception. One day, after Maureen had been warned many times not to smoke in her upstairs bedroom, Mom decided she had to take more drastic measures, and she proceeded to whip Maureen with a belt. Maureen stood there in stoic silence, almost oblivious to what Mom was doing, showing no emotional response or stress. She seemed to be saying to all of us as we watched, "It doesn't hurt—it doesn't matter." Increasingly, it also seemed to me that Maureen could not take responsibility for her actions—perhaps she did not realize that she ever did anything wrong.

Seeing that Maureen's behavior did not change day after day no matter what disciplinary measures were used, Mom became frustrated and one day blurted out to Maureen, "I don't know how it is that I have failed with you—none of the other kids are as stubborn as you."

Maureen said nothing and just looked back at Mom with bewilderment—Mom's evaluation of her did not register—she appeared to have no comprehension of what Mom was saying.

With Maureen still absent from our supper that night, Mom finished before the rest of us and left the table to call my sisters Helen and Pat, who were living together in a Longmont apartment.

"She's not here," said Pat on the other end of the line. "Helen and I both got home a little after five, and we haven't seen her."

"Wait a little longer," said Pat. "She'll probably be home later tonight. If she's not home by midnight, give us a call, and we'll notify the police."

At eleven thirty, Mom again called Pat and Helen. Helen answered.

"She still's not home," said Mom.

"We'll call the Weld County sheriff," said Helen.

The next day, as Rollie and I walked home from school, Rollie said, "I wonder if Maureen's home yet?"

"I don't know," I said. "I saw Kathleen at noon hour, and I asked her if she had seen Maureen at school, and she said she hadn't."

The two of us walked into the dining room, where Mom was sewing, and Rollie asked, "Did Maureen come home yet?"

"No, she didn't, but Rosemary called just a while ago," said Mom. "She said that Maureen had taken the bus to Kansas City. Rosemary said she got a phone call from her sayin' she was there at the Kansas City bus station and she wanted to know if Rosemary could come and pick her up. Maureen got there a little after lunch—had ridden the bus all night. All she had with her was her baton—I guess she skipped her twirling lesson yesterday and hitched a ride to Longmont with somebody. She bought a bus ticket to Denver and then bought another one to Kansas City."

Rosemary, still working for the American Telephone & Telegraph Co., had transferred to Kansas City from Denver a year before. Maureen stayed with Rosemary in Kansas City for several days until Rosemary could get time off to drive her back to Colorado. A week later, Rosemary drove her Buick convertible into the front yard with Maureen sitting beside her. Maureen wore a new blouse and skirt—Rosemary had taken her shopping. Maureen looked content and happy—as if she had just returned from a restful vacation.

By the time Maureen and Kathleen were high school juniors, it was apparent to us and to all who knew them that they were two very different people. They were the diametrical opposite of the proverbial "two peas in a pod" Bobbsey twins of childhood literature. Kathleen frequently played in our summer softball workup games in our backyard, but Maureen chose to participate in less physical activities such as jacks and Chinese checkers. Kathleen, following in the footsteps of our sister Pat, was canning and sewing and entering her jars of fruits and vegetables and dresses in county 4-H club competitions; Maureen, with very little interest in handicrafts and needlework, preferred to spend her time sketching and coloring. Kathleen was the class news reporter for the yearbook, while Maureen was assigned to be the art editor. Kathleen was elected to the Mead High School cheerleading squad, but Maureen did not even bother to try out. Kathleen was selected as queen at the MHS Homecoming Dance; Maureen stayed home—no one had invited her. Kathleen was dating Eddie Heterle, her steady boyfriend; Maureen had only been asked out once—she was David Borgman's date to the MHS prom. Eddie Heterle escorted Kathleen to the MHS Pep Club Sweetheart Ball—Kathleen was a queen candidate; Maureen stayed home—again she had not been invited.

Mom, always aware of Maureen's social isolation from her twin sister, encouraged Kathleen to be more inclusive. When Kathleen, a frequent babysitter of Kurt Olson, was asked to go on a vacation to the Midwest with Kurt's parents, Don and Mary Olson, and to be Kurt's "nanny," Mom said Kathleen could go if they also took Maureen. The Olsons said no, and Kathleen went anyhow; Maureen stayed home.

Kathleen married Eddie Heterle and moved to Denver, and after her graduation, Maureen stayed home.

One day my bookkeeping teacher, Mrs. Thelma Bachman, asked me, "How are the twins doin'?"

"Kathleen lives in Denver and now has a baby girl," I said. "They named her Candace. Eddie works for Bill Drieling Motors in the parts department."

"What about Maureen? Is she makin' it?"

"I think so," I said. "She's at home doin' housework and stuff—she says she's goin' to Longmont one of these days to find a job."

"I sure hope Maureen finds something," said Mrs. Bachman. "I was really worried about what was going to happen to her when she graduated. She's a very <u>unusual</u> girl."

One day when all of us were at school, Maureen went out of control, screaming, crying, and throwing things. Luckily, our brother Tom was there, and he finally calmed her down. He and Mom decided that they had better get Maureen to a doctor, so they took her to the emergency room of the Longmont Hospital, where Maureen was sedated and examined. She was diagnosed with a psychiatric disorder and was transferred to Denver's Porter Hospital and admitted to the psychiatric ward.

One of the first to realize that Maureen was suffering from something that she herself could not control was our sister Rosemary. Rosemary had some distance from the situation, both geographical and emotional, and had begun her own study and reading about the behaviors she observed in Maureen. Rosemary had also discussed her findings with Helen, who had

had conversations about Maureen with Longmont's Dr. Cooke, Helen's former boss. All concurred that Maureen's behavior was symptomatic of a very serious mental disorder.

It was late evening, and Rosemary, with several days still left of her vacation, was sitting alone at the kitchen table, smoking a cigarette. Mom and Dad had already gone to bed. Eating a light supper, I was still hungry, so I prepared myself a bowl of Cheerios and milk and sat down at the table.

Knowing that Rosemary was one of the few people whom Maureen even talked to, I asked her, "What do you think is goin' on with Maureen? Why do they have her in the hospital?"

"She's *schizophrenic*," said Rosemary.

"What's that mean?" I asked.

"It means that she is mentally ill with a disease that they used to call a split mind," Rosemary responded. "However, the more they learn about it, it's more complicated than that. It's a combination of 'haywire' thinking that is disorganized and delusional."

"What's delusional?" I asked.

"It's believing something that isn't true," said Rosemary. "Most schizophrenics believe someone is out to get them when it's really not the case. They don't trust anyone."

"Many of them also hallucinate," added Rosemary. "They think someone is there with them, who actually is not—if it's a person they think is there, they may start talkin' to 'em."

"I guess too," said Rosemary, "that they're always depressed—they're sad and always down in the dumps."

"Well, I get that way sometimes," I said.

"We all do," said Rosemary. "But we snap out of it—Maureen doesn't."

"Schizophrenics also don't react to things like you and I do," said Rosemary. "If somethin' real bad happens—it doesn't seem to bother 'em."

"Well, Maureen sure seemed like that sometimes," I said. "When Francis Vogel was killed by that train, the whole school was affected. But not Maureen—his death didn't seem to bother her. She didn't even go ta the funeral—but Kathleen did."

"They don't fit in with their families—they seem to be on the outside," said Rosemary.

"That's the way Maureen seems," I said. "She's different from all of us."

"What caused Maureen to be that way?" I asked. "How come she has it and the rest of us don't?"

"Well, nobody knows for sure," answered Rosemary.

"They say it's a disease and the only way you can get it is to be born with it," said Rosemary.

"One of the parents has the disease—even though they may not show it."

"I've never seen Mom or Dad act like Maureen does," I said. "If they have the same disease, they sure don't act like they do."

"What are they goin' to do about Maureen?" I asked.

"It looks like after they treat her at Porter Hospital, they may have to send her to the insane asylum in Pueblo. Maybe the doctors there can help her," said Rosemary.

"What can they do?" I asked.

"They will give her medication and electric-shock treatments," Rosemary answered.

"What's electric shock?" I asked.

"It's when they send electricity through the brain," said Rosemary. "It sounds so horrible that I don't even want to talk about it."

"You know," said Rosemary, "I've been thinkin' about Maureen—I don't really think I know who she is—I don't know her like I know the rest of my brothers and sisters."

Rosemary took a long puff from her cigarette and said, "I don't think she is really Maureen—I think she is really somebody else."

"What d' ya mean? Somebody else?" I asked.

"Well," said Rosemary, pausing while she exhaled, "they say schizophrenics have split minds and personalities. I think she really is two persons. There's somebody else inside her—that's who she really is."

"Now when I think of Maureen—I don't call her Maureen," said Rosemary. "In my mind, I call her <u>Agnes</u>—ya know that's the name that Mom and Dad gave her when she was born, Agnes Maureen Newton."

Tears came to Rosemary's eyes, and she didn't speak for a moment—she just stared ahead and dragged on her cigarette.

Then she said, "Agnes is her real name, and that's really who she is—she's really Agnes—the person that none of us knows. Agnes is the person she won't tell us about."

As I walked over to the kitchen sink and put my empty cereal bowl in it, I heard Rosemary say, "There must be a light somewhere inside Agnes—but she doesn't let it out—not even a glimmer."

I said good night to Rosemary and went up the stairs to bed. I lay awake thinking about what Maureen told me one time when her fingers touched a frayed area on the electrical cord of her bedroom lamp.

"It scared the wits outta me," said Maureen. "And it hurt—there was this sharp pain that went straight up into my arm."

I knew that when they got ready to put that electricity to Maureen's head, she was going to be real scared. I hoped it wouldn't hurt. I knew how she would sound if it did.

Maureen and Kathleen Newton, 1944. *Newton Family Album*

Maureen Newton, 1953. *Mead Consolidated Schools Yearbook*

Rosemary Newton, 1956. *Newton Family Album*

Kathleen Newton, 1952. *Mead Consolidated Schools Yearbook*

CHAPTER 37

Christmas

In mid-December, Mom asked Jerry, "Before you come home tonight, can you pick up a Christmas tree for us? We need to get it decorated soon—the presents are already startin' to arrive in the mail, and I want to place them around the tree."

Jerry, working at the Longmont Drug, brought home a blue spruce and set it up in the corner of the living room where Mom had removed Dad's chair and radio to another location in the room. Standing next to the window, the lighted tree could be easily seen from those viewing from outside. The next evening, Mom and my six brothers and I decorated it. Jerry carefully placed the lights evenly over the tree, and the rest of us hung the colored balls and tinsel on its sparsely arranged branches.

"I get to hang the glass bell," said Marc, pointing to the prized ornament that was deemed the most elegant of the lot.

"Here's 'Tom's angel'," said Jerry as he unwrapped the tissue paper surrounding it. Two years before, brother Tom had bought this cherubic figurine embedded in a cloud of spun cotton fiber for us to place on the top of the tree.

"I get to put the angel on," said Richie, always quick to stake his claim to do something before any of the rest of us.

When the tree was finally decorated and smothered with tinsel, Richie, on tiptoe, placed the angel on the topmost central branch. Tom's angel was a beautiful sight. She was looking upward with her arms crossed in front of her, appearing majestically serene as a pretty young girl suspended in the heavens. She was a spectacular family icon, inspiring us with the spirit of Christmas.

The Christmas holiday season was a welcome break from the rigorous academic routine of school and the physical toils of basketball. As we began our Christmas vacation, we seven brothers helped Mom clean the house. Our three sisters and a brother would be coming home to spend the next weekend, so their bedrooms had to be scrubbed and their beds made up with clean sheets that Mom had washed. As usual, I opted to clean the downstairs' spare bedroom and the living and dining rooms so I could listen to the top-50 tunes on KGMC radio featured on Saturday mornings. That morning, Rodney Markham dropped off a load of coal in the coal shed, and Marc and Frosty found some kindling in the alley behind Mr. Alexander's house. There would be plenty of fuel to keep the house warm when all the Newton family members arrived on Saturday for a cold Christmas Eve.

On Saturday afternoon, Mom and Dad and we seven boys departed the house at different times and walked to Guardian Angel Church. Father Martin was there to hear our confessions. We hurried back home to polish our shoes and take our baths and to help Mom make the final dinner preparations before our far-flung family arrived.

On Christmas Eve, we Newtons assembled from afar for our customary opening of presents. Brothers-in-law Jack Curran, Wilbur Thornton, Dale French, and Ed Hetterle came with our four sisters (Betty, Eunice, Pat, and Kathleen), accompanied by a dozen or more nieces and nephews. Our sister Rosemary had taken the train from Kansas City to be there, and sister Helen, now a stewardess with United Airlines, had flown in from New

Jersey. Brother Tom, just out of the army and now working for a finance company, picked up our sister Maureen from the state mental institution in Pueblo, and both of them arrived just in time for supper. Walt Slee, our trusted and benevolent friend, came. Our brothers Orbin, Ray, and Jack were absent, but fifteen of us siblings were there for that '56 Christmas.

For two days, Mom had worked to prepare the main supper course of pressure-cooked pinto beans and ham and homemade rolls, which we all topped off with fresh-churned butter. For those to whom beans were not of their choosing, Mom had cooked up a pot of chicken soup flavored with egg noodles she had made from scratch. For dessert, she would offer her family fresh-baked sweet rolls, just out of the oven and oozing with rich caramel syrup and a dash of cinnamon.

When all the in-laws, nieces, nephews, brothers, and sisters had arrived, supper was served—first to the younger set—us seven younger brothers and our nieces and nephews. We carried our filled bowls and glasses to any place in the house where we could find a place to sit. The adults assembled around the large dining-room table—all except Walt Slee, who ate with my six brothers and me. When everyone had finished eating, the women washed the dishes, and the youngsters watched a Christmas special on TV.

And then the throng of more than thirty of us gathered in our small dining and living rooms. Some sat on the floor or in chairs or on the sofa. Gifts in boxes of every size, wrapped in paper of every design in the colors of red and green and white and blue, were piled high around the tree. Brothers Marc and Frosty were designated by Mom to hand them out to all of us waiting with eager anticipation and excitement. Nephews and nieces jockeyed one another for seats on the floor, hoping to be the first to receive a present with their name on it. And then we all embarked on the annual family frenzy of tearing wrappers and ribbons off boxes and dropping them to the floor.

Being very practical, Richie, Rollie, and I pooled our meager resources to buy Mom a new steam iron for Christmas. A replacement was needed—Mom and my four brothers and I were constantly pressing starched shirts and table linens. We gave Dad a box of Roi-Tan cigars and a box of chocolates. We gave a tie with a rainbow trout painted on it and Roi-Tan cigars to Walt. I gave a sweater to my nephew Dennis, whose name I had drawn. My brothers and I each received two pairs of socks and knitted gloves from our sister Helen and sport shirts from our sister Rosemary. Walt gave each of us two pairs of sweat socks and two white T-shirts. I got a shirt from Susan Curran, who drew my name.

"You boys be sure and tell those who gave you presents 'Thank you,'" said Mom, seeing the gifts we had received. However, she and Dad were not ones who were prone to give an outright thank-you to their young children. But we did not need that reinforcement message—if Mom or Dad used the gift that we gave them, that was all the thanks we needed. We knew they were grateful for what they had received.

When the gift-opening furor ended, Richie and I gathered all the torn paper and curled ribbons into large grocery boxes and put them on the porch where the crumpled remnants would later be used to start the morning fires.

On Christmas morning, we saw that Santa Claus had left a new basketball and tennis shoes under the tree for Marc and Frosty, as well as wax-paper-wrapped parcels of chocolate and divinity fudge and sacks of hard candy, nuts, and oranges. Rollie and I left the house early—it was our turn to serve Mass. As altar boys at Guardian Angel Church, we had to prepare the altar, fill goblets with wine and water, and light the candles. Helen and Rosemary sang in the choir, beautifully augmenting the local voices warbling familiar Christmas carols while Mom sang along and played the organ. Father Martin Arno read St. Luke's account of the birth of Jesus and gave an extemporaneous homily on the significance of Christ's birth.

Light of Her Children

"Christ is God's <u>most</u> precious gift to mankind," said Father Martin. "God could have presented his begotten Son to the world as a king, crowned with gold and adorned in silk and diamonds, but he chose instead to send his Son as a babe in a manger, born to a virgin and surrounded in poverty."

Pausing a moment to adjust his tight tunic under his outer vestment and to withdraw his handkerchief from his left sleeve, he wiped his nose and continued, "It is Jesus's virgin birth that is perhaps the most significant miracle that God has shown to his people on earth and showing the almighty power and majesty he has."

Father Martin paused once again, and he looked to his left and to the front pew, where brothers Marc and Frosty were sitting with their friends.

"And you youngsters out there," he reminded them, "Christmas is not just about 'Santy Claus' and receiving gifts—it is much more than that—it's about the birth of Jesus Christ and what he will do on this earth in the short thirty-three years of his life. As you grow older and learn more about Jesus, you will understand more about the true meaning of Christmas."

"So remember all of you out there, kids and oldsters alike," Father concluded. "Christmas is about Christ—that's why we celebrate Christ's Mass on this beautiful day—this twenty-fifth day of December."

After Communion with the taking of bread, the choir and the whole congregation concluded the service singing "Silent Night." Father Martin's off-key voice could be heard above all of the others.

I lay in bed that Christmas night thanking God for making it a joyful Christmas vacation for me. The joyful conversations and experiences I had had with my siblings, parents, and in-laws over the last two days swirled in my head. The emotional closeness that I felt with my family members was always exemplified best at Christmastime, when we were all together. Unlike my friends, I was the lucky one—I had so many more brothers and sisters than they did—I had so many more connections of familial care and love than they did. Although I was grateful for the generous gifts I received from my siblings, it was their presence that I appreciated most. I lamented with regret that my three oldest brothers could not be there with us. I thought how wonderful the Christmas vacation was going to be—I could sleep in for the next several days with no school to go to. I thought about basketball and the fun and success I had in playing the game so far. The combination of the Christmas and basketball seasons mixed together was of the finest of times in my short life.

Rosemary Newton, 1956. *Newton Family Album*

Back row, L–R: Dennis Thornton, Marc Newton, Robert Thornton, James Thornton. *Front row, L–R*: Jean Thornton, Patricia Thornton, Laura French, Victoria Thornton. 1956. *Newton Family Album*

Maureen Newton, 1956. *Newton Family Album*

Helen Newton, 1956. *Newton Family Album*

Frosty Newton, Marc Newton, Walt Slee, Ronnie Newton, and Robert Thornton, 1956. *Newton Family Album*

Chapter 38

Winning

Our final basketball season at Mead High School began without Jerry, who had graduated. Rollie had been given the green light by the doctor to play once again, and Dave, as a sophomore, would be playing with the three of us seniors. Again Mead was picked by the *Greeley Tribune* to win the conference championship, but it said the major contender to unseat us was Gilcrest, the only conference team that had defeated us the previous year. Like us, Gilcrest had most of its major starters back; unlike us, they were much taller. We played them on their court in the first round at the time when their top scorer was leading the conference with more than twenty points a game, with Richie at a close second with more than eighteen. Gilcrest had the lead for most of the game and, in the final minute, was ahead by two points. With thirty seconds left, I potted a long set shot to tie the score. Gilcrest then moved the ball down the floor to their end of the court and immediately hit a jump shot to win; it was Mead's first loss, and thus, early in the season, we found ourselves in second place.

My own strengths as a basketball player were my ball-handling and defensive skills. My weakness was my temper and frustration that flared when a call by the referee was perceived by me to be wrong. This habit of questioning authority was a characteristic not only exhibited on the basketball court but also at home and in the classroom, and it got me into trouble often.

One game Coach Adams had us play what he called a "rabbit" zone defense, where four players defended four zones of the opponent's offensive half-court and where the fifth player, the rabbit, roamed from zone to zone, following the ball wherever it went. I was the rabbit, a role I dearly loved, and I went about it aggressively and perhaps, in the eyes of the referee, too aggressively.

Early in the first quarter, my opponent and I grabbed the ball simultaneously, and as we muscled each other for it, he lost his balance and fell to the floor, leaving me standing with full possession of the ball—the referee blew the whistle and motioned his body with a swivel to one side as he called the foul on me, implying I had pushed the opponent. I protested only with a silent thought, being certain that I had not fouled and concluding in my mind that this referee was not experienced. With the second foul, the same referee pointed at me after I slid my body across the floor going after a loose ball; my upright opponent, attempting to go after the ball as well, stumbled and fell over my outstretched body, giving the impression to the referee that I had knocked his legs out from underneath him.

"Come on, ref," I protested loudly as he descended on me to retrieve the ball I held in my hand. "I didn't touch 'im."

"Be careful what you say there, Mr. Newton," he said to me with a stern look. "I'm callin' this."

On the offensive side of the game, I had had success on one occasion in putting the ball on the floor with my dribble and driving past my opponent to score with an easy layup. On a second occasion, while attempting the same thing, my opponent fouled me, and I sank both free throws. I attempted a third drive toward the basket, but this time another opponent moved in front of me, and I bowled him over as I went in for the layup—landing on top of him. I was called for a charging foul, again by the same referee. I thought that it was an unbelievable call. I looked him straight in the eye as I handed him the ball and said with exploding rage, "Ref—there ain't no way that I fouled 'im! He jumped right in front of me!"

The referee dropped the ball, looked over to the scorer's table, and placed his hands into the form of a T—I now had four fouls—all in the first quarter. Coach Adams immediately removed me from the game, and I sat on the bench until the final quarter, where I committed a fifth foul and had to leave the game. I was grateful that in spite of my own performance, our team was able to squeak by with a victory.

Afterward, Coach Adams said to me, "Ronnie, don't ever pop off again like that again. I'm surprised that you acted that way. It doesn't seem like your style."

I was disappointed in myself knowing that Coach Adams was disappointed in me. I never questioned the call of a referee again—I simply raised my hand—informing the scorer and everyone else in the gym that I was submitting to the authority of the referee. Once again, I had to come to realize that the referee might be mistaken, but when it came to the game, the referee was always right. It had taken me twelve years of playing basketball to accept the fact that in sports, that principle always prevailed.

As we came to the end of conference play, Mead had a chance to avenge our loss to Gilcrest when Gilcrest, still undefeated, came to Mead to play on our home court.

"This is a big game for you guys," said Ronald Weber. "I'm getting' there early and get a good seat—there's goin' to be a lot of people there. I bet there's a huge crowd comin' over from Gilcrest."

"Yal," I acknowledged. "There's supposed to be such a big crowd there that Mr. Carlson [school superintendent] thought we ought to play in the Memorial Building in Longmont. But Coach didn't want to—he wanted to stay in Mead—he says we'll play better at home."

Light of Her Children

The Mead gym was packed with the largest crowd ever assembled. Unable to find an empty seat, folks were standing at both ends of the court. The importance of the event caught the attention of Dad, and he attended his first basketball game, arriving right before it started. Our brother Marc, seeing that Dad was unable to find a seat, gave him his, and Marc sat on the floor between his legs. Mom and our brother Frosty had already taken their seats in the bleachers across the floor from the Mead players' bench.

"We're goin' to surprise them and start with a full-court press," said Coach Adams as he gave his customary pregame talk in the locker room.

"Ronnie—you do as you always do—get on the one who's takin' the ball out. And Richie, you jump on the guy who takes it inbounds—and Ronnie, you help him out—both of you try to take the ball away from him."

Richie and I forced their guards to turn the ball over several times, resulting in easy layup scores for us. The Gilcrest players were rattled into a frenzied pace, and they hurried their shots, shooting poorly; Mead tripled the score on them by the end of the first quarter and then doubled it on them by the end of the first half. We ceased pressing them in the second half, but our tight man-to-man still kept them from scoring effectively, and we beat them by more than twenty points.

Mead ended conference play with a record of thirteen and one, tied with Gilcrest for the conference crown. We now had the opportunity to enter the district tournament for the second year in a row, and also for the second year, Mead was the top-seeded team.

My brothers and I were surprised and pleased when our brother Jack, a career marine, called home to tell us that he was taking leave so that he could be there to see us play.

"Jack's comin' home," said Mom as she hung up the phone. "Says he wants to be here to watch you birds play in the district tournament."

"Really?" I said, not believing what I heard.

"That's right," said Mom. "He said he'll be here long enough to watch you in the state tournament if you make it that far."

I was most surprised; the thought of Jack coming home just to watch us play had never occurred to me. Hearing this news, it confirmed to me that my brothers and I were doing something very special—it had to be in order for Jack to travel thousands of miles just to watch us. I knew how special the next several weeks were going to be for me, and I hoped that they were going to be special for Jack as well. I quickly recalled that it was Jack who introduced us to basketball, bought us sweat socks and tennis shoes, and built a basketball goal for us in our backyard.

Mom, Dad, Jack, Tom, Jerry, Marc, and Frosty were our family members who attended every game as we swept through the district tournament, winning all three games. We won the first two handily by wide margins, but in the finals, we could not put the opponents away until the final minutes. It was another significant moment for all us Newtons when Mead was awarded the district-tournament trophy for the second year in a row.

"I was so scared they were goin' to beat you birds," said Mom the next day. "That would have been awful—I couldn't bear to think about it."

"You were only up by five points with three minutes left to play," said Jack. "But I knew you had it won when you guys stole the ball from 'em and made a layup to put cha ahead by seven with only a minute left."

"I don't like it when the score is real close like that," said Mom. "I don't think my heart can take it."

Then in the second week of March in 1957, forty-eight teams from all over the state assembled in Denver for the state tournament in the second week of March in 1957. The year before, tournament games had been played in a high school field house, but this year they would be played at the Denver Coliseum, a facility with a seating capacity of ten thousand.

We played our first quarterfinal game before a sparse crowd in midafternoon on Thursday, winning easily, and Coach Adams played our reserves most of the game. Unlike the year before when our team stayed in a hotel, we drove home to Mead after each game; Coach Adams had concluded that perhaps our early elimination from the tournament the year before was our being enamored with luxurious accommodations and food—causing us to lose our focus on the game.

"I want you guys at home sleepin' in your own beds," said Coach Adams. "I want you rested and ready for each game—you're goin' to need it."

Mead won its semifinal game on Friday, and now for the first time in Mead High School's forty-year history, Mead would be playing for the state championship on Saturday. Four final games were slated that evening, and we were the second on the docket. There must have been eight thousand fans there when our game started. Our opposing team, Wiggins High School, was much bigger with three players hovering around six foot four, while Mead averaged just six feet. I was not optimistic that we would beat this team of giants.

"Dear God," I prayed. "Let us hang in there with these guys—help us to make a good showin'—don't let them blow us out."

Mead started out with a man-to-man defense, and Coach Adams assigned me to guard the opponent's leading scorer, a six-foot-three sharpshooter. By the end of the first half, we were only down four points. I had scored only two baskets, but my opponent I had guarded had twelve points, scoring nearly half of his team's total. As I entered the locker room, I felt winded and exhausted—a feeling I had never experienced before. How could that be? I knew I was the most conditioned player on our team. Had I been challenged by my swifter and taller opponent like never before? Also, I was deflated psychologically because I had failed to thwart his offensive output, and at the same time, I had contributed very little to my own team's scoring.

However, my body was energized with the short halftime rest, and my psyche was too when Coach Adams barked confidently, "Men, we can take these guys—they're only up by four—we've got the whole second half ahead of us—I know we can do it. We've been okay on the boards, but they are getting some easy shots inside. I think we can stop their scorin' if we switch to a zone."

I emerged for the second half with a new confidence. Offensively, Mead's second-half opportunities mostly came to me. I sank six buckets, a majority from drive-in layups as I maneuvered through Wiggins's man-to-man defense. The score was tied several times until the final two minutes when Mead surged ahead by four points; we went into a stalling mode, holding on to the ball and not shooting, forcing Wiggins to foul. Their only hope was that we would miss our shots at the free-throw line and that they then could regain possession of the ball. Controlling the ball with my dribbling, I was repeatedly fouled, and I ended up sinking seven out of eight free throws. Mead won the game by four points—it was the finest game I ever played offensively—ending up with twenty-three points.

But I was not the only star that night—my three brothers accounted for all but two of our other thirty points. I was proud that many of my family members, especially Jack, were present to see us awarded with the large championship trophy. I suspected that Jack had one of the most exhilarating military leaves of his career and perhaps one that was most satisfying. My three brothers and I were selected to the all-state team by the Denver newspapers.

Richie, Rollie, and I were all given the opportunity to play beyond our high school days: Coach John Bunn of Colorado State College of Education in Greeley invited us to play for him. Richie and I accepted the offer, and Rollie opted for Colorado A&M College.

Front row, L–R: Richie Newton, Mike Eckel, Lanny Davis, Ronnie Newton, Allen Thompson. *Back row, L–R*: Coach Jack Adams, Rollie Newton, George Rademacher, Carl Hansen, Lyle Schaefer, Dave Newton. 1957. *Mead Consolidated Schools Yearbook*

Frosty and Marc Newton, 1957. *Mead Consolidated Schools Yearbook*

Jack Newton, 1957. *Newton Family Album*

CHAPTER 39

Dragging Main

My final days in high school and graduation were somewhat troublesome for me because they occurred at a time when I had broken off my relationship with Kathy Nottingham, a Longmont girl I had dated for several months and had grown to like very much. Now with college looming ahead and me leaving my family, my school, and my friends, I felt alone and insecure. I was dreading the loss of the opportunities I always had in sharing the intimacies of life with my friends, my brothers and sisters, and my mother.

However, I was suddenly emotionally uplifted when Kathy showed up again in my life with a visit one Sunday afternoon to Mead with several of her friends. Her surprise appearance in my front yard resurrected my reveries of her, and two days later, I called and asked her out once again.

Kathy never knew what car I would show up in. I often borrowed my brother Tom's '56 Ford, but I sometimes drove my brother Jerry's Plymouth or the '49 Ford we triplets had purchased together. This time I would have a surprise for Kathy. I would be driving a brand new '57 "special model" Plymouth Fury that belonged to Dean Seewald, the farmer I was working for that summer.

Light of Her Children

Although I was still working on the Eckel farm, I was also working for Dean. He and Frank Eckel had begun to collaborate in both the farm and dairy operations. Dean had planted corn and barley, and I was helping him to cultivate and ditch the corn and to irrigate both the corn and the barley.

Dean asked me one day, "Would you like to borrow my car sometime? If ya got a hot date, let me know—I'll let cha have it."

"I sure would," I said. "How 'bout next week? My girlfriend's getting back from vacation then, and I'd like to take her out in it."

I wanted to take Kathy out in Dean's car in the worst way. I wanted to drag Main Street of Longmont with her sitting next to me in a new car—a car like no one else had—a special model—only a thousand had been made that year—and Dean Seewald had one.

Chrysler had introduced a limited-edition model called the Fury, introduced at a premium price and designed to showcase the Plymouth marque and to draw consumers into showrooms. Dean Seewald was the ideal owner. He loved to show off his new expensive car wherever he went and to anybody who wanted to see it. Dean was part of the acceleration of the pace of American small-town existence, which reverberated simultaneously with American automotive advances; there was a kind of a new rapid shift, fast-forwardness to life.

The Fury had a push-button automatic transmission—a first in an American automobile. It was a two-door hardtop coupe with its off-white color elegantly trimmed in gold anodized aluminum. The sleek, streamlined body was dramatically highlighted with upward turned tailfins (the beginning of the space race influenced so many aspects of life then), and the car had fuel injection, a large 318-cubic-inch V-8 engine, and dual, four-barrel carburetors.

"Hell," said Dean, "I had this son of a bitch up to 120 miles per hour in just a few seconds out on the Washington Highway."

With this car, I wanted to show off my relationship with Kathy to all her Longmont friends. I asked Dean if I could borrow the Fury for my Friday night date with Kathy. On that Friday afternoon, I saw Dean's car coming down the road toward me as I was stooped over cutting irrigation furrows in his barley field. Dean brought the car to an abrupt stop right next to the fence where I was working.

"Here's the car for ya," said Dean. "I took it to Longmont to get it washed, and I filled it up with gas. Com'on over here—I wanna show ya how to drive it."

Dean wanted to be sure that I was comfortable with the push-button gearshift, and besides, he wanted to show off all the car's features to me.

"Git in here and drive it, and take me back to the Eckels," he said. "My pickup is parked there."

I pushed the Drive button and steered the sleek vehicle down the gravel road.

"Boy, my girlfriend is sure goin' to be surprised when she sees this!" I exclaimed.

"Who is she?" Dean asked

"Kathy Nottingham—her dad said he knows you—his name is Walter—they live in Longmont."

"Yes, I know 'im," said Dean. "He sells insurance there in Longmont, doesn't he?"

"Yal—he used to farm himself," I said. "He gave it up and moved to town."

Longmont, a town of twelve thousand population, was just ten miles from Mead, and it was sprawled north and south along Highway 85, which was its Main Street. The street was about a mile long, and each evening in the summer, carloads of teenagers could be seen moving north and south, looking for friends and talking to one another at the stoplights. My brothers and I had done this many times with our Mead friends, wishfully hoping that we would somehow meet a girl of our liking.

Kathy sat close to me as we headed north on Main Street. At the north end of town, we turned around at North Johnson's

Corner to head back through downtown. As we passed the cemetery, I mentioned to Kathy, "That's where my sister Martha is buried—she lived only a week."

"What was wrong with her?" asked Kathy."

"I guess her intestines didn't develop right. She lost a lot a blood—died before I was born."

On our left, we saw a sign with lights outlining a large cowboy boot and spur.

"My sister Eunice works in the Spur," I said. "My brothers and I and our friends eat there sometimes when we come to Longmont on Friday nights. I always order a tomato, lettuce, and cheese sandwich—it isn't on the menu—Eunice makes it especially for me—my brothers order grilled cheese—ya know we Catholics can't eat any meat on Fridays."

"Your high school's brick is just like ours in Mead," I commented as we drove by Longmont High.

"I'm sure glad we moved to Longmont," said Kathy as we the passed the two-story structure. "Goin' to high school there has been the happiest days of my life."

The neon marquee lights of the Trojan Fox Theater glowed brightly as we cruised by.

"My triplet brothers and I saw our first movie in that theater," I said. "We saw *Snow White and the Seven Dwarves* and later we saw *Pinocchio*."

"I saw them too," said Kathy. "My mother took my sister and me to see them—the theater was in Limon—Limon was just thirty miles away from our farm in Genoa. Didn't you just love Geppetto in *Pinocchio*?" Kathy asked.

"Yes, I did," I answered. "But I thought Snow White was the most beautiful girl I had ever seen—I fell in love with her as if she were a real person. We saw the *Jackie Robinson Story* too in that theater, and Mrs. Eckel took us one time to see *The Harlem Globetrotters* on Mike's birthday."

"Isn't that where your friend works? Over there in Lewis Furniture?" Kathy asked.

"Yal, that's Walt Slee—he sold a television set to my sister Helen, who gave it to us for Christmas. He sells nothing but Philcos—we have two Philco radios and a Philco phonograph also."

"I have a phonograph in my bedroom, but I couldn't tell you what the brand is," said Kathy. "But we have a Zenith TV. It's a good one—Daddy paid a lot of money for it."

In the next block, we saw Ann's Style Shop.

"You remember, don't you?" I asked, pointing to the sign for Ann's Style Shop. "That's where I bought your Christmas present."

"Yes, I do, and over there is Snyder's Jewelry—that's where I bought yours."

"I've always wanted to go in that canning plant over there," I said. "I'd like to see how they can all those peas and pickles that they haul in from Mead."

"I've been in there!" exclaimed Kathy. "My biology class took a tour there—we were studying how food is preserved—they were canning pumpkins then."

Reaching the end of Main Street at South Johnson's Corner, I pulled in to turn around and head back north on Main Street.

Sitting right next to me, Kathy said, "Here, let me push the buttons." She pushed in the reverse so that we could maneuver around the gas pumps.

Back on the street and with the windows down, Kathy moved over to the passenger-door side to wave to her friends as we slowly cruised by them, only to move back to the center of the seat and hold on to my arm with both hands. I was exhilarated with Kathy close at my side.

Not wanting me to spend my hard-earned money that she knew was in short supply, Kathy usually did not expect anything to eat or drink when we went out. But this night I said, "Let's go to the A&W, I'm thirsty from sweatin' outside all day. Would you like to go?"

"If you want to—sure," said Kathy.

I gulped down my root beer and said, "Let's take this thing out on the county-line road and see how fast we can go—do you want to?"

"Sure!" she said as she handed me her unfinished root-beer mug. "Let's go!"

I drove out of town and took Highway 66 east to the Weld-Larimer County Road, where I turned south and brought the Fury to an immediate stop. With Kathy looking at her watch, we timed to see how many seconds it took to reach sixty miles per hour—the tires screeched and spun on the pavement as we started.

"Six seconds!" yelled Kathy. "Wow!"

"That's a heck of a lot faster than Mike's Olds," I said.

"The engine sounds like we're in a jet airplane," said Kathy.

I wanted to see what if felt like to drive the car at one hundred miles per hour—I stepped on the gas as we headed south down the county line. The hot air of the night swirled around our heads, fluttering Kathy's short hair. I slowed the vehicle down and turned into a remote area by the Saint Vrain River. Kathy and I had been there before—lots of kids had used this area—my brother Rollie and his girlfriend, Joann, had parked there. We all went there when we wanted a spot where we could spend time alone.

Kathy took both of her legs and propped them up over my lap—we embraced only for a moment before our lips eagerly met once again. It was always exciting for me when I kissed her. She was the only human being I ever told that I loved.

"When do you leave for college?" I asked, not wanting to bring up the subject.

"September third," she said. "Daddy bought me a plane ticket to Columbia, Missouri—that's where Stephens is."

"That's where the University of Missouri is too," I said reluctantly. "Now you're goin' to have all those college boys to take you out."

"Well, you're goin' to have all those pretty girls in Greeley too," she said, smiling. "I hear there's a lot more women there than men—you'll have a lot to choose from."

"I don't think I'll have much time for girls," I said. "I'll be playin' basketball, workin', and studyin'—it looks like I'll be workin' on weekends too—I don't wanna flunk out the first quarter."

Kathy and I talked into the night. The river gurgled loudly as we talked. We heard the mournful mooing of cows and the sloshing of their hooves as the animals came down to the river to drink. Bats flapped their wings; they swept over the river snatching insects in flight. Poplar-tree leaves fluttered in the breeze and cast flickering shadows on our faces as we talked, and tree branches were temporary landing sites for sparrows that had not yet made up their minds where they would settle for the night. However, mosquitoes seemed to have a precise knowledge of where they wanted to be, feasting on our bare arms before we slapped and smashed the pesky pests into oblivion. We heard the squawks of ducks swimming in small ponds cut out from the river and the screeching of the long-billed killdeer as they scurried along the sandbars digging for food in the moonlight. I noted to myself the sharp contrast between the distinctive methane swamp odor of the plains along Saint Vrain River and the fresh mint and juniper smells along the higher elevations of that same river where I fished high in the Rockies.

Immersed in our talking, we were oblivious to the occasional roar of cars traveling down the county-line road or heading east toward the Washington Highway and the Del Camino Restaurant.

"Oh my gosh," said Kathy, looking at the clock on the dashboard, "I've got to get home."

"But I've got to go the bathroom—I can't wait till I get home. Promise you won't look?" she asked.

"I promise," I said.

Main Street, Longmont, CO, circa 1950. Longmont Museum and Cultural Center

First National Bank, Longmont, CO, circa 1950. Longmont Museum and Cultural Center

South Johnson's Corner, Longmont, CO, circa 1950. Longmont Museum and Cultural Center

St. Vrain River (east of Longmont, CO), 2012. Sheila Koenig

CHAPTER 40

Time to Go

Ever since I had been a ninth-grader, my goal was to go to college. Now that I had graduated from high school, I spent the summer working and saving my earnings so that I could pay my own way. I knew that I was on my own—it would be unrealistic for me to expect Mom and Dad or my sisters and brothers to help me with finances. I had earned an academic scholarship that covered my tuition at the college of my choice in the state of Colorado. I had decided on attending Colorado State College of Education in Greeley, because my triplet brothers and I had been invited to play basketball for CSCE coach John Bunn. Coach Bunn also said that he would see to it that I would have a job in the college dining hall when I arrived.

In the summer, I worked on the Frank Eckel farm about a mile and a half from Mead. The farm operation was now managed by Dean Seewald, to whom Frank gave total control. Besides row-cropping, Dean raised cattle—feeding them corn ensilage he produced on his farm and on the other land he rented.

I worked for Dean all summer, irrigating crops, feeding milk cows, cultivating corn, and hauling hay and ensilage. I felt fortunate that Dean had offered me the job—making ten dollars a day. I wanted to save as much as I could for college.

"Do you need some money?" Dean asked me several times.

"No—you can pay me later," I answered.

I did not want to be paid—to me it was like savings—he could pay me at the end of the summer—I wanted a big fat check then.

When September came, Dean had me drive his Dodge truck following along the side of a corn harvester spewing slices of corn ears and stalks into the bed of the truck. The truck-bed sideboards had been augmented with five-foot upward extensions that doubled the capacity of the bed and allowed several tons of fresh-cut green silage to be loaded at one time. I had to maneuver the truck forward cautiously, being careful not to bump into the moving harvester being pulled by the tractor that Dean was driving.

One morning as I drove alongside an irrigation ditch, the weight of the truck's payload abruptly caved in the ditch's bank, and the whole truck turned on its side, spilling fresh-cut corn onto the ground. Luckily, there was no water in the ditch.

Dean came running up to me as I climbed out of the tilted cab to survey the damage.

"What the hell are you doin'?" shouted Dean.

"You know that you shouldn't be drivin' that close to the ditch," said Dean. "You know better than that."

"I don't know nothin'!" I shouted back at him. "And I'm quittin'—you can get somebody else to do this crap for you!"

I had had a bellyful of Dean Seewald—I had worked daylight to dark, Sundays and holidays—he had never thanked me for my diligent work. I didn't want to work that week anyhow—I had wanted some time off before I went off to school.

"Well, look what's happened here!" yelled Dean. "You've bent the whole goddamn frame—you twisted the hell of it—Christ Almighty, Ronnie—that'll cost me some dinero to get that fixed!"

I stood there with regret and bewilderment, looking at what I had done. There before me was a giant mound of spilled ensilage and a damaged truck with its wheels on one side completely off the ground. I was remorseful that I, unlike my farm-friend classmates, had not developed sufficient skill in manipulating farm equipment; I was a city kid—not a farm boy. I knew that Dean would be telling his friends how inept and stupid I was—I imagined how he would be talking them: "I shouldn't've hired that damn kid in the first place—he may know how to play basketball, but he doesn't know shit about farmin'!"

I said nothing more to Dean—I was wanting to leave and walk home—I felt helpless and apologetic.

"Ronnie, go get Eckel's truck," commanded Dean. "We'll load this corn into it—and for god's sake, keep the son of a bitch outta the ditch."

We finished harvesting the cornfield, and I told Dean I couldn't work anymore—I had some things to do before I left for college.

"What do I owe you?" asked Dean.

I was afraid to answer him—I knew I had cost him several hundred dollars with damage to his truck. But I had worked nearly four months for him—hardly taking a day off—I calculated that I should be paid $900 for the summer—a month earlier he had written me a hundred-dollar check—I had needed lunch money.

"How much?" he persisted.

"I don't know," I said.

"How 'bout $600?"

"Okay," I said.

I gave my answer reluctantly—I was hoping for more—but I knew I had caused him a lot of grief and had cost him money. It was time for me to go—and I had enough money to get me through most of my first college year.

Ronnie Newton, 1957. *Newton Family Album*

CHAPTER 41

Leaving Town

While walking through town on Main Street one Sunday morning on our way home from church, I said to Richie, "Before long, we're goin' to be outta here—we'll be leavin' this old place—ya know as long as I can remember, this town has always looked old."

"Well," said Richie, "most of these buildings had been here for thirty years before Mom and Dad moved here. Dad sez this town has gone through some tough times—survivin' through the Depression and all that, but Mom sez Mead has never recovered—she sez she wonders if it ever will."

Richie, Rollie, and I spent the first eighteen years of our life in Mead, Colorado, and although we had personally prospered with time, the physical landscape of Mead had not. Main Street was still covered with gravel and scattered with potholes. Dust rose into the air behind any vehicle traveling Main Street no matter what the speed was. Signs saying that intersection U-turns were required when a northbound driver wanted to park on the west side of Main Street were faded and mostly illegible. Drivers ignored the signs (made years before by my brother Tom under a contract with the town) and turned in the middle of the street. With relatively little traffic, town officials had not bothered to have the signs repainted.

Not far from the church and on the corner of Main and across from the Mead High School football field stood Tony Dempewolf's abandoned Texaco station. It had been closed since the late 1940s, but the cylindrical glass pumps were still there. Long before, Tony had begun distributing non-highway gas from his red Texaco truck as he drove from farm to farm.

"I worked for Tony after school when I was in the ninth grade," I commented.

"What'd you do?" asked Richie.

"I rode around with him in his truck to deliver gas. He was sick back then—he had something wrong with his lungs—couldn't breathe very well—didn't have any strength to crawl up on the truck and pump the gas. He drove, and I pumped for 'im. He paid me a buck an hour."

Next to the empty gas station was the Mead Town Hall—it had been used only rarely since we Newtons had moved out in 1940, right after we triplets were born. The windows were covered with sheets of plywood, and tall ironweeds grew around its foundation and the front steps facing Main Street. On the south-side wall, honeysuckle climbed its way up the covered windows, even reaching to the roof and then winding its way along the east-side eave. The branches of the dead elm tree on the west side of the building formed a kind of steeple. Even the once-bright orange color of the building's brick had weathered to a dull, dirty brown. Since we Newtons had moved out years before, I had not been back inside.

"Orbin said he played basketball in there," said Richie.

"I wonder if the basketball goals are still there?" I asked.

"I bet they are. Some night we ought to sneak in there. I'd like to see what it was like in there where we were born. I bet over these last eighteen years, it hasn't changed a bit."

Gigantic ironweeds, two and three feet tall, stood along each side of Main Street, where we walked, surviving on what little moisture was left in the parched soil. Although only midmorning, their small oblong leaves, thirsting for water, drooped as the heat of summer lingered from the day before, confirming to Richie and me that life in this small town was harsh and unforgiving.

Passing by, we were reminded that the broad sides of the Clark Lumber Company were in need of a fresh coat of paint—the Sherwin-Williams logo and the black Clark Lumber Co. letters were pale gray and almost unreadable.

"The mayor's house is the only building that's been painted on this whole street," said Richie.

"It sure stands out bein' next to ole Jim Halpin's house," I said. "I don't think the Halpin house has ever been painted."

"It probably was at one time," said Richie. "It's like the blacksmith shop over there—you can tell that once it was painted green—but now there isn't much green left on it."

However, despite the stagnant physical landscape of Mead, the town's human perspective had constantly shifted with time. Ben McCoy had moved his family into the rental house vacated by schoolteacher Roy Stoddard, who left town as soon as school was out in '49. Stoddard's wife had been missing for a week—her whereabouts was unknown. Finally, it was revealed that she had run off with Hap Howlett; however, the love affair did not last, and it was several years later before Hap finally found the love of his life and married.

Jackie Thompson's dad had come to town and converted the vacant appliance store in the Doke Building into a grocery store and set up living quarters in the back. But after two years, Jackie, a classmate of us triplets, was not in class—her dad had given up trying to make the grocery-store venture work, and the family moved away. Mr. Thompson had started a scout troop in Mead—we triplets joined and received our tenderfoot badges, but that was as far as it went—the troop folded.

Joe Jones was no longer the mechanic at Mead Motor Company—he had left there and, in 1950, built his own garage on the lot behind his new café. He also hauled in an old, abandoned café building all the way from Longmont and propped it onto a foundation right on Main Street, next to the pool hall, setting his wife, Lila, up in the restaurant business, while the family lived in the basement. Both garage and restaurant were thriving.

Sandy Adler had left his farm near Highland Lake, moved into the Amen house next to the school, and bought the Handy Corner from Roy George. Sandy let his wife run the place while he counted the money. Grover Roberts was still cutting hair and operating the pool hall. Mrs. Bunton had died, but Ole Man Bunton was still keeping the Red & White Grocery Store open. He seemed lonely and bitter, his scowl permanent—and there were more Roma wine bottles in the garbage can in the alleyway. The IGA grocery store had closed, and the building had been converted into an apartment. Our former classmate Mary Helen Olson and her new husband had just moved in.

At the Mead Motor Company, Duck Newman was still selling Texaco gas and was now married to Myrtle, and Johnny Carlson had taken over the blacksmith shop on the other side of Main Street. But he committed suicide, and now Harvey Potts was doing the blacksmithing. Wilbert Peppler married Mead Junior High English teacher Bonnie Muhm. He bought the house of Rodney Markham's mother on Main Street, next to the lumberyard, and moved his new bride in with him. In '54, he was elected as the town mayor—defeating incumbent James Elmer Newton.

Across from the Guardian Angel Church, Mary Helen Olson's mother and her aunt were still selling burgers, beer, and liquor in the Mead Inn. The pea huller and the pickle factory still operated for several weeks each summer, and each fall, the beet dump opened.

By 1957, Tony Dempewolf had died, and his widow, Margaret, married Bub Howlett—Bub moved in with her in her house two doors down from Ronald Weber's house. Weber was still living at home and was learning the carpentry trade, working with his dad; he was playing fast-pitch softball for Longmont's Harsh Lumber Company team, and his brother Vernon was working at an auto-repair shop in Longmont.

The Williams family bought Ed Dempewolf's old house from the Warners—science teacher Edwin Warner was now teaching elsewhere. Mr. Warner, like most teachers who taught at Mead, did not stay long—they were always looking for better opportunities. Mary Johnson had died and had willed her estate to Guardian Angel Church. Iva Stotts, who had bought the now-deceased Mary Johnson's house, sold it, and she and her daughter, Irene (our former classmate), moved to Nebraska. The house, just south of the Stotts, had been renovated and rented to Coach Jack Adams and his wife, Arden. Besides Joe Jones's house and garage, the only new construction on Main Street was the basement home of Leo Bencomo on the north end of town—Leo never pulled together enough money to build the upper portion of the house.

Delbert Thompson, our classmate Allen's father, had bought the Peterson house, located south of the Mead Inn. The Schaefers had moved into the Doke house, two doors down from our house, and classmate Lyle's father, Russell, was teaching industrial arts and science at Mead High School, while his wife, Marcella, worked in the cafeteria and drove a school bus. Marcella had been recruited by Betty Lee's mother, Lucy, who was now the head cook for the school's new cafeteria.

Lucy Lee offered a cafeteria position to Laura Dreier Newton, who was no longer employed at the Mead Post Office. Laura had successfully taken the civil-service test for the vacant postmaster position at Hap Howlett's retirement, but when Dwight Eisenhower was reelected president, Bill "Cork" Clark, a registered Republican, was appointed to that job. Laura, a confirmed Depression-era Democrat, knew her application efforts were futile and moved on to the school-cafeteria job.

Emily Newman was still teaching fifth grade, and her husband, Curly, was still on the road working for the Denver Elevators Company; their son Herb was a student at Colorado University, and their son Clarence had left the School of Mines and had taken a job in Longmont. Loe Hernandez's sister Mary still lived with her mom and dad on Main Street, but Loe was now living in Denver. Vernon Widger was seen only occasionally at his parents' home next to the town park—he was now riding bulls and competing in the rodeo circuit.

After two years of frustrating service to the Evangelical United Brethren congregation, the Reverend Willis Geottel left Mead. He had tried in vain to make a living serving the Lord and driving a school bus. Sunday services at the EUB Church became sporadic, and sometimes Mr. Carlson (Mead School superintendent) had to lead the dwindling congregation in worship.

Father Martin Arno was no longer serving the Mead and Frederick Catholic churches—he had been transferred to serve as pastor of St. John's in Longmont. His replacement was Father Maurice Zauro—a conservative priest in his sixties, who backed up his homilies by reading from the Roman Catholic Code of Canon Law. Frosty and Marc Newton had replaced their older brothers, and now they were now serving Mass at Guardian Angel Church.

Said Marc of this hard-line priest, "Father Maurice never wanted to call me Marcus—he said I should be named Mark—he said I should spell my name with a *K*. He told me there never was a saint named Marcus." The seeming omnipotence of priests was under pressure from the speed and magnitude of changes in post–World War II American culture. Father Maurice might have tried, like King Canute, to hold back the tides (in this case, the tides of changing attitudes), but that attempt was not really successful.

But amidst all of the town's visible deterioration in the late 1950s, the Mead Consolidated Schools building (originally constructed in 1918) was still the crown jewel and "polestar" of the community. Unlike the other buildings of the town, the school-building complex was continuously well maintained by custodian Marion Humphrey. Its wooden structures had new coats of paint, and window frames had just been painted a cream color. After thirty-nine years, the bricks of the school proper had retained their rich red color, and the gym built in 1939 still had its sturdy gray exterior stucco walls. The Pearl-Howlett country schoolhouse had been moved to the school grounds, placed just south of the two-and-a-half-story brick structure, and had been freshly painted. Next to it, a single-story wood-sided industrial-arts building was built along with a separate bus garage. Mr. Humphrey also maintained the school lawn and playing fields, keeping them watered and manicured; he would have the field ready for the fall football season. Mr. Humphrey's children—Robert, Ethel, and Alberta—had all graduated and left home, so he had to hire others to help him get the school ready for the fall of '57.

And now, for the first time in the lives of my two triplet brothers and me, we would not be attending Mead Consolidated Schools that '57 fall. As the first week of that September '57 rolled around, I was struggling with myself to come to terms with the fact that I would be leaving Mead—in that very next week, my brother Rollie would be taking Richie and me to Greeley to attend college.

Sitting in the pool hall visiting with Ronald Weber while we drank pop, I said to Weber, "It's goin' to seem funny not livin' here anymore—I'm goin' to miss this place—ya know the buildings haven't changed all that much, but the people have—people have been dyin' and movin' in and out of this town ever since I can remember. What about you, Weber?" I asked. "When are you leavin'?"

"Probably when I get married," said Weber. "I met this girl one night after a basketball game I was reffin' in Longmont last year—she was a cheerleader—if we're still goin' together in a year or two, we'll probably get married, and then I'll move to Longmont."

"I'll bet she's really good-lookin', isn't she?" I said.

"You damn right she is," said Weber. He slapped me on the shoulder and grinned widely and said, "Ronnie, do ya think I'd marry her if she wasn't?"

Weber gave me a ride home in his Buick convertible that night—he had the top up—we were experiencing an early cold snap resulting from the frigid air that had moved into Northeastern Colorado from the North. As we drove into our front yard—I noticed how dark the night had become. The heavens revealed nothing—there was not even a twinkle in the sky.

Handy Corner and post office, Mead, CO, 1954. *Mead Consolidated Schools Yearbook*

Farmers Union Town Hall, Mead, CO, 2004. Sheila Koenig

Main Street (looking north), Mead, CO. *On the left from north to south*: the Handy Corner / post office, Baker's IGA Grocery, barbershop / pool hall, Jones's Restaurant, Doke Building, Bunton's Red and White Grocery, Mead Motor Company, circa 1950. *Historic Highlandlake Inc.*

Epilogue

My triplet brothers and I did not continue our basketball careers in college. Our need to work to pay our expenses precluded spending the required extra time on the basketball court. Also, in my own case, my academic interests gravitated toward the biological sciences, and my studies, coupled with work, took precedence over basketball. And now in 2015, as I reflect on the first eighteen years of my life with sports and basketball dominating my very existence, I am reminded of the truth of UCLA basketball coach John Wooden's statement: "What you are as a person is far more important than what you are as a basketball player." This is a bit of wisdom that my parents, my teachers, the clergy, my older brothers and sisters, and the townspeople knew all along—this wisdom was so self-evident that they seldom took the opportunity to articulate it. Yet this wisdom was their motivating principle as they guided my triplet brothers and me through those eighteen years. Our small town of kind and forgiving folks, our school of wise and compassionate teachers, and our large family ensemble of parents and older siblings provided fortuitous direction to my triplet brothers and me as they steered us through the myriad of life's experiences. It was these people who shaped our character, and we were lucky and privileged to have had them do so. The community of town, church, school, and family provided the ideal environment for molding young people—and my triplet brothers and I were the fortunate recipients of the nurturing of that environment. Yes, there were negatives, but these were more than balanced by good things.

With Mom at the helm and with my older sisters serving in a co-parenting role, my unusually large family was the most important nurturing unit for me. My triplet brothers and I were among a group of seven brothers all separated from a group of seven older sisters; this separation in age and gender resulted in a maternal parenting role for all my sisters in the upbringing of us seven brothers. For us triplets, the parenting by our oldest sisters started early: changing our diapers, giving us baths, preparing our bottles of Pet Milk before bed, watching over the three of us while Mom did her baking and canning, mashing our hard-boiled eggs for dinner, and reprimanding us for opening an off-limits cabinet door or for running away out of their sight.

As we triplets grew older and our three younger brothers were born, it was the role of our younger sisters to look after us while Mom and our oldest sisters did the housecleaning, the cooking, the washing, and the canning. And with time, we seven brothers began to look after one another but always under the watchful eye of an older sister. When Mom was to be absent from home, before she left, it was always an older sister who was designated to be in charge of the household.

With our sisters as co-parents, my triplet brothers and I learned from them. Our sister Helen taught us the prayers we said as we knelt over our beds each night; our sister Pat read nursery rhymes to us from Mother Goose; our sister Rosemary bought a Winnie the Pooh book for us, and our sister Maureen read out loud from it as we huddled around her on our living-room sofa; our sister Kathleen assumed the role of teacher as she quizzed us on our catechism lessons; and sister Helen, knowing I liked to draw just as she did, pointed out images in the newspapers that I could copy. Our sisters told us what they had learned from the day's school lessons as we sat at the supper table; our sisters constantly corrected our careless and inappropriate speech and our unrefined behavior, and they were quick to reprimand us when we misbehaved.

Our sisters often played an intercession role acting on the behalf of us triplets. As I tried to understand and deal with my childhood and adolescent romances, it was sisters Helen and Kathleen who stepped in to give me guidance and assurance and bolster my confidence to overcome my feelings of shyness and embarrassment. By their actions and encouragement, the two of them conveyed to me that they understood the importance of those relationships in my young life, perhaps because they too had had similar experiences.

As the three of us triplets moved into our teen years, our sisters took on counseling and advising roles, and they became our confidantes. When I told sister Helen, then an airline stewardess, that I might want to be a pilot and join the air force when I finished college, Helen, knowing that I really didn't know what I was getting into and that I had no aptitude for this, wisely said, "You know, to be a good pilot—you really have to want to be one—be real sure that's what you want to do. Of all the pilots I've known, flying has been what they've wanted to do all their life."

"I thought you told me that you wanted to be a priest," Helen added.

"I do," I said.

"You may be more suited to be a priest than a pilot," said Helen. "You need to think about it a lot more. But you've got time—you still have four years of college to finish."

Although many studies have shown that co-parenting by siblings leads to the success and survival of a family unit in guiding children to adulthood, it is the mother, as pointed out by Jeffrey Kluger in his book *The Sibling Effect*, who provides the most influence. Kluger cites other authors who have found that successful mothers have relied on two principles to keep their children in line: a sense of responsibility to family and respect for parental authority. Kluger emphasizes that the most successful mothers are those who govern with an established rule book and tell the kids what is expected of them. Says Kluger,

> Such a take-no-prisoners parenting style may not always be fun for the kids but, done right, it can lead to twin benefits: better behavior in the short run, and a deep sense of family responsibility and loyalty in the long run. This builds very strong ties among all members of the household—particularly the siblings.

Through her firm and resolute management style, Laura Dreier Newton instilled a deep sense of family responsibility in all the eighteen children whom she prepared for adulthood. In fact, that sense of family responsibility prevailed with her children even after they left home. Laura's older children continued to provide financial support and compassion to their younger siblings until the younger too embarked into the adult world.

My six brothers and I, the seven youngest of the twenty children Laura Dreier Newton bore, were the recipients of that loyal and compassionate generosity provided by our older brothers and sisters; through their kind acts of family responsibility, the seven of us were the most fortunate ones—we were spared from the great hardship and deprivation that the eldest of our brothers and sisters had all endured.

Now it is 2015, and the strong ties established with my siblings still remain, both with the living and the deceased. Thirteen of my brothers and sisters have lived out their lives and have passed on. My two triplet brothers, Roland and

Richard, are still here on this earth with me, along with my sisters Helen and Patricia and my brothers Marcus and Forrest; the seven of us still remain, reaping the benefits of large-family and small-town life and continuing the legacy of James Elmer and Laura Dreier Newton. Today, the second and third generations descending from that marriage union of James Elmer Newton and Laura Celia Dreier ninety-five years ago number more than a hundred—twinkling stars in their own right—and forming new constellations of brilliance. The light of Laura's children continues as a beacon to brighten the future of Newton generations to come.

Table 1. Newton Family

James Elmer Newton* 22 Nov. 1889 Farmworker and housepainter, Mead, CO
Laura Celia Dreier* 24 Nov. 1901 Mail clerk and cafeteria cook, Mead, CO
Orbin "Urban" Dreier Newton* 16 Nov. 1920 Career Marine Corps officer, Longmont, CO
Raymond Lee Newton* 04 Sep. 1922 Import artifact salesman, New York, NY
Eunice Elaine Newton* 18 Sep. 1923 Restaurant worker, Hygiene, CO
Robert Newton* 16 Oct. 1925 Deceased at one year of age, LeRoy, CO
Georgia Roberta Newton* 16 Oct. 1925 Beautician, Longmont, CO
Rosemary Newton* 23 Jun. 1927 Corporate personnel officer, San Francisco, CA
Jack Eugene Newton* 15 Feb. 1929 Career Marine Corps officer, Huntington Beach, CA
Helen Cecilia Newton 29 Aug. 1930 Medical secretary / airline stewardess, Rockford, IL
Patricia Ann Newton 16 Mar. 1932 Dental assistant / preschool teacher, Longmont, CO
Thomas James Newton* 30 Jul. 1933 Finance manager, Grand Junction, CO
Martha Newton * 06 Jan. 1935 Deceased at one week of age, Mead, CO
Mary Kathleen Newton* 15 Mar. 1936 Sales clerk, Redmond, WA
Agnes Maureen Newton* 15 Mar. 1936 Hospital kitchen worker, Longmont, CO
Gerald Anthony Newton * 20 May 1938 Clerk and custodian, Longmont, CO
Roland Joseph Newton 29 Sep. 1939 Bank officer, Whitefish, MT
Ronald James Newton 29 Sep. 1939 Professor, Greenville, NC
Richard John Newton 29 Sep. 1939 Business owner, Aurora, CO
David Allen Newton* 19 Mar. 1941 Corporate executive, Washington, DC
Marcus Emerit Newton 23 Mar. 1944 Journalist, Greeley, CO
Forrest Benedict Newton 09 Mar. 1946 Bank officer, Oxford, MI

*Deceased

James Elmer and Laura Dreier Newton with firstborn son, Urban, 1921. *Newton Family Album*

James Elmer Newton, 1960. *Newton Family Album*

Laura Dreier Newton, 1918. *Newton Family Album*

James Elmer and Laura Dreier Newton, circa 1920. *Newton Family Album*

Laura Dreier Newton, 1960. *Newton Family Album*

Bibliography

Anderson, Vincent L. In: Battle of the Coral Sea: May 4–10, 1942. *The true story of young Marine corporal Vincent L. Anderson and his survival after the loss of the aircraft carrier USS Lexington.* http://home.vicnet.net.au/~gcasey/welcome.html.

Battle of the Coral Sea. http://en.wikipedia/wiki/Battle_of_The_Coral_Sea.

Berg, Raymond Arthur. 1997. *My Memories of Arthur and Daisy Turner.* Histories of the Berg and Turner Families, Alice Berg York, ed. Mead, Colorado. Pp. 13–15.

Berg, Veva. 1982. *Backward Glances.* Memoir. Greeley, Colorado. 17 pp.

Braeman, J., Bremmer, R. H., and D. Brody (Eds.). 1975. *The New Deal: The State and Local Levels.* Vol. II. Ohio State University Press. Columbus, Ohio. ISBN 0-8142-0201-2 (vol. 2). 434 pp.

Denver Post. 101 W. Colfax Avenue. Denver, Colorado 80202-5315.

Etl, Sophie. 1980. *The Good Old Days: Our Pioneer Heritage.* Fleming, Colorado. pp. 37–47.

Fleming Historical Society. 1971. *Forward; Incorporation; Fleming School History 69 & Re 3; Churches.* Memories of Our Pioneers. General Publishing, Iowa Falls, Iowa. Pp. 9–24.

Fleming Historical Society. 1971. *Dreier Family: Memories of Our Pioneers.* General Publishing, Iowa Falls, Iowa. Pp. 45–53.

French, P. A. N. 2013. *Childhood Memories.* 1235 Baker Street, Longmont, Colorado, 80501. 6 pp.

Gammill, Homer L. 1978. *A Little History of the Early Days of Mead.* Historic Highlandlake: Preserving the Rich History of the Highlandlake/Mead Area. Copyright 2009. Historic Highlandlake Inc. http://historichighlak.org/mead/mead.

Greeley Tribune. 501 Eighth Avenue. Greeley, Colorado, 80631.

Hallas, James H. 1994. *The Devil's Anvil: The Assault on Peleliu.* Praeger Publishers. Westport, Connecticut. ISBN 0275946460.

Hoyt, Edwin P. 1975. *Blue Skies and Blood: The Battle of the Coral Sea.* Simon and Schuster Inc. 1230 Avenue of the Americas. New York, New York. 10020. ISBN: 0-7434-5835-4. 217 pp.

Kluger, Jeffrey. 2011. *The Sibling Effect: Brothers, Sisters, and the Bonds That Define Us.* Riverhead Books (Penguin Group, USA, Inc.). New York, New York. 307 pp. ISBN 978-1-59448-831-3.

Longmont Times Call. 350 Terry Street. Longmont, Colorado, 80501.

Liguori, Alphonsus (St.). 1969, 1974, 2006. *The Fourteen Stations of the Way of the Cross with Meditations.* Catholic Book Publishing Corp. New York. 31pp. ISBN 978-0-89942-014-1.

Leonard, S. J. 1993. *Trials and Triumphs: A Colorado Portrait of the Great Depression, with FSA Photographs.* University Press of Colorado. Niwot, Colorado, 80544. ISBN: 0-87081-311-0. 313 pp.

Newton, M. E. 2015. *Meadean Standard Time*. 5213 W. Eleventh Street Road, Greeley, Colorado, 80634. 140 pp.

Ready for Sea Handbook. http://www.fas.org/irp/doddir/navy/rfs/index.html.

Rocky Mountain News. Denver, Colorado.

Ross, B. D. 1991. *Peliliu: Tragic Triumph*. Random House. New York, New York. ISBN 0394565886.

Ross, J. H. and Heath, M. G. (Comps). 1919. History of Company E, 355th Infantry, AEF, Omaha, Nebraska. 97 pp.

Schmidt, G.; Dreier, C.; Morison, F.; and Williams. L. 1988. *LeRoy United Methodist Church, Fleming Colorado: 1888–1988*. 205 pp.

Sekich, Vera. 1993. *A Coal Miner's Daughter Who Became a Farmer's Wife*. CQG Ltd. Books. Longmont, Colorado. Lib. Cong. Cat. No. 93-072265. 111 pp.

Sekich, Nick Sr. 1980. *Growing Up and Living in Mead: A History of the Town*. Historic Highlandlake: Preserving the Rich History of the Highlandlake/Mead Area. Copyright 2009. Historic Highlandlake Inc. http://historichighlak.org/mead/mead.

Sherman, Frederick C. 1950 and 1982. *Combat Command: The American Aircraft Carriers in the Pacific War*. (1950) E. P. Dunton Inc. 2 Park Avenue. New York, New York. 10016. (1982) Bantam Books Inc. 666 Fifth Avenue. New York, New York. 10103. ISBN: 0-553-22917-6. 377 pp.

Smith, Pauli Driver. 2009. *History of Mead, Colorado*. Historic Highlandlake: Preserving the Rich History of the Highlandlake/Mead Area. Copyright 2009. Historic Highlandlake Inc. http://historichighlak.org/mead/mead.

Students of Mead High School. *Mead Bulldog*. 1946–1958. Publishers: Students of Mead High School. Mead Consolidated Schools. Mead, Colorado.

United States Army. 1953. *355th Infantry Regiment*. The Army Lineage Book. Vol. II: Infantry. US Government Printing Office. Washington 25, D. C. pp. 690-691.

USS *Lexington*. http://wikipedia.org/wiki/USS_Lexington_(CV-2).

Wickens, J. F. 1964. *Colorado in the Great Depression: A Study of New Deal Policies at the State Level*. PhD dissertation. University of Denver. Denver, Colorado. 432 pp.

Williams, L. L. 1990. *Generations of Heists and the Dreiers*. Family Ancestors. LeRoy, Colorado. 22 pp.

Wooden, J. R. with Jamison, S. 1997. *Wooden: A Lifetime of Observations and Reflections on and off the Court*. The McGraw-Hill Co. New York, New York. 201pp. ISBN 0-8092-3041-0.

INDEX

A

Achenbach, Earl, 3
Achenbach, Ernestine Dreier, 3
Adams, Arden, 345, 398
Adams, Jack (Coach), 6, 8, 331, 343–45, 347–49, 376–77, 379–80, 398
Adam's Ant, 259, 279
ADCA (Aid to Dependent Children Act), 46
Adler, Sander "Sandy," 80
aircraft carrier, 61, 411
Akers, Carl, 200
Akers, Mamie, 86, 96, 119–20, 133, 157, 171, 204–5, 254, 299, 317
Allenspark, 252–53, 257, 262, 268, 274, 276, 278, 287–88
Amen, Jake, 117, 134
American Telephone & Telegraph Co., 361
"America the Beautiful," 265, 267
Ann's Style Shop, 386
Argonne Forest, 25
Arno, Martin (Father), 74, 77, 104–5, 108, 112, 115, 136–37, 151–53, 156, 158–59, 164, 186–87, 192–93, 214, 303–5, 322, 368, 370–71, 399
aspen, 258, 269–71, 276, 279–80, 288
atomic bomb, 72
attic, 135, 150, 198
automatic phonograph, 100
A&W Root Beer Drive-In, 215

B

Bachman, Thelma (Mrs.), 362
Baker, Dale, 83, 88, 91, 104–5, 252
Baker, David, 79
Baker's IGA Grocery, 75, 88, 91, 100–101, 179, 397
Baltimore Catechism, 188
Bantheville, France, 26
baptism, 34, 39, 54–56, 108, 188
Baraco, Edward (Father), 265–66
barley, 80, 83, 86, 132, 222–23, 232, 350, 383–84
Base Depot, 69
Basic School, 72
basketball, 5–9, 13–14, 43, 51, 56, 75, 85, 95–96, 125, 178–84,

187–88, 190, 196, 203, 205, 225–26, 232, 247–48, 253, 303, 307, 313–14, 335, 339, 341–44, 352, 368, 370, 372, 374–78, 388, 390, 392, 395, 400, 403
bayonet, 13, 86, 92
beans, 22, 36, 47, 77, 89, 98, 110, 155–56, 166, 168, 213, 239, 255–57, 284, 357, 369
beatific vision, 136–37
Becker, Joann, 232, 303, 387
Beers, Jim (Coach), 341
Beese, Samuel (Reverend), 31–32, 37
beet dump, 44, 248, 397
bell tower, 85
Bencomo, Leo, 398
Bernhardt, Betty, 301, 310
Big Narrows, 256
Big Springs, Kentucky, 15
Big Thompson River, 8
bindweed, 233, 240
bingo, 156–59
birth, vii, 1, 34, 36, 45, 47–48, 51–56, 108, 370–71
Black Gnat, 280
Blazon, Marvin, 181
blizzard, 198–201, 204–5
blue spruce, 88, 149, 270, 367
Bossie (cow), 89, 109, 117–19, 121, 146, 168, 177, 202, 230, 250, 322, 324, 357
Boulder County, Colorado, 48, 53, 334
brandy, 194
brook trout, 171, 252, 260, 269, 370
Brossman, Edward, 48
Brown, Mrs., 313–14, 322
Brust, Connie, 39
Bunn, John (Coach), 5, 9, 380, 390

Bunton, Alice, 91, 411
Bunton, Bill, 23, 91, 197, 220–27, 347–48, 398
Bunton's Red & White Grocery, 83, 88, 91, 297, 318, 397
Burger Bros. Texaco, 82
Burlington and Quincy Railroad, 19

C

Cabin Creek, 263–64
Camp Elliott, 69
Camp Saint Malo, 263–65
Camp Zachary Taylor, 25
canning, 74, 77, 79, 84, 110, 165, 212, 361, 386, 404
Capper's Weekly, 202
Carlson, Carl (Superintendent), 181, 200, 376, 397, 399
cart, 123, 141–45, 148
catalpa, 145
Catholic Church, 5, 23, 33–34, 39–40, 55, 101, 104–5, 319, 326
cemetery, 16, 35, 45, 385
chickens, 22, 33, 75, 96, 110, 117–19, 121, 167, 169–73, 202, 211, 299
chinook, 205
choir, 23, 43, 75, 96–97, 104, 112–13, 136, 151–52, 186, 267, 271, 304, 370–71
chokecherry, 270, 278
Christmas, 75, 87–89, 96, 135, 141, 147, 180, 182–83, 202, 246, 254, 323, 367–72, 386
Cinnamon, Marvin, 253
Civil War, 14
Clark, Ansel, 83, 91, 142, 324
Clark, C. H. (Mr.), 183
Clark, Chick, 254, 259
Clark, Donna, 208

Light of Her Children

Clark, Doreen, 324
Clark, Robert "Cork," 144
Clark Lumber Co., 83, 88, 324, 396
Clarkson, Kentucky, 24, 27
Claus, Clayton, 223–28
Clymer, Joseph (Dr.), 34, 39
Colburn, Joann, 232
Collins, Bill, 315, 317
Colorado A&M College, 223, 380
Colorado School of Mines, 399
Colorado State College of
    Education, 5, 253, 380, 390
Columbia, Missouri, 387
Company E, 355th Infantry, 25–27
confession, 151, 186
Confirmation, 188–89, 192–94, 198
Congregational Church, 253
Conoco Service Station, 82
Cooke, Malcom (Dr.), 344, 363
Coors beer, 90, 221
Copeland Mountain, 262–63
Coral Sea, 63, 411–12
corn, 22, 24, 33, 47, 79, 86, 110,
    119, 131–32, 138–39, 166–67,
    169, 172–73, 202, 209, 211,
    213, 239, 242, 266, 328, 351,
    383, 390–92
Country Road 13 (CR 13), 332
Country Road 32 (CR 32), 332
County Road, 387
cribs, 2–3, 57, 60
Crystal Springs, 257, 267
Curran, Betty Newton, 98
Curran, Jack, 98, 106, 368
Curran, Susan, 370

D

dago, 190–91
dairy barn, 349, 351
dance, 301, 307–10, 361

Daniels and Fisher Store Co., 118
Davis, Lanny, 381
Del Camino Restaurant, 388
Dempewolf, Ed, 107, 348, 398
Dempewolf, Tony, 82, 323, 326,
    395, 397
Dempsey, Charles, 82
Dempsey, Eva, 82
Denver, Colorado, 310, 411, 413–14
Denver Catholic Register, 202, 213
Denver Coliseum, 379
Denver Dry Goods, 247
Denver Elevators, 83, 157, 317, 399
Denver Post, the, 58, 172, 201, 267,
    339, 358, 411
Depression, the. *See* Great
    Depression
disability benefits, 323
district tournament, 180, 342, 345,
    377–78
Doke, Grace, 144
Doke, Isaac, 82, 144
Dreier, Edna "Mikie," 22–23,
    30–32
Dreier, Ella "Jimmie," 22
Dreier, Emerit Arlo, 19, 21, 77, 408
Dreier, Ernest, 4, 22
Dreier, Ernestine "Ernie," 3
Dreier, Grandma, 4
Dreier, Idaletta "Petie," 22–23
Dreier, Laura Celia "Johnnie,"
    21–24, 28, 30–40, 42–48,
    51–59, 62, 66–68, 72, 194
Dreier, Lydia Elizabeth (Heist), 19,
    21–23, 30–32, 35, 45–46, 58
Dreier, Lydia "Freddie," 22–23,
    155, 159, 207–17
Dreier, Margaret "Maggie," 22–23
Dreier, Melinda "Sammie," 22–23
Dullaghan, Joe, 18–19
Durango, Colorado, 47

E

eastern slope, 205
Eaton, Colorado, 226, 250
Eckel, Frank, 348–49, 352, 354, 383, 390
Eckel, Mike, 222–23, 308, 312, 340, 351, 381
Eckel, Patricia, 228, 354
Eisenhower, Dwight, 321, 324, 398
electric shock, 364
Elitch Gardens, 307–8, 310
elm, 33, 124, 132–33, 149, 154–55, 211, 395
Elodea, 302
Empire of the Rising Sun, 97
engagement, 69
English Channel, 25
Erie, Colorado, 224
erysipelas, 1, 37
Evangelical Free Church, 31
Evangelical United Brethren Church, 399

F

Farmers' Union Town Hall, 48, 85
Ferncliff, Colorado, 253, 267–68, 271, 276
Field Depot Company, 69
First Communion, 40, 53, 114–15, 191, 205
First National Bank of Longmont, 242, 244, 351, 389
flare, 374
Fleming, Colorado, 18–19, 36, 297, 411–13
flies, 71, 254, 258–59, 270, 272, 279–80, 282, 292–94
fly-fishing, 252–53
food stamps, 79
Foremost, 154, 244
Fort Collins, Colorado, 47, 200, 227
Fort Douglas, Utah, 97
Fort Hood, Texas, 74, 87
Fort Lupton, Colorado, 47, 226, 250
Fox Creek, xi, 263, 270–71, 287, 296
France, 25, 27
Frazier, Colorado, 199
Frederick, Colorado, 53, 153, 155, 180, 189–90, 194, 224, 413
French, Dale, 104, 106, 252, 368
French, Laura, 373
French, Patricia Newton, xvii

G

Gallegos, Dulcinea, 356
garden, 22, 32, 35–36, 77, 83, 109–10, 123, 128, 132, 138–39, 145, 165–67, 169–70, 225, 238, 241–42
Genoa, Colorado, 385
Geottel, Willis (Reverend), 399
German brown trout, 272
German Russians, 225
Germans, 13, 25–26, 58, 86, 90, 225
Gettman, Darrel, 181
Gettman, Fred, 86, 119
Giardia, 276
Gilcrest, 374, 376–77
Glass and Bryant Dry Goods Store, 30
godfather, 188
Graham, Barbara, 156, 159–60, 162–63, 209, 212–13
Graham, John Gilbert, 337
Graham, Mary Sekich, 156, 159
Grand Junction, Colorado, 408
Grand Ole Opry, 101

Gray Hackle with a Yellow Body, 258, 285
Grayson County, 24
Great Depression, 1, 42, 44, 46, 55, 82–83, 97, 315–16, 320, 394, 398, 412, 414
Great Plains, 199
Great Western Sugar Co., 248
Greeley, Colorado, 7, 9–10, 39, 53, 57–58, 83, 96, 227, 250, 313–14, 343, 374, 380, 388, 390, 400, 408, 411–13
Greeley Elks Club, 57
Greeley Tribune, the, 57, 343, 374, 412
Guadalcanal, 68–69, 72
Guardian Angel Catholic Church, 34, 38–39, 55, 57, 74–75, 82, 89, 104, 112–13, 135–36, 150–53, 163, 186, 214, 216, 303, 317, 319, 368, 370, 397–99
Gust, Christine, 55
Gust, John, 82, 157

H

Hagemeier, Leonard, 24
Half-Breed, The, 213–14, 218
Halloween, 131, 133–35, 137, 139, 331
Halpin, Jim, 396
Handy Corner, 127–29, 397, 402
Hansen, Carl, 381
Harry O'Lynch's Clothing Store, 246
Hawaiian Islands, 61
heart murmur, 344
Hearvy, Ethel Roman, 124, 400
Hearvy, Gary, 124–25
Heater, Gabriel, 100

heat exhaustion, 70, 235, 379
Heil, Harold, 333
Heil, Jake, 226, 333
Heil, Kenneth, 181
Heist, Lydia Dreier, 58, 175
Hepp, Shirley, 113
Hernandez, Donald, 202
Hernandez, Loe, 126–27, 135, 147, 182, 399
Hernandez, Max, 327
Hernandez, Molly, 327
Hetterle, Candace, 362
Hetterle, Eddie, 213
Hetterle, Kathleen Newton, 213, 368
Highland Lake, 47–49, 91, 172–73, 297–300, 306, 308, 397, 413
Highlandlake, Colorado, 47–48, 91, 94, 172–73, 297–300, 308, 397, 412–13
Highlandlake Church, 308
Highway 7, 256, 262–63, 268
Highway 66, 216, 246, 248, 256, 332, 387
Hispanic, 191
Hitler, Adolf, 57–58, 90
Holy Communion, 44, 102, 113
Holy Family, 114
Homecoming Dance, 361
hoop, 75, 178–79, 182
Hopp, Conrad "Connie," 335
Hopp, Kenneth, 335
Horrell, Zachary (Uncle), 33
hot dogs, 256, 284, 320–21
Howard, Bill, 39
Howard, Eddie, 307, 310
Howlett, Mamie, 96, 317
Howlett, Theodore "Hap," 95, 136, 315, 317, 319, 324, 396, 398
Howlett, Vernon "Bub," 83, 317, 398–99
Humphrey, Alberta, 400

Humphrey, Ethel, 400
Humphrey, Marion, 400
Humphrey, Robert, 171

I

ironweed, 233, 240–41
Italian, 153, 155, 190–91, 264

J

Japanese, 62–63, 66–70, 72, 74, 86–87, 93, 95, 97, 327
JCPenney Co., 12, 154, 230, 244
Jensen, Anita, 297–98, 300, 302, 306
Jensen, Lawrence, 299–301
Jensen, Mary Mead, 297
Jensen, Roland, 299
Jepperson, Isabel (Mrs.), 16, 181
Jitney, 309
Johnson, Cotton, 109
Johnson, Edmund, 46
Johnson, Gladys, 109
Johnson, Mary, 58, 136, 166, 172, 326, 398
Johnson's Corner, 215, 384
Johnstown, Colorado, 39, 45, 50–51, 97, 184, 227, 249
Jones, Ardith, 90
Jones, Glen (Dr.), 45, 50–53, 55, 76, 108, 144
Jones, Joe, 83, 90, 107, 144, 221, 228, 348, 396, 398
junior high, 180, 190, 339, 397

K

Kansas City, Missouri, 18, 360–61, 368
Keller, Bernard, 327

Keller, Glen, 128, 155, 327, 348
Kentucky, 14–16, 24–25, 31, 37, 47, 145, 195, 225
KGMC Radio, 307, 368
Kluger, Jeffrey, 405
KOA Radio, 199, 310
Korean War, 327
Kuner-Empson Canning Co., 84, 125–27

L

LaFollette, Mr., 142
Lamberson, Wilse (Marshal), 85, 87, 135, 149–50
Larimer County, 387
Latta, Dr., 37
Laurance, Sister, 102, 188, 192
Laybourn, Rusty, 291
Lee, Betty, 192, 398
Lee, Louis, 151–52
Lee, Lucy, 152, 304, 398
Le Havre, France, 27
Leitchfield, Kentucky, 24–25
LePore's Tavern, 194
LeRoy, Colorado, 18, 22–24, 30–31, 33, 35–38, 53, 408, 413–14
LeRoy Evangelical Church, 23, 29, 31, 37
letter, 6, 24, 67, 147, 160–62, 217
Lewis Furniture, 253, 385
lilac, 108, 149
limbo, 37
Little Narrows, 256
lodge-pole pine, 118
Longmont, Colorado, 2, 12, 23–24, 33–34, 39, 45, 47, 53, 66, 82–84, 98, 104, 109, 114, 126, 141, 166, 175, 183, 186, 189–92, 213, 215, 226–27,

232, 242, 244, 246, 249,
  252–54, 259, 301, 309,
  317, 323, 328, 351–53, 355,
  361–63, 367, 376, 382–85,
  397–401, 408, 412–13
Longmont Drug, 244, 323, 367
Longmont High School, 352
Longmont Sporting Goods, 254,
  259
Long's Peak, 8, 86, 236, 266
Loos, Edna "Mikie," 30, 32
Loos, Harry, 30, 32, 38
Loretto Heights College, 43
Louisville, Kentucky, 25, 27, 145
Loveland, Colorado, 47, 53, 166,
  200, 227
Luther, Father, 34–35
Lyons, Colorado, 224, 256, 277, 291

M

Maestos, Johnny, 85
Maher, James (Father), 55–57
Main Street, Longmont, 82, 213,
  383–84, 386
Main Street, Mead, 78, 87, 90, 107,
  136, 394–95, 397–99
Malchow, Charles, 175
Malevich, Frank, 349
Marjorie, Sister, 8, 37, 53, 102,
  113–15, 186–87, 239, 264,
  319
Markham, Charles, 141
Markham, Effie, 220
Markham, Rodney, 135, 323, 368,
  397
marriage, 31–32, 104, 407
Mary Martha, Sister, 205
Mathews, Henry, 58
Mathews, Mary, 58
Maurer, Ernie, 22

Maynard, Dean, 239–42, 328,
  383–84, 390–92
Maynard, Mary Ellen Newton, 49,
  328
McCormick, Roscoe (Dr.), 36
McCoy, Ben, 396
Mead, Colorado, xvii, 5, 7–10,
  17–18, 24, 33–34, 38–39,
  44, 47–48, 50–51, 55–56,
  58–59, 61, 72, 74–75, 77–80,
  82–88, 90–91, 93–95,
  97, 100, 104, 108–9, 118,
  123–25, 127, 131–36, 142,
  144, 149, 153, 160, 174, 180,
  182–84, 186, 188–91, 201,
  208, 214, 216, 220–21, 223,
  227–28, 232, 243, 248–49,
  256, 277, 288, 297–98,
  300–301, 308, 314, 317, 319,
  321, 324, 326, 330–32, 334,
  336, 339, 342–45, 348, 356,
  361, 366, 374, 376–80, 382,
  384–86, 390, 394–400, 408,
  411–14
Mead, Malcom, 48
Mead, Paul, 58, 227
Mead Appliance, 100, 144
Mead Consolidated Schools, 11, 56,
  79, 85, 131, 399–400, 414
Mead Garage, 83, 144
Mead High School, xvii, 5, 8, 10–
  11, 48, 61, 180, 223, 232, 301,
  339, 344, 361, 374, 379, 395,
  398, 414
Mead Inn and Liquor, 83
Mead Motor Company, 88, 90, 94,
  134, 136, 221, 396–97, 402
Mead National Bank, 39
Mead Pool Hall, 80, 86, 125, 277,
  301
Mead Post Office, 324, 398

Mead Town Hall, 56, 395
medal, 78, 192
Meeker, Mount, 8, 86, 212, 236, 263–64, 266, 274
Meeker, Nathan C., 17
Memorial Building, 376
Memorial Day, 252, 265, 267, 290
Meuse River, 25, 27
Mexican nationals, 126–27, 226
Midway Island, 62
Miller, Linda, 352
Mills Brothers, 311
Minch, John, 299
Miracle of Our Lady of Fatima, 238
morning glory, 233, 240
Mother's Oats, 179, 203
Muhm, Bonnie, 397
Mulligan Lake, 172

N

National Legion of Decency, 213
Nehi soda, 154
Newman, Bernard "Duck," 90, 92, 138–39, 189–90, 201, 244, 246–47
Newman, Clare "Curly," 399
Newman, Emily (Mrs.), 92, 138–39, 189–90, 201, 244, 246–47
Newman, Herbert, 139, 399
Newman, Myrtle, 335
Newton, Agnes Maureen, 47, 97, 111–12, 173, 199, 202, 207, 209, 212, 320–21, 355–66, 369, 373, 404, 408
Newton, Benedict, 14, 31, 33
Newton, Bill, 328
Newton, Carl, 47
Newton, David Allen "Dave," 6, 96–97, 104, 111, 113, 142, 146, 158, 167, 173–75, 179, 198, 200–201, 206, 210–11, 217, 229–31, 233, 235–36, 238, 240–44, 246–47, 249–50, 252, 256, 258–60, 263, 267–72, 275–80, 282–84, 287–89, 292–93, 301, 321–22, 330–32, 335, 343, 374
Newton, Ellenda, 15
Newton, Eunice Elaine, 36, 39, 41, 43–44, 49, 55–56, 74, 87, 89, 96–98, 118, 146, 172, 218, 315, 317, 368, 385, 408
Newton, Ferne, 102–3, 106, 357–58
Newton, Forrest Benedict "Frosty," 108, 345, 377
Newton, Georgia Roberta "Betty," 35–36, 39, 43–44, 49, 55–56, 74, 79, 89, 98–100, 106, 111, 113, 189, 211, 301, 315, 368
Newton, Gerald Anthony "Jerry," 6, 48, 50, 56–57, 88–90, 96–97, 104, 111, 126, 142–44, 171, 174, 180–81, 202, 206, 229, 252, 287, 308, 323, 327, 341–43, 349–50, 353, 355, 358, 367, 374, 378, 382, 408
Newton, Helen Cecilia, xvii, 2, 39, 45, 58–59, 74, 76, 88, 101, 104–5, 112, 115, 161–62, 166, 172, 180, 182, 191, 217, 311, 314, 316–17, 321, 323, 326, 335–36, 355, 360, 362–63, 368, 370, 373, 386, 397, 404–5, 407–8
Newton, Ida Carrico, 14, 20, 27
Newton, Ignatius, 31
Newton, James, 31, 41, 408

Newton, James Elmer "Elmer," 5, 12, 17–28, 30–39, 41–48, 50–59, 61–62, 66–68, 72, 81, 108, 111, 153, 177, 324, 338, 397, 407–9
Newton, James Irvin, 15, 31
Newton, Jim, 51
Newton, Joey, 191
Newton, Kathy, 102
Newton, Laura Dreier "Johnnie," 1, 5, 40, 58, 61, 108, 314, 324, 398, 406–9
Newton, Lynne, 102, 106
Newton, Marc, xvii, 77, 148, 195, 243, 338, 373, 381, 399, 407–8
Newton, Mary (aunt), 14, 16, 38–39, 54–55, 87, 188, 190–92, 194–95, 213, 239–40, 329
Newton, Mary Kathleen, 47, 87, 92, 97, 101–2, 111–12, 116, 125, 138, 159–61, 173, 190, 199, 202, 207, 210, 212–14, 217–18, 297–98, 320–23, 355, 357, 359–62, 364, 366, 368, 404–5, 408
Newton, Merle, 51
Newton, Mike, 51
Newton, Orbin "Urban" Dreier "Dunk," 1, 12, 34–36, 38, 43, 48–49, 51, 56, 59, 62, 69, 72, 74, 85, 92, 95, 102–3, 160, 180, 189, 315, 369, 395, 408–9
Newton, Patricia Ann "Pat," xvii, 2, 42, 45, 74, 76, 88, 103–5, 111–12, 166, 172, 180, 314, 323, 326, 354–55, 360, 368, 408
Newton, Patrick, 102–3, 106
Newton, Raymond Lee "Ray," 1, 36, 39, 43–44, 48–49, 53, 56, 59, 61–62, 66, 74, 95, 124, 257, 408, 411
Newton, Richard John "Richie," xviii, 2, 5–7, 9, 11, 54, 60, 74, 76, 78, 97, 99, 111, 119–22, 124–25, 139, 154, 158, 170–71, 174–75, 177, 181, 189, 191–92, 194, 197, 199–203, 205–6, 210–11, 229–32, 235, 238, 240–41, 243–47, 249–50, 254–55, 258–59, 261–63, 267–68, 270–71, 273, 275–77, 282–93, 298–301, 304, 314–15, 321, 330–31, 334–35, 341, 343–45, 349, 367–68, 370, 374, 377, 380, 394–96, 400, 408
Newton, Robert (brother) "Bobby," 1, 36–37
Newton, Robert (uncle), 24, 33
Newton, Roland Joseph "Rollie," xvii–xviii, 2, 5–7, 9, 53–54, 74, 76, 97, 101, 113, 124–25, 136, 151, 154, 156, 158, 171, 174, 190, 192, 194, 199–203, 205, 210–11, 229–32, 235–38, 241, 244, 246–47, 249–50, 256, 259, 267–68, 276–77, 282–86, 288–95, 300, 303–4, 314–15, 321, 330–31, 335, 341, 343–45, 349, 360, 370, 374, 380, 387, 394, 400, 406, 408
Newton, Ronald James "Ronnie"
  birth, 52
  taking the First Communion, 115
  receiving Confirmation, 193
  first made cart, 141
  meeting Ginger Staffieri, 155
  first win in basketball, 180
  first loss in basketball, 183

first time seeing a dead person, 326
winning the conference championship (1955–1956), 344
winning the state championship (1957), 380
leaving Mead (1957), 5, 394
Newton, Rosemary, 37, 39, 43–44, 49, 54–56, 74, 76, 79, 88–89, 96–97, 99, 105–6, 108, 113, 115, 118, 140, 145, 147–48, 173, 307, 309, 315–16, 322, 325, 358, 360–66, 368, 370, 373, 404, 408
Newton, Shively "Tex," 328
Newton, Spaulding (uncle), 14, 24, 33, 38–39, 45, 47–48, 54–56, 188–95, 239, 328–30
Newton, Thomas James "Tom," 2, 6, 14, 30, 42, 75, 110, 115, 132, 136, 147, 151, 166, 182, 199–201, 229, 248, 297, 308, 311, 327, 329, 350, 357, 362, 367, 369, 382, 394, 408
New York City, 96, 101
New York Tribune, the, 17
night riders, 15–16
Nimitz, Chester (Admiral), 63
Norene, Ed, 84
North Central College, 45
North Platte River, 291
North Saint Vrain, 255, 268, 289–90
Nottingham, Kathy, 7, 352, 382, 384
novena, 44
Nygren, Bill, 220
Nygren, Walter, 226
Nygren, Willie D., 222

O

Olathe, Colorado, 47
Olson, Don, 362
Olson, Gary, 136, 140
Olson, Margaret, 134, 202
Olson, Mary, 362
Olson, Mary Helen, 397
Omaha, Nebraska, 18–19, 28, 413
orchestra, 308, 310
orphanage, 42–43, 46, 67, 71, 315

P

Palinkx, Connie, 301, 308–10, 335–36
Palinkx, Francis, 221
Palinkx, Ginger, 300, 306, 308, 312
Pancraitius, Sister, 53, 205
pea huller, 84, 125, 165, 167, 397
Pearl Harbor, 61–62, 74
peas, 84–85, 125–26, 165, 167, 213, 361, 386
Peetz, Colorado, 18
Peliliu Island, 69
Peppler, Wilbert, 132, 235, 246, 248, 252, 349, 397
Peterson, Fred, 75, 82
Peterson, Tom (Coach), 340
Pet Milk Co., 75
Philco radio, 58
Philco television, 386
Pike's Peak, 265
plane crash, 333
Platte River, 18, 100, 132, 175, 291
Platteville, Colorado, 47, 239, 291, 328, 332
plums, 74, 151, 166, 317
Plymouth Fury, 382
ponderosa pine, 87

pool hall, 80, 84, 86, 88, 91, 107, 123, 125, 128, 134, 136, 184, 220, 277, 301, 315–16, 340, 347–48, 351, 397, 400, 402
Popular Mechanics, 202
Porter Hospital, 362, 364
post office. *See* Mead Post Office
Poudre River, 224
prayer, 37, 44, 112–15, 305
pumpkins, 110, 132, 137–38, 167, 386
push-button automatic transmission, 383–84

R

Rademacher, Eddie, 158
Rademacher, George, 381
Rademacher, Josephine, 113, 189, 192, 238, 297, 308–9, 312
Rademacher, Louie, 154–55, 159, 230, 252, 254
Rademacher, Rita, 238–39
Rademacher, Ted, 80, 226, 232, 240, 244, 246, 330, 347, 350
Rademacher, Theresa, 189, 238, 309
Ralph Miller's Shoe Store, 245
rationing, 68, 79
Reader's Digest, 202
Red & White Grocery Store, 83, 88, 91, 94, 107, 134, 136, 145, 202, 297, 318, 351, 397
Redmond, Martha, 39–40, 42, 45
Redmond, William, 39–40, 42–43
Redmond farm, 86, 108, 119, 171
Replacement Battalions, 69
Rio Grande King, 272, 280, 292
Roberts, Grover, 80, 84, 91, 107, 125–26, 221, 228, 397
Roberts, John, 184

Roberts, Kate, 53
Roberts, Raymond, 53
Roberts, Roland, 53
Robinson, Lorraine, xiii, xvii
Robinson's Chicken Hatchery, 118
Rock Creek, xi, 252–56, 263–64, 267–71, 275, 277, 279, 287–96
Rocky Ford, Colorado, 47
Rocky Mountain National Park, 290, 296
Rocky Mountain News, 104, 127, 138, 201, 210, 230, 247, 309, 327, 336, 413
Rocky Mountains, 10, 86, 224, 252
Roger, Father, 39
Roman, Hulda, 76, 108, 124
Roman, Louis "Louie," 50, 146, 222, 231–35, 238, 249, 255, 299
Roman Catholic Church, 33
Roosevelt, Franklin (President), 62, 67–68, 314–15, 317
Roosevelt National Park, 290
rosary, 59, 72, 112–13, 154–55, 186, 192, 327
rose, 39, 69, 105, 109, 193, 203, 311, 394
Rose, Father, 39
Royal Coachman, 258
Ryan, Lynn, 98
Ryan, Monica, 98, 197

S

Safeway Grocery, 141
Saint Vrain, 224, 291
Saint Vrain River, xi, 48, 117, 249, 252, 256, 263, 275, 290, 298, 332, 335, 387–88
Saks Fifth Avenue, 96

sand burr, 240
Schaefer, Lyle, 381, 398
Schaefer, Marcella, 398
Schaefer, Russell, 398
Schell, Bill, 107, 154, 159, 347
schizophrenic, 363, 365
second hoeing, 234
Seewald, Dean, 382–83, 390–91
Seewald, Joe, 226
Sekich, Frederick "Freddie," 159, 207–8
Sekich, Jimmy, 193
Sekich, Mike Sr., 125, 176
Sekich, Nicholas Jr. "Nicky," 155–56, 216
Sekich, Nicholas Sr. "Nick," 125, 155, 176, 207
Sekich, Vera, 156, 159, 193
Sekich, Violet, 151–52, 159, 304
Sherman, Frederick (Captain), 63, 65, 413
Shriver, Bob, 310
Sibling Effect, 405, 412
Sieman, Bobby, 37
silver poplar, 123–24, 149, 154, 172, 236, 330
siren, 135, 344
Sisters of Loretto, 43, 120
Sisters of St. Francis, 43, 71
Skeeks, 133, 140
Slee, Walter, 252–60, 262–64, 266–78, 280, 282–85, 288–94, 299–300, 369–70, 373, 386
Smith, Joseph, 113
Snider, Elizabeth, 84
Snider, George, 84, 135, 321
Snider's Drugstore, 48, 50, 87, 134, 155
Snyder's Jewelry, 386
Social Security, 322–23

Sonnenberg, Carrie, 36
South Pacific, 62, 72
South Platte River, 18, 132, 175, 291
South Saint Vrain River, 256
spic, 191, 218
spiritual bouquet, 44
Staffieri, Ginger, 161, 208
St. Anthony's Fire, 37
Stapleton Airport, 200
state tournament, 344, 378
Stations of the Cross, 303
St. Catherine's Chapel, 263–64
St. Clara's Orphanage, 43, 67, 71
Stephens College, 387
Sterling, Colorado, 18–19, 28, 30, 32, 35, 37, 175, 223
Stevenson, Adali, 321
stewardess, 335, 368, 405, 408
St. John's Catholic Church, 34, 100, 114, 186, 191–92, 399
Stoddard, Roy, 315, 396
Stotts, Irene, xvii, 327
Stotts, Iva, 398
Stotts, Nadine, 327
St. Petersburg, Colorado, 23, 33
St. Peter's Catholic Church, 23, 33
strawberries, 19, 22, 132
straw stack, 18, 88, 118–21, 134, 154, 171, 222, 231, 238, 299
St. Theresa's Catholic Church, 153, 189, 192
St. Urban, 34
sugar beets, 9, 17, 24, 44, 86, 216, 223, 226–27, 233, 240, 248, 250, 260, 266, 330
sugar-beet topper or digger, 216, 228
sunflower, 240
Swedish Lutheran Church, 189
Sweetheart Ball, 361
Swenson, Chris, 268

swing, 103, 124, 171, 310
swing band, 310

T

technical foul, 178, 182, 184, 341, 375–76, 380
thinning, 233–34, 237–38, 348–49
third hoeing, 240, 248
thistles, 240
Thompson, Allen, 3, 209, 247, 313, 340, 381
Thompson, Delbert, 398
Thompson, Jackie, 396
Thompson, Jessie Boyles, 335
Thornton, Byron "Wilbur," 74, 87, 97–98, 118, 166, 169, 172–75, 218, 368
Thornton, Dennis, 373
Thornton, James, 148, 373
Thornton, Jean, 373
Thornton, Patricia, xvii, 373
Thornton, Robert, 373
Thornton, Victoria, 373
threshing, 18–19, 21–22, 33–34, 86, 109, 333
Times Call, 290, 412
tomatoes, 74, 136, 166–68, 239–42, 246
tornado, 19, 223
torpedo, 61, 63, 65
town hall, 48, 50, 55–56, 59, 85, 205, 326, 395
town park, 38, 109, 132, 136, 164, 216, 399
tree house, 104, 123
Trocadero Ballroom, 307, 310
Trojan Theater, 213
twin sisters, 266

U

Ulibarri, George, 181
Union Pacific Railroad, 18, 28, 85
United Airlines, 325, 335, 368
United States Pacific Fleet, 61
University of Colorado, 48
US Army Eighty-Ninth Division, 25–27
US Army Thirty-Second Division, 25
USAT *Barnett*, 66
US Highway 287, 213
US Marine Corps, 12, 62, 72, 74, 185, 325, 408
US Marines Division, 69
US Navy, 66, 69, 73
USS *Lexington*, 61, 411, 414
USS *Monticello*, 67
USS *Portland*, 66

V

Vehr, Urban J. (Archbishop), 189, 192–94
Virgin Mary, 44, 105, 239
Vogel, Francis, 364

W

Walker, Billy, 144–46, 148
Walker, Phoebe Doke, 145
Warner, Edwin, 398
Warriors, 186, 190, 193, 195
Washington Highway, 7, 190, 200, 232–33, 236, 249, 299, 332, 383, 388
Weatherman Bowman, 199
Weber, Ronald, 134–35, 139–40, 156, 245, 303, 314–16,

332–36, 338, 340, 376, 397, 400–401
Weld County, xii, 9, 57–58, 75, 83, 109, 131–32, 216, 223–26, 233, 241, 248–50, 266, 317, 334, 349, 360
Weld County Sheriff, 57
welfare, 46–47, 57, 314–16, 319, 323
Western Front, 25
Western Slope, 199
Western Union, 66
wheat, 4, 9, 17–18, 21, 23, 28, 35–37, 44, 79, 83, 86, 223, 266, 284
wheatgrass, 270, 272
White, Redland, 83
Widger, Vernon, 399
Wiggins, Colorado, 223, 379–80
Wiggins High School, 379
Wild Basin, 253, 263, 290, 296
Williams, Laurel Dreier, xvii
willows, 254, 263, 268–70
Windsor, Colorado, 53, 225–26, 250
Wonder Bread, 231
Wooden, John, 403
World War I, 13, 28, 32, 34, 55, 58
World War II, 1, 16, 72, 82, 99, 253, 327, 399
worms, 172–73, 254, 258, 270, 277, 282, 292

Y

Yakel, Albert, 124

Z

Zauro, Maurice (Father), 399
zone defense, 340, 375

Coming soon—the sequel to
Light of Her Children: Here's the Score

Here's the Score

A family of twelve siblings coming out the depths of Great Depression poverty finds itself living in an abandoned town hall that once served as a basketball gymnasium in a small Colorado town. There, with basketball hoops hanging over their heads, an all-male set of triplets is born, marking the beginning of their destined journey toward high school basketball stardom. Growing up in the '40s and '50s with basketball as the dominant sport played during the cold of winter in the rural school gymnasiums throughout Northeastern Colorado, the triplets' obsession with basketball is inspired and nurtured by their older siblings. The triplets and two other brothers participate in a historic event in our nation's basketball history—they form and play as the starting five for their high school basketball team. Throughout their young lives, the triplets and their brothers experience adulation and newspaper notoriety, causing their mother to constantly remind them to refrain from self-absorption and to work together. This story, told through the eyes of sixteenth-born and triplet **Ronald James Newton**, recounts his struggles in the classroom and on the basketball court and portrays his arduous pursuit in the development of meaningful and satisfying relationships with classmates, family, and friends. The story's thematic threads of spirituality and facing and rising above adversity are enveloped in the bonding relationships that small-town and small school athletics provide, and they are crowned by the success the Newton brothers experience playing basketball.

Edwards Brothers Malloy
Thorofare, NJ USA
August 29, 2016